# Issues in Geography Teaching

*Issues in Geography Teaching* examines a wide range of issues which are of interest to those teaching geography from the 'early years' through to higher education. The issues discussed include:

- the role of research and the use of ICT in teacher training;
- the significance of developing critical thinking skills;
- broader educational issues such as citizenship and development;
- the importance of environmental education;
- the position and role of assessment;
- the present state and status of geographical education and issues that are likely to be of concern in the future.

At a time of great change in geographical education, it is vital that practitioners should develop their own awareness and perspective on a variety of curriculum concerns and developments and evaluate how these might impact upon their work. The issues raised in this book are those confronted regularly by geography teachers, NQTs and student teachers in their professional work; yet there is often insufficient time to consider them in detail. *Issues in Geography Teaching* provides an opportunity to do that, detailing the contexts, presenting the facts and raising thought-provoking questions which should stimulate further interest and discussion.

**Chris Fisher** is Senior Lecturer in Geography Education at Canterbury Christ Church University College. **Tony Binns** is Senior Lecturer in Geography in the School of African & Asian Studies at the University of Sussex.

**Issues in Subject Teaching series**
Edited by Susan Capel, Jon Davison,
James Arthur and John Moss

**Other titles in the series:**

# Issues in Geography Teaching

Edited by
Chris Fisher and Tony Binns

London and New York

First published 2000 by RoutledgeFalmer
11 New Fetter Lane, London EC4P 4EE

Simultaneously published in the USA and Canada
by RoutledgeFalmer
29 West 35th Street, New York, NY 10001

*RoutledgeFalmer is an imprint of the Taylor & Francis Group*

© 2000 Chris Fisher and J.A. (Tony) Binns

Typeset in Goudy by Keystroke, Jacaranda Lodge, Wolverhampton
Printed and bound in Great Britain by TJ International Ltd, Padstow, Cornwall

*British Library Cataloguing in Publication Data*
A catalogue record for this book is available from the British Library

*Library of Congress Cataloging in Publication Data*
Issues in geography teaching / [edited by] Chris Fisher and Tony Binns.
    p.  cm. – (Issues in subject teaching)
   Includes bibliographical references.
    1. Geography–Study and teaching. I. Fisher, Chris, 1952– II. Binns, Tony. III. Series.

  G73 .I87 2000  00-020762
  910'.71–dc21

ISBN 0–415–23077–2 (pbk)
    0–415–23268–6 (hbk)

# Contents

# Figures

# Tables

# Contributors

**Kathy Alcock** taught for more than twenty years in a variety of schools covering the age range from 4 to 18 years. Kathy then moved into Higher Education and is now Senior Lecturer in Primary Education, with particular responsibility for primary geography at Canterbury Christ Church University College. She is currently acting as programme consultant writing teacher notes and resource packs for BBC Education and has also written for Folens, Scholastic and the Geographical Association.

**Jeff Battersby** has taught in secondary schools for twenty-six years. He is currently Lecturer in Geography at the University of East Anglia where he is Co-Director of the secondary PGCE course in Initial Teacher Education, with particular responsibility for geography and environmental education. Jeff was a member of the SCAA Advisory Group for geography in the first revision of the National Curriculum and involved in the production of Optional Tests and Tasks Units. He is currently part of the QCA writing team preparing materials to support the revised Geography Orders. He has extensive experience with a wide number of geographical publications, editorial responsibilities, and advisory and consultancy work in Britain and elsewhere.

**Tony Binns** has lectured in Geography at the University of Sussex since 1975 and was Curriculum Tutor on the PGCE programme from 1981 to 1995. He is a Senior Lecturer and governor of a large comprehensive school in Hove. He has written on a wide range of educational and developmental issues. In 1994–5 he was elected President of the Geographical Association and was a founder member of the Association's International Committee, becoming its Chair in 1999. He has also served on the Educational Advisory Panel of the Commonwealth Institute and on the Council of Worldaware. He has taught in a number of African universities in Kenya, Nigeria, Sierra Leone and South Africa. Tony has developed an international reputation for his work in 'development', but he has always maintained a strong interest in geographical education.

**Graham Butt** is a Senior Lecturer in Geography Education and Senior Tutor for PGCE courses at the School of Education, University of Birmingham. He is an active member of the Geographical Association and previously chaired its Assessment and Examinations Working Group. He currently edits the 'Assessment Matters' section of one of the Association's journals, *Teaching Geography*. Graham has a variety of research interests and has written widely on aspects of geographical education, particularly in the fields of assessment and language.

**Roger Carter** has worked in primary and secondary schools and in teacher education. For some years he was adviser for geography in Staffordshire. He is now the geography adviser for Jersey Education. He was President of the Geographical Association in 1998–9, and editor of the *Primary Geography Handbook*.

**Simon Catling** is tutor in geographical education and, currently, Acting Head of the School of Education, Oxford Brookes University. He taught in primary schools in London for eleven years. He has published widely on primary geography and environmental education, including the *Outset Geography* and *Mapstart* series for pupils and *Placing Places* for teachers. He is a past President of the Geographical Association, for which he chairs its New Initiatives Fund. His research interests include children's understanding of maps and geography.

**Gill Davidson** runs the Secondary Geography PGCE course at Oxford Brookes University. She has broad experience of teacher education with extensive experience in Higher Education and the provision of professional development courses for teachers. She is also an OFSTED inspector and runs regional courses for teachers on the improvement of the quality of teaching and learning in geography. Gill was formerly Head of the Humanities Faculty in a large comprehensive school and has published on a range of topics including teaching and learning styles, evaluation and various aspects of geography education.

**Chris Fisher** is a teacher of Geography with a strong interest in classroom processes. He is currently Senior Lecturer in Geography Education at Canterbury Christ Church University College where he is responsible for the PGCE Geography (Secondary and Middle years) courses. His teaching activities also include teachers' professional development programmes such as Subject Leadership at Diploma Level, geography and other generic 'in-service' work. Before his move to Higher Education, he taught geography for twenty-one years in secondary schools, becoming a subject mentor and leading a successful geography department. While a senior teacher whose responsibilities included student teachers, he assisted with the Sussex PGCE Geography course which stimulated his interest in Initial Teacher Education. Recent teaching has included work with Rhodes University, South Africa that has initiated a new research project in graphicacy and a partnership with Canterbury. Chris is vice-chair of governors at a large community college in East Sussex and is a member of the Teacher Education Working Group of the Geographical Association.

**Tony Fisher** is IT coordinator at the University of Nottingham School of Education, which he joined as a PGCE geography tutor with eighteen years' experience as a school geography teacher. He has been head of a large humanities faculty in a comprehensive school, where he was also a mentor and professional tutor. He was also for two years an advisory teacher with Nottinghamshire LEA. He has research interests in the area of new technologies in education, and has undertaken case-study research into geography teachers' use of computers. He was a member of the team that carried out the evaluation of the Multimedia Portables for Teachers Pilot. Among his recent publications is *Developing as a Teacher of Geography*.

**David Hassell** was originally a geography and games teacher in Hertfordshire. In 1986, he joined the Advisory Unit for Computer Based Education, Hatfield, as an advisory teacher and project officer for Information Technology, with the focus on computer-based modelling. He later spent some time as a consultant, managing a remote sensing project at the Institute of Education before being appointed as Software Manager at the National Council for Educational Communications Technology (NCET) in 1993. As NCET became the British Educational Communications and Technology Agency (BECTA), Dave became Head of Curriculum and Institutional Development for schools where he now has responsibility for all curriculum activity, software liaison, work with school senior managers and institutional ICT development policies.

**David Kinninment** has been teaching for seven years and is head of geography at Blyth Tynedale High School, Northumberland. He has served on a Schools Curriculum and Assessment Authority advisory panel and has written A-level texts and a CD-ROM. He was one of the founding members of the *Thinking Through Geography* book and is a member of the Northumberland 'Thinking Skills in Humanities' Group.

**David Lambert** is a Reader in Education at the University of London Institute of Education where he is coordinating tutor for the geography PGCE. He is also involved in the teaching of INSET, various short courses and the MA in Geography Education. His research interests include assessment policy and practice, and the concept of prejudice in geography education. He also has an interest in textbooks and produced the Cambridge Geography Project which won the 1992 TES Schoolbook of the Year Award. He is currently Honorary Publications Officer of the Geographical Association.

**David Leat** taught for twelve years, including four years at an LEA field centre. He is now a geography PGCE tutor at the University of Newcastle, and his research interests lie in teachers' thinking and professional development. David works with a group of teachers on a project titled 'Thinking Through Geography', preparing a series of books on how to make geography more challenging to pupils. He has been engaged in various curriculum projects in Northumberland examining critical thinking, with a view to devising more powerful in-service models. He is a member of the Teacher Education Working Group of the Geographical Association.

**Melanie Norman** is currently Senior Lecturer in Geographical Education at the University of Brighton. Her teaching career spans twenty years in comprehensive schools in London and East Sussex where she held a number of posts including Head of Geography, Head of Year and Senior Teacher. Melanie's current responsibilities include teaching on undergraduate QTS and leisure studies degree routes; School of Education coordinator for geography; Course Leader for 2 Year BAQTS degree routes; and Faculty of Education Link Tutor for the 'Partnership in Education' programme operated by the University of Brighton with all its partner schools and colleges. She is also a Fellow of the Royal Geographical Society, a member of the Geographical Association Teacher Education Working Group and an LEA representative on two governing bodies of schools in the Eastbourne area.

**Eleanor Rawling** MBE is currently Leverhulme Research Fellow at the University of Oxford Department of Educational Studies, on secondment from the Qualification and Curriculum Authority (QCA) London. Her work with QCA includes reviewing the National Geography Curriculum, developing curriculum support materials for teachers of geography, advising government on geography's place in the curriculum and involvement with work on citizenship and sustainable development education. She is a prominent figure in geography, being a Council member for both the Royal Geographical Society with the Institute of British Geographers and the Geographical Association. She is a past President of the Geographical Association and has been Chair of the Council of British Geography (COBRIG), whose biennial seminars she organizes to link school geographers with those from higher education. Eleanor has produced a wide range of books, and papers since 1976. Her distinguished career and contributions to geographical education were duly recognized with the award of an MBE in 1995.

**Margaret Roberts** is a Senior Lecturer in the Department of Educational Studies at the University of Sheffield. She is the coordinator of the geography PGCE course and has taken a keen interest in the establishment of the University of Sheffield PGCE partnership with schools. Most of her research has been on the geography National Curriculum, with recent research focusing on the nature of geographical enquiry at Key Stage 3. She is chair of the Teacher Education Working Group of the Geographical Association.

**Stephen Scoffham** has been involved in geography and environmental education for many years. A long-standing member of the Geographical Association, he has served on a range of GA committees, writes regularly for *Primary Geographer* and helped pioneer national initiatives in action research. He has produced many successful publications in geographical education including *Keystar Atlas Programme*, *World Watch Geography* and the *Blueprints* and *Learning Targets* series. Stephen has experience as a classroom teacher at both primary and secondary level. He is the Schools' Officer for the Canterbury Environment Centre and Chair of the World Education Development Group (East Kent). He is currently Senior Lecturer in Primary Geography at Canterbury Christ Church University College.

**Rex Walford** OBE teaches at the University of Cambridge and is a Fellow of Wolfson College. Rex was appointed to lead the post-graduate teacher education course in Geography in 1973. The Cambridge course is now one of the major providers of secondary geography teachers. This followed time spent teaching in schools and training teachers at Maria Grey College, Twickenham. He is a past President and trustee of the Geographical Association and a past Vice-President of the Royal Geographical Society on whose Education Committee he sits. Rex was the first Chair of the Council of British Geography (COBRIG) from its foundation in 1988 to 1993. He was also a member of the Working Group appointed by the government to write the original National Geography Order in 1988. Rex has also been involved in creating the national Worldwise Quiz and Geography Action Week. He was honorary national secretary to the GA's Land-Use UK survey in 1996 and now directs the research phase of that project. Rex's long and very distinguished career in geographical education was recognised in January 2000 with the award of an OBE.

**David Waugh** is a leading author of school geography textbooks used in schools, including some 26 different editions in the 11–19 age range. He was educated at Dame Allan's School in Newcastle on Tyne, graduated at Swansea University and obtained his PGCE at the Institute of Education in London. He taught initially in Warwickshire and Sheffield before becoming head of geography at Trinity School, Carlisle. He held this post for twenty years before concentrating full-time on writing textbooks. He now spends much of his non-writing time travelling to collect materials and photographs for his books.

# Introduction to the Series

This book, *Issues in Geography Teaching*, is one of a series of books entitled *Issues in Subject Teaching*. The series has been designed to engage with a wide range of issues related to subject teaching. Types of issues vary among subjects, but may include, for example: issues that impact on Initial Teacher Education in the subject; issues addressed in the classroom through the teaching of the subject; issues to do with the content of the subject and its definition; issues to do with subject pedagogy; issues to do with the relationship between the subject and broader educational aims and objectives in society, and the philosophy and sociology of education; and issues to do with the development of the subject and its future in the twenty-first century.

Each book consequently presents key debates that subject teachers will need to understand, reflect on and engage in as part of their professional development. Chapters have been designed to highlight major questions, to consider the evidence from research and practice and to arrive at possible answers. Some subject books or chapters offer at least one solution or a view of the ways forward, whereas others provide alternative views and leave readers to identify their own solution or view of the ways forward. The editors expect readers of the series to want to pursue the issues raised, and so chapters include suggestions for further reading, and questions for further debate. The chapters and questions could be used as stimuli for debate in subject seminars or department meetings, or as topics for assignments or classroom research. The books are targeted at all those with a professional interest in the subject, and in particular: student teachers learning to teach the subject in the primary or secondary school; newly qualified teachers; teachers with a subject co-ordination or leadership role, and those preparing for such responsibility; mentors, tutors, trainers and advisers of the groups mentioned above.

Each book in the series has a cross-phase dimension. This is because the editors believe it is important for teachers in the primary and secondary phases to look at subject teaching holistically, particularly in order to provide for continuity and progression, but also to increase their understanding of how children learn. The balance of chapters that have a cross-phase relevance, chapters that focus on issues which are of particular concern to primary teachers and chapters that focus on issues which secondary teachers are more likely to need to address, varies according to the issues relevant to different subjects. However, no matter where the emphasis is, authors have drawn out the relevance of their topic to the whole of each book's intended audience.

Because of the range of the series, both in terms of the issues covered and its cross-phase concern, each book is an edited collection. Editors have commissioned new writing from experts on particular issues who, collectively, will represent many different perspectives on subject teaching. Readers should not expect a book in this series to cover a full range of issues relevant to the subject, or to offer a completely unified view of subject teaching, or that every issue will be dealt with discretely, or that all aspects of an issue will be covered. Part of what each book in this series offers to readers is the opportunity to explore the inter-relationships between positions in debates and, indeed, among the debates themselves, by identifying the overlapping concerns and competing arguments that are woven through the text.

The editors are aware that many initiatives in subject teaching currently originate from the centre, and that teachers have decreasing control of subject content, pedagogy and assessment strategies. The editors strongly believe that for teaching to remain properly a vocation and a profession, teachers must be invited to be part of a creative and critical dialogue about subject teaching, and encouraged to reflect, criticize, problem-solve and innovate. This series is intended to provide teachers with a stimulus for democratic involvement in the development of subject teaching.

Susan Capel,
Jon Davison,
James Arthur and
John Moss
May 1999

# Introduction

*Chris Fisher and Tony Binns*

Geography is a fast-changing subject, yet teachers seem to cope readily with change, since it is recognized that much of the attraction in studying and teaching the subject is due to the fact that good geographical education feeds off topicality. In recent years, however, developments in subject knowledge, together with the application of broader skills, concepts and values have added a new dynamism to geographical education. Though the need to be aware of and respond to change has always been a feature of good geography teaching, this is now a widely recognized quality among 'Advanced Skills Teachers' in all subjects. Recent major innovations in many aspects of the education system, particularly at school level, have resulted in a considerable transformation in teaching content and strategies. Today therefore, perhaps more than ever before, teachers of geography are faced with the need to be fully briefed on the facts and opinions surrounding debate on a range of issues which might affect their teaching of the subject. Teachers also need to be in a strong position to pose challenges to both their pupils and teaching colleagues.

The editing partnership for this book had its origins over a decade ago in the collaboration of teaching geography in both school and university through the Postgraduate Certificate in Education (PGCE) programme at the University of Sussex, one of the first Initial Teacher Education (ITE) programmes to be based predominantly in schools. Tony Binns was the university-based Curriculum Tutor at Sussex (1981–95), while Chris Fisher was a school-based mentor (1984–96) managing a large geography department at Hailsham Community College in East Sussex. This early collaboration continues to have as much significance today, as we both continue to work towards strengthening the important links between schools and higher education institutions, and we see this book as a natural expression of our aspirations. We believe that we bring to this work our contrasting, but complementary, interests and experiences within the subject, which include the international awareness of geographical issues, as well as considerable practical expertise in both school and university. We both also share a strong belief in pupil entitlement to high quality learning and in the provision of a curriculum which has appeal and relevance, whilst also making a meaningful contribution to the broader education process. It is on the basis of these important considerations that we embarked on assembling a team of expert practitioners and writers in geographical education to make contributions to this volume.

This book seeks to address some of the key issues which we believe currently face teachers of geography, from the 'early years' through to initial teacher education. The team of contributors includes a broad diversity of specialisms within geographical education across the full age range of compulsory education. Though some of the writers are very well known in their respective fields, others are relative newcomers with refreshing perceptions and approaches, a combination which in itself reflects the breadth and dynamism of the subject. The contributors have each sought to present evidence, provoke thought and stimulate debate among teachers of geography. Few have provided definitive answers – indeed that was not their brief. All, however, address key issues and present the reader with a range of questions which they believe need to be answered. We are most grateful to all members of the 'writing team' for their cooperation and good humour in dealing with numerous editorial requests and the inevitable deadlines. This book is certainly not intended for the 'passive' reader, but instead is geared towards inspiring both action and reflection. We firmly believe that developing a personal and critically informed viewpoint on a range of broad and subject-specific educational issues is a prerequisite for good teaching and we very much hope that this book goes some way towards encouraging this.

As editors, we have had to work within a number of guidelines, most notably the three-part structure adopted by all other books in this series, and also the strict limitation we have had to place on authors in terms of the length of their contributions. Undoubtedly the greatest challenge in our editorial responsibilities has been to restrict the contributions to just one volume! We are all too aware that the key issues of concern in geography teaching will change in the future as they have done in the past, and therefore at any other time the contents of such a book as this could well be very different. We are also aware that although the book is 'located' primarily within the context of geographical education in England and Wales, there is nevertheless a much wider international relevance to many of the issues debated. Our overseas experience suggests that many common issues and areas of concern exist elsewhere.

Initial 'brainstorming' and subsequent discussions with colleagues identified a profusion of issues across a broad spectrum of topics which were felt to impinge on the teaching of geography at the beginning of the twenty-first century. We do recognize that in our final selection of topics presented here, there will inevitably be aspects of geographical education which have been either omitted or only partially examined. In terms of recent developments concerning geography, we firmly believe that the increasing dialogue between the main 'professional associations' (the Geographical Association and the Royal Geographical Society with the Institute of British Geographers), has represented a significant step forward in reaching some common agreement on the key issues and areas of concern in geographical education.

This book, as with others in the series, is divided into three broad sections and most of the contributions are either 'classroom-based' or examine 'wider issues'. The book both starts and finishes with broad 'overview' chapters written, respectively, by Eleanor Rawling and Rex Walford, which provide a useful context for many of the specific issues considered in other chapters. The early chapters examine issues which are particularly, though by no means exclusively, related to Initial Teacher Education (ITE). Within this element of the education system, we felt that the growing impact of Information and Communication Technology (ICT) was raising concerns about the ability of school-based ITE courses to respond appropriately at a time when so many other initiatives, such as, for example, enhanced programmes in numeracy and literacy, also demanded inclusion. Issues of concern include the relationship between ICT and the education system, the curriculum and geography in particular. Such issues extend into the classroom, where, having been at the forefront of ICT initiatives, geography now seems to be struggling to access the increasing range of technological resources in schools as the 'core' (compulsory) subjects in the curriculum tend to dominate both the timetable and access to funding. Overcoming such problems, together with identifying how ICT might enhance geographical learning and be more effectively integrated into the curriculum, are aspects that Tony Fisher and (in Part II) David Hassell have addressed in their contributions.

A second area of current widespread concern to those in geographical education is the problem of recruitment to ITE. Though this issue is by no means peculiar to our subject, it is now sufficiently severe for geography to be deemed a 'shortage subject' by the UK government's Department for Education and Employment (DfEE). It is a fact that geography graduates are now being actively sought by the world of business and commerce, where salaries, working conditions and career prospects often bear little comparison with those of the teaching profession. However, we do believe that the causes of the recruitment shortfall are not merely subject-specific, but are more related to the generally negative perceptions of teaching as an unattractive and low-esteem career. As a number of ITE schemes are urgently attempting to address this issue, Melanie Norman offers an interesting insight into a 'cross-phase' strategy designed to improve teacher recruitment.

Undoubtedly one of the greatest impacts on the teaching of geography in schools in the 1990s has been the introduction of the National Curriculum from September 1991. Since then there has been much discussion about the impact of the new curriculum, and on no fewer than three occasions the geography curriculum has actually been revised. A number of contributors focus on different aspects of the implementation of the National Curriculum on geographical education. These include such issues as learning difficulties created by the curriculum and the notion of pupil entitlement (Jeff Battersby), implications of the content base and the need for a greater focus on classroom processes, autonomy in learning and critical thinking (David Leat and Chris Fisher), and the impact on professional development and school geography (Gill Davidson and Simon Catling). With so many 'top-down' initiatives currently preoccupying teachers, it is unfortunate that many other aspects of good professional practice have suffered. These include the need for practitioners to be continually reflective about their work, as well as opportunities for ongoing professional development and the effective use of educational research. In response to the latter, Margaret Roberts offers a view of how ITE can generate worthwhile research opportunities through her own experience with PGCE students. Eleanor Rawling, in her initial overview, also responds to such issues, taking a very positive view of how the curriculum can, once more, be 'shaped' by teachers to suit the needs of their own pupils, an issue which is further explored by Chris Fisher in his chapter on 'resourcefulness'.

The particular circumstances surrounding the evolution of the geography National Curriculum have also resulted in considerable debate about teaching strategies, not least concerning the structure, scope and utilization of modern textbooks. This has become a particularly controversial issue at Key Stage 3 (11–14 years), where teaching quality is often weakest and non-specialist teachers are most numerous. Such concerns and important related questions are examined in David Lambert's consideration of textbook pedagogy. Alongside this, David Waugh offers an author's perspective on textbook use, providing an interesting insight into the parameters and constraints affecting textbook writers.

In Part III a range of broader issues is considered which frequently have implications beyond the classroom. The first three contributions – global citizenship (Roger Carter), development education (Tony Binns) and environmental education (Stephen Scoffham) – are key elements in geographical education, whose positions have generally been enhanced across all age ranges. Such topics might be regarded as separate disciplines in their own right, yet by their very nature they offer a distinctive route and significant opportunities to foster cross-curricular links. In examining these important issues, the challenge to the writers was to justify their positions within the school curriculum and also to look forward to their future contributions and positions in relation to geography. The growing significance of the European dimension in geography teaching is examined by Stephen Scoffham, who raises important questions of perception and place knowledge among both pupils and teachers.

Another broad issue concerns the considerable recent change in geography's contribution across the primary curriculum and, in particular, its roots in the 'early years'. Kathy Alcock examines how geography might be integrated within the early years' curriculum and the benefits of its introduction at this early stage. Other chapters in Part III examine still wider issues. The important role of geography in preparing young people for adult life is initially expressed by Eleanor Rawling in her introductory overview, while the implications of increasing 'vocationalism' are explored by Graham Butt, who sees future vocational developments as providing possible opportunities for geography and geographers. The thread of research into geographical issues, raised in a number of earlier chapters, continues in this final section by examining the need for an effective methodology in assessment in the light of considerable variation in school practice (Graham Butt). In the context of the introduction of the National Curriculum, Gill Davidson and Simon Catling explore concerns about both the development of school geography, and the simplistic notion of education, emphasizing the need to acknowledge the 'nature' of learning. Their suggestion of a 'question-led' curriculum also links effectively to views expressed by David Leat and others in earlier chapters.

To conclude the book, Rex Walford has provided an overview of recent developments, raising important questions concerning the value of flexibility in geography and the need for a longer-term view of educational philosophy and curriculum structure. Walford, like other contributors, encourages readers to take on a leading role in developing geography into the new century.

We hope the book will provoke interest and debate among geography educators in all sectors of the education system. At a time of continuing pressure, with one educational initiative after the other being implemented and monitored, we feel confident in saying that geography is a dynamic and highly relevant subject which has a distinctive role to play in preparing young people for citizenship in the twenty-first century. We trust that this book will encourage readers to reach the same conclusion.

# 1 School geography 5–16

## Issues for debate

*Eleanor Rawling*

## Introduction

With the National Curriculum Review 1998–2000 now completed and the revised, less prescriptive programmes of study for geography ready for implementation in September 2000 (DfEE, 1999), it is timely to examine the state of the subject for pupils aged 5–16. Geography has now been re-established in Key Stages 1–3 (after the temporary disapplication of its Key Stages 1–2 programmes of study 1998–2000), so it is now a full part of the statutory ten-subject National Curriculum for pupils aged 5–14 years. Despite the traumas of the past ten years of curriculum change, gains have been made for geography, as a direct result of the National Curriculum (Rawling, 1999). Geography is also a popular optional subject with high entries for public examinations at 16-plus (GCSE) and 18-plus (A-level), and new one-year Advanced Subsidiary Levels are about to provide further possibilities for geography in the 16–19 curriculum. There are now central guidelines for the subject at all these levels (National Curriculum Order, GCSE and A/AS-level Criteria), containing considerable detail about the subject content to be taught in physical, human and environmental aspects of the subject and about the standards expected (see summary diagram, Table 1.1 for the 5–16 situation). There is then a framework as a basis for development into the next century.

However, despite this apparent strength, there are a number of concerns about the future status and quality of geographical education in England. It will be argued that school geography has lost status since the initial establishment of the National Curriculum (1988), is in danger of losing curriculum ground to so-called 'basic' skills and the new National Curriculum subject of Citizenship, and provides considerably less evidence of creative flair and curriculum innovation than was the case pre-National Curriculum. Many of these trends are a direct result of central policies designed to improve the school curriculum, so it may be salutary to consider the unintended impacts on one particular National Curriculum subject.

Four issues concerning the status and well-being of school geography in England will be considered. In each case, an attempt will be made to draw out wider implications and a concluding section will summarize the possibilities for action. The issues are:

Table 1.1 School geography 5–16: A summary for 2000

| | 5–7 years (Key Stage 1) | 7–11 years (Key Stage 2) | 11–14 years (Key Stage 3) | 14–16 years (Key Stage 4) |
|---|---|---|---|---|
| Status in the curriculum | Compulsory [re-established in Sept 2000 after temporary disapplication of the programmes of study 1998–2000] | Compulsory [re-established in September 2000 after temporary disapplication of the programme of study 1998–2000] | Compulsory and with statutory teacher assessment at 14 years | Optional but popular subject for public examinations at 16 (GCSE) [some aspects of geography in general national vocational qualifications (GNVQs) e.g. Leisure & Tourism] |
| Central guidelines | National Curriculum Geography Order (programme of study) | National Curriculum Geography Order (programme of study) | National Curriculum Geography Order (programme of study) | GCSE Criteria for Geography [details of syllabuses left to examination boards] |
| Main emphasis | • enquiry approach/skills<br>• locality of the school and a contrasting locality<br>• environmental change/ sustainable development<br>• basic locational knowledge<br>• mainly local scale but awareness of wider world | • enquiry approach/skills<br>• two contrasting localities<br>• three themes, i.e. water and landscape, settlement, an environmental issue<br>• environmental change/ sustainable development<br>• locational knowledge<br>• mainly local, regional and national scale | • enquiry approach/skills<br>• two countries in different stages of development<br>• a wide range of physical human and environmental themes (10 themes)<br>• environmental change/ sustainable development<br>• locational knowledge<br>• full range of scales, local to global | • full range of geographical enquiry and skills<br>• balance of physical/ human/environmental geography<br>• range of places and scales<br>• issues about places/ environments |
| Issues | • increasing marginalization due to National Literacy and Numeracy Strategies and emphasis on English, Maths, Science<br>• unknown effects of the re-establishment of geography PoS from 2000<br>• potential impact of the new framework for PSHE and Citizenship | • increasing marginalization due to National Literacy and Numeracy Strategies and emphasis on English, Maths, Science<br>• unknown effects of the re-establishment of geography PoS from 2000<br>• potential impact of the new framework for PSHE and Citizenship | • school inspections reveal low grades for pupil progress and poor quality of teaching/ learning relative to other subjects<br>• unknown effects of the implementation of the new NC subject, Citizenship and the PSHE framework | • declining numbers and competition from other academic subjects with protected status<br>• competition from general national vocational courses<br>• unknown effects of the new NC subject, Citizenship and the PSHE framework<br>• potential effects on 14–16 choices of broadening the 16–19 curriculum with AS |

- geography and the threat of the 'basics';
- geography and 'preparation for adult life';
- the decline of school-based curriculum development;
- school geography as part of a wider geography education system.

## Geography and the threat of the basics

In 1997, nine years after the introduction of a National Curriculum designed to raise standards, the incoming Labour Government found continuing concern about basic literacy and numeracy in English schools. National Curriculum test results for English and Mathematics (used as measures of literacy and numeracy) seemed to show that large numbers of primary school children were still not reaching the required levels of achievement in these subjects. Media attention given to this situation and to some international comparisons (Martin *et al.*, 1997) fuelled concern and it was not surprising that the new government decided to make literacy and numeracy its own priorities. The first White Paper of the new government (DfEE, 1997a) was an educational one which stridently claimed that 'the priority for the curriculum must be to give more emphasis to literacy and numeracy in primary education'. As a direct result, government educational policy has focused on the twin track of setting demanding targets for schools to achieve by 2002, and on initiating prescriptive national teaching strategies for both literacy and numeracy. The targets state that by 2002, 80 per cent of 11-year-olds should reach National Curriculum level 4 in English and 75 per cent of 11-year-olds should reach level 4 in Mathematics (DfEE, 1997b). The National Literacy Strategy (DfEE, 1998) is being implemented in schools from September 1998 and the National Numeracy Strategy (DfEE, 1999) follows suit from September 1999.

Though the intention to address perceived shortcomings in these important basic skills is generally welcomed, the consequent impact on the wider curriculum is giving more cause for concern. In January 1998, the government announced that it intended to release schools from the National Curriculum requirements in 'the non-core six' – i.e. History, Geography, Design and Technology, IT, Art and PE – so that schools could give more time to literacy and numeracy. Although this was publicized as being a temporary two-year measure, the recent (1998–2000) review of the National Curriculum subjects has been focused on reducing content in precisely these non-core six subjects (QCA and DfEE, 1999) so that, although the subjects will be reinstated, it is unlikely that the full statutory breadth and balance of the National Curriculum will return in 2000. What is more, the National Curriculum subject Orders for English and Mathematics have now been brought directly in line with the Literacy and Numeracy strategies. Effectively, the broad and balanced National Curriculum of 1988 has now been replaced by a much narrower vision and one which elevates one particular definition of the basics and apparently downgrades other subject contributions.

For geography, just beginning in 1998 to show the benefit of ten years of recognition in the National Curriculum in improved teaching and learning in geography for 5–11-year-olds (OFSTED, 1998a), this change of emphasis is of great concern. Despite QCA guidance on the need to maintain a broad curriculum (QCA, 1998), many schools have, not surprisingly, decided to delay full implementation of the Geography Order. Even in those where geography was flourishing, local education authority advisers have reported a decrease in time dedicated to the subject and a narrowing of emphases. Creative ideas about geography's many contributions to literacy and numeracy, published in *Primary Geographer* (e.g. two full issues, January and July 1998) and elsewhere (e.g. Development Education Association leaflet, 1998) have been valuable, but it has proved difficult to encourage schools to diverge from the tightly prescribed guidelines for the government-approved literacy and numeracy hours. Recent informal surveys undertaken by LEA advisers show that geography has been a particular casualty of this new policy, even though what limited evidence there is about the primary curriculum seems to suggest that, contrary to the government's thinking, schools which retain a broad and balanced curriculum actually perform better in National Curriculum English, Maths and Science tests (OFSTED and DfEE, 1997).

In April 1999, it was announced that the National Literacy Strategy was to be extended to Key Stage 3. Although the plans and guidance for this Key Stage are still being developed and, certainly, Key Stage schemes of work for non-core subjects will include reference to language and literacy, the main emphasis is likely to remain on the English curriculum. At Key Stage 4, there are already signs that a narrower view of the curriculum holds dangers for geography. The broad ten-subject National Curriculum for 14–16-year-olds was already amended in 1994, after schools found it impossible to cover the detailed requirements set out in the first versions of the subject Orders. The notion of a hierarchy of subjects was introduced by Sir Ron Dearing at that time, with the core subjects of English, Mathematics and Science occupying a central position and, more controversially, some element of Design and Technology, Information Technology and Modern Foreign Languages also being protected. Geography became an optional subject, in competition for curriculum time with other National Curriculum subjects (e.g. History, Art), non-National Curriculum subjects (e.g. Business Studies) and the newly developed general vocational courses. The inevitable decline in numbers of pupils opting for GCSE geography is taking place with 4 per cent, 8.5 per cent and 3.1 per cent reductions in candidates being registered in 1997, 1998 and 1999 respectively. History numbers have seen a similar decline and Bell (1998), in a paper to the British Educational Research Association, noted that constrained option choice for 14–16-year-olds has also resulted in a substantial decline in numbers taking both history and geography (22 per cent, 1984; 11 per cent, 1997).

As Marsden points out for primary geography (Marsden, 1998), important wider issues are raised by these situations. It is not merely a question of 'heads down and fighting our corner' for geography in an increasingly competitive situation. It is crucial that geographers, along with other subject specialists, challenge the assumption that learning in the basics or the core subjects is somehow opposed to and independent of learning in other subject areas. Geography can undoubtedly be an effective and motivating medium for learning basic as well as subject-specific skills, as the recent Schemes of Work for primary geography make clear (DfEE and QCA, 1998). Matthew Arnold's observations on the deadening effect of the basic 'Revised Code' primary curriculum in England reveals that he felt that this was true in the late 1880s as well:

> I find in them [schools] in general, a deadness, a slackness and a discourage-
> ment, which are not the signs and accompaniments of progress. Meanwhile
> . . . geography and history, by which, in general, instruction first gets hold of
> a child's mind and becomes stimulating to him, have in the great majority
> of schools fallen into disuse and neglect.
>
> (Arnold, 1910)

In addition, it can be argued that at all Key Stages there are other basic entitlements which should find a place in any curriculum. Indeed, the original National Curriculum seemed to recognize this by its breadth of subjects, although the overloaded requirements made it impossible to deliver. Perhaps, as geographers, we should be asking ourselves 'What is the minimum entitlement in our subject which is essential for every future citizen?' How important are, for example, basic map skills, some locational knowledge, environmental awareness and understanding of global interdependence for the twenty-first century and how clearly linked are these by the general public with the school subject, geography? A flurry of articles in the press, in early May preceding the 1999 National Curriculum consultation, seemed to show that the public image (or at least the media's image!) of geography is still one of a predominantly factual subject, with little recognition of its contribution to understanding major environmental, social and political issues. It is interesting to note that the science community in England has also been undertaking such a rethinking exercise about entitlement to Science (Nuffield Foundation,1998) and some of this seems to have borne fruit since the Secretary of State's letter introducing the National Curriculum consultation (May 1999) has recognized that 'keeping National Curriculum Science in step with the changing world of the 21st century' is a major issue still to be addressed. Can geographers make the same case? Initial signs from the review of the National Curriculum are not promising. The primary curriculum is likely to remain in the grip of narrowly defined literacy and numeracy, with other subjects reduced to brief lists of required content. The Key Stage 3 curriculum will not escape the pressures of literacy and numeracy. Although some interesting ideas were considered for Key Stage 4 during the Review (e.g. about a curriculum based on entitlement to broad areas of experience with schools free to plan the detail), the government intends to maintain the existing view of 'core and others', leaving more adventurous changes for the longer term (QCA and DfEE, 1999). Unless we can make and justify a convincing case for a geographic entitlement for all (possibly using the new requirements for Citizenship and Personal, Social and Health Education as one lever), geography's future in England may be as a minor extra to the primary curriculum 'if time permits', and a marginal academic offering for some 14–16-year-olds.

## Geography and 'Preparation for Adult Life'

Preparation for Adult Life (PAL) is the term coined in England to refer to the 'new agenda' of the Labour Government, covering personal, social and health education, citizenship, education for sustainable development and the spiritual, moral, social and cultural dimensions. In reviewing the National Curriculum for the year 2000, Ministers have wished to 'create space' for these aspects of education, alongside the existing ten-subject National Curriculum, already perceived as overloaded by many schools (SCAA, 1997a).

Since 1988, geography has suffered in England from this continuing tension between the desire to prescribe detailed subject content to be taught for individual National Curriculum subjects and the need to recognize, and leave room for, some of the wider purposes of schools in preparing pupils for adulthood. The Education Reform Act of 1988 stated that every pupil should be entitled to a curriculum which was balanced, broadly based and 'prepares (such) pupils for the opportunities, responsibilities and experiences of adult life' (DES, 1989a: 7). The guidance booklet produced by the Department of Education and Science (1989b) explained that the National Curriculum, as specified, was not intended to be the whole curriculum – 'they [the foundation subjects] are necessary but not sufficient. – More will however, be needed to secure the kind of curriculum required by Section 1 of ERA.' The booklet identified a whole range of areas which schools would need to address, including targeted activities such as careers education and guidance, broader dimensions such as multicultural education, and cross-curricular themes like political understanding. Such matters were taken very seriously by the government's advisory body (then the National Curriculum Council) which, during 1989 and 1990, developed a full set of Curriculum Guidance booklets to help schools teach five cross-curricular themes. Ministers, however, saw this as distracting attention from the main task of implementing the National Curriculum subjects and, after a major disagreement between the NCC's Chief Executive, Duncan Graham, and the Secretary of State for Education (described in detail in Graham, 1993), the status of the booklets was downgraded and schools were left in no doubt that the National Curriculum subject content was the main priority.

The problem has remained throughout the 1990s. Whatever the Act states about preparation for adult life, a highly detailed and subject-based National Curriculum has left schools little room for manoeuvre in curriculum planning. With no clear statement of aims and priorities for the education of each age group, schools have assumed that the ten National Curriculum subjects (and particularly the core subjects with their detailed Orders, testing arrangements, and impact on league tables) are the top priority. For geography, this situation has caused dilemmas. The National Curriculum specification seems to require a narrow concentration on subject-specific content and skills, so this is how schools have responded. School inspection reports in the 1990s have frequently commented on the missed opportunities for teaching about environmental matters or developing economic awareness. Yet geography, with its wide-ranging content, its coverage of physical and human geography topics, its relevance to current environmental, social and political issues and the opportunities it provides for critical enquiry, could potentially make a major contribution to many cross-curricular areas including the now fashionable citizenship. Over the past ten years, these matters have not been valued but now, suddenly, the political agenda is changing and, not surprisingly, all subjects, including geography, are seen to fall short of delivering these wider purposes.

The details of the new PAL agenda, which Ministers now wish to promote, were outlined during 1998–9 by four Advisory Groups or Panels covering education for sustainable development; personal, social and health education; citizenship; and creative and cultural education. An existing QCA project on spiritual, moral social, and cultural education also continued its work. These groups between them produced a total of 106 recommendations and proposed almost 300 new learning outcomes to add to the curriculum. A QCA overarching 'PAL' task group attempted to summarize the proposals and recommended that schools should be given non-statutory guidance on curriculum planning rather than further statutory requirements. Despite this, however, Ministers have now approved more prescriptive solutions, including an overarching framework for Personal, Social and Health education for all Key Stages 3 and 4 and the creation of a new 'National Curriculum subject' called Citizenship to be implemented at Key Stages 3 and 4 from 2002 (QCA and DfEE, 1999: 17–31). Geography may find its contribution to environmental education and education for sustainable development have been confirmed since environmental topics are already part of the National Curriculum content, and the government is keen to be seen to be addressing the recommendations of its Advisory Group on Education for Sustainable Development (1998), not dealt with directly in the PSHE and Citizenship frameworks. However, other developments are not so encouraging for existing National Curriculum subjects. With a new National Curriculum Order called Citizenship in existence, schools may find it easier to add a 5 per cent curriculum time slot to the school curriculum at Key Stages 3 and 4 (11–16 years), rather than consider meeting the requirements mainly by contributions from existing subjects. This will increase the pressure on existing subjects and possibly exacerbate geography's decline as a GCSE subject. What is more, it may be that many social, political and economic issues and teaching/ learning approaches designed to foster critical thinking and reflection will find a place in something new called Citizenship rather than in geography. Guidance on the implementation of personal, social and health education and citizenship are still awaited by schools, as these will give a steer on the relative importance given to subjects.

Mary Cawley (1998) describes the worrying situation in the Republic of Ireland where recommendations for a revised junior secondary curriculum have omitted geography as a direct result of moves to broaden the school curriculum and to address areas such as social, political and technological education. The geography education community needs to ask some searching questions. Despite a weighty literature on geography's contribution to these broad cross-curricular areas (see Foskett and Marsden, 1998), we seem to have failed to impress policy makers or to make clear that schools can use existing subjects to address some of the wider curriculum purposes (see Wragg, 1996). Or is it merely that, for politicians with a relatively short term of office, a 'quick fix' solution is more newsworthy and less bother to implement? The survival of good quality geography may require that we give this matter some serious thought.

## The decline of school-based curriculum development

Central curriculum guidelines increasingly provide the framework within which teachers operate in many developed countries, as governments attempt to influence perceived economic and social ills by means of educational policy. Ultimately, however, the quality of education offered and the standards achieved depend primarily on the way in which teachers implement these guidelines within their own schools and classrooms – that is, it depends on their professional expertise in school-based curriculum development. In geography education in England, there is a long tradition of curriculum development. During the 1970s, the three Schools Council Geography projects[1] (GYSL, 14–18 Bristol and 16–19) provided curriculum frameworks, teaching materials and most importantly, professional support and in-service education so that teachers could review and develop their own teaching and learning. Although project dissemination did not reach all schools, those that were involved provided a generation of school pupils with access to a wide range of contemporary issues through geography and with active enquiry styles of learning. Teachers were also enthused by the new ideas from geography and from education, and an air of challenge and innovation was disseminated through project conferences and publications. Project approaches gradually influenced GCSE and A-level syllabuses in the 1980s and, judging by subject entries and results in the 1989–95 period,[2] geography was popular and successful in raising standards.

The situation changed dramatically in 1988 when the ERA introduced a Geography National Curriculum. Although there have been some gains, particularly in ensuring an entitlement to geography in the primary curriculum (Rawling, 1999), one of the biggest casualties has undoubtedly been involvement in school-based curriculum development and the resultant innovation and creativity that are associated with it. Writing in 1996 about the impact of the National Curriculum on geography (Rawling, 1996), I showed how the highly prescriptive 1991 Geography Order, and the context within which it was introduced, had a detrimental effect on all four conditions necessary for school-based curriculum development to flourish (see Table 1.2). The introduction of the National Curriculum was not so much an exercise in changing content (though there was an element of that for geography), but about redefining and relocating curriculum control. Teachers were denied a shared role in curriculum planning, since the Order seemed to appropriate all three levels of planning (national, school and classroom). It also seemed to reject previous good curriculum practice,

*Table 1.2* School-based curriculum development

| Important conditions | Situation after 2000<br>[revised Geography NC] |
|---|---|
| (A) *Shared curriculum control*<br>Recognition and respect for three levels of curriculum planning | *Improving*<br>Less prescription in the Geography National Curriculum, more flexibility and greater recognition of teacher input |
| (B) *Teacher teamwork*<br>Teachers work together in supportive environment on curriculum planning | *Stagnation or decline*<br>Inadequate support infrastructure (e.g. fewer subject advisers)<br>   Emphasis on competition between schools reinforced by funding and league tables |
| (C) *Building on good practice*<br>New developments draw on existing good practice and teacher commitment | *Improving*<br>Some central guidance drawing on good practice (eg QCA Schemes of Work)<br>   Greater role for subject associations |
| (D) *The curriculum system*<br>Content, teaching/learning approaches and assessment recognized as integral parts of one system | *Improving*<br>The Geography National Curriculum has a more integrated curriculum model and is more obviously a minimum national entitlement |
| (E) *Professional development*<br>Teacher development seen as an essential part of curriculum development<br>   Confidence in status and contribution of geography | *Stagnation or decline*<br>Confidence and trust of geography teachers diminished by other national policies (e.g. Literacy Strategy) and by geography's declining status in primary and 14–16 curriculum |

*Source*: Adapted from Rawling, 1996

to confuse the relationship between curriculum content and assessment strategies and to offer no coherent policy of guidance and support. In 1996, I expressed the hope that the 1995 (Dearing) review of the National Curriculum might address some of these concerns. In the event, although the geography curriculum itself became less prescriptive, the other conditions were not met. In particular, essential curriculum planning guidance did not arrive until a year or more after implementation (SCAA, 1996, 1997b), it was labelled confusingly as advice on consistency in assessment (although its application was much wider), and it was not accompanied by any major dissemination or professional development programme for teachers. Teachers were still not made to feel partners in developing the curriculum.

It is difficult to make a direct link between the decline in curriculum development activity and the state of geography in schools. Given the curriculum history of the past ten years, geographers could not have avoided involvement in the National Curriculum, and there have been gains in confirming its existence as one of the ten statutory subjects for 5–14 years. The National Geography

Curriculum is being delivered and the first tentative teacher assessment results for geography (1997 and 1998) show that these are largely similar to those of other comparable non-core subjects. However, it is not hard to find problems with implementation and quality. OFSTED inspection findings at Key Stages 1, 2 and 3 over the past three years (1996a, 1996b, 1997,1998a, 1998b) point to continuing weaknesses for geography. Although, at primary level (Key Stages 1–2) there are examples of lively well focused geographical work, the 1998 OFSTED summary commented that 'within the primary curriculum, progress and teaching in geography are weak in comparison with most other subjects'. 'The organisation of the curriculum [is weak] in some schools, with infrequent study of geography' (1998a). Similarly, at Key Stage 3, although there is a good deal of satisfactory work and some high quality investigative activities, geography compares unfavourably with most other subjects when standards of achievement, progress and quality of teaching are examined (OFSTED, 1998b). Given the significance of Year 9 (14-year-olds) choice of subjects for the 14–16 curriculum and beyond, geography's current inability to stimulate pupils to achieve higher standards, *compared with other subjects*, must be seen as a danger signal for the future. The overall picture emerging is one of uninspiring and unimaginative teaching for this crucial period in secondary education. At all Key Stages, the weaknesses are linked in some way (SCAA, 1997a; OFSTED, 1998a, 1998b) with the need for further professional development in curriculum and assessment practice, but also (particularly at Key Stages 1–2) in subject knowledge.

Further points reinforce the concern. One particular geography textbook, presenting a relatively narrow uncritical view of the subject, holds a stranglehold on the market. In-service education is focused almost exclusively on the technicalities of delivering and assessing the required content, with no time for the kind of reflection about teaching strategies or excitement about developing new ideas from academic geography which used to characterize activities in the 1970s. The number of geography-specific advisers in local education authorities is declining year by year and recent figures reveal that the supply of entrants to teacher training for geography has declined dramatically (Roberts, 1999). The picture painted is one of curriculum stagnation and the signs are that this will eventually affect quality and status. This contrasts with the situation in higher education, where there has been an upsurge of interest in teaching and learning geography (Healey, 1998), stimulated by the teaching quality audit exercise (Chalkley, 1998) and, more recently, the decision to establish a geography 'subject centre' to promote good practice in teaching, learning and curriculum planning. The 'buzz' of curriculum development activity seems now to be found in higher education, not in schools. It is particularly well exemplified in the new Teaching and Learning Guides published by the Geography Discipline Network (GDN, 1998). These are full of sound curriculum advice and case studies of good practice and, ironically, they would be equally applicable in most cases to schoolteachers. However, there will need to be considerable publicity to persuade teachers that these are relevant, given the stranglehold of National Curriculum and examination guidelines (Rawling, 1999a).

In fact, the conditions may become more favourable in schools. The latest review (1998–2000) of the National Curriculum has made minimal changes to the content of subject Orders, but it has reduced prescription and increased flexibility both within subjects and across the wider curriculum (QCA and DfEE, 1999). The Geography Order has also undergone a subtle change of structure, potentially more conducive to creative curriculum implementation (see Rawling, 2000a). In this respect, it may be argued that the tide of state control in England is beginning to 'roll back'. Indeed, *The Sunday Times* (16 May 1999) in an article titled 'Revenge of the Progressives', has characterized, probably unhelpfully, the latest National Curriculum Review as demonstrating a revival in the fortunes of the progressive educational lobby. As far as geography is concerned, SCAA/QCA Monitoring shows that schools never really appreciated the amount of freedom provided in the 1995 Review. From 2000, there will be even less control over what and how they teach, particularly at Key Stage 3, although, despite *The Sunday Times*, the revised Geography Order still does demand a basic framework of locational knowledge and factual content from which more expansive contributions can be built. The two are not, and never have been, mutually exclusive. It would seem that the time is right for the subject community to relaunch geography as a motivating and relevant subject in Key Stages 1–3 and to promote a new drive for school-based curriculum development in geography. Such a move might serve not only to improve the quality of teaching and learning in schools, but also to reconnect the subject with the current citizenship and sustainable development initiatives, at least at school level. Given the enthusiasm and excitement surrounding developments in teaching and learning in higher education geography, it might also provide the right stimulus to reopening productive dialogue with our higher education colleagues. The forthcoming publication, in 2000, of a Key Stage 3 Scheme of Work for geography provides another reason to remind schools of their autonomy in curriculum terms. This joint initiative of QCA and the DfEE Standards and Effectiveness Unit is designed to provide examples of units of geographical work covering the whole Key Stage 3 programme of study. Though it will present invaluable support for the less confident geography department, is there also a danger that it will become the 'state-approved' approach to implementing geography for this age group (i.e. an even more prescriptive curriculum than 1991, entering by the back door)? One positive point is that the Teachers' Guidance, appearing with the Scheme of Work, will clarify the principles of curriculum planning and draw attention to the scope for teachers to develop their own units from the models provided.

The existence of central curriculum guidelines does not rule out creative school-based curriculum development – the key seems to lie in achieving a balance in which a national framework is accommodated while creative development activities are revived at local and school levels.

## School geography as part of a wider geography education system

This chapter has stressed the need to look outward from school geography, both at broader educational trends and at different levels of education. This is necessary in order to understand the problems we face and to find solutions. It will also be argued that it is important to see the whole geography education system, rather than focusing on one part of it. In a recent article, Gersmehl referred to the need for geographers in the USA to view the educational enterprise as a complete system (Gersmehl, 1996). He used the analogy of a four-wheeled cart to draw attention to the four essential aspects of the system (the wheels) as he saw it. My own version of the cart (Figure 1.1) is designed to relate to the situation in England and suggests that school geography is only one part (one wheel) in an interdependent system. The other 'wheels' are teacher education, academic geography and lifelong learning, in each of which the subject is, or should be, strongly represented. It is crucial that geographers are aware of current issues and concerns in the other parts of the system – for instance, teacher supply shortage in secondary geography teacher education; renewed emphasis on teaching/learning and the benchmarking exercise (1999) in higher education geography; proposals to widen educational opportunities and extend access in lifelong learning. At present, every part of this system operates independently, having its own systems of funding, assessment, regulation, monitoring and public accountability so, to continue the analogy, the wheels of the cart are operated and serviced separately. A greater degree of cooperation might ensure that this particular cart runs more smoothly, to the benefit of all levels of education.

The Council of British Geography is making progress in developing cross-sectoral links, particularly through its biennial COBRIG Seminars (see Rawling and Daugherty, 1996) aimed at geographers from all levels of the education system. There are similar initiatives in other countries, for example, the Geography

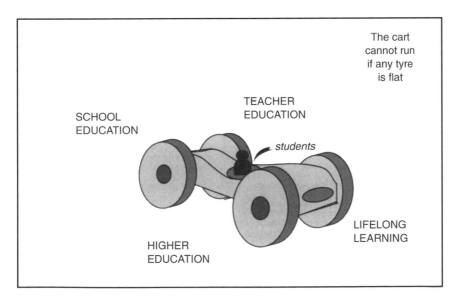

*Figure 1.1* Geography education is like a cart with four wheels (adapted from Gersmehl, 1996)

Education National Implementation Project (GENIP) in the USA. Some current examples of cross-sectoral cooperation reveal how it can work to mutual benefit. The Royal Geographical Society with the Institute of British Geographers (RGS–IBG) recently organized a high-profile day conference to investigate the issue of teacher supply and shortage of geography entrants. Delegates and speakers included representatives from academic geography, schools and teacher education and from various national bodies like the Teacher Training Agency and the Qualifications and Curriculum Authority. A joint TTA/RGS–IBG Conference Report has highlighted strategies for action at all levels of education (Rawling, 2000b).

Another example concerns the Higher Education Study Group of the RGS–IBG which organized a joint schools/higher education conference in May 1999, on the theme of Exploring Pedagogy and the Teaching and Learning of Geography (Rawling, 1999b). At this conference, delegates identified several aspects of teaching and learning where there was potential for collaborative cross-sectoral research, including the use and misuse of textbooks, fieldwork approaches in schools and higher education, and effective ways of promoting the development of independent learning at different ages. Given the existence of the ESRC fund for teaching and learning initiatives, might it be possible to take some of these ideas through to fruition? A start in identifying broad areas of common interest across the sectors has, for example, been made in the paper, *Reflections on School Experience* (Bednarz et al., 1999)[3] prepared for the international Teaching and Learning Symposium held in Hawaii, March 1999.

## Conclusion

Confirmation of a place in the National Curriculum does not ensure continuing security for the subject. This brief chapter has shown that threats to geography can come from outside the subject, particularly in recent years from initiatives designed to address basic skills and pupils' preparation for adult life. They can also come from within the subject, in the sense that unless innovation and creativity about teaching and learning are maintained, the health, vigour and status of the school subject may decline. It has been argued that strategies to strengthen geography's position must include a revival in school-based curriculum development and renewed attention to the whole geography education system. These are encouraging signs, noted above, but there are also some issues for immediate discussion and action which are summarized below:

- Re-launching geography at Key Stages 1–3

  How can we relaunch geography in schools in the year 2000 as the revised Statutory Order is introduced, to ensure that its value and potential are realized afresh? Can we reintroduce it to primary schools where, in many cases, it has been marginalized since 1998? Can/should the subject associations work to make this a priority?

- Public image of geography
  How can we re-educate the public and the media about the character and diversity of the modern school subject, without losing the strengths generated by its old image? (Geography is about sustainable futures and global citizenship as well as, and because of, its concern with place knowledge, maps and fieldwork.) Can we start policy makers talking about a geographic/environmental entitlement, rather than just equating geography with locational knowledge?
- Geography at Key Stage 4
  How can we halt the dramatic decline in geography take-up and GCSE entry at Key Stage 4? Can this be done without fighting other subjects (e.g. history)? How effectively can we build on geography's contribution to cross-curricular areas if fewer pupils are able to take the subject to GCSE? Will geography gain from the opportunity for more pupils to take the Advanced Subsidiary level at 16–19, despite difficulties at 14–16? Will the proposed more radical look promised for the 14–19 curriculum in 2002 be too late to halt the decline at 14–16?
- Geography in the whole curriculum
  How can we ensure that newer concerns like thinking skills, citizenship and education for sustainable development are a part of geography's responsibility? Can we convince senior managers as well as geography coordinators and teachers? Are there new possibilities for geography in qualifications at 16–19 (e.g. short course combinations; AS syllabuses)?
- Curriculum development and pedagogy
  How can we revive interest and involvement in school-based curriculum development and promote new initiatives in teaching and learning? Will a relaunch of the National Curriculum help? Where will the time, funding and opportunity for professional development and research come from? What benefits might derive from links with higher education colleagues? Are there potential cross-sectoral initiatives that can be followed up?
- Cross-sectoral liaison
  How can we establish cross-sectoral liaison and cooperation on a more formal footing within the geography education system? What role can be played, for example, by COBRIG activites such as the biennial Seminar, subject association initiatives, international dialogue and funding from agencies like the Teacher Training Agency and the Economic and Social Research Council?

My own view is that this latter point is crucial. Mutual understanding and cooperation across the levels and sectors of education are not luxury 'extras' which can wait for calmer times; they are essential strategies to ensure the health and quality of geography into the next century.

## Notes

1   Geography for the Young School Leaver (Avery Hill), Geography 14–18 (Bristol) and Geography 16–19 (London) were the three influential curriculum development projects of the 1970s and early 1980s in England. For an account of their activities and influence see Rawling (1991).
2   Entries for GCSE geography stayed stable at 290,996 candidates in 1989 and 290,365 candidates in 1995. GCSE grades A–C awarded for geography increased over this period from 46.1% candidates to 52.7% candidates. Entries for Advanced level geography increased from 38,555 to 43,454 candidates 1989–95; 26.1% candidates received A or B grades in 1989 and 30.6% received grades A and B in 1995 (source of data, QCA).
3   The papers for this symposium are available on the World Wide Web at <http:/www. chelt.ac.uk/gdn/hawaii/>.

## References

Arnold, M. (1910 edn) *Reports on Elementary Schools 1852–1882*, London: HMSO.

Bednarz, S., Burkill, S., Lidstone, J. and Rawling, E. (1999) 'Developing an international network for learning and teaching geography in higher education: reflections on school experience', paper produced for International Symposium on Learning and Teaching Geography in Higher Education, Honolulu, March 1999. Also available at <http:// www.chelt.ac.uk/gdn/hawaii/>.

Bell, J. F. (1998) 'Patterns of subject uptake and examination entry 1984–97', paper presented to BERA Annual Conference, August 1998, Belfast.

Cawley, M. (1998) 'Geography under threat in Irish second level education', *International Research in Geographical and Environmental Education*, 7, 1: 5–13.

Chalkley, B. (1998) 'Geography and quality in higher education', special issue of *Geography* focused on Quality and Standards in Geographical Education, 83, 1: 53–62, Geographical Association, Sheffield.

Department for Education and Employment (DfEE) (1997a) *Excellence in Schools*, Cm 3691, London: The Stationery Office.

Deprtment for Education and Employment (DfEE) (1997b) *From Targets to Action: Guidance to Support Effective Target Setting in Schools*, London: DfEE.

Department for Education and Employment (DfEE) (1998) *The National Literacy Strategy: Framework for Teaching*, London: Standards and Effectiveness Unit of DfEE.

Department for Education and Employment (DfEE) (1999) *The National Numeracy Strategy and Framework for Teaching*, London: Standards and Effectiveness Unit of DfEE.

Department for Education and Employment (DfEE) and QCA (1999) *The National Curriculums Handbook for Primary Teachers and Handbook for Secondary Teachers*, London: QCA.

Department for Education and Employment and Qualifications and Curriculum Authority (1998) *A Scheme of Work for Key Stages 1 and 2: Geography*, London: QCA. (Revised version forthcoming 2000.)

Department of Education and Science (1989a) *The Education Reform Act 1988; Circular no. 5/89*, London: DES.

Department of Education and Science (1989b) *The National Curriculum from Policy to Practice* (para 3.8), London: DES.

Development Education Association (1998) *Literacy: The Global Perspective*, London: DEA.

Foskett, N. and Marsden, W. E. (1998) A *Bibliography of Geographical Education 1970–1997*, Sheffield: The Geographical Association.

Geography Discipline Network (GDN) (1998) *Geography Teaching and Learning: A Series of Ten Booklets*, HEFCE Fund for Development of Teaching and Learning, Cheltenham: Cheltenham and Gloucester College of Higher Education.

Gersmehl, P. (1996) 'Opinion: more like a cart than a factory: understanding resistance to educational change', *Journal of Geography*, 95, 3 (May/June): 130–1, NCGE, Indiana, PA.

Graham, D. (with Tytler, D.) (1993) A *Lesson for Us All: The Making of the National Curriculum*, London: Routledge.

Healey, M. (1998) 'Developing and internationalising higher education networks in geography', *Journal of Geography in Higher Education*, 22, 3 (November 1998): 277–82.

Higher Education Funding Council for England (HEFCE) (1998) *Learning and Teaching: strategy and funding proposals*, Consultation Paper 98/40, Bristol: HEFCE.

Higher Education Funding Councils (HEFCs) (1998) *Consultation: Subject Centres to Support Learning and Teaching in Higher Education*, Circular letter no. 36/98, Bristol: HEFCE.

Judd, J. (1999) 'Schools to teach citizenship lessons', *Independent on Sunday*, 21 February 1999.

Marsden, W. E. (1998) 'The Blair necessities', *Primary Geographer*, 34 (July 1998): 26–8, The Geographical Association, Sheffield.

Martin, M. O. *et al.* (1997) *Science Achievement in the Primary School Years: IEA's Third International Mathematics and Science Study (TIMSS)*, MA: Center for the Study of Testing Evaluation and Educational Policy, USA.

Nuffield Foundation (1998) *Beyond 2000: Science Education for the Future*, London: Kings College.

OFSTED (1996a) *Subjects and Standards: Issues for School Development Arising from OFSTED Inspection Findings 1994–95 Key Stages 1 and 2*, London: HMSO.

OFSTED (1996b) *Subjects and Standards: Issues for School Development Arising from OFSTED Inspection Findings 1994–95 Key Stages 3,4 and post 16*, London: HMSO.

OFSTED (1997) *The Annual Report of Her Majesty's Chief Inspector of Schools: Standards and Quality in Education 1995–96*, London: HMSO.

OFSTED (1998a) *Standards in the Primary Curriculum* (Geography leaflet), London: HMSO.

OFSTED (1998b) *Secondary Education: A Review of Secondary Schools in England 1993–97*, London: HMSO.

OFSTED and the Department for Education and Employment (DfEE) (1997) *National Curriculum Assessment Results and the Wider Curriculum at Key Stage 2*, London: DfEE.

Qualifications and Curriculum Authority (QCA) (1998) *Maintaining Breadth and Balance at Key Stages 1 and 2*, London: QCA.

Qualifications and Curriculum Authority (QCA) and DfEE (1999) *The Review of the National Curriculum in England: The Secretary of State's Proposals*, London: QCA.

Rawling, E. (1991) 'Innovations in the geography curriculum 1970–1990: a personal view', in Walford, R. (ed.) *Viewpoints on Geography Teaching: The Charney Manor Conference Papers 1990*, Harlow, Essex: Longman.

Rawling, E. (1996) 'The impact of the National Curriculum on school-based curriculum development in secondary geography', *Geography in Education*, Cambridge: Cambridge University Press.

Rawling, E. (1999) 'Geography in England 1988–98: costs and benefits of National

Curriculum change', *International Research in Geography and Environmental Education*, 8, Clevedon: Channel View Books/Multilingual Matters.

Rawlin, E. (1999b) 'Exploring pedagogy and the teaching and learning of geography' – report of a seminar organised by the Higher Education Study Group of the Royal Geographical Society with IBG, May 1999. (Unpublished, but available from elerawling@aol.com.)

Rawling, E. (2000a) 'National curriculum geography: new opportunities for curriculum development' in Kent, A. (ed.) *Reflective Practice in the Teaching of Geography*, Sage Publications.

Rawling, E. (2000b) 'Understanding teacher supply in geography', report of a conference organized jointly by the Teacher Training Agency and the Royal Geographical Society with the Institute of British Geographers, April 1999.

Rawling, E. M. and Daugherty, R. A. (eds) (1996) *Geography into the Twenty-first Century*, Chichester: John Wiley.

Roberts, M. (1999) 'Report of a survey to investigate recruitment to secondary geography PGCE courses and into job prospects for those completing such courses', unpublished survey report, School of Education, University of Sheffield.

School Curriculum and Assessment Authority (SCAA) (1996) *Consistency in Teacher Assessment: Exemplification of Standards – Geography at Key Stage 3* , London: SCAA.

School Curriculum and Assessment Authority (SCAA) (1997a) *Monitoring the School Curriculum: Reporting to Schools*, London: SCAA.

School Curriculum and Assessment Authority (SCAA) (1997b) *Expectations for Geography at Key Stages 1 and 2*, London: SCAA.

Wragg, T. (1996) *The Cubic Curriculum*, London: Routledge.

# Part I

# Issues in training geography teachers

# 2 The re-emergence of middle years initial teacher training

*Melanie Norman*

## Introduction

Currently, 43 per cent of teachers in the UK are in the 45–60 age range (DfEE, 1998a). In the next few years it is anticipated that there will be a severe shortage of teachers in the UK for two main reasons. First, many teachers in the 45–60 age group will retire in the next ten to fifteen years, and second, current teacher recruitment is well below the target set by the Teacher Training Agency (TTA). The shortage of teachers is more severe in some subjects than in others, geography being a subject officially recognized as a shortage area from September 1999. There is therefore an urgent need to encourage geography students into the teaching profession. Most geography teacher provision comes from those who follow the postgraduate certificate in education (PGCE) route, but perhaps it is time to also increase the undergraduate entry into geography teaching.

The current shortfall of students being recruited to teacher training courses has prompted the TTA to offer various Higher Education Institutions (HEI) Initial Teacher Training (ITT) departments student numbers in addition to those already allocated to them for ITT courses. These additional numbers are allocated to encourage these HEI to develop courses which train students to become experts in 'cross-phase' teaching (i.e. spanning the primary and secondary age ranges) in the recognized shortage subject areas. ITT providers in the recent past have organized their courses to train students for particular age ranges which generally accord with the primary/secondary age phases reflected in most UK schools. Thus, ITT courses, whether PGCE or undergraduate qualified teacher status (QTS) courses, train students to teach in either the primary sector (ages 5–11 years ) or the secondary sector (ages 11–18 years). The newly revived 'cross-phase' courses train students to teach in the upper years of the primary school and offer a subject specialism at both Key Stages 2 and 3.

In this chapter I look at the general issues of cross-phase understanding/ misunderstanding, and discuss a new provision to train geography teachers to strengthen a subject which, having nearly been lost to the curriculum in the 1980s when the National Curriculum consultation was taking place, is once again in danger of extinction.

## Background to the issue

The age at which it is deemed appropriate for pupils to transfer from one type of school to another type of school has generated debate for several decades. There are positive aspects of transferring from one school or college to another at different stages of one's development. Such changes of institution may be indicative of the changing needs of the individual, society, or employment.

The traditional age of transfer between primary and secondary sectors in the UK education system has been 11-plus, since the recommendation of the Board of Education Consultative Committee in *The Education of the Adolescent*, in 1926:

> It is necessary to explain why we think that the most desirable course is that children should pass to a new school at the age of 11. It is, briefly, that we desire to mark as clearly as possible the fact that at the age of 11 children are beginning a fresh phase in their education, which is different from the primary or preparatory phase, with methods, standards, objectives and traditions of its own. We want both them and their parents to feel that a hopeful and critical stage in their educational life is beginning in a school environment specially organised to assist it.
>
> (Board of Education Consultative Committee, 1926: para. 96: 89)

There is evidence that such transfers can have a negative impact in which children may suffer as a consequence of being unable to adapt to the change of environment. This has a subsequent impact on the child's ability to learn, which can have a long-term negative effect on a child's education. Nevertheless, the Board of Education Consultative Committee report of 1931 recognized that primary education should lead on to post-primary education as a matter of course and not be separate from it:

> In framing the curriculum for the primary school, we must necessarily build on the foundations laid in the infant school and must keep in view the importance of continuity with the work of the secondary school.
>
> (Board of Education Consultative Committee, 1931: para. 74)

It is also interesting to note that the 1931 Board of Education Consultative Committee Report recognized the importance of teachers in all types of secondary school keeping in close contact with teachers in the contributory primary schools and departments through regular meetings, conferences and placement exchanges to see the nature of each other's work. The report also recommended that such collaboration might include members of training colleges directly concerned with teaching methods (Board of Education Consultative Committee, 1931: para. 61).

These recommendations sound very much like the recommendations which supported the National Curriculum initiatives of the late 1980s, which begs the question, how far have ideas in education actually progressed this century, or have they merely been recycled over the decades? The following paragraphs support this notion that very little is new when changes are actually implemented.

Recognizing that transfer between schools does cause problems for some pupils, the DES circular 10/65 stated:

> A change of school is a stimulus for some pupils but for others it means a loss of momentum; the break imposed by transfer therefore calls for a deliberate effort to bridge it. To achieve continuity close co-operation between the staff of the different schools will be necessary, particularly where several junior schools feed to one senior school, in the choice of curriculum, syllabus and teaching method.
>
> (DES circular 10/65, cited in Stillman and Maychell, 1984:16)

There was encouraging feedback in the Bullock Report (DES, 1975) to suggest that cooperation between schools had, at least in part, contributed to an improvement in the levels of English-language curriculum liaison. However, the Cockroft Report (DES, 1982) indicated that cooperation between schools in different sectors had eased transfer difficulties from a pastoral and social perspective, but little had been achieved in terms of curriculum continuity (Stillman and Maychell, 1984: 16).

The Central Advisory Council for Education Report *Children and their Primary Schools* (1967) (commonly known as the Plowden Report) investigated the transition between primary and secondary schools and concluded that the age of transfer at 11 was too early and that 12 or 13 was a more realistic age to transfer to the secondary sector. Primary age pupils need to be given the fullest opportunities to develop their potential skills and abilities before the pressures of adolescence come in to force (Derricott, 1985: 2–4).

*Children and their Primary Schools* (1967) advocated middle school education to further develop the positive aspects of primary education, at the same time as gradually moving forward into secondary school work. However, it was suggested by some that this recommendation would seemingly increase the possibility of upset to pupils' learning by expecting them to cope with two transfers between schools at a time of their lives already identified as causing pressure, that is having to cope with adolescence. The primary, middle school, secondary school structure requires pupils to transfer to another school at the age of 9 and then again at the age of 13. The Plowden Report made twelve recommendations about continuity and consistency between the stages of education. The following list extracts those recommendations pertinent to the issues discussed in this chapter:

(iii)   The initial and in-service training of teachers should overlap more than one stage of education.

(iv)   There should be a variety of contacts between teachers in successive stages of education.

(v)   Local education authorities should close schools for one day to arrange conferences for teachers, when there is evidence of lack of contact between those in successive stages.

(vii)   There should be a detailed folder on each child which could provide a basis for a regular review with children's parents of their progress. The folder should accompany the child into the middle and secondary schools and should be available to the child's class teacher. Information about former pupils should be sent back from secondary to primary schools.

(ix) Authorities should send parents a leaflet explaining the choice of secondary schools available and the courses provided within them.

(xii) Discussions should be held between primary and secondary teachers to avoid overlap in such matters as text books and to discuss pupils' records.
(The Central Advisory Council for Education Report, 1967: para. 448)

The 1980s brought many changes in the education system; the introduction of the National Curriculum was mainly aimed at raising pupil standards, but its principles, which embraced all areas of education from the ages of 5 to 16 years, inevitably addressed issues of continuity:

A national curriculum will secure that the curriculum offered in all maintained schools has sufficient in common to enable children to move from one area of the country to another with minimum disruption to their education. It will also help children's progression within and between primary and secondary education and will help to secure the continuity and coherence which is too often lacking in what they are taught.
(DES, 1987, cited in Moon and Mayes, 1994: 357)

It is beyond the scope of this chapter to discuss the issues of primary/secondary transfer in general; however, it can be seen from these paragraphs that it is an issue which has prompted long-standing debate. It is clear that there has been a concern which has instigated a variety of responses to deal with primary/secondary transfer; it is a matter for further debate as to whether the National Curriculum has indeed addressed the question of curriculum continuity.

## A revival of primary/secondary initial teacher training routes

During the 1960s and early 1970s many teachers were trained in Colleges of Education to teach across the primary/secondary age range, or junior/secondary (J/S) routes as they were then known. As teaching became an all-graduate profession during the 1970s these J/S routes began to disappear, such that newly trained teachers had very little idea of cross-phase issues. To some extent, during the 1980s, schools developed their own solutions to this problem, when it became commonplace to have an appointed person in a secondary school who dealt with feeder primary schools and developed links to make the transition for pupils from one sector to another as smooth as possible. The advent of the National Curriculum in the late 1980s reinforced and extended these links as subject clusters were encouraged. There was initial interest but, as ever, the time needed to make such groups a success was never officially allocated although there was widespread recognition of their importance.

Initial Teacher Training courses have long recognized the importance of incorporating elements which introduce students to the notion of transition and the issues surrounding progression through the stages of education. It has been usual to include primary placement experience in secondary training courses, although it has never been common practice to include a secondary experience for those training to teach in the primary sector.

The advent of DfEE Circular 4/98 (1998b) has now officially emphasized the importance for trainee teachers to understand issues of progression. Annex A, Section A, Knowledge and Understanding, identifies for those training to teach in the secondary sector:

> Those to be awarded Qualified Teacher Status must, when assessed, demonstrate that they:
>
> vii understand, for their specialist subject(s), progression from the KS2 programme of study.
>
> (DfEE, 1998b: 9)

And for those training to teach in the primary sector:

> For all courses, those to be awarded Qualified Teacher Status must, when assessed, demonstrate that they:
>
> d. iv understand the progression from SCAA's 'Desirable Outcomes for Children's Learning on Entering Compulsory Education' to KS1, the progression from KS1 to KS2, and from KS2 to KS3.
>
> (DfEE, 1998b: 10)

As a consequence of the revived interest in an understanding of cross-phase issues, new cross-phase courses have recently been introduced into several Initial Teacher Training departments, now referred to as Key Stage 2/Key Stage 3 courses. In 1995, the TTA invited ITT providers to bid for numbers for cross-phase training in shortage subject areas. There was a recognition by the TTA that teacher subject specialisms needed boosting at Key Stage 2 and that there was a shortage of teachers of certain subjects in the Key Stage 3 sector. Only three HEI in England and Wales took up the initial offer to develop cross-phase degree routes in upper primary/lower secondary (UPLS) teacher training. However, there are currently 20 HEI in England and Wales offering such routes, showing a rapid growth in this sector of ITT and indicating a renewed understanding of the value of cross-phase trained teachers.

The division that can be created by the National Curriculum, and by the separation of primary and secondary phases of schooling, tends to promote discontinuity for pupils in their learning, and fails to acknowledge the varying levels of achievements of pupils at the end of Key Stage 2 in particular. This may have repercussions for pupils' progression in learning from Key Stage 2 to Key Stage 3 as identified by the School Curriculum and Assessment Authority (SCAA), whose report *Promoting Continuity between Key Stage 2 and Key Stage 3* states:

A concern often expressed during the recent review of the National Curriculum was that there was a loss of momentum in pupils' progress between the end of Key Stage 2 and the beginning of Key Stage 3. Primary schools often felt that their achievements have not been recognised and that secondary schools did not take sufficient account of the progress that pupils had made. Secondary schools on the other hand, have to plan for pupils coming from a range of different primary schools and ensure that the curriculum in Year 7 builds on what may be a wide range of experience.

(SCAA,1996b: 3)

Newly Qualified Teachers graduating from middle years initial teacher training courses will be in a strong position to forge links between primary and secondary sectors and hence facilitate pupil learning and minimize pupil disorientation and disaffection.

*Promoting Continuity between Key Stage 2 and Key Stage 3* recognizes that:

continuity will not flow from these curricular and assessment arrangements as a matter of course – continuity of pupils' educational experience can be significantly enhanced by the quality of the professional links established between primary and secondary schools.

(ibid.: 4)

Middle years trained graduates, with teaching practice experience in both primary and secondary schools, will understand how each sector operates and will be able to make a significant professional contribution to fostering links between schools and establishing continuity of experience for pupils.

The Annual Report of Her Majesty's Chief Inspector of Schools *Standards and Quality in Education 1994/95* (OFSTED, 1996) especially focused on the quality of teaching in Key Stages 2 and 3. The Chief Inspector stated that his evidence indicated that everything possible must be done to improve the quality of teaching given to children, particularly in Key Stages 2 and 3.

A prevailing theme is that standards of achievement at the upper end of Key Stage 2 and in Key Stage 3 are too low, for two reasons:

- 'curriculum liaison between primary and secondary schools is often insecure or non-existent' and
- 'Key Stage 3 pupils are often taught by the least qualified, or least experienced teachers'.

At the end of the four-year cross phase initial teacher training programmes, Newly Qualified Teachers will have considerable expertise in their subject specialisms and will have also developed an insight into and understanding of the curriculum, of teaching and learning, and of matters which enhance the concept of transition between primary and secondary schooling. Graduates should know what constitutes good practice at primary and secondary levels and will be able to carry principles of effective practice from one Key Stage to another.

There is concern from the TTA that Key Stage 2 teachers' subject expertise is often insufficient to promote quality learning in older and more able pupils. Increasingly, schools need to draw on deeper levels of expertise and understanding from a graduate teacher with a particular subject strength. In recognizing this need, and in acknowledging the grave concern over secondary level teacher supply in shortage subjects, students on Key Stage 2/Key Stage 3 degree routes will have a specific subject strength and will know how to apply this to promote quality teaching in the 7–14 age range.

Middle years ITT aims to produce graduates who will make a positive contribution to the raising of standards of education in the widest sense at Key Stages 2 and 3. The strengths of teachers who graduate through middle years routes will lie in their ability to bring to this key transitional phase of education the wide understanding of the whole curriculum of a good primary teacher, together with the enthusiasm and expertise in their own subject required of a good secondary teacher.

Students who follow Key Stage 2/Key Stage 3 routes therefore will have experienced whole curriculum work and also subject specialist work. They will have the skills of differentiation and cross-curricular project work associated with a primary teacher, and also the ability to specialize in a particular subject area associated with a secondary teacher. Additionally, they will have an understanding of the issues and problems for both students and staff of changing the style of learning between key stages.

## A geographical dimension in middle years training

For many years, the main avenue into geography teaching has been through PGCE pathways. There are currently 39 institutions in England and Wales offering PGCE geography courses, producing approximately 400 new geography teachers each year. A survey carried out by the Teacher Education Committee of the Geographical Association (GA) during the 1998/9 academic year, revealed widespread under-recruitment to geography PGCE courses. In 32 responses to questionnaires from geography PGCE departments, the number of students who gained QTS during the academic year of 1997/8 was only 83.1 per cent of the target set by the TTA. In January 1999 the number of students still on PGCE courses amounted to only 74.2 per cent of the target numbers set by the TTA. This situation is not explained only by an increase in target numbers this year, as the actual number of students on PGCE courses is less than the number who gained QTS in the previous year. In forecasting for 1999/2000 on similar target numbers as for 1998/9, over half the HEI indicated that recruitment is more difficult than in previous years. It appears that a serious recruitment problem is actually getting worse (Teacher Education Committee, 1999).

It is clear that graduate geographers are not being recruited into teaching in the numbers desirable to maintain the specialist teaching of the subject in schools. In 1998 only thirteen trainees were accepted onto undergraduate routes nationally for secondary geography ITT. The situation is such that from September 1999 the TTA has declared geography as one of the secondary shortage subjects.

The serious teacher supply situation cannot be allowed to deteriorate further. Much teaching of geography at Key Stage 3 is classified as 'poor' in OFSTED reports. There is a tendency for qualified teachers of most subjects to be used to 'bridge gaps' in shortage subject areas in the lower school curriculum. Geography teaching suffers greatly in this respect and non-specialists are frequently asked to teach geography to Key Stage 3 classes. Senior management, desperate for staff coverage, too often adopt the opinion that 'anyone who can read and write can teach geography'. This attitude says a lot about the status and the perception that others have of geography as a subject in its own right. It is this perception which has influenced the decline of the quality of geography teaching in the lower secondary school (11–14 year age group). Inevitably this has a knock-on effect in the upper school and beyond.

Perhaps more worrying are the recent initiatives which emphasize literacy and numeracy in the primary school to the apparent detriment of non-core subjects. The introduction of the Literacy Strategy in September 1998 and the 'Numeracy Hour' from September 1999, though not statutory, has certainly put constraints on the primary school curriculum as teachers try their best to respond to the initiatives. The 'literacy and numeracy hours' can have a wide interpretation and need not necessarily marginalize other subjects. However, evidence suggests that curriculum time for geography has diminished as a direct result of primary schools preparing for these initiatives. Research currently being undertaken by the University of Northumbria (at Newcastle) shows that 78 per cent of teachers interviewed report a reduction in the time spent on geography in the curriculum (Rawlinson et al., 1999). The research has gathered evidence from 86 primary schools and 40 secondary schools in the northeast of England. The results indicate that the reduction in geography curriculum time is not just confined to the primary sector, but geography teaching in secondary schools is also diminishing as the timetable continues to be squeezed.

Although recruitment to geography degrees is currently buoyant, more undergraduates are now opting for science-based geography degrees and it has been traditionally the arts geography graduates who have gone into teaching. The situation at A-level is still healthy, with large numbers of students still selecting to study geography. The situation at GCSE, however, is less encouraging, with a steady decline in take-up. Projecting the current situation in primary geography and geography teaching at Key Stage 3, it will not be many years before student applications for geography degrees decline, because pupils simply will not have had the opportunities to study the subject at earlier stages of their education with specialist geography teachers. Government legislation is strangling geography in the primary school, and in the overfull curriculum in the secondary school managers are forced to timetable non-specialists to teach the subject to lower school classes. In Scotland, the General Teaching Council requires geography to be taught to pupils by geography specialists. It would be gratifying to see the same commitment to the subject in England and Wales. Geography has already 'died' as a separate subject in the school curriculum of Australia and the USA, and it must not be allowed to meet the same fate in the UK.

## A new ITT undergraduate geography degree: a case study

The current situation with regard to the supply of geography teachers has prompted the University of Brighton School of Education (UBSE) to bid for numbers for an upper primary/lower secondary (UPLS) route in geography. The bid was successful and the first cohort began in September 1999.

The 1996–8 round of OFSTED inspections of thirty-six geography PGCE courses, found that 'areas of weakness in a minority of courses are the trainees' understanding of progression from Key Stage 2 to Key Stage 3', and OFSTED generally recommends providers to 'develop trainees' understanding of progression from Key Stage 2, and of the standards associated with Key Stage 3 level descriptions' (OFSTED, 1999).

The middle years route into geography teaching aims to improve the quality of geography teaching both in the primary school and in the lower secondary school, where evidence clearly shows that the subject is being poorly taught. It will, however, go only a small way to meet what appears to be a huge dearth in provision.

Why are there currently so few undergraduate main subject geography teacher training courses? Surely this is an excellent route into teaching, combining subject knowledge and application with the principles and practice of education studies?

The UPLS geography route at UBSE will offer students core studies in maths, science and English so that they can meet the standards of Annexes C, D and E (DfEE, 1998b). There will also be general Professional Studies modules and Professional Development in Geography.

Geography subject modules will provide the students with their academic geography studies. Some of this provision will come through the University of Brighton's School of the Environment in the Faculty of Engineering and Environmental Studies, where undergraduates are studying for a B.Sc. in geography and other related subject areas. Modules in fieldwork and GIS, which would be difficult to run with small group numbers, will be serviced by the geographers in the School of the Environment, with support from the School of Education geographers. UBSE has forged strong links with other Faculties in the University in order to give the best possible provision to students on ITT courses. These cross-faculty links have been very valuable in terms of expanding ITT provision and are recommended to other ITT providers to fully exploit internal resources for everyone's benefit.

Modules will also develop students' application of geography at Key Stages 2 and 3 and of course ICT skills to meet the requirements of Annexe B (DfEE, 1998b). In addition, a specific dimension of the proposed UPLS geography route at UBSE will be a direct link in years 3 and 4 to developing the trainees as Subject Leaders.

The school experience modules provide trainees with two primary placements and two secondary placements during the four-year course. Overall, students who follow the upper primary/lower secondary route should have a tremendous amount to offer, whether they choose to work in the primary sector, the secondary sector, or in middle schools.

The students entering this course will have a lot to achieve to meet the standards required by the DfEE for Qualified Teacher Status, as set out in Circular 4/98 (DfEE, 1998b). They will qualify in all the general standards, plus the specific standards of Annexes B, C, D and E and the geography subject-specific standards. Are we asking too much? Are the goals achievable?

## Conclusion

Middle years training is re-emerging, but is still generally misunderstood. The old J/S routes referred to earlier are long forgotten by most teachers as the profession has for so many years concentrated on the primary/secondary divide rather than looking at issues of progression and identifying ways each sector can support the other. Whenever the UBSE Key Stage 2/Key Stage 3 degree route is discussed among colleagues from other educational institutions or with teachers in schools, the question that is always asked is 'Are there a lot of middle schools in your area?' No, there are not a lot of middle schools in the partnership placement area of UBSE, although West Sussex still operates a middle school structure, but this is too narrow an interpretation of middle years trained teachers. The training of middle years graduates does not focus exclusively on teaching in middle schools. They are trained to have a much broader brief, which encompasses a wide and much needed understanding of issues of progression. Middle years trained graduates will bring skills and specific subject expertise to Key Stage 2 teaching which primary trained teachers will not have. OFSTED evidence suggests that the teaching of geography at Key Stage 2 is weak, although a slow improvement is recognized. Geography teaching in primary schools has undoubtedly been affected by the numeracy and literacy initiatives, though it is hoped that work in geography will improve with the re-instatement of the full curriculum from September 2000. Middle years trained geography subject specialists in the primary school will have been trained to exploit all curriculum areas in the pursuit of improving literacy and numeracy standards; they will be able to advise others how geography can be incorporated into many aspects of the curriculum.

Middle years trained teachers in the secondary sector will bring knowledge and understanding of the key skills to teaching at Key Stage 3 which secondary subject specialists do not have. Their subject expertise will allow them to be employed in a specific subject department, but they will also be able to contribute to the mathematics and English departments as a result of their training, giving employers considerable flexibility when middle years graduates are appointed to posts. Graduates will also have invaluable expertise in ICT.

There needs to be a concerted effort from those institutions training teachers in the middle years to advertise and celebrate the particular contributions that these graduates can make to both the primary and the secondary sector. Unless this is a reality, institutions will be doing a disservice to their middle years trained graduates and schools will be unaware of the distinctive potential of these graduates.

Given the crisis situation in the supply of geography teachers and the possible long-term effects on the subject, the middle years trained geography teachers should make a valuable contribution to the teaching profession in general and make a particularly positive contribution to the continued long-term success of geography.

## Questions

1   Can 'High Status, High Standards' geography teachers be achieved through cross-phase training, or will they be 'jacks of all trades' and masters of no specific field?
2   Given the support for an understanding of cross-phase education by all teachers, dating back to the 1920s, is it not time that ITT courses made better provision for cross-phase experiences?
3   Should ITT providers be given more opportunities to develop primary and secondary geography undergraduate education courses, in order to foster subject teaching across Key Stages 1–4?
4   Will 'Secondary Shortage Subject Status' help to entice geography students into geography teaching?
5   Will cross-phase trained geography graduates be attractive to:
    (a)  primary school heads and governors?
    (b)  secondary school heads of geography departments?
    (c)  secondary school heads and governors?

## References

Board of Education Consultative Committee (1926) *The Education of the Adolescent*, London: HMSO.

Board of Education Consultative Committee (1931) *The Primary School* (Hadow Report), London: HMSO.

Central Advisory Council for Education (1967) *Children and their Primary Schools* (Plowden Report), London: HMSO.

Derricott, R. (ed.) (1985) *Primary to Secondary: Curriculum Continuity*, Windsor: NFER-Nelson.

DES (1975) *A Language for Life (Bullock Report Great Britain)*, London: HMSO.

DES (1982) *Report of the Committee of Inquiry into the Teaching of Mathematics in Schools (Cockroft Report Great Britain)*, London: HMSO.

DfEE (1998a) *Statistics of Education: Teachers England and Wales*, London: DfEE.

DfEE (1998b) *High Status: High Standards Circular 4/98*, London: DfEE.

Moon, B. and Mayes, A. (eds) (1994) *Teaching and Learning in the Secondary School*, London: Routledge.

OFSTED (1996) *Standards and Quality in Education 1994/95*, London: HMSO.

OFSTED (1999) *Secondary Initial Teacher Training: Secondary Subject Inspections 1996–98; Overview Report*, London: HMSO.

Rawlinson, S., Essex-Cater, E. and Regan, E. (1999) *Geographers into Teaching*. The School of Education, University of Northumbria at Newcastle; on-going research reported at the University Departments of Education Geography Tutors' Conference, University of Birmingham, March 1999.

SCAA (1996a) *Review of Qualifications for 16–19 Year Olds*, London: School Curriculum and Assessment Authority.

SCAA (1996b) *Promoting Continuity between Key Stage 2 and Key Stage 3*, London: School Curriculum and Assessment Authority.

Stillman, A. and Maychell, K. (1984) *School to School*, Windsor: NFER-Nelson.

Teacher Education Committee (1999) *Report of Survey to Investigate Recruitment to Secondary Geography PGCE Courses and into Job Prospects for those Completing such Courses*, Sheffield: Geographical Association.

# 3  The role of research in the initial education of geography teachers

*Margaret Roberts*

Research, which disciplines curiosity and calls certainty into question, is a proper basis for teaching.

(Rudduck and Hopkins, 1985: 112)

## Introduction

In 1996 the Teacher Training Agency (TTA) published a policy statement titled *Teaching as a Research-based Profession*. The TTA saw part of its role as 'helping teachers to play a more active role in conceiving, implementing, evaluating and disseminating research' (TTA, 1996). In 1998 a study set up by the DfEE concluded that 'the actions and decisions of policy-makers and practitioners are insufficiently informed by research' (Hillage *et al.*, 1998). Implicit in the report's recommendations was the idea that educational research should have an impact on practice in schools. The official current rhetoric is all in favour of classroom teaching being supported by research. The phrases used vary: 'research-led', 'research-based', 'evidence-based', 'classroom-focused research' and 'classroom-relevant research evidence'. The underlying message is the same: classroom teaching should be related in some way to research.

Interest in teaching as a research-based profession is, however, not new. During the 1970s and 1980s teacher research was developed through the Humanities Curriculum Project (Stenhouse, 1970) and through the Ford project (Elliott and Adelman, 1976). Lawrence Stenhouse titled his inaugural lecture in 1979, 'Research as a basis for teaching' (reproduced in Rudduck and Hopkins, 1985: 113). Later, Elliott wrote about 'teaching and teacher development and evaluation, research and philosophical reflection' being integrated through action research (Elliott, 1991:54).

If the teaching profession is to develop as a research-based or evidence-based profession, whatever range of meanings that might have, then this must have implications for the initial teacher education of teachers.

I begin this chapter by examining the extent to which statutory influences on initial teacher education support the notion of teaching as a research-based profession. Then I explore what research-led teaching could mean in a

Post-Graduate Certificate of Education (PGCE) geography course, using examples from one particular institution. I examine:

- ways in which existing research can be used on a PGCE course;
- ways in which student teachers can become engaged in their own research;
- the way in which a course can be research-led in its practices and processes.

This chapter, although drawing examples from one PGCE course, is relevant to all those involved in the professional development of geography teachers, during the PGCE course, during the induction period, and during continuing professional development.

## The statutory framework for initial teacher education in England and Wales

Courses of initial teacher education in England and Wales have come under increasing central control and scrutiny during the past decade. There are statutory requirements for courses, there are standards for student teachers to achieve, there is a curriculum to be taught and there is a framework for the inspection of PGCE courses.

### Requirements

The current course requirements, standards and curriculum are set out in Circular 4/98 (DfEE, 1998). Over 90 per cent of those gaining Qualified Teacher Status (QTS) as secondary geography teachers in England and Wales do so through courses set up by Higher Education Institutions (HEIs). The requirements state that such courses must be a minimum of 36 weeks in length, of which 24 weeks must be spent in schools. The imbalance between time spent in higher education and time spent in school would seem to discourage a research orientation towards teaching. HEIs, through their libraries and computer facilities, have greater access to reports of research. HEIs are staffed by people who generally have a greater knowledge of relevant educational research than most classroom practitioners. Most HEI geography tutors have developed research knowledge and skills through their own research activities. The short length of time spent in HEIs by PGCE students, a period of only 12 weeks, places severe limits on what geography PGCE tutors can do to promote teaching as a research-based profession. However, the requirement in Circular 4/98 for HEIs to develop partnerships with schools encourages close links which open up possibilities for research-based activities within the partnership.

### Standards

Circular 4/98 contains a list of standards to be achieved by students by the end of the PGCE course. The standards are subdivided into separate statements that refer to what student teachers must know, understand, be aware of and be able to do before they can be awarded Qualified Teacher Status (QTS). They are written to be 'specific, explicit and assessable' (DfEE, 1998: 8). They set out what has to be 'demonstrated'. They present a model of learning guided by the outcomes of learning, rather than by the principles of processes to guide learning. The statements, although intended to be clear, are all open to interpretation and debate and could mean different things in different teaching and learning contexts (Bale, 1999). Student teachers are, for example, expected to identify 'clear teaching objectives' (DfEE, 1998: 12). Student teachers are not expected to investigate this approach to teaching and learning, to be aware of the arguments for and against the use of objectives in planning, or to consider the problems of identifying clear objectives for mixed ability classes. The statements are presented as something to be accepted, not something to be investigated and certainly not something to be challenged. They do not encourage an open questioning attitude to what the preface to the standards describes as 'the complexity of the teaching process' (DfEE, 1998: 4). The guidelines, however, do not specify how these outcomes are to be achieved, and it is in the process of achieving the standards that there is scope for initial teacher education courses to develop a research-led approach to teaching.

### Standards related to research

In the 64 statements in Circular 4/98 that are relevant to secondary geography PGCE students, the word 'research' occurs twice.

> Those to be awarded Qualified Teachers Status must, when assessed, demonstrate that they:
>
> *are aware of and know how to access*, recent inspection evidence and *classroom-relevant research evidence on teaching secondary pupils in their specialist subject(s), and know how to use this to inform and improve their teaching* [and:]
>
> *understand the need* to take responsibility for their own professional develop-ment and *to keep up to date with research and developments in pedagogy and in the subject they teach.*
>
> (DfEE, 1998: 9 and 16) (my italics)

Although the relevance of research is acknowledged in the standards, the paucity of statements referring to research does not encourage trainees to consider research as a major contribution to their development. Furthermore, in both these statements, research is presented as something that has already been carried out by others. Student teachers have to 'be aware of', or 'access', or 'keep up to date' with research. This is a limited view of the role of research in professional development. PGCE students are not required to demonstrate that they have the skills to investigate their own practice or indeed that of the 'good teachers at work' that they are expected to watch. The standards do not encourage the student teachers to develop an investigative approach to teaching. If the notion of teaching as a research-based profession is to be taken seriously, then these are serious omissions.

### The Information and Communications Technology curriculum for ITT

From September 1998 all PGCE students have also had to meet the requirements presented in the 'Initial Teacher Training Curriculum for the use of Information and Communications Technology (ICT) curriculum in subject teaching' (DfEE, 1998: Annex B). The first part of the ICT curriculum sets out what 'trainees must be taught and be able to use' (DfEE, 1998: Section A, p. 18). The emphasis is on classroom practice using 'those methods and skills described in this section'. There is no mention of research. In Section B, which sets out 'the knowledge and understanding of, and competence with, ICT which trainees need to support effective teaching' there is one reference to research:

> Trainees must demonstrate that they know how to use ICT to improve their own professional efficiency and to reduce administrative and bureaucratic burdens, including:
>
> *Knowing about current classroom-focused research* and inspection evidence about the application of ICT to teaching their specialist subject, and where it can be found.
>
> (DfEE, 1998: 31) (my italics)

The reference to research only in the last paragraph of the ICT curriculum suggests that most of the requirements are not research-based, and that they are not in any way problematic. As with the general standards referred to earlier, the emphasis is on knowing about research that has already been carried out, and not about student teachers engaging in their own investigations into the use of ICT.

### The inspection framework

The only reference to research in the 'Framework for the Assessment of Quality and Standards of Initial Teacher Training' (TTA, 1998) is to the two standards quoted earlier. The language used in the framework does not suggest a research-based approach to professional development. The framework refers to the quality of 'training' and to course 'delivery'. In evaluating quality, inspectors are required to find out whether 'opportunities are given to trainees to observe good teachers at work', but not that 'trainees' are given opportunities to develop the skills of observation. 'Trainees' are expected to be 'shown clearly how to teach their subject, to deploy effective teaching methods', not to be given opportunities to consider the value of different ways of teaching. 'Trainees' are expected 'to receive effective feedback' on their own teaching, not to be provided with the skills and conceptual frameworks to evaluate and discuss their own practice.

In summary, the official frameworks of requirements, standards, curriculum and inspection all fail to emphasize the potential role of research in the professional development of student teachers. There is a mismatch between the rhetoric of the TTA and the DfEE in favour of teaching as a research-based profession and in the implicit messages of the official frameworks that the very same institutions have devised for initial teacher education. In this chapter I argue for a more critical view of teacher development, in which teaching and learning is seen as something to be constantly queried and investigated by teachers throughout their professional development.

## Using the research findings in initial teacher education

There is a substantial body of research findings relevant to geographical education in schools. The Geographical Association has published a bibliography containing 3,708 references to books, journal articles and Higher Level degree theses, written between 1970 and 1997 (Foskett and Marsden, 1998). The list is by no means inclusive, as short articles, items in newspapers, and many publications from other countries have been excluded. This bibliography also did not include the large body of general educational research, much of which is highly relevant to beginner geography teachers. Existing research can be used in a course of initial teacher education in several ways:

- It can inform the content of the course.
- It can inform the teaching and learning processes used on the course.
- It can be used by student teachers as a point of reference for their own investigations.
- Theoretical frameworks developed through research can be used to increase understanding of teaching and learning.

The examples to be discussed are all taken from the 1997–1998 PGCE geography course at the Department of Educational Studies, the University of Sheffield.

### Example A: Course content informed by research

The content of all the sessions of the geography PGCE course was underpinned by research. One example of a session informed both by research in geographical education and by educational research in general was on written work. The session introduced PGCE students to the concept of 'audience' in geographical writing (Butt, 1996) and the extent to which this encourages geographical understanding. Examples of pupils' writing were examined with this concept in mind. The session also explored problems pupils have in writing in geography and referred to ways in which 'writing frames' could be used as part of a process of supporting pupils' written work (Wray and Lewis, 1997). These were applied in a geographical context. Because of time constraints, details of the research were not presented to the PGCE students, although this would have been preferable.

## Example B: Course process informed by research

PGCE course tutors at the University of Sheffield visited each student teacher three times during the block periods of school experience. The process of debriefing geography student teachers after observation of lessons was strongly influenced by research on clinical supervision (Acheson and Gall, 1980). In this style of supervision, the supervisor collects non-judgemental data during the observational period. Following the lesson, the data are discussed and interpreted by the student teacher and the supervisor. Student teachers are not 'given feedback'. They are participants in a discussion at the end of which conclusions are drawn and judgements are made and from which targets are negotiated. Instead of being dependent on the views of others, they learn to make their own judgements and to develop professional autonomy. If teaching is to develop as a research-based profession, it seems important that the processes used to promote learning on a course of Initial Teacher Education are themselves informed by research.

## Example C: Replication of research

PGCE geography students were introduced to lesson planning in the context of a lesson they were about to teach in one of the partnership schools. In pairs, PGCE students were required to plan and implement a lesson about contours for a small group of 12-year-old pupils. As part of the preparation, PGCE students were presented with findings of research carried out by Boardman on pupils' understanding of contours (Boardman, 1989). Some student teachers chose to attempt to replicate part of this research as part of the lesson and, in their evaluations they compared their findings with those of Boardman. Although the primary purpose of this activity was to provide a real context in which to learn about planning, implementing and evaluating a lesson, it also had other purposes. It demonstrated to PGCE students, early in the course, first, that teaching and learning can be investigated and second, that classroom practice can be usefully informed by research.

## Example D: Discussing theoretical frameworks with student teachers

PGCE geography students were introduced to several theoretical frameworks during the course of the year. One of those presented was developed for the evaluation of the TVEI project (Technical and Vocational Educational Initiative) (Barnes *et al.*, 1987). The report of the evaluation included a framework that categorized the extent to which teachers controlled subject content and activities. A style of working in which the teacher kept a tight control of content, procedures and outcomes was categorized as 'closed'. A style in which the teacher provided an explicit framework for the selection of content, procedures and evaluation of outcomes was categorized as 'framed'. A style in which the teacher negotiated all aspects of the teaching and learning with the learner was categorized as 'negotiated'.

PGCE students were introduced to the possibility of combining 'closed', 'framed' and 'negotiated' teaching styles within one lesson (Roberts, 1996a). They were then asked to consider this framework when planning and teaching a decision-making lesson with A-Level students (Roberts, 1996b).

Groups of between four and six student teachers worked collaboratively planning and teaching a half-day lesson for A-level students based on an A-level geography decision-making examination paper. The PGCE students' task was to use the resources and activities provided for the examination to develop an interactive lesson. Although the main purpose of the activity was to increase knowledge and experience of working with a particular A-level syllabus, an additional purpose was to enhance understanding of the use of different teaching styles through the use of a theoretical framework. For some PGCE students the framework transformed the way they thought about teaching and learning. It enabled them to re-conceptualize the classroom situation. It encouraged them to explore the underlying purposes of different ways of working with pupils. It encouraged them to question rather than accept. If teaching is to be a research-led profession, it seems important that PGCE students be encouraged to develop new understandings through the exploration of theoretical frameworks.

The four examples discussed show ways in which the DfEE requirements for PGCE students to become aware of 'classroom relevant research' and to 'know how to use this to inform and improve their teaching' (DfEE, 1998) can be fully integrated into many aspects of a PGCE geography course. Once the research evidence, theoretical frameworks, and the concepts derived from the research of others have been introduced, then they can become constant points of reference. Research findings can underpin the content of what is studied, the way teaching and learning take place, and the way teaching and learning are understood.

## Investigative work by PGCE students

The statutory standards and curriculum for ITT do not require PGCE students to carry out research into classroom practice. However, the school/university partnerships that have developed since 1992 provide opportunities for research. The following examples were all negotiated with partnership schools for the 1997–8 geography PGCE course at the Department of Educational Studies at the University of Sheffield. They enabled student teachers to carry out small-scale research by:

- interviewing a pupil
- observing a pupil
- observing an experienced teacher
- peer observation.

### Example A: Interviewing one pupil

During the first week of the course, geography PGCE students visited a school in which over 90 per cent of pupils were from ethnic minority backgrounds. During the visit each student teacher interviewed one 11-year-old pupil for an hour. The student teachers investigated the pupil's direct and indirect knowledge and experience of places in Sheffield, in Britain and in the world (Roberts, 1998). They investigated attitudes of pupils towards places mentioned. After the visit, the findings were shared and discussed and related to a theoretical framework devised by Goodey (1973) and to work developed by Matthews (1992) on children's maps, Spencer, Blades and Morsley (1989) on environmental perception and Wiegand (1991) on knowledge of the world. The activity had many purposes including: learning how to relate to pupils; how to listen; learning about pupils' place knowledge in relation to the requirements of the geography National Curriculum; and learning about the ethnic minority groups in our society. In addition to these purposes, however, a key purpose of the visit was to introduce the concept of teaching as an essentially investigative process. The teacher always needs to investigate to some extent what is in the learners' minds. This session also motivated PGCE students to read research findings and to consider theoretical frameworks. After the visit, the student teachers wrote reports for the school on the pupil they interviewed, providing the school with information on 11-year-old pupils that would have been difficult to obtain in any other way. The research was a very rich learning experience for the student teachers, as the following quotations from the reports suggest:

> When I first met Fatima I had no idea as to the extent of her knowledge. I have learned that it is important to make connections with the child to make sure work is of the right ability level for that particular child.

> Personal experience was of great importance for the accumulation of place-knowledge and this personal experience is in part determined by gender, ethnicity, economic and social status, mobility and opportunity.

> It is easy to assume a child has similar points of reference in town, country or world as yourself. I assumed H would know about the cathedral and the football stadiums, about France and know that Australia is at the other side of the world. I was wrong. It would be important to know what your class genuinely does know before you try to teach them.

Among other things, they learnt about forming relations with pupils, about the significance of cultural difference, and about the need to become aware of their own assumptions as teachers.

### Example B: Close observation of one pupil

PGCE students spent a lesson with a class of 13-year-old pupils in a partnership school in which parts of the geography National Curriculum and the technology

National Curriculum were planned jointly by the geography and the IT departments. The pupils developed their capabilities in using databases at the same time as studying issues of development (reported in QCA paper, 1998). During the lesson each PGCE student sat alongside one pupil, who was using a self-instructional booklet. The PGCE student teachers' task was to investigate, by observation and discussion with the pupils, the pupils' IT skills, their geographical understanding and the extent to which using computers contributed to their learning of geography. After the lesson, the student teachers compared their findings and discussed issues arising from the activity. Each student teacher wrote a report on his or her particular pupil. Some extracts from the reports illustrate what could be learnt from such close observation:

> It was obvious that R could produce simple data representative graphs at the touch of a button. However, I was impressed with his level of understanding of these graphs and he explained their distribution with a variety of geographical reasoning.

> I think a lot was learnt from observation of the pupil. You can tell when they are not too sure what they are doing, when a lot of unnecessary work is done on the computer in the hope that something which looks right appears on the screen. However, without discussion you cannot really tell what exactly they are thinking and whether they really have a full grasp of the information. Ideally, the best way to combine both techniques is to observe the child working and then discuss with them what they have done. This gives them the chance to explain and allows you double opportunity to assess their understanding.

These short extracts show that student teachers learnt about pupils' skills and about their levels of understanding. They also learnt about how to learn about pupils, about how to investigate. It is significant that the second quotation refers to assessment. The process of close research observation and discussion are skills needed by teachers for formative and diagnostic assessment.

### Example C: Observing an experienced teacher

During the first week of school experience, pairs of PGCE students observed an experienced geography teacher teaching a mixed ability class, to investigate how teachers planned for differentiation. One student teacher observed a higher achieving pupil, while the other observed a lower achieving pupil, in an activity originally developed by Corney (reported in Ellis, 1997). They negotiated with the teacher about which pupils to observe closely. The student teachers made detailed field notes about what 'their' pupil was doing during the lesson. Afterwards, they discussed their findings with the teacher in relation to the teacher's plan for differentiation. At the university the student teachers shared their observations and then discussed and evaluated the strategies they had observed. The main purpose of this activity was to evaluate strategies of differentiation. An additional purpose was to convey the idea that pedagogic knowledge can be increased through systematic investigation. One PGCE student wrote:

> Focusing on two pupils was really good because I realised you can never do that when you're teaching . . . you could see exactly where their concentration lapsed and came in. You could really work out how they interacted with other pupils. Later, I spoke to the learning support teacher about learning difficulties, and I learned a lot from that.

### Example D: Peer observation

Geography PGCE students were placed in pairs for both periods of school experience, a situation which provided opportunities for peer observation. For one of their geography assignments PGCE students were required to investigate their own classroom practice with the help of the teaching partner. They had to select a suitable lesson for the investigation, identify a focus for the observation, decide what data they wanted collected, decide how they were to be collected (after consulting the research literature) and to discuss all this with their partner. The partner carried out the observation and collected data. The PGCE student then analysed the data related to his or her practice, and compared them with other research findings. The types of focus chosen by student teachers included:

- the use of questioning in geography lessons;
- the relative attention paid to boys and girls;
- the relative attention paid to higher and lower achievers;
- patterns of teacher–pupil interaction in relation to the layout of the room.

Most student teachers, in their reports, pointed out several limitations of the activity: the possible unreliability of data from only one lesson; the subjectivity of some of the categories used; and the influence of the research activity on what is being observed. However, this small investigation made most student teachers far more aware of processes within their own classroom. They became aware, for example, of the way they responded to pupils' answers, or of their tendency to ask particular types of questions, or of great inequalities in the attention they gave to different pupils. They were expected, by reading some of the related literature, to relate their own findings to those of other researchers. Several students followed up the assignment with further peer observations.

Through this piece of action research on a very small scale, PGCE students became aware of their own practice as something which could be easily investigated to provide evidence for their own professional development, as the following extract from an assignment shows:

> It did provide some insight into my classroom practice in that there did appear to be some gender imbalance in the classroom interaction. More importantly, however, I feel this enquiry holds more significance in the whole learning

process of teacher training. This is because it is another means to encourage you to examine your classroom and employ self-assessment and explanation. Also I found it important as an introduction to classroom research . . . which will prove invaluable when reading educational literature in the future.

## An enquiry approach to teaching and learning

There is a third sense in which a PGCE geography course could be considered to be 'research-led'. A course can be developed in such a way as to encourage an inquisitive approach to pedagogic knowledge. Clearly, PGCE students have to be introduced to information and ideas on many aspects of education. Yet new information can be presented not as knowledge to be accepted, but as knowledge to be questioned. Stenhouse wrote about this kind of 'instruction' as 'sceptical, provisional, speculative in temper' (Rudduck and Hopkins, 1985: 118). In the PGCE geography course from which my examples were taken, everything presented was open to discussion, debate and critical judgement. For example, when the PGCE students were introduced to 'audience-centred writing' and to 'writing frames', they were not expected to accept the concepts and strategies uncritically. They were expected to examine them, to apply them in their own practice and to make their own professional judgements about their value. In this, as in other sessions, the content was discussed in a spirit of enquiry. To stimulate critical exploration of the content of the course, PGCE students were required to keep journals in which debate and discussion were encouraged.

Such an approach is consistent with the requirements of the geography National Curriculum, and the GCSE and A-level geography syllabuses. The importance of enquiry is emphasized in the geography National Curriculum. It requires that pupils should be given opportunities to identify issues and questions, to identify and collect evidence, to analyse and evaluate evidence. The core requirements for GCSE and A-level geography demand investigative work. The message of these requirements for school geography is that enquiry is a crucial part of the learning process. The way a PGCE course is taught and learnt can provide a model for an enquiry approach. PGCE students can apply *how* they learn on the PGCE course, as well as *what* they learn in classroom practice.

More important, however, is the contribution such an approach makes to professionalism. Such an approach emancipates student teachers from the authority of university tutors, of school mentors and of externally imposed standards, and provides them with encouragement to make their own independent professional judgements in seeking new understandings.

## Conclusion

The statutory framework for initial teacher education in England and Wales does not encourage courses of initial teacher education to be research-led. It is, however, possible for a PGCE geography course to emphasize research in its content, through the inclusion of investigative activities and in the way the course is taught. I have argued that this is beneficial for professional development. A research-led course can provide student teachers with greater access to pedagogic knowledge, by making them familiar with some of the research literature and by developing the critical skills for them to access and examine research findings. A course can provide student teachers with new frameworks for thinking about teaching and learning and this can provide insight into classroom processes. A research-led course provides opportunities for student teachers to investigate their own practice systematically, providing a foundation for future action research to improve practice. It encourages student teachers to pay close attention to pupils, to their activities, to their thinking, and to their viewpoints, a prerequisite for good teaching and assessment. A course in which the activities are investigative in nature provides a model of a way of working which is highly relevant to enquiry-based work in secondary school geography. A research-led course can encourage students to develop professional independence and the ability to make their own professional judgements.

If teaching is to develop as a research-based profession, as the TTA and the DfEE seem to want to encourage, then it seems important that the process of critical, investigative professional development should begin during courses of initial teacher education. In England and Wales it is possible to do this within the existing statutory frameworks, but it is also possible to avoid doing this. The statutory frameworks for the development of partnerships, for qualifications and for inspection should attach far more importance to the potential contribution of research to the process of becoming a teacher.

## Questions

1   Which pieces of research into geographical education would be most valuable for geography PGCE students to be aware of and why?
2   What research skills do geography PGCE students need to have, in order for them to benefit from observing other geography teachers in the classroom? What aspects of a teacher's practice are difficult to understand simply from observation?
3   What theoretical frameworks, related to geography, environmental education, or education generally, would be valuable for geography PGCE students to be aware of and why?
4   To what extent are the processes that can be used to investigate teaching and learning similar to the processes of geographical enquiry?

## References

Acheson, K. and Gall, M. (1980) *Techniques in the Clinical Supervision of Teachers*, New York: Longman.

Bale, J. (1999) 'Excavating Circular 4/98', paper presented at the annual conference for University Geography Tutors, Birmingham, 1999.

Barnes, D., Johnson, G., Jordan, S., Layton, D., Medway, P. and Yeomans, D. (1987) *The*

*TVEI Curriculum 14–16: An Interim Report Based on Case Studies in Twelve Schools*, Leeds: University of Leeds.

Boardman, D. (1989) 'The development of graphicacy: children's understanding of maps', *Geography*, 74, 4: 321–31.

Butt, G. (1996) '"Audience-centred" teaching and children's writing in geography', in Williams, M. (ed.) *Understanding Geographical and Environmental Education*, London: Cassell Education.

DfEE (1998) *Teaching: High Status, High Standards. Requirements for Courses of Initial Teacher Training. Circular 04/9*, London: DfEE.

Elliott, J. (1991) *Action Research for Educational Change*, Milton Keynes: Open University Press.

Elliott, J. and Adleman, C. (1976) *Innovation at the Classroom Level: A Case Study of the Ford Teaching Project*, Unit 28, Open University Course E 203: Curriculum Design and Development, Milton Keynes: Open University Press.

Ellis, B. (ed.) (1997) *Working Together: Partnership in the Education of Geography Teachers*, Sheffield: The Geographical Association.

Foskett, N. and Marsden, W. (eds) (1998) *A Bibliography of Geographical Education 1970–1997*, Sheffield: The Geographical Association.

Goodey, B. (1973) *Perception of the Environment: An Introduction to the Literature, Occasional Paper No. 17*, Birmingham: University of Birmingham Centre for Urban and Regional Studies.

Hillage, J., Pearson, R., Anderson, A. and Tamkin, P. (1998) *Excellence in Research in Schools, DfEE Research Report No. 74*, London: DfEE.

Matthews, M.H. (1992) *Making Sense of Place: Children's Understanding of Large-scale Environments*, Hemel Hempstead: Harvester Wheatsheaf.

QCA (1998) *Geographical Enquiry at Key Stages 1–3, Discussion Paper No 3*, Sudbury: QCA Publications.

Roberts, M. (1996a) 'Teaching styles and strategies', in Kent, A., Lambert, D., Naish, M. and Slater, F. (eds) *Geography in Education*, Cambridge: Cambridge University Press.

Roberts, M. (1996b) 'An exploration of the role of the teacher within enquiry based classroom activities', in Van der Schee, J. and Trimp, H. (eds) *Innovation in Geographical Education*, Amsterdam: Centrum voor Educatieve, Geografie Vrije Universiteit.

Roberts, M. (1998) 'Different worlds: student teachers' investigation of place knowledge of pupils in a multicultural classroom', in Smit, M.J. (ed.) *Geography Education in Multicultural Societies: A Selection of Papers from the IGU/CGE Conference*, Stellenbosch: University Press, University of Stellenbosch, South Africa.

Rudduck, J. and Hopkins, D. (1985) *Research as a Basis for Teaching*, London: Heinemann Educational Books.

Spencer, C., Blades, M. and Morsley, K. (1989) *The Child in the Physical Environment*, Chichester: John Wiley.

Stenhouse, L. (1970) *The Humanities Project*, London: Heinemann.

TTA (1996) *Teaching as a Research-based Profession*, London: Teacher Training Agency.

TTA (1998) *Framework for the Assessment of Quality and Standards in Initial Teacher Training*, London: Teacher Training Agency.

Wiegand, P. (1991) 'The known world of primary children', *Geography*, 76, 2: 143–9.

Wray, D., and Lewis, M. (1997) *Extending Literacy: Children Reading and Writing Non-fiction*, London: Routledge.

# 4 Developing the educational use of information and communications technology

## Implications for the education of geography teachers

*Tony Fisher*

## Introduction

In September 1998 the UK Initial Teacher Training National Curriculum for the use of Information and Communications Technology in Subject Teaching[1] came into force (DfEE, 1998). Though not the first computer-related requirement for new teachers (see, for example, DFE, 1992), it is by far the most detailed and prescriptive, coming at a time of increasing government intervention in teacher education. This curriculum represents a clear conviction that not only should pupils in schools learn *about* computers and their uses, but also that their education in all subjects, including geography, will benefit from teaching and learning *with* computers.

In addition to being a curriculum for beginning teachers, it is also the basis for the New Opportunities Fund (NOF) 'lottery-funded training' for serving teachers. It thus comprises a blueprint for all teachers' knowledge and under-standing of the educational use of new technologies, and a specification for teachers' personal 'computer capability'. It demonstrates the government's belief that the future of education is closely bound up with an increasing use of computers and associated technologies. Therefore skills in, and an understanding of, the use of such technologies are considered necessary for all teachers, regardless of subject and are now required for the award of Qualified Teacher Status (QTS).

Computers have been in UK schools for some years. Claims and predictions have been made about the potential benefits, but attitudes vary. Enthusiasts have forged ahead, whilst others more sceptical still remain to be convinced. Since the early 1970s, various projects to research and develop the use of computers in teaching and learning have been established. More recently, information technology (IT) has appeared as a statutory subject of the National Curriculum. The Dearing review of the National Curriculum in 1995 made the use of IT a 'general requirement' of the Programme of Study for each National Curriculum subject (including, of course, geography), in addition to being a separate subject in its own right.

In this chapter I investigate the following questions:

- What is the relationship between geography and the use of new technologies?
- What general educational issues arise from the ICT National Curriculum and the system into which it is being introduced?
- Are there geography-specific issues, relating to an increase in the use of ICT?

These questions will be explored in relation to the education of new and practising geography teachers.

## Geography and I(C)T – the story so far

The relationship between the study of geography and the use of computers is uncontrived and uncontroversial. The development of increasingly powerful 'mainframe' computers assisted the development of the 'quantitative revolution' of the 1960s and early 1970s. Since then there has been a strong quantitative strand in geography, and an increasingly multifaceted and close relationship between aspects of geography and the use of computers. We live in an increasingly data-rich world, in which computers play a key part in the collection and processing of diverse data for a variety of purposes, from remote-sensing of the rates of clearance of tropical forests, to recording the contents of the supermarket shopping trolleys of individual consumers. However, a central concern is the organization of mere *data* so as to provide intelligible *information*, and subsequently the interpretation of this information so as to give it meaning, in order to add to human *knowledge*. (Some would add another step: Knowledge is not the goal, but a stage on the path to *wisdom*.)

The interaction of the discipline of geography, and the computer-based data handling tools at its disposal, has influenced the development of 'geography as spatial information technology' (Mather, 1991: x). Geography as an academic discipline has made use of computer-based data handling software, statistical processing packages and cartographic programs. Remote-sensing data from satellites is organized and presented using computers. Simulations enable phenomena to be modelled and the interplay of variables to be examined, for instance the behaviour of water in a drainage basin. Beyond all these, geography has given its name to a powerful computer-based approach for the multivariate analysis and display of spatially referenced data: the *geographic information system* (GIS), an application of great research and commercial significance.

Were it not, however, for the development of the affordable, space-efficient 'microcomputer', such developments would have had little impact on geographical education in schools. The advent of the 'micro' in the 1970s led to the possibility of 'computer-assisted learning' (CAL) in school geography. The 1980s saw the publication of a number of books documenting geography teachers' progress in integrating computers into the geography classroom (e.g. Midgley and Walker, 1985; Shepherd, Cooper and Walker 1980; Watson, 1984). The possibility of a profound impact on education was recognized:

> The microcomputer represents a revolution in educational technology, not only in the classroom, where it can radically transform teaching and learning situations, but also in administration, with its capacity to store and process information.
>
> (Midgley and Walker, 1985: 14)

Not all geography teachers embraced the use of the microcomputer enthusiastically. However, geography teachers, faced with the perennial problem of bringing the subject's object of study – the world – into the classroom, have long had a 'multimedia' approach to teaching and learning in the subject. They have employed text, photographs, slides, video, maps, diagrams, sketches, models, globes, newspapers and other media in their work. For some geography teachers, the computer fitted in as another medium, another means of bringing the world into the classroom. Also, the perceived link between computers and a purely quantitative approach to geographical analysis began to weaken in the 1980s, as computer-based information came to be used in social, political and values education (Tapsfield, 1991: 58).

The ImpacT Project (Watson, 1993) identified a number of benefits from computer use in geography teaching. In the mid-1990s school geography's claim for a special relationship with computers was given further impetus. The 'Geography and IT Support Project' involved the Geographical Association (GA) and the then National Council for Educational Technology (NCET), and sought to take forward the use of IT in geography, one of four secondary subjects to benefit from joint initiatives funded by the Department for Education (DFE). The project identified aspects of the relationship between school geography and IT. Pupils, it asserted, are entitled to use IT in geography in order to:

- enhance their skills of geographical enquiry;
- gain access to a range of geographical knowledge and information sources;
- deepen their understanding of environmental and spatial relationships;
- experience alternative images of people, places and environments;
- consider the wider impact of IT on people, places and environments.

(GA/NCET, 1994)

(See the 'To take you further' section for the project's publications.)

Geography provides a meaningful context for the use of computers at all levels of study, from the primary school to the highest levels of research. Some of these opportunities and contexts are indicated in the exemplification materials published to support the ICT National Curriculum (TTA 1999). At their most effective, such opportunities enhance teaching and learning in the subject, and develop IT capability at the same time.

However, despite the projects and dissemination materials, and the evident progress made by some geography teachers and departments, the development of the use of microcomputers in school geography, as in other subjects, has been patchy. Watson (1997) argues that teachers have been caught in a 'dichotomy of purpose', between a pedagogic, subject-focused rationale on one hand, and a more vocational, technocentric rationale on the other. This has resulted, she argues, in confusing messages to teachers about why to use computers in their work: should they be embracing CAL to enhance teaching and learning in their subject? Or should they, and their subject, be doing their bit to develop the technologically literate work-force of the future? These are not incompatible aims, but they represent different starting points and imply different approaches.

Since the early 1970s a sequence of initiatives can be identified, with the underlying aim of increasing the use made of computers (see Watson, 1997: 76 for a summary). Throughout this time, teachers have been exhorted to become computer-literate and to use IT in their work. However, at no stage has there been any financial incentive, for example tax breaks for teachers to become computer owners – though some have, of course, bought computers for either or both family use and work-related use. So, in the absence of a personal home computer, many teachers have had their computer use restricted to what has been possible in school, with the additional possibility of taking a cumbersome desktop computer home for an evening, weekend or holiday.

This brings us to the present, with the introduction of the new National Curriculum for ICT in Subject Teaching, and its use as the basis for the programme of NOF training. The government clearly believes that the teaching profession has gone neither far nor fast enough, in incorporating computers into day-to-day education.

## Issues relating to the ICT National Curriculum

Information and Communication Technology (ICT) is a curriculum subject in its own right, with its own programme of study and assessment arrangements. ICT is also a generic term, referring to these technologies (emphasizing, but not restricted to computers) which are used in the context of other subjects, including geography. It is this which the new National Curriculum seeks to describe. It is written as a generic statement of what all new teachers should understand about, and be able to do with, ICT. Many of the issues arising are also of a generic nature.

The Curriculum sets out the detailed requirements in two sections:

• Section A: effective teaching and assessment methods;
• Section B: trainees' knowledge and understanding of, and competence with, information and communications technology.

Section B is about the *personal ICT capability* of the teacher, albeit mediated via a subject context, whereas Section A is much more about *pedagogy* – the use of ICT to support teaching and learning. This curriculum, and hence the initial and in-service training based on it, will focus on equipping teachers, both new and serving, with 'the knowledge, skills and understanding to make sound decisions *about when, when not and how to use ICT effectively in teaching particular subjects'* (DfEE, 1998: 1, emphasis as in original).

It is interesting to compare the earlier quotation from Midgley and Walker (1985) with the following extract from the introductory paragraphs of the ICT National Curriculum:

> ICT is more than just another teaching tool. Its potential for improving the quality and standards of pupils' education is significant. Equally, its potential is considerable for supporting teachers, both in their everyday classroom role, for example by reducing the time occupied by the administration associated with it, and in their continuing training and development.
>
> (DfEE, 1998: 1)

We see that both make similar claims for the beneficial impact of ICT, not only on teaching and learning, but also on other aspects of teachers' work. However, both tend towards a 'technologically deterministic' perspective, which implies that things will happen *because of the technology*. 'At its simplest, technological determinism considers technology to be an exogenous and autonomous development which coerces and determines social and economic organisations and relationships' (Grint, 1992: 151). In technological determinism, human agency is not explicitly identified, either in connection with the production of the technology, or in connection with decisions about its use.

Technological determinism represents a trap into which it is all too easy to be lured. Used cynically, it can be employed to mask the role of vested interests. 'Use this technology and everything will be not only different, but also better', some proponents seem to say. However, 'technological development does not have pre-set social effects which are predictable, universal or, for that matter, just or beneficial' (Lyon, 1991: 106). We can say confidently that the technology is a tool which makes some things possible, including some things which were not possible before, but alone it does not have the agency implied by technological determinism. In the end it is teachers who make the changes (or do not).

The rise and proliferation of the computer are interwoven with the transition from the modern era to 'postmodernity'. In particular, the development of increased computer memory and faster processing, together with the extension of the Internet, has been closely associated with the compression of time and space, key characteristics of postmodern social, economic and cultural conditions (Harvey, 1989).

Schools are essentially modernist institutions (Hargreaves, 1994), left as structural and procedural anachronisms whilst the world around them becomes increasingly postmodern in how it operates. Computers have made possible fundamental changes in how that world operates, but they have not (yet?) had the same impact on schools. Many aspects of the way schools are structured – subject departments, timetables, classrooms – mirror the characteristics of Fordist-type mass production. Yet much of the economic activity of advanced economies has changed with the impact of new technologies. Championed by some and accepted as inevitable by others, such change has not been without controversy, conflict, and unwelcome consequences. Can schools, indeed should schools, undergo the same transformation? It is essential for teacher education to engage with such issues and questions, so that teachers and teacher educators, in addition to being able to use the technologies as and when appropriate in their work, can also confidently and authoritatively join the wider debate.

But schools do not suffer only from being 'out of synch' with such large-scale changes in society. Many modern societies are themselves in difficulty, economically and socially. In such societies, and their increasingly hard-to-afford systems of public education, schools are charged with the responsibility to 'administer the innovative treatment if the ailing society is to recover' (Winer and de la Mothe, 1987: 64). Part of that 'innovative treatment' is to produce a flexible, highly qualified, technologically literate work force. This has been fuelled by government concern with the economy and with international competitiveness (Ridgway, 1997: 6). In the UK traditional manufacturing has declined, with movement towards what some have termed an 'information economy'. The drive for education to produce a skilled, technologically literate work force has gained impetus.

> The aim of many policy-makers in the UK and around the world is to encourage evolution into a learning society for the next century: one in which all people are responsible for their own learning throughout their lives. Access to information and learning will often depend on new technologies as well as on an approach to teaching which supports collaborative professional development.
>
> Governments in Europe and around the world have already recognised the need to review educational practices and incorporate new technologies. Their view is of a vocational imperative and one in which IT will increase the quality and efficiency of learning itself.
>
> (Somekh and Davis, 1997: 3)

Castells (1996) takes the argument a stage further. Society itself, he argues, is changing fundamentally as a result of the impact of new technologies. He proposes the term 'informational society' to describe this new social order. Information of one sort or another has characterized all societies, but in the present case, 'information generation, processing and transmission become the fundamental sources of production and power' (Castells, 1996: 24). Such processes in society have spatial dimensions and manifestations. Geography teachers, in addition to being a part of education's response to the changes, will also wish to describe and explain what is happening from the perspective of the subject, for instance in their teaching of globalization.

Computers, and all other technologies, are physical and social artefacts. Produced by human endeavour, their meaning and purpose are socially constructed. There is thus a fundamental role played by discourse in shaping knowledge about computers in general, and their place in education in particular. As we have seen, a dominant discourse is the 'economic rationalist' discourse which asserts that the future lies in the information economy, and that therefore education must prepare those who will work in this economy. But the case, it has been argued, does not rest at this point:

> Microelectronics and computing are presented as economically indispensable, yet the criterion slips – economic utility is portrayed as educational usefulness. Thus, the new technology promoted by the state and by industry as one panacea for economic recession becomes, in the context of schooling, a necessary part of teaching and learning. The economic arguments for the wholesale support of Information Technology are crude; the educational arguments fallacious. This slippage, from a technological and economically determinist commentary on new technology in society to the necessity for computers in schools, is evident in a number of contexts – most particularly where curriculum design reflects the presumed needs of the economy.
>
> (Linn, 1991: 201)

Whether or not we agree that 'the educational arguments are fallacious', the preceding quotation makes clear the dangers inherent in a situation in which 'technicist assumptions substitute for educational debate' (Linn, 1991: 200). So, is the ICT National Curriculum built on such technicist assumptions, or something more substantial by way of proof of the educational value of computers? There are studies and evaluations of the ways in which computers have been used in schools, and in teaching and learning in geography (e.g. GA/NCET, 1994; Watson, 1993). However, 'evaluation is not enough: rather, analysis leading to theory is needed if the impact of technology in education is to be fully understood' (Beynon, 1993: 228). There is still a lack of a substantial research basis for the claims being made about the educational value of computers. Thus we can interpret government spending (about a billion pounds sterling over the period 1999–2002) to increase and extend the educational use of computer technology as something of an act of faith in response to the economic imperative referred to above.

The foregoing paragraphs are not intended as an argument against the educational use of computers in general, or in geography in particular – rather they are a reminder of the need to retain a critical, questioning stance in the face of sometimes extravagant claims as to their potential. As Michael Apple has put it, 'Our task as educators is to make sure that when it [IT] enters the classroom it is there for politically, economically and educationally wise reasons, not because powerful groups may be redefining our major educational goals in their own image' (Apple, 1992: 120). Teacher education has a clear role in this task.

The situation in schools, though it will change as a consequence of current initiatives, merits further consideration in order to shed light on some of the issues around the full implementation of the new curriculum, and the greater use of new technologies to support teaching and learning. Many of those same schools charged to 'administer the innovative treatment' have themselves been slow to innovate when compared to the rate of technological change in business and industry. This is partly a result of insufficient investment in hardware and training over recent years, but also reflects the inherent conservatism of the school as an institution, exacerbated by what has been termed 'innovation fatigue'. Educational policies and initiatives come thick and fast and,

> as the pressures of postmodernity are felt, the teacher's role expands to take on new problems and mandates – though little of the old role is cast aside to make room for the new changes. [Further,] innovations multiply as change accelerates, creating senses of overload among teachers and principals or headteachers responsible for implementing them. More and more changes are imposed and the timelines for their implementation are truncated.
>
> (Hargreaves, 1994: 4)

The introduction and extension of the use of computers into teachers' work are one such innovation. Change has taken place, but the impact between and within schools has been uneven. Unsurprisingly, then, some experienced teachers have found themselves overtaken by events. Their own earlier experience at school and in initial teacher education preceded the development and educational use of the microcomputer. So, unless they have been reached by in-service training, they may well still lack the pedagogical models and conceptual frameworks (in addition to confidence and IT capability) needed to support the introduction of computers into their teaching. Though 'training for practising teachers was recognised as important from the start, [it] was mainly in the form of inadequate short courses' (Davis, 1992: 7–21).

This brings us to another issue in relation to the new ICT National Curriculum: the ability of the system to cope with the new requirements. The notion of initial teacher *education* (ITE) has been replaced, at least in 'official' discourses, by a specific conception of the preparation of teachers as *training*. This in turn has been influenced by philosophies of workplace-based learning, so the requirement for student teachers to spend more time in school has increased. A postgraduate student teacher on a 36-week course leading to Qualified Teacher Status (QTS) must by regulation spend 24 weeks in school-based work. Yet these 24 weeks must be spent in those same schools and classrooms where, according to an official commentary on inspection findings, 'much remains to be done to improve professional practice in the teaching of IT and in its productive use' (Goldstein, 1997: 2). Many serving teachers lack basic skills in the use of computers, in addition to their lack of pedagogical understanding of the use of ICT in their teaching. The NOF training referred to earlier is intended to address this. Nevertheless, for many student teachers, their more experienced teacher colleagues in schools are not in a strong position to assist and guide them in their first steps with using computers in their teaching.

Further, these teachers work in a context where 'schools vary greatly in the extent to which they are able to afford to upgrade their IT resources regularly' (Goldstein, 1997: 2). This is clearly a source of difficulty in the preparation of new teachers to use new technologies in their teaching. Ageing hardware and software, and problems of access to resources, may result in disappointment among IT-capable student teachers, at the restricted opportunities to capitalize on their expertise. And the combined effect of a lack of adequate resources, plus restricted computer expertise among experienced staff, may result in situations in which those working in the school have expectations that the student teacher will be the one to bring new, ICT-based teaching and learning approaches to bear (Fisher, 1996: 33–7).

The situation in schools should change as a result of in-service training and the development of the National Grid for Learning and associated hardware improvements. However, the present situation inevitably shifts the load for dealing with the requirements of the ICT National Curriculum towards the teacher education institutions. Yet those same institutions have just twelve weeks to do all that they must with the student teacher! The shortfall in teachers able to use ICT to the benefit of teaching and learning has been recognized for some time. It has been suggested that, previously, little attention was directed at ICT in initial teacher education from central government, and that 'had initial education been supported from the start, rather than concentrating on in-service courses, then it is possible that the UK could have had a better-trained workforce today' (Davis, 1992). But it may be that the new curriculum is a case of 'too much, too late'.

The new Curriculum for ICT in Subject Teaching is written as a single, generic curriculum. However, the requirements do not apply to ICT in isolation, but must be set within the specific context of the student teacher's main curriculum subject. The requirements must be interpreted from the perspective of subject pedagogy in geography (and each other subject), yet all must be met. This inevitably throws up some difficulties in interpretation across the range of subjects.

The ICT National Curriculum contains nearly 120 specific requirements. There are doubts among those working in ITE that the detailed requirements of this curriculum can currently be met in the case of all student teachers, particularly those starting from a low base in terms of their own personal IT capability. This problem is exacerbated by the situation in schools, where many student teachers find good use of IT in subject teaching difficult to observe, or where levels of resourcing make it difficult to comply with the requirement that 'trainees must be given opportunities to practise, in taught sessions and in the classroom, those methods and skills described' (DfEE, 1998). Yet in order to make use of IT during teaching practice, student teachers need an insight into classroom uses of computers, together with the confidence to use them. Such confidence is importantly related to *competence* in the use of computers (Wild, 1995: 7–20). A one-year course in which the Standards must be met, and in which a great deal of time is spent planning, marking and evaluating one's first steps in teaching, does not provide much time in which also to develop personal competence in the use of computers.

One response to the introduction of the National Curriculum for ICT has been an increase in the practice of 'auditing' for levels of ICT capability among entrants to initial teacher education courses. Such audits reveal, predictably, a considerable range of personal ICT capability among intending teachers. The author's own research indicates that considerable variation in ICT capability is found among prospective geography teachers, notwithstanding the 'special relationship' between geography and ICT described earlier! This raises a further issue.

For a student teacher with extensive personal IT capability, Section A of the new curriculum provides more than enough challenge. The pedagogy of ICT use in the geography classroom is currently under investigation. The various sub-sections of Section A are all prefaced with the phrase 'trainees must be taught . . . '. This implies that there is a body of knowledge about the appropriate use of computers in geography teaching, which is commonly known by ITE lecturers and school-based colleagues, and which can unproblematically be passed on to student teachers. There is *experience* in using computers in geography teaching and this is being disseminated by, among others, the regular IT column in the Geographical Association journal, *Teaching Geography*. This experience is a mixture of innovative ideas and reports on practice. It is, of course, an essential part of the profession's learning about the use of ICT in geography teaching. But it is not a systematic, theorized approach to the use of computers in the subject. Hence, it remains true that much of what is currently known about the sound educational use of computers should be regarded as tentative and provisional.

For the student teacher lacking in personal IT capability, the problem is greater still. Such a student teacher, in addition to getting to grips with the pedagogical questions and learning how to use computers in the geography classroom, has also to develop the full range of personal computer skills listed in Section B. It is widely recognized that, in learning how to use computers, decontextualized skill training has little lasting impact. It is important to integrate what is being learnt into one's work, and to reinforce learning by subsequently using the skill in the context of real purposes. Otherwise, what has been supposedly learnt quickly goes stale and is easily forgotten.

Further, we need teachers who not only have personal IT capability, and who understand the pedagogy of computer use in their own subject, but who are also 'technologically literate'. Technological literacy means much more than familiarity with the computer and its use. It involves critical awareness and an understanding of the relationship between the technology and its social, economic, cultural and political setting. 'The "how?" associated with skills training must always be secondary to the "why?" associated with technological literacy' (Beynon, 1993: 228). Strong on skills and pedagogy, the new ICT curriculum is silent on technological literacy.

Another aspect of current government strategy to develop the use of ICT by geography teachers and others, is that of the development of the National Grid for Learning (NGfL) and the Virtual Teacher Centre. The Grid will connect all UK schools and other educational establishments by way of the Internet. The Virtual Teacher Centre will be a very large web site, with materials for teachers to use and opportunities to join in 'on-line' discussion. Together these have the potential to support teacher professional development, but require not only access, but also a cultural shift for teachers to see themselves as members of a wider, on-line educational community.

## The ICT National Curriculum and geography

The previous section has looked broadly at issues and implications relating to the ICT National Curriculum. All of these, because of their generic nature, bear on the education and day-to-day work of geography teachers. A case has also been made that geography and those who teach it have a particular role to play. Geography teachers are well placed to teach about some of the impacts of increasing use of networked technologies on people, places and the environment. Further, the use of such technologies in geography may also be consistent with their use as an aspect of 'education for citizenship' (see Advisory Group on Citizenship, 1998: Appendix B).

Geography provides a fertile context for exploring the use of ICT in teaching and learning. 'Geography teachers have a unique role in the forefront of educational development / applications of new technologies' (Phillips, 1997: 221). This is something of a two-edged sword and raises a problem of breadth versus depth of experience. We have described the pressure of time on initial teacher education courses, and the same problem has confronted teachers in schools. Yet, 'for the introduction of all innovations, the most necessary ingredient for successful change is time' (Tapsfield, 1991: 59). There is an enormous range of possibilities for the use of ICT in geography. It falls to teacher educators to establish a balance between breadth, to give a sense of these possibilities, and depth, to get to grips with some of the teaching and learning issues specific to the subject.

One such teaching and learning issue in geography is the enquiry approach. Enquiry is seen as a very important aspect of school geography, and is specified in the National Curriculum Programmes of Study; in addition, it is woven into the National Curriculum assessment structure by way of the level descriptions. We have already seen that ICT can 'enhance . . . skills of geographical enquiry' (GA/NCET, 1994). However, questions remain about the quality of enquiry within some school geography. If enquiry is inadequately conceptualized as an approach, then simply adding ICT is not likely to improve matters. Indeed, there is a danger that using the technology can make matters worse, as it may create a superficial impression that something more sophisticated is happening, when in reality it is not. Similarly, using a word processor to 'type up' a fair copy of work which has already been drafted on paper is unlikely to benefit geographical attainment or indeed ICT capability in any meaningful way.

However, the potential of ICT to support and enhance geographical enquiry is enormous. For instance, a single program which enables:

- questionnaires to be developed,
- data to be entered so as to create a database,
- analysis of the data and presentation of graphs and charts,

offers the possibility of supporting virtually an entire enquiry. In *Geographical enquiry at Key Stages 1–3* (QCA, 1998), one of the examples given is a Key Stage 3 scheme of work on 'development' in which ICT features prominently as a means of manipulating and presenting data relating to development indices.

ICT, however, does not create good geographical enquiry of its own accord: it has to be planned for. To plan for enquiry incorporating the use of ICT requires on the part of the teacher an understanding of how ICT can support the enquiry process, rather than blind faith that it will! This involves not only an understanding of the enquiry process and knowledge of what ICT can do to support it, but also an understanding of the nature of progression in both enquiry and IT capability. Thus, to capitalize fully on the potential of ICT in enquiry, the geography teacher needs also to be aware of the content and requirements of the National Curriculum for IT and their practical implications. The *Exemplification of Standards* (SCAA, 1996) is useful in this regard. Liaison between the geography and IT departments in schools will be important in supporting and extending such progression.

Another issue for the education of geography teachers is that of making good educational use of geographic information systems (GIS). Geographical education has for many years investigated the spatial distribution of phenomena, so in an analogue sense a GIS is nothing new. A set of maps of several different phenomena in a given area may invite 'visual correlation' or mental overlaying to reveal coincidences of pattern and the presence of anomalies. However, a computer-based GIS, using digital map and survey data, allows the manipulation of maps to reveal and analyse such patterns quickly and easily (see for example BBC Education, 1997).

GIS has much potential for enhancing work in the subject, but its use in school is unlikely to be developed or reinforced beyond geography. Much used in the world beyond school, the use of GIS in the classroom could make a contribution to fulfilling both the pedagogical and vocational imperatives described earlier. For instance, GIS could be used in a geographical enquiry investigating the potential customer base for alternative locations for a new supermarket. This would also model the processes used by retail businesses and develop understanding of the processes and potential of the GIS application. Experience with GIS is now relatively common among prospective geography teachers with recent first degree experience, but it is still uncommon in schools. Yet it has considerable potential for school geography (and was indeed specified in the earlier versions of the National Curriculum for Geography).

ICT can also bring a vast amount of information into the geography classroom, for instance on CD-ROM and via the World Wide Web (WWW), to supplement other sources. 'ICT provides pupils with access to people and places that they may not otherwise reach' (Canterbury Christ Church College, 1998: 38). Another issue for the education of geography teachers, then, is that of developing the skills needed to manage the flow of information, so as to support active learning in the subject rather than mild curiosity and casual browsing. More information is not necessarily better! Teaching strategies should require engagement with the information, involving processing and reformulation to meet specified requirements.

This relates to the use and management of enquiry approaches mentioned earlier, and also has broader implications for approaches to teaching and learning. For instance, if a more research-based methodology comes to characterize teaching and learning in the subject, some geography teachers, both new and experienced, may need support in incorporating aspects of 'flexible learning' into their approach. Projects may be supported by the teacher in the role of tutor, rather than as provider of direct instruction 'from the front'. Eventually this in turn may have implications for school decisions about timetabling, and resource allocation and management.

As with any new approach, the use of the WWW needs careful preparation. The issue of preventing access to undesirable material is often voiced as a concern, and any plans must take account of a school's policy regarding such matters. However, other issues such as:

- bias and veracity of material,
- downloading times (e.g. for large satellite images and other complex graphics),
- and language level of written text,

should also be addressed when allowing access to the WWW for individual or group research.

Much WWW use involves fetching information from elsewhere via the Internet. But of course the Internet also allows communication in the other direction. The Internet supports e-mail, which enables person-to-person contact and exchange of information. This has great potential in geography, as does publishing the outcomes of local work on a section of the school's web pages. This gives purpose and a sense of audience to communicating the results of local enquiry, and provides up-to-date information for others to use.

The ICT curriculum requires a broad engagement with ICT in the teaching of geography, but it may well be that a more fruitful approach is to take one or two particular approaches and investigate them in depth. It is important to do this from the perspective of the teaching objectives for the subject. Once there is clarity about the learning outcomes which a sequence of lessons seek to achieve, the teacher is then in a better position to judge whether ICT can make an appropriate contribution. This is entirely in accord with the intent of Section A, but it presupposes that the teacher is conversant with what is possible. Inevitably, then, personal ICT capability is a necessary precondition to making informed judgements about appropriate uses of the technology to support teaching and learning.

## Conclusion

We live in interesting times. With the new ITT National Curriculum for ICT, the NOF Training Programme for serving teachers, the development of the National Grid for Learning and the associated extension of Internet connectivity to every school, education in general could be poised on the cusp of significant change.

But it is not guaranteed. Edgar Stones has written of the impact of technological innovation in education that solutions to pedagogical problems have very often been sought by the use of various types of technology . . . currently, computers, video-disks, lasers, multimedia "presentations" . . . In due course some have been absorbed into the teacher's armamentarium; others gather dust in stock rooms. None has brought the prophesied pedagogical millennium.

(Stones, 1992: 8)

So far, the change process has been gradual, but it may be that now something more significant – a quantum step – is possible. If so, geography teachers will play an important part, for the potential in geography is considerable.

## Questions

* Why might geography claim to have developed a 'special relationship' with the use of new technologies, and is the claim justified?
* To what extent does the geography teacher have a responsibility to teach about broader aspects of the impact of ICT on people, places and environments, and to be aware of broader educational debates about the use of ICT?
* In which areas of geography is the use of ICT particularly appropriate, and are there any aspects of the subject which constitute a 'no-go area' for ICT?

## Note

1 Because of its rather cumbersome full title, in this chapter the curriculum is referred to as 'the ICT National Curriculum'.

## Materials to take you further

Donert, K. (1997) *A Geographer's Guide to the Internet*, Sheffield: The Geographical Association. This guidance booklet for teachers discusses what the Internet is and how it may be incorporated into geography teaching. It identifies relevant skills and teaching strategies.

Hassell, D. and Warner, H. (eds) (1995) *Using IT to Enhance Geography: Case Studies at Key Stages 3 and 4*, Sheffield, The Geographical Association. This booklet summarizes key aspects of the use of computers in geography teaching, identified by the Geography and IT Support Project. It provides case studies representing some of the work done in schools and gives pointers for development.

NCET/GA (1994) *Investigating Weather Data*, Coventry: NCET.

NCET/GA (1995) *Shopping and Traffic Fieldwork*, Coventry: NCET.

NCET/GA (1996) *Human Geography*, Coventry: NCET.

This series of three booklets together with computer materials on floppy disk (for PC, Acorn and Macintosh computers) provides some ready-made approaches to the use of computers in geography, including photocopiable items. The materials were developed as part of the Geography and IT Support Project.

Webster, K. (1998) *Internet to Go*, Godalming: WWF UK. This booklet takes a multidisciplinary (geography, science, English) approach to using the Internet in environmental education. It provides a number of activities and includes teachers' guidance notes and student worksheets.

## CD-ROMs

BBC Education (1997) *Teaching Today: Geography and IT*, BBC Education. This multimedia CD-ROM, published with an associated booklet and videocassette, provides a set of in-service training materials for the geography department wishing to develop its use of ICT. The CD-ROM shows how ICT can be used in school geography, making particular reference to the use of spreadsheets, geographical information systems and the Internet.

Population Concern (1998) *The Population and Development Database 1998*, London: Population Concern. This multimedia CD-ROM and booklet provide material and suggestions for teaching about population change. It will run on most computers; a web browser is used for navigation.

*The Sunday Times* (1998) *Window on the World*, British National Space Centre. This multimedia CD-ROM works like a web site, but needs no Internet connection. It uses a standard web browser to allow access to 2000 pages exploring the uses made of remote sensed data about the earth. Teachers will want to consider how such a rich IT-based resource can best be made use of in geography.

## References

Advisory Group on Citizenship (1998) *Education for Citizenship and the Teaching of Democracy in Schools*, London: QCA.

Apple, M. (1992) 'Is the new technology part of the solution or part of the problem in education?', in Beynon, J. and Mackay, H. (eds) *Technological Literacy and the Curriculum*, London: Falmer Press.

BBC Education (1997) *Teaching Today: Geography and IT*, London: BBC Education.

Beynon, J. (1993) 'Technological literacy: where do we all go from here?', in Beynon, J. and Mackay, H. (eds) *Computers into Classrooms: More Questions Than Answers*, London: Falmer Press.

Canterbury Christ Church College (1998) *Talking About ICT in Subject Teaching: Secondary*, Canterbury: Christ Church University College.

Castells, M. (1996) *The Rise of the Network Society*, Oxford: Blackwell.

Davis, N. (1992) 'Information technology in United Kingdom Initial Teacher Education', *Journal of Information Technology for Teacher Education*, 1, 1: 7–21

DFE (1992) *Circular 9/92*, London: DFE

DfEE (1998) *Circular 4/98 'Teaching: High Status, High Standards'*, Annex B, London: DfEE.

Fisher, T. (1996) 'Information technology and the curriculum: IT capability and the new teacher', *British Journal of Curriculum and Assessment*, 6, 2: 33–7

GA/NCET (1994) *Geography – A Pupil's Entitlement to IT*, Coventry: NCET.

Goldstein, G. (1997) *Information Technology in English Schools: A Commentary on Inspection Findings 1995–6*, London: OFSTED.

Grint, K. (1992) 'Sniffers, lurkers, actor networkers: computer mediated communications as technological fix', in Beynon, J. and Mackay, H. (eds) *Technological Literacy and the Curriculum*, London: Falmer Press.

Hargreaves, A. (1994) *Changing Teachers, Changing Times: Teachers' Work and Culture in the Postmodern Age*, London: Cassell.

Harvey, D. (1989) *The Condition of Postmodernity: An Enquiry into the Origins of Cultural Change*, Oxford: Blackwell.

Linn, P. (1991) 'Microcomputers in education: dead and living labour', in Mackay, H., Young, M. and Beynon, J. (eds) *Understanding Technology in Education*, London: Falmer Press.

Lyon, D. (1991) 'The information society', in Mackay, H., Young, M. and Beynon, J. (eds) *Understanding Technology in Education*, London: Falmer Press.

Mather, P. (1991) *Computer Applications in Geography*, Chichester: John Wiley and Sons.

Midgley, H. and Walker, D. (1985) *Microcomputers in Geography Teaching*, London: Hutchinson.

Phillips, A. (1997) 'IT resources', in Powell, A. (ed.) *Handbook of Post-16 Geography*, Sheffield: The Geographical Association.

QCA (1998) *Geographical Enquiry at Key Stages 1 to 3: QCA Discussion Paper No. 2*, London: QCA.

Ridgway, J. (1997) 'Vygotsky, informatics capability and professional development', in Passey, D. and Samways, B. (eds) *Information Technology: Supporting Change Through Teacher Development*, London: Chapman and Hall.

SCAA (1996) *Consistency in Teacher Assessment – Exemplification of Standards, Geography: Key Stage 3*, London: SCAA.

Shepherd, I.D.H., Cooper, Z.A. and Walker, D.R.F. (1980) *Computer Assisted Learning in Geography: Current Trends and Future Prospects*, London: Council for Educational Technology.

Somekh, B. and Davis, N. (eds) (1997) *Using Information Technology Effectively in Teaching and Learning*, London: Routledge.

Stones, E. (1992) *Quality Teaching: A Sample of Cases*, London: Routledge.

Tapsfield, A. (1991) 'From computer-assisted learning to information technology', in Walford, R. (ed.) *Viewpoints on Geography Teaching: The Charney Manor Conference Papers*, London: Longman.

TTA (1999) *Using ICT to Meet Teaching Objectives in Secondary Geography*, London: TTA.

Watson, D. (ed.) (1984) *Exploring Geography with Microcomputers*, London: Council for Educational Technology.

Watson, D. (1993) *The ImpacT Report*, London: King's College.

Watson, D. (1997) 'A dichotomy of purpose: the effect on teachers of government initiatives in information technology', in Passey, D. and Samways, B. (eds) *Information Technology: Supporting Change Through Teacher Education*, London: Chapman and Hall.

Wild, M. (1995) 'Pre-service teacher education programmes or information technology: an effective education?', *Journal of Information Technology for Teacher Education*, 4, 1: 7–20

Winer, L. and de la Mothe, J. (1987), 'Computers, education and the "dead shark syndrome"', in Rushby, N. (ed.) *Technology Based Learning: Selected Readings*, London: Kogan Page.

# Part II

# Issues in the geography classroom

# 5 Does differentiation provide access to an entitlement curriculum for all pupils?

*Jeff Battersby*

The focus of this chapter will be to identify the reasons why differentiation has become such an important issue for teachers to address. I aim to identify the strengths and weaknesses of differentiation strategies within the debate over teaching and learning, curriculum content and process. Regardless of the number, age and ability of the pupils in any class group, I will offer pointers to what we might aspire to in a curriculum entitlement for all – a difficult, but not impossible, goal to attain. I will also address the question of whether learning difficulties are a problem for the curriculum or for the pupil and how our view of this issue impacts on the quality and variety of learning opportunities that are offered to our pupils.

An education system that claims to meet the learning needs of all children and young people and that claims that all pupils have an entitlement to the 'broad, balanced, relevant and differentiated' curriculum promoted by HMI and the 1998 Education Act, has to be designed to meet a diversity of learning needs. At present, most education systems around the world start from the assumption that all children are taught in groups. Consequently 'teaching is focused on some concept of the aggregate learning needs of the pupils in a group, which in turn, leads to an assumed homogeneity in those pupils' learning needs' (Wedell, 1995: 100).

The fundamental principles of the National Curriculum and the Code of Practice, as set out in Section 1.2 of the Code, are that all children with or without special educational needs should have 'the greatest possible degree of access to a broad and balanced education, including the maximum possible access to the National Curriculum' (Webster, 1994: 1). How far are we providing this for each and every one of our pupils? To what extent are we managing the curriculum or managing pupil learning? Webster and others concerned with pupils with special educational needs claim that managing the learners is more important than managing the learning process. What makes a difference in terms of pupil achievement, is a focus on how targets are going to be reached through the learning process, rather than what the targets themselves might be (Webster, 1994). We should look from the curriculum to pupils' needs, rather than the other way round.

An entitlement curriculum, accessible to all children, was how the government saw the introduction of the National Curriculum. However, no two children are the same, as they differ in their abilities, aptitudes and needs, and therefore equality of opportunity cannot be achieved by treating all children the same. The goals of education may be common to all, but the means of achieving them cannot, and probably should not, be identical for all. 'The purpose of education for all children is the same. But the help that individual children need in progressing towards them will be different' (Warnock, 1978: Ch 1, para 1.4). 'The responsibility of schools is to adapt the curriculum to take differences into account' (Hart, 1992: 132).

Each of the National Curriculum Orders opens with details of the Common Requirements which include important statements about the varying or modifying provision to enable all pupils to access the National Curriculum. It refers to the programme of study to be taught to 'the great majority of pupils in the key stage, *in ways appropriate to their abilities*' (QCA, 1997: 11). There is a requirement for teachers to recognize and provide for a small number of pupils by selecting 'material from earlier or later key stages where this is necessary to enable individual pupils to progress and demonstrate achievement' (ibid.: 11). Appropriate provision should also be made for pupils who need to use means of communication other than speech, non-sighted methods of reading and technological aids. Judgements made about pupil achievement in relation to the level descriptions should allow for any such provision (ibid.). Differentiation is therefore essential if all pupils are to have access to the programmes of study. Goals that are set relating to teaching, learning and assessment of the curriculum need to take account of pupil needs to allow them access to appropriate work, have genuine opportunities for achieving success and have real access to the entitlement curriculum.

## What is the entitlement curriculum?

Are we aware of what we need to teach so that we can clarify what we want our pupils to learn? An analysis of the curriculum demands of the programmes of study identifies enquiry as an important strategy to adopt, with the emphasis on encouraging and enabling the pupils to think. Thinking skills, based on Bloom's (1956) six levels of learning, or learning opportunities which allow the pupil to learn along the lines of Vygotsky's (1978) 'zone of proximal development' or of Bruner's (1966) 'scaffolding' of learning, all support the notion of differentiation for pupils. Teachers therefore need to know the curriculum requirements and know their pupils' needs and plan accordingly to meet these needs. In a study of primary practice (Alexander, 1991) pupils who worked hardest were to be found in classrooms where teachers had carried out meticulous planning, so that both pupils and teachers knew what they had to do and no time was wasted. Working hard is not a prerequisite for high achievement, but it is perhaps a measure of successful practice in which pupils are learning effectively and purposefully.

Black and Dockrell (1986) assert that the teaching process is also the assessment process. Assessment finds out the place where pupils have arrived at in their learning process, and then builds in time for remedial or extension work. They found that when teachers were planning a unit of work, they started off with a list of knowledge, concepts and skills which they wanted their pupils to acquire. 'As they built their learning materials around this, so they were sure that everything they wanted to teach was included. Furthermore they knew at which point in the learning sequence they should seek to find out their pupils' difficulties' (Black and Dockrell, 1986: 12).

There is a need to know our pupils if we are to enable them to learn. There is also a need to know, or at least consider, the knowledge, skills and abilities that the pupils bring to their learning; the language understood by the pupils; pupils' feelings, motivation, emotional needs and any physical impairments that may handicap them or which might impact on their ability to engage and be successful in their learning.

Hall claims that

> it is important to consider what knowledge the learners should possess if they are to tackle a particular task successfully. Their general abilities, such as listening, talking, reading, writing, and skills requiring physical co-ordination as well as their attitudes to learning and to themselves must also be borne in mind.
>
> (Hall, 1992: 21)

She also asserts that teachers should know what experiences pupils bring to their learning which might affect the match of the task to their needs. Teachers can pick up clues when questioning pupils about why they have tackled a task in a certain way and when they mark homework. However, coursework and end-of-module tests perhaps offer the best opportunities to probe pupils' attainments and offer real opportunities for differentiated assessment of their learning.

National Curriculum guidance defines differentiation as the process by which 'curriculum objectives, teaching methods, assessment methods, resources and learning activities are planned to cater for the needs of individual pupils' (NCC, 1989). Differentiation is seen as the essential means of achieving entitlement for all children within a common curriculum framework. However, it could be argued that differentiation will simply 'reinforce and perpetuate existing inequalities' (Dowling 1990).

## What is differentiation?

Differentiation in the National Curriculum is meant to be an enabling process focused on the development of the curriculum and concerned with creating optimum learning conditions for each child regardless of age, gender, race or any ability. Differentiation fulfils a pedagogic rather than an organizational strategy. The main focus is on teaching, to allow for differences in pupils' capacities and abilities to learn within a teaching group, rather than on the distribution and allocation of children into supposedly homogeneous groups which could be taught as a separate unit, all together and all in the same way. 'More and better differentiation is required, more careful assessment and monitoring of children's needs as individuals and the development of teachers' skills in providing a learning environment which is sufficiently flexible to allow all children's needs to be taken into account' (Hart, 1992: 132) to enable them to learn effectively and to the best of their abilities. 'To ignore or deny differences, or make a virtue out of treating all children the same, is not a solution but a retreat from a solution' (ibid.: 135).

Hart's central idea is based on what we have learnt about providing appropriate teaching for children experiencing difficulties. She suggests that we now appreciate the limitations of differentiation and the risks of differentiation, and have reconceptualized the territory which has been appropriated by differentiation in line with our own knowledge, understanding and beliefs. The reconceptualizing of curricular content to match pupils' learning ability is 'an intellectual challenge for the teacher which is never sufficiently acknowledged' (Wedell, 1995: 103).

Different levels and kinds of pedagogical expertise are required to support pupils' learning, their achievement and progress. Teaching demands differ according to whether a pupil is faced with new learning, consolidating existing learning through practice, or extending his or her prior learning. The teacher may deal with these phases of learning by direct involvement in teaching or by managing pupil learning mediated by other means. Differentiation is about matching what teachers want pupils to learn to the curriculum, and what experiences, knowledge, understanding, attitudes and skills pupils bring to their learning.

'Assessment is inseparable from the teaching process, since one of its prime purposes is to improve pupils' performance. It should help teachers to diagnose pupils' strengths and weaknesses, to match the work of the classroom to their capabilities, to guide them to appropriate courses and groups and to involve them in discussion and self appraisal' (DES, 1985: 51). Differentiating the curriculum, learning experiences and assessment strategies ought to lead to improvements in pupil performance and in their achievement. However, HMI (DES, 1989) found evidence of poor differentiation and stated that if teachers are to improve their skills in assessment, various interrelated questions need to be addressed. What do we need to clarify about the curriculum in order to help pupils to learn? What do we need to know about the experiences, knowledge, skills and attitudes that pupils bring to the classroom that may affect their learning, and how do we find out about these? How do we match the two in order to plan for pupils' learning and enable each pupil to make progress?

Differentiation is best thought of as an ongoing process that needs to be planned for and is characterized by flexibility. It is the means of maximizing learning for all children by taking account of individual differences in learning style, interest, motivation and aptitude, and reflecting these variations in the classroom. Differentiation is the process whereby teachers meet the need for progress through the curriculum by selecting appropriate teaching methods to match the individual child's preferred learning strategies, within a group situation (Visser, 1993). 'Differentiation calls for teachers to be more varied in all aspects of their teaching, so that all children, including those with learning difficulties or with special educational needs, are able to take part, given appropriate challenges, and extended in ways which meet their abilities, existing skills and aptitude for learning' (Webster, 1994: 4).

Teachers need to bring the content of lessons alive by different means, so that all children are engaged from the outset, to organize and structure learning to fit the demands of the learning outcomes, the tasks in hand and the skills of the pupils taking part. Resources and activities need to be designed so that pupils of varying abilities can get something from them, working at different speeds and levels. Learning needs to be organized to take account of pupil differences: some pupils work best alone, others in a small group. Equally, some learning is better done when pupils work alone, other learning occurs where pupils are working in groups and yet others where pupils work as a whole class. Similarly, there is a rich variety of ways of recording, sharing and displaying the results of pupils' work and giving feedback to them. Most children, including those experiencing learning difficulties, benefit from a teaching and learning environment where flexibility is the norm, rather than the exception, representing differentiation in action.

Differentiation should not be confused with 'individualized learning', because there are distinctions. One major disadvantage of individualized learning programmes is that all pupils can end up working on different materials, whilst interactions between teacher and children may become superficial, brief and infrequent. Webster (1994) and others have found that individualized learning often turns out to mean that the majority of pupils are working on separate topics and activities, whilst pupils with specific learning difficulties could labour alone for long periods. It also becomes difficult to draw the whole class together for discussion, identifying key concepts, giving feedback on ways of working and summarizing what pupils have achieved. There may be no opportunities for pupils to work with more able peers, with the result that some might lose interest and experience a sense of failure.

## Differentiation in practice?

Differentiation by outcome arises naturally as the end product of a common task set to all pupils and depends on the capabilities of each pupil to address the task. This is easy to plan and set up and assumes that all pupils will be successful in the task as there are no criteria for failure. All pupils will be able to complete the tasks, though not all to the same standard. With this strategy, pupils tend to expect less individual attention from the teacher as there is an assumption by them that they are expected to work at their own level. Differentiation by outcome offers opportunities for the teacher to assess different levels of attainment within any group whatever the ability range contained within it. However, some pupils may be restricted in what they are able to achieve if they are not given some support or guidance from the teacher. There are few opportunities to use differentiation by outcome to diagnose a pupil's strengths and weaknesses, and some pupils will inevitably feel a sense of failure when they measure their performance against their peers.

Some of the difficulties pupils experience in their learning and in demonstration of their capabilities relate to their ability to read and write. Some pupils may not be able to read sufficiently well to follow instructions or to grasp the meaning of text or ideas presented in a written format. Other pupils may not be able to write well enough to be able to complete the work or present it in a form that the teacher can assess. They may be unable to demonstrate their capabilities to the teacher.

This raises questions about the appropriateness of the teaching, learning and assessment strategies and techniques which are available to both teachers and pupils. Decisions about the suitability of each of these should meet the judgement of 'fitness for purpose'. Consideration needs to be given to providing learning opportunities and assessment tasks which are accessible to, and meet the needs of, both pupils and teachers.

Differentiation by task is an attempt to provide work and tasks which are suited to the needs of the individual pupil, and is particularly useful for the formative assessment of pupils in order to set targets for further learning progression. This strategy can be very demanding on the efficiency of the teacher's organizational capabilities. Differentiation by task can often impede the variety and the quality of learning, by reducing opportunities for pupils to work collaboratively, which is essential for some learning activities such as role plays and debates about controversial issues.

Differentiation by process combines the best of the two previous strategies because various aspects of the tasks and outcomes can be differentiated according to the pupils' needs. This is particularly useful in helping pupils to identify their strengths and weaknesses and to set targets to make progress. This strategy allows the teacher to work with individuals and groups of pupils through part of the lesson and appears an excellent strategy to help teachers and pupils structure their learning. It is very demanding on the teacher, as trying to provide support for all members of the class requires detailed record keeping of pupils' achievements and their future needs.

Differentiation by response by the teacher is probably the most frequently used strategy and is probably done almost subconsciously. It provides opportunities for the teacher to give specific advice to individual pupils as and when and for however long they need it, offering support, encouragement, clarification, focus, remedial action, revision, prompting and challenge.

Teachers need to consider the content, delivery, pace and accessibility of the lesson and whether it has more or less appeal to different interest groups, to females or to males, to particular preferred learning styles or to preferred teaching styles and classroom organization. Do the style and structure of questions and tasks enable and encourage all pupils to participate in the learning and its assessment? Do the sequence and structure of the questions, tasks and learning benefit all, some or few of the pupils? How can the teacher offer equal access to all learning to all the pupils? Do some tasks and activities demand that pupils work alone, in pairs, in a small group as well as in a whole class? Can all pupils readily engage in this variety of approaches to learning? What of the pupils who have poor interpersonal skills and find it difficult to work with other pupils? Are some pupils disadvantaged if there is no opportunity for collaborative work or are some disadvantaged because there is too much?

At what level does the teacher pitch the work for the pupils? What is the appropriate level of complexity of language to be used in teacher exposition, in instructions, in questions asked and questions written for the pupils? Decisions about the range, complexity and readability of texts and other resources such as maps, photographs, tables and graphs will advantage some and disadvantage others in gaining access to the curriculum content of the lesson. What support is offered to pupils, to those with and without specifically identified learning difficulties, and to those who are on the margins of needing support? Who is given extra help by the teacher and by learning support assistants? 'How? Why? and When?' represent further questions to ask and thereby strategies of differentiation, especially if they are carefully planned and considered.

Given the complexity of learning in the classroom, teachers need to be able to recognize the wide variety of pupils' needs to plan their teaching and their pupils' learning. This requires an appropriate delivery, lesson content, structure and tasks which balance the needs of the individual to the needs of the whole group. When this occurs, pupils are most likely to learn effectively and purposefully, to make progress and achieve positively. However, on occasions when this does not occur for all pupils, then some might experience learning difficulties which need to be addressed. These need to be interpreted in relation to the curricular contexts and opportunities to which those 'difficulties' are a response. Have these occurred as a result of the teacher attempting, or failing to differentiate the curriculum and the learning opportunities and the assessment of that learning?

Action taken to alleviate these difficulties may reinforce the very problems teachers seek to address if they do not question or significantly alter features of the general curriculum content, organization and pedagogy which may be limiting learning opportunities in the first place. Does the presence of learning difficulties require a reappraisal of curriculum entitlement? Do we need to teach pupils who are experiencing learning difficulties differently? How can we create conditions for successful learning to occur for all? The process of questioning and rethinking benefits all children through an evaluation of the variety of teaching, learning and assessment strategies employed in the lesson that might otherwise be overlooked.

We need to be careful about attributing 'abilities' to children without examining how the responses on which those judgements are made may be conditioned by the particular qualities and characteristics of the curriculum provided for the pupils. We call some pupils less able as if their limited attainments are directly attributable to individual limitations. How far is this an accurate analysis or have we somehow failed to notice that the pupils are not actually being provided with appropriate opportunities to learn, differentiated to meet their needs?

## Learning difficulties – a problem for the curriculum or for the pupil?

When pupils experience learning difficulties, are they a problem for the curriculum or a problem for the pupil? The most frequent reaction is that learning difficulties are the fault of the pupil and that pupils are exhibiting some deficiencies rather than the curriculum. Instead of asking 'What is it about this pupil which is preventing him/her from taking advantage of the educational opportunities provided within the general curriculum?', we need to turn the question around and ask 'What is it about this curriculum which is making it difficult for this pupil to learn?' Exploring the link between learning difficulties and the curriculum highlights the need to provide appropriate learning opportunities for those pupils experiencing difficulties. This requires a more fundamental rethinking of the curriculum than simply making adaptations on an individual basis.

According to Galton, Simon and Croll (1980), differentiation by pedagogy, task and curriculum content would be counter-productive because additional pressure on the teacher in the preparation of additional materials and the management of lessons might impair the quality of teaching for the class generally. The strategy might also fragment the class group and isolate the children who most need support from the stimulus of working with their peers. Some pupils could be marginalized by being deprived of some curriculum content and experiences that would make it difficult for them to be included in some future learning experiences with other children. Changing the task for everyone makes it possible to alleviate these difficulties while creating a learning experience which all can share. Creating more opportunities for learning through discussion and practical experiences, with more emphasis on cooperative work and self-directed activities might be more effective and appropriate for all pupils, not just those experiencing learning difficulties.

Pupils who achieve success in the tasks presented to them and who can do the work, do not provide any feedback which could alert the teacher to the need to reconsider the appropriateness of the task and overall learning experiences offered to the pupils. Successful pupils rely on their peers who are experiencing difficulties to alert the teacher to the need to reconsider the opportunities which they are providing for the group as a whole. Learning difficulties can therefore perform an important service on behalf of all pupils by drawing attention to the possibilities for development, or changes to content, pedagogy and tasks which might otherwise pass unnoticed.

Learning difficulties should help teachers develop an appropriate and equitable curriculum for all. Is a pupil's 'short attention span', 'slow working pace' or limited response to a task an assessment of an individual's attributes or is it possibly telling us more about the qualities and characteristics of learning experiences which have not so far succeeded in tapping a pupil's curiosity, interest and imagination? Evidence of children's concentration on tasks provides a resource for evaluating the ability of the curriculum to sustain the interest of learners.

If we are to achieve equality and excellence in the education we provide for all pupils, then we need an approach to the task of providing appropriate teaching which shifts the focus of attention from the abilities and characteristics of children to the abilities and characteristics of the curriculum. We need to differentiate the learning opportunities we provide and present to our pupils to enable them to gain greater access to the curriculum, and for them to be able to demonstrate their capabilities when measuring their success against the National Curriculum assessment criteria in the shape of the level descriptions.

Recognizing the interconnectedness of everything that happens in classrooms, teachers should be continually reviewing any judgements they make in the light of experience. This development aspect of teaching is central to, not additional to our professional responsibilities, as we seek to provide a curriculum appropriate to all children. There is always more to learn about how to create conditions for successful learning for all children. Those experiencing difficulties in learning provide the cutting edge for the development of professional thinking and practice to develop a curriculum which is appropriate to all irrespective of gender, race, disability, class, bilingualism or giftedness. The 'aim of equality also serves the aim of excellence for all' (Hart, 1992: 142).

## Differentiation and *your* teaching?

Teachers can differentiate through the teaching styles they adopt with their pupils, the ways in which they present information, the level of language complexity in any materials used and in their own instructions, how tasks are set, the pace and level of complexity of learning. A range of tasks, activities and learning outcomes can be planned to make different demands, to be completed at different rates and in different ways by different pupils. New vocabulary, technical terms or unfamiliar concepts can be introduced, revised and developed in a variety of ways. Some pupils benefit greatly from being given extra support from the teacher or a learning support assistant. ICT, video and multi-media methods used in the classroom together with active learning strategies help to bring learning alive for most, if not all pupils. Teachers should also give some consideration to the general learning conditions and overall classroom environment, including the listening conditions, positioning of the white/black board, general lighting, and the arrangement of pupil work areas for different activities.

How are pupils asked to learn and to carry out their work? Planning for different groupings of the pupils, classroom interactions, use of information technology, feedback and help during learning are all important and represent differentiation strategies. A range of pupil pairings and a balance of small group, resource-led or whole-class teaching can be introduced for a majority of lessons to deliver the curriculum and offer opportunities for learning. It is important to consider the role of additional adults in the classroom – who, when, what, and how do they provide support? The role of both the teacher and learning support assistants is an important one and should enable the pupils to demonstrate what they know, understand and can do. All too often, support can be of the inappropriate kind, where the work is completed by the support staff and not by the pupil. Much care and attention needs to be given to the way in which questions are asked of pupils, whether openly or through worksheets. Does the wording of questions and tasks encourage the pupils to think (genuine open-ended) or close down pupils' thinking (test or fixed choice)?

The ways pupils are allowed or encouraged to show the results of their learning, including different formats of presentation, recording and assessment, demonstrate a further example of differentiation. The teacher should plan to provide opportunities for pupils to present what they have learnt in different ways and to different audiences through the use of video, flow charts, strip cartoons, posters, leaflets and magazine formats. Feedback and discussion with children about their work also need to be planned for and varied to meet the different demands of the pupils, the tasks or the assessment and reporting requirements. Strategies including both written and verbal observations and reflections by both the teacher and the pupil, which include reference to the strengths and weaknesses of the learning outcomes and which incorporate some reference to future targets, are both enabling and flexible and further exemplification of good practice.

## Conclusion

What is the whole school or a department's commitment to its pupils? One that is constantly developing new and flexible strategies to meet pupils' changing needs is, according to Ainscow (1992), a 'moving school'. How far is this a realizable and realistic goal for any school or department? Some pupils, who have identified special educational needs, have an Individual Education Plan (IEP) which builds on the curriculum that the child is already following and makes use of programmes, activities, materials and assessment techniques readily available to the child's teachers. It sets clear targets with monitoring arrangements and clarity about any additional pastoral and medical requirements or information which may be needed. IEP's are 'living documents', designed to show clearly what progress children make; to update information and advice; and to plan for further action (Russell, 1994). To what extent can we, or should we, provide all pupils with an individual action plan? Would this represent good practice in differentiation? As long as these plans draw a distinction from individualized learning, then they are to be encouraged.

Differentiation is about giving access and entitlement. It should also lead to an end to dependency. Differentiation should be based on collaboration between pupils with different learning styles and strengths and not on a hierarchy of abilities, where a variety of abilities is seen as an asset not as a problem. There should be an end to matching tasks to pupils and instead a beginning of pupils deciding for themselves what they need to achieve. In this way pupils can take some ownership of, and responsibility for, their learning, development and achievement. An informed awareness of the individual needs of pupils presents the best chance for both teachers and pupils being able to meet these needs through appropriate provision, response and access to the entitlement curriculum in its widest interpretation.

## Questions to ask in relation to the issues explored in this chapter

- To what extent do your schemes of work offer a variety of teaching and learning opportunities for all the pupils, irrespective of ability?
- What is it about your curriculum and pedagogy which is making it difficult for some of your pupils to learn and to achieve success in geography?
- How will you 'set up success' to enable all your pupils to learn effectively and positively, to the best of their abilities?

# References

Ainscow, M. (1992) 'Aboard the moving school', *Educational Leadership*, 50, 3: 79–81.

Alexander, R. (1991) *Primary Needs Evaluation Project. Interim Evaluation Reports 10 and 11*, Leeds: Leeds University.

Black, H.D. and Dockrell, W.B. (1986) *Diagnostic Assessment in the Secondary School*, Edinburgh: SCRE Publications.

Bloom, B.S. (1956) *Taxonomy of Educational Objectives: Cognitive Domain*, London: Longman.

Bruner, J.S. (1966) *A Study of Thinking*, Chichester: Wiley.

DES (1985) *The Curriculum 5 to 16*, London: HMSO.

DES (1989) *National Curriculum Task Group on Assessment and Testing*, London: DES and Welsh Office.

Dowling, P. (1990) 'The Shogun's and other curriculum voices', in Dowling, P. and Noss, R., *Mathematics versus the National Curriculum*, Basingstoke: Falmer Press.

Galton, M., Simon, B. and Croll, P. (1980) *Inside the Primary Classroom*, London: Routledge and Kegan Paul.

Hall, E.F. (1992) 'Assessment for differentiation', *British Journal of Special Education*, 1: 20–3.

Hart, S. (1992) 'Differentiation. Part of the problem or part of the solution?', *Curriculum Journal*, 3, 2: 131–42.

NCC (1989) *The National Curriculum and Whole Curriculum Planning*, York: NCC Publications.

Qualifications and Curriculum Authority (1997) *Supporting Pupils with Special Educational Needs: Key Stage 3*, Sudbury: QCA Publications.

Russell, P. (1994) 'The Code of Practice: new partnerships for children with special educational needs', *British Journal of Special Education*, 21, 2: 48–52.

Visser, J. (1993) *Differentiation: Making it Work*, Stafford: NASEN Enterprises Ltd.

Vygotsky, L.S. (1978) *Mind in Society: The Development of Higher Psychological Processes*, Cambridge, MA: Harvard University Press.

Warnock, M. (1978) *Meeting Special Educational Needs*, London: HMSO.

Webster, A. (1994) *The Code of Practice Stage One*, Special Children, No. 79, Managing Special Needs in Mainstream Schools Supplement, 1–8.

Wedell, K. (1995) 'Making inclusive education ordinary', *British Journal of Special Education*, 22, 3: 100–4.

# 6   Issues in ICT and geography

*David Hassell*

## Introduction

Information and Communications Technology (ICT) may be a term that has only become popular in the past few years, but the notion of ICT has a long history within the teaching and learning of geography. The use of ICT as a tool for teachers and learners has never had such prominence and is something that must be addressed by all phases of education, reaching across formal and informal education. Despite the importance of the technology, there are many issues for all geographers, ranging from access to the technology, to identifying its effective use and application. More importantly it could be claimed that ICT is changing geography continually, be it in the patterns of work that geographers study or the formal understanding of how the subject can and should be taught. Another key issue is the 'half-life' of change within the technology, which means that new teaching and learning opportunities appear at an ever increasing rate and this has considerable implications for the initial training and continuing professional development of teachers.

There is a huge range of opportunities for enhancing the teaching and learning of geography and discussion often concentrates on these benefits. However, there are also many ways that ICT can support teachers in the execution of their professional duty, which can improve the teaching and learning process, the teachers' efficiency or their activity behind the scenes. The big questions for all involved in geography is how can the issues which restrict the use of ICT be overcome and when they are, how can ICT be integrated effectively to enhance geography? Finally, will ICT have any fundamental impact on the subject itself?

## Why ICT?

Many teachers have managed to teach effectively for years without using ICT, so why bother? This is a question that has been asked many times and for which there is a range of answers. There is a considerable body of research (NCET, 1994) which has looked at a wide range of factors, which can be divided into intrinsic and extrinsic reasons. Research has shown that the learning process can be improved in a number of ways:

- ICT can provide a safe and non-threatening environment for learning with the flexibility to meet individual needs and abilities of each student;
- ICT gives students immediate access to richer source materials;
- difficult ideas are made more understandable when information technology makes them visible;
- ICT can affect the power to try out different ideas and take risks, encouraging analytical and divergent thinking.

However, it is not only the hardware and software that enhance the process, for as many commentators have explained, it is not the technology but what it is used for that is most important. Students must have well designed, meaningful tasks and activities and they will make the most effective use of computers only if teachers know how and when to intervene (NCET, 1994; NCET and GA, 1996). Extrinsically, ICT is already pervasive in society and many feel there is a duty to ensure that pupils leave school prepared for life in the technological world of the twenty-first century.

In 1993 the Department of Education (as it was then) brought together a conference of geographers to debate the issue. Two questions that emerged were: Can geography lessons be enriched with information technology? Are there some IT skills and capabilities which pupils should expect to be taught in school geography? Having looked at how ICT might enhance the subject as well as the role of ICT in the world at large, the answer to the questions was undoubtedly yes! It was proposed that a statement was needed to crystallize the essence of what ICT might offer the subject, and the document *Geography – a pupil's entitlement to IT* (NCET and GA, 1994) was the result. This was jointly published by the Geographical Association (GA) and the National Council for Educational Technology (NCET, now BECTa) and two versions, one for primary and one for secondary, were distributed to all maintained English schools. The idea of entitlement is valid for all ages and the documents propose that pupils studying geography are entitled to use ICT:

- to enhance their skills of geographical enquiry;
- to gain access to a wide range of geographical knowledge and information sources;
- to deepen their understanding of environmental and spatial relationships;
- to experience alternative images of people, place and environment; and
- to consider the wider impact of IT on people, place and environment.

The term 'pupil entitlement' focuses on those uses of ICT in which pupils should expect to gain competence during their school geography course and although there may be an overlap they do not have to match core IT skills.

## The changing climate for ICT

The role of ICT in geography has been recognized for many years with a wide range of activity supported by evangelists promoting its use. However, the adoption of

ICT has been restricted by the lack of access to equipment, training and other issues, many of which are beyond the gift of the average geography teacher. Though governments have spent considerable funds on the use of ICT there has never been a systematic strategy to make the most of technology. Since 1997 the government has realized the need to have a strategic approach to developing ICT use in schools, and has put in place a range of initiatives which aim to improve the situation whilst providing a number of issues for teachers.

Prior to 1997, the Labour Party commissioned an investigation and report (The Independent ICT in Schools Commission, 1997) under the chairmanship of Denis Stevenson, which identified that ICT was a key issue for the future and put forward a range of proposals, including that the government should:

- announce that addressing the issue of ICT is a top priority;
- construct an overall strategy, and appoint a departmental minister to drive it;
- make national agencies key players in this strategy;
- enable all organizations to participate in a coherent and productive way;
- encourage every school to formulate, implement whole-school ICT policies;
- sustain and give coherence to the many small and low-key initiatives to be undertaken over a five–ten-year period required to achieve the long-term objective.

After the general election the government adopted a number of Stevenson's proposals in a consultation paper 'Connecting the Learning Society' (DfEE 1998a) which set out its targets for the following five years. These included:

- by 1998 plans for a National Grid for Learning (NGfL) should be in process of implementation;
- by 1999 all Newly Qualified Teachers would need to become ICT-literate;
- by 2002 serving teachers should feel confident, and be competent to teach, using ICT;
- by 2002 all schools, colleges, universities and libraries should be connected to the NGfL;
- by 2002 most school leavers should have a good understanding of ICT;
- by 2002 the UK should be a centre for excellence in software content for education;
- from 2002 the majority of administrative communications in schools should be electronic.

There are a number of executive government activities that together form the National Grid for Learning (NGfL) initiative which is designed to ensure the targets are achieved. There are four key elements to the initiative.

*Training* – there are two major initiatives, the first being a new ICT national curriculum for initial teacher education, which is expected to ensure that all NQTs are trained in the use of ICT to enhance their curriculum teaching. Second, £230 million is being spent between 1999 and 2003 on providing the opportunity for every teacher to have training in the use of ICT to support the teaching and learning in the curriculum (Hassell, 1999). This money comes from the National Lottery via the New Opportunities Fund and is managed by the Teacher Training Agency. The scheme aims both to bring teachers up to a minimum standard (as described in *The Use of ICT in Subject Teaching – Expected Outcomes for Teachers in England and Wales* (TTA, 1999a)) and also to ensure that teachers finish the programme with improved competence and confidence and with an action plan for future continuing professional development. However, the funding only amounts to approximately £450 per teacher, which cannot be spent on teacher cover or travel to any centres, so the training will mainly be based on distance learning techniques and on teachers contributing some of their own time. The Green Paper on the teaching profession, *Teachers – meeting the challenge of change* (DfEE, 1998a), also provides an indicator of the future with the notion that all teachers will have to ensure they keep their ICT skills up to date. Many heads are already looking carefully at applicants' ICT skills as they appoint new staff.

*Infrastructure* – Many schools do not have the computers or the external network connections to satisfy the government's target. Between 1998 and 2002 an element of central government funding (Standards Fund), with match funding from LEAs (over £760 million) is being spent on enhancing school infrastructure. LEAs have a wide range of approaches to dealing with their Standards Fund grants. These include devolving the grant to schools to make their own decisions, working in partnership with all schools to achieve better purchasing deals, and providing an integrated system with on-line LEA support. However, there will always be inconsistencies in the effectiveness of approaches, which could see some schools working on their own with little support and having to 'reinvent' the wheel. Another strand to the larger initiative is that of Managed Services which was introduced in 1999. This initiative (*Open for Business, Open for Learning*, DfEE, 1998b) aims to provide schools with more effective purchasing by accrediting a number of providers and setting up national framework contracts for the purchase of equipment and services along with training and technical support. Any school can take advantage of the service that should provide better value for money and greater confidence in developing a school's ICT infrastructure.

*The National Grid for Learning (NGfL) web sites* – As part of the government's initiative there are a number of web sites to support schools' education. The British Educational Communications and Technology Agency (BECTa) has a central role to provide a web infrastructure that supports all learners, and in particular schools. The NGfL web site (http://www.ngfl.gov.uk) has been established to provide an architecture into which a wide range of providers can deliver material that will support learners. BECTa also has responsibility for the Virtual Teacher Centre (http://vtc.ngfl.gov.uk) and there are similar sites for Scotland (http://www.svtc.org.uk/), Northern Ireland (http://www.nine.org.uk/) and Wales (http://vtccymru.ngfl.wales.gov.uk/) supported by other agencies. These aim to provide access to a range of materials, guidance and services for teachers. The materials range from official documents such as the National Curriculum and schemes of work, through support for the use of ICT in every subject, to conferencing facilities and links to a wide range of other providers. The sites will develop over coming years and whilst there is an enormous potential for geographers, in the short term there are going to be issues about access and teacher and pupil skills.

*Other initiatives* – There are a range of other initiatives that are designed to reduce the teacher's bureaucratic burden through the use of ICT, to encourage inter-agency activity and to improve software and content provision. Geographers have problems with effective access to data and suitable software and equipment to support the subject, and over coming years the software initiative may improve the situation.

The NGfL is providing over £1 billion of new funding, which seems a lot of money, but it will not solve all the problems for geographers trying to make the most of ICT in their teaching. Everybody should be aware of the initiatives to ensure that they make the most of them, but there will be limits to their effects. However, changes in the ICT industry and patterns in home and personal ownership of computers will also have a large influence. Some analysts predict the cost of personal computer ownership dropping dramatically over the next fifteen years to the price for a basic machine reaching the cost of a video player, which could influence accessibility enormously, for example every pupil could have a suitable portable in their bag.

## The range of ICT

If teachers should be using ICT and there are improving opportunities for geographers to use the technologies, where does one start? In a short chapter such as this it is difficult to describe the range of opportunities in detail, but Table 6.1 provides an overview of the scope and some of the applications of ICT. For a more detailed treatment of the use of ICT, the IT pages of *Teaching Geography* and the references at the end of the chapter will provide a source of further ideas. Technology is advancing at an ever increasing speed and whether this reflects new opportunities or delivers existing ones more effectively, it confronts teachers with an ever-changing panorama of issues. The table of examples is neither static nor is it mutually exclusive, because one of the major changes in ICT is the notion of converging technologies. In the recent past you needed a different software tool for every job, for example a word processor was only for drafting and redrafting text and then laying it out in a rudimentary fashion. With the latest word processing software you can combine multimedia, write collaboratively on-line, calculate and display information in variety of ways – the software is becoming more integrated as well as gaining new features. Also, a number of the ideas could be integrated in a single geographical activity. Finally, the table is not comprehensive. There is a lot of specific software which could be used effectively in geography, but hopefully the examples provide an overview of the range of opportunities that exist.

*Table 6.1* Examples of the ICT opportunities to support geography

| Technology | Sample geographical application |
| --- | --- |
| Presentation packages (word processing, DTP and presentation software e.g. Powerpoint) | when researching information for an investigation use a word processor to analyse and manipulate a text, e.g. to edit and extract useful information from an article copied from a CD-ROM or the Internet; |
| | as one of the products from an investigation to use a desktop publishing package to produce a leaflet promoting the case for or against a local by-pass; |
| | to support decision-making on sustainable use of rainforests, use a word processor to present a coursework report (combining text, maps and graphics); |
| | use a presentation package to combine various types of information to argue the case to the class on the new superstore location. |
| Data logging | in an investigation into depressions to record hourly weather information with an automatic weather station to investigate the passage of a depression; |
| | use data logging equipment to record and compare river flow along a river's length; |
| | use a weather satellite system to collect, record and investigate the daily timing of equatorial rain cells (this could also be completed as an Internet activity). |
| Data handling (databases and spreadsheets) | to analyse the environmental impact of housing developments on a number of sites by using a spreadsheet to analyse and present fieldwork scores; |
| | use a data-handling package to analyse information collected from a land use survey in an urban area; |
| | as part of a locality study to compare and contrast climatic data using a spreadsheet to present data graphically; |
| | use a database with graphing facilities to display information about global economic development in graph/chart form. |
| Simulations and modelling software | use a simulation package to investigate the effects of migration on population change in a region; |
| | as part of course work use a modelling package to investigate the length of time it takes for a drainage system, e.g. the Aral sea, to find equilibrium; |
| | use a spreadsheet to calculate the costs of alternative development proposals for a derelict site. |
| Mapping and geographic information systems (GIS) | use a mapping package to present comparative socio-economic data about the European region; |

Table 6.1 continued

| Technology | Sample geographical application |
| --- | --- |
| Mapping and geographic information systems (GIS) continued | to investigate the changing traffic pressure in a locality using a mapping package to present flow rates over time from a series of observations of major roads; |
| | use a GIS as a tool to support decision-making in a local issue such as the location of a new retail park. |
| Digital images (from the Internet, digital cameras, or scanned images from film cameras, Photo CD, or other sources) | to record information on fieldwork either to exemplify what has been seen or to use in presentations, such as views of the buildings, areas to be assessed for environmental quality or physical features; |
| | to provide materials, either for class or individual work, these can be used to stimulate discussion and the images can also be used in pupils' work or annotated to develop and illustrate understanding. |
| Electronic communication (e-mail and web links) | as part of an exercise to compare contrasting localities pupils can exchange information with other schools on agreed topics or by asking questions; |
| | to investigate contrasting climate or to investigate the movement of weather systems schools can set up a partnership to exchange weather data by e-mail. |
| Multimedia authoring (on machines or via the Internet) | as part of a class activity on tourism the class cooperate to produce a multimedia package to present information on a number of holiday destinations to help other students; |
| | developing web pages on the school site to display the arguments on a local issue and to collect views from others. |
| Information rich sources (CD-ROM and the World Wide Web) | to provide up-to-date information such as weather satellite images or weather information on any country of the world; |
| | to investigate leisure and tourism through access to information on localities, services and travel in this country and abroad; |
| | as part of an investigation into employment use a CD-ROM of UK census data to find and display information on patterns in chosen areas; |
| | use the Internet to find information on recent tectonic activity before exploring the impact, causes and effects of a specific earthquake somewhere in the world. |

Looking at the examples in Table 6.1 from a geographical standpoint there are a range of processes which ICT can support, including to:

- collect, keep and use individual or class collected data;
- monitor the environment;
- explore and extract relevant information;
- create, edit, manipulate and use appropriate maps, diagrams and graphs;
- investigate, develop and present geographical ideas;
- predict and solve problems; and
- help make decisions.

Linking this back to the entitlement document, how many of these opportunities are provided in schools at the moment? Although all schools should provide opportunities to address these issues using traditional methods, they can all have value added through the use of ICT.

## The challenge for geography

Discounting the subject of IT, geography could be the place in the curriculum where the range of ICT technologies has the greatest impact. The discussion so far in this chapter has concentrated on the role of ICT to enhance the teaching and learning of the subject. However, the impact of ICT is much more pervasive and is an issue which geography as a subject must come to terms with. This impact can be seen in the changing patterns in society, the tools that exist to support decision-making in the real world and the way ICT could alter what we teach, when we teach it, and how we teach it.

Changes in the types of jobs, the distribution of workers across industry sectors and the types of work and skills are having a growing influence on work patterns and the location of industry. Examples of these changes include the concentration of transatlantic companies in Ireland, the development of computer programming and printing in widely distributed locations, such as India and Hong Kong. Some of these changes affect the local business community, for example the closure of local insurance and other services due to the vast increase in remote service activity such as call centres. These changes, combined with aspects such as the ability to telecommute are changing the face of travel requirements as an increasing proportion of economic activity is based on e-commerce and less is based on traditional industries and in particular manufacturing.

Throughout a huge range of human activity, including commerce and the public sector, ICT is playing an increasing role in decision-making, ranging from locating a road or superstore to the identification of flood or weather hazards. ICT can enable better decision-making as it is possible to take into consideration a wider range of variables, as well as supporting the monitoring of natural hazards and systems to provide greater warning and providing the opportunity to take action to reduce impact. As a result, ICT can provide better and faster tools for decision-making. These changes have an impact in two ways; first, they change the geography we teach, but second, they change the decision-making skills and processes that we should be developing in children. The key issue in this area is how can the subject community ensure that the geography of formal curricula that is taught and examined keeps up with these changes?

A second issue is how the technology has the power to change what goes on in the geography classroom. Geography is a complex subject which relies on the development of spatial awareness and skills, and an understanding of a wide range of abstract concepts. Many of these concepts cannot be illustrated 'live' whilst providing opportunities for developing enquiry and decision-making skills. All teachers would expect that as pupils progress through school they should be able to complete increasingly complex geographical enquiries more effectively and make more appropriate decisions based on the evidence. Most people would agree that for pupils to become more autonomous in this work they have to have a good grounding in a wide range of geographical concepts, and this often determines what and in which order things are taught. However, if you have ever watched young children play a computer game such as *SIMCITY* (Electronic Arts, 1990) the city planning game, and then questioned them to find out how and why they made certain decisions, the answers can be very revealing. Once children have used the software for a while they start to make complex decisions based on their understanding of how the underlying 'model' works. The software has the benefits of explicit interaction where there is instant feedback. The children also have an environment where they can discover relationships themselves and where abstract concepts can be illustrated in a simplified form (Bliss, 1994). Of course, pupils using this sort of software are motivated by the game element and spend a long time on the computer developing their understanding. But, normally would we try and teach 9- or 10-year-olds about settlement planning (whatever one thinks of the *SIMCITY* model) at the level of detail in this software? This is only an anecdote, but it illustrates that with the right tools where students have access to methods of demonstrating, exploring, posing questions and decision-making with effective feedback, the need for a detailed knowledge may no longer be a barrier to the development of higher-order skills. For example, if one were teaching about the change in agricultural land use, a map-based package with data on different areas over time could be a valuable tool. Students would be able to investigate and identify patterns and explore how patterns changed, by displaying data for a specific year, whilst the system would be able to demonstrate visually any dynamic changes. A more sophisticated system could allow students to model changes and ask 'what if . . . ?' questions, which would enable them to investigate the relationship between the variables involved. Finally, it would be possible to predict future change in different scenarios and evaluate the predictions. As a result of having such systems, we could see different teaching approaches, with a change in the emphasis in learning outcomes, from product to process, and in the content that is taught. The challenge for geography in the future will be to build on these opportunities whilst providing a curriculum which is viable and supportable by the teaching force.

## The challenge for developers and providers

Whilst the technology moves on in leaps and bounds, schools still suffer from the lack of access to effective software, data and other information. Software is a particular problem, for example the majority of mapping software or GIS available for schools is either not suitable or priced at a level which is prohibitive. There are a few exceptions and the development of software technologies will mean that GIS which runs over the Intranet or Internet may start to solve some of the problems. Another of the considerable concerns is the lack of modelling or simulation software which enables students to gain better understanding of the hidden processes which geographers need to study. However, even if the software were available, a key problem for schools is the access to data, in particular cartographic and statistical data. It is worth comparing the UK situation with that in the USA. In the US the freedom of information legislation and government policy to make data available mean that it can be easier to visit a US web site to find information about our own country. Digital map data are technically available, but for most schools they are just not accessible. The challenge here seems to be for developers and providers of data, but it is even more important for teachers to communicate what they need and to take any opportunities that arise to guide developers.

## The challenge for teachers and schools

As a geography teacher of children with a range of ages and abilities to be taught and the pressure of local and national imperatives on standards and many other issues, ICT provides considerable challenges. Despite the hype and the range of articles imploring teachers to use the technology, it is vital that ICT be used only where it really does add value to the geography. The first issue is to ensure that ICT will make a difference. It is possible to ask the following questions (from the BECTa/GA Geography project) when reviewing whether the use of ICT is adding value:

- Is it a non-trivial use of ICT which enhances good geography?
  For example, typing climate figures into a spreadsheet and graphing them, without any consideration of the reasons for graphing and the type of graph selected, might be considered a trivial use.
- Is it an effective way of delivering the defined learning outcomes in geography?
  For example, students may have a better understanding of an abstract concept because the ICT application has given them the opportunity to investigate it more fully.
- Is it efficient use of classroom time?
  For example, some IT applications free the students from mechanical and repetitive tasks, enabling them to spend longer on the analysis or investigational aspects of their work. A lot of time may be taken up initially when implementing something new, but this may 'pay off' in the longer term through benefits in learning.
- Do students have opportunities to evaluate and reflect on their use of ICT?

A key issue for geography departments will be to map what resources they have access to, the skills the teachers have and then to try to develop a plan to provide the entitlement for students. It is important to remember that teachers have an entitlement as well to ensure they have the confidence and competence to make the most of ICT. This does not just concern what is used with the students in class, but how the ICT can help the teacher carry out his or her professional duties. ICT can:

- support the development of materials, making it easier to produce differentiated worksheets and reduce preparation;
- provide access to resources, statistics and other information;
- enable teachers to exchange good ideas and obtain peer support;
- aid the assessment, reporting and recording of student progress including supporting target setting;
- provide access to research and inspection evidence as well as professional development.

Obviously, the NOF training initiative will have an impact on teacher confidence and competence, but establishing a departmental development plan is an ongoing issue for all.

Another issue to think about, is the range of facilities which a department should have to ensure that students can be provided with their entitlement to geography and ICT and to identify an action plan to help the department work towards this goal. Although the list of facilities a department should have will change as new technologies appear, a good starting point for a department to aim for would be the list below:

1   Generic ICT facilities which include multimedia computers (with printing facilities) with:
    - word processing; database; spreadsheet; desk-top publishing and multimedia authoring tools;
    - an Internet browser for access to resources on the World Wide Web, and associated e-mail and on-line services.
2   A digital camera.
3   Geography-specific facilities:
    - quality CD-ROM electronic atlas and encyclopaedia;
    - modelling software suitable for geographical models;
    - Geographic Information System (GIS) with digital map data;
    - automatic data-logging weather station;
    - map and statistical data for local and place studies.

In addition, departments will also build up a selection of content-rich resources, which will include specific geography software, CD-ROMs, Internet sites, and so on.

## The challenge for us all

It is easy to look at the use of ICT and say there are so many problems and issues that ICT just cannot be integrated successfully. This approach is not viable, since our students deserve to have a geographical education which reflects the world in which they live, where ICT is completely pervasive and more importantly changing the nature and processes involved in the subject.

Obviously, there is not enough money in the system, but there are a number of key initiatives that geographers must make the most of. What is important is for geographers to work together and for there to be some strategy for the future. The Geographical Association has produced a position statement, *Geography in the Curriculum* (GA, 1999) which might provide the starting point for this strategy. The statement includes an understanding of ICT, but may not have made explicit the underlying changes in geography that ICT brings about. Geographers can play a vital role for placing ICT in context, to provide the perspective for technologies in decision-making, taking into account values and attitudes and at the same time strengthening the subject. What is required is for all the participants to work together to find a strategy and solutions which are appropriate and effective. If this chapter stimulates the reader to think further about ICT, here are some questions that might provide some starting points for your thoughts.

- How will ICT continue to change geography?
- What role does the use of ICT in society (e.g. in planning or hazard management) have for the school curriculum?
- What opportunities does ICT provide to enrich the teaching and learning experience?
- How can we train and support geography teachers to use ICT effectively?
- Do I make the most of ICT for myself and my students?
- What do I need to make a difference?

The challenge for all of us is not necessarily to answer these questions today, but to think about how we might evolve solutions and manage the change which comes about from the impact of ICT.

## References

Bliss, J. (1994) 'From mental models to modelling', in Mellar, H., Bliss, J., Boohan, R., Ogborn, J. and Tompsett, C. (eds) *Learning with Artificial Worlds: Computer Based Modelling in the Curriculum*, London: Falmer Press.

Department for Education and Employment (1998a) *Teachers – meeting the challenge of change*, London: HMSO, http://www.dfee.gov.uk/teachers/greenpaper/index.htm.

Department for Education and Employment (1988b) *Open for Business, Open for Learning*, London: HMSO, http://www.dfee.gov.uk/grid/challenge/index.htm.

Electronic Arts (various dates for different versions from 1990) *SIMCITY*, San Mateo: Electronic Arts.

The Geographical Association (1999) *Geography in the Curriculum*, Sheffield: The Geographical Association.

Hassell, D. (1999) 'Will you get some training?', *Teaching Geography*, 24, 2: 92–3.
National Council for Educational Technology (1994) *IT Works*, Coventry: NCET.
NCET and The Geographical Association (1994) *Geography: A Pupil's Entitlement to IT*, Coventry: NCET.
NCET and The Geographical Association (1996) *Investigating Patterns in Human Geography*, Coventry: NCET.
Teacher Training Agency (1999a) *The Use of ICT in Subject Teaching – Expected Outcomes for Teachers in England and Wales*, London: TTA.
Teacher Training Agency (1999b) *The Use of Information and Communications Technology in Subject Teaching, Identification of Training Needs – Secondary Geography*, London: TTA.

## Web sites

| | |
|---|---|
| National Grid for Learning | http://www.ngfl.gov.uk |
| Virtual Teacher Centre | http://vtc.ngfl.gov.uk |
| Scottish VTC | http://www.svtc/org.uk/ |
| Northern Ireland Network for Education | http://www.nine.org.uk/ |
| Welsh VTC | http://vtccymru.ngfl.wales.gov.uk/ |
| BECTa | http://www.becta.org.uk |
| Department for Education and Employment | http://www.dfee.gov.uk |
| The Geographical Association | http://www.geography.org.uk |
| The Geography and ICT web site | http://vtc.ngfl.gov.uk/resource/cits/geog |
| Qualifications and Curriculum Authority | http://www.qca.org.uk |
| Teacher Training Agency | http://www.teach-tta.gov.uk/ |

# 7 Writing geography textbooks

*David Waugh*

## Introduction

In this chapter I explore some of the issues involved when using and in writing geography textbooks for the 11 to 19 age range. In doing so I have expressed my own personal views and opinions fashioned during thirty years of teaching geography and over eighteen years of writing geographical textbooks. I hope that these views will stimulate debate concerning geography textbooks, especially about the way in which textbooks serve the needs of geography teachers (both specialist and non-specialist), students and pupils. The chapter addresses the following issues:

- How have geography textbooks evolved since the 1950s?
- What should be the main roles of a geography textbook?
- What are the limitations in using geography textbooks?
- How is a geography textbook written?

## How have geography textbooks evolved since the 1950s?

The simplest dictionary definition of the term 'textbook' is a 'Manual of instruction, standard book in any branch of study' (*The Little Oxford Dictionary*, 1988: 582). To an educational publisher, a textbook refers to any material that can be sold in multiple packages, that is in bulk. To the geography teacher, such as myself, a textbook is (or should be) a major educational resource. Despite the introduction of wider forms of media (e.g. the Internet and CD-ROMs), I am strongly convinced that the textbook is likely to remain the most valuable teaching resource. This assumes that teachers realize that the textbook is only a 'resource' and as such can never replace the skills, knowledge, enthusiasm and expertise of the classroom teacher.

A quick glance at the numerous, and ever increasing, geography textbooks available on the market shows a wide range in approach. At one extreme are books that encourage students to investigate and to enquire for themselves, often through the use of numerous questions or the setting of activities. At the other extreme are textbooks that provide information and resources, e.g. photographs, maps, graphs and other data, which can then be adapted by the teacher to suit their individual

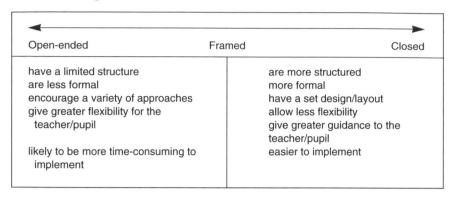

*Figure 7.1* The range of geography textbooks

needs. These two extremes have been defined as open-ended and closed (Figure 7.1) by several lecturers in geographical education, such as David Lambert and Margaret Roberts; Roberts used similar criteria in providing a framework for teaching styles and strategies (Roberts 1996, chapter 8).

Though I agree that there are indeed two extreme types of resource book available to geography teachers, I prefer to use what I consider to be the more appropriate, and user-friendly, terms, that is workbook/activity book rather than open-ended and resource book instead of closed.

A 'workbook' may be full of activities or enquiries where a specific author sets tasks that usually seem to assume that all pupils possess similar ability and motivation, and have the time and resources to complete those tasks. I strongly believe that such activities (i.e. questions, investigations and enquiries) should ideally be designed by individual teachers, as they know the abilities, interests and needs of their pupils and are aware of their own, and their department's, level of confidence and competence. I tend to include activities and questions only because that is what most teachers demand, rather than what I feel they should have! Even so, most of the tasks that I write are meant as:

- time savers for teachers, especially at certain pressure-points;
- ideas for follow-up work, especially at Key Stage 3;
- exemplars of examination questions for General Certificate of Education (GCSE) and Advanced Level (A-level).

A 'resource book' gives teachers accurate, up-to-date and wide-ranging data for them to use in a way that they think best. It should be presented to stimulate and interest pupils as well as give them self-confidence. Also, as both the National Curriculum (NC) and most GCSE and A-level syllabuses tend to be overcrowded, in relation to both time on school timetables and increased competition from compulsory subjects, the textbook should ideally cover all the prescribed content.

It would seem fairly obvious, however, that no textbook in isolation can satisfy the different needs and the wide-ranging approaches of all geography teachers.

Indeed, total reliance on a single textbook, or textbook series, can be as restrictive to a pupil as if that pupil had the same geography teacher throughout his or her entire secondary education from 11 to 18 years.

## What should be the main roles of a geography textbook?

In my own school days, back in the 1950s, there was little choice within the limited range of geography textbooks. They were, to stereotype, always in black and white and usually consisted of lengthy sections of text, sometimes extending uninterrupted for several pages. The pages themselves were packed with facts, overcrowded maps, the occasional poor quality black and white photo and very few activities. They rarely contained descriptions and the limited number of questions usually only tested pupil knowledge, meaning that children were not encouraged to think for themselves. Looking back, these books appeared to have advanced little from the 'capes and bays' geography, with its rote learning of places and data, that was typical of half a century earlier. There seemed little effort:

- to design or to make the books look interesting;
- to get pupils to understand processes;
- to involve pupils;
- to get them to ask questions or to be critical;
- to apply their knowledge;
- to see and explain patterns;
- to develop their own values and attitudes.

It was, arguably, the Honeybone, Long and Roberson series of the late 1950s/early 1960s that began the modern evolution of geography textbooks. However, to me, the real breakthrough came in the early 1970s with the development of the School's Council Geography for the Young School Leaver Project (GYSL), which later became the Avery Hill Project (AHP). Had I not been involved from the outset with this project, it is doubtful if I would have ever become an acceptable teacher and I would certainly never have been capable of writing geography texts. Before this involvement with the AHP, my own teaching style was dominated by a formal, fact-giving, 'chalk and talk' approach – although had I been paid by results I would have been pretty successful! The AHP completely changed my teaching style and approach by making me realize the importance of pupil involvement. The key elements of the AHP were knowledge, understanding, application and the development of values and attitudes; together with the value of using a wide range of geographical resources. Basically, the AHP helped me, initially, to discover and, later, to develop what were to become my main classroom strengths.

I now perceive the role of the textbook to include the following:

- The book should provide a relevant core or 'tailor-made' teaching scheme of work for either the National Curriculum or for GCSE. This means covering all, or most, of the basic content and skills, whilst simultaneously allowing and encouraging teachers to develop their own style, approach and strategies to suit the needs, interests and abilities of their own pupils. A textbook should be the 'skeleton' to which the teacher can readily add the 'flesh', and this should include the teacher's own ideas and use of local examples, updated case studies and more recent data. As was stated in the 'Key Geography Foundations Teachers' Resource Guides':

> In these days of little or no planning time, many teachers will find that the scheme of work for Key Geography as it stands will meet their needs, and will provide a good structure and direction for their teaching. Others, however, may prefer to adapt the scheme of work to their own personalised programme and develop, lesson by lesson, work schemes that detail more exactly their own choice of teaching strategies and learning activities.
>
> (Waugh and Bushell, 1992b)

This I believe can also apply to all my more recent publications.

- The book should also be practical, giving teachers and student teachers ideas for alternative approaches to a topic. It should save the teacher time in lesson preparation, in having to seek new or updated resources, and in having to convert new data into an appropriate teaching format. This has greater significance at times of National Curriculum implementation or revision or following changes in the examination system. According to Roberts:

> the over complex and unmanageable 1991 NC and the lack of prescription in the Programmes of Study (PoS) on how courses should be constructed meant that the task of producing schemes of work was more difficult (in geography) than for some other NC subjects. Some teachers felt that they did not have the time or confidence to construct their own schemes of work. In addition, over half the departments had some non-specialist teaching geography and, as one (nameless) head of department commented 'non-specialists feel safe with a textbook'.
>
> (Roberts, 1998: 24)

- The book must be factually accurate, relevant and up to date, so that teachers and pupils alike can feel completely confident in the reliability and quality of information.
- It must also be interesting in both design and content, utilizing the latest publishing technology. It is often said, within publishing circles, that geography textbooks are amongst the most attractive in the educational market.
- There is a need for the book to be accessible to as wide a range of pupils as possible.
- The book should be seen by pupils:

    o in the short term, as helping them to achieve as high a grade as possible;

○ in the longer term, as having a relevance to their future lives and way of life. Pupils seem to get great satisfaction in being able to say 'We saw something on TV last night that you were talking about in class last week.'

○ as part of an interesting and enjoyable subject that is worthwhile pursuing at successively higher levels. In the Key Geography series, the authors made a conscious decision to put 'earthquakes and volcanoes', which many pupils enjoy studying, into 'Interactions' so that it might be taught at that time when pupils were choosing their GCSE options.

- Where a book forms part of a series, it should show progression, for example in geographical knowledge, vocabulary and skills. If it is a 'stand alone' text then it is even more important that it should show differentiation through, for example, language, explanation, comprehension and in pupil tasks.
- The book should provide a fundamental resource for teachers, student teachers and pupils, rather than for groups of people not actively involved in classroom work, e.g. Office for Standards in Education (OFSTED) Inspectors and Advisers. It should also show a flexible approach offering a range of possible methods of use from providing the basis for a structured course, contributing to the construction of a teaching syllabus through to being used largely as a resource. Such a range of uses can be accessed by a range of teacher experience from the least confident and newly qualified, through to the most experienced and confident teachers.
- The book should also increase geographical awareness and improve educational standards.
- There is a growing need for textbooks to have links with other relevant media, e.g. the Internet, CD-ROMs and videos. For example *The New Wider World* (Waugh, 1998) has several case studies taken from the BBC *Geography 2000* series. Through cooperation between the BBC and the publishers several 'screen grabs' (i.e. still photos taken from the programmes) were included and links made between the video and the textbook. A new Channel 4 educational series on China includes comparative case studies planned to be included in a related text. Further, in *Extensions* (Waugh and Bushell, 1999), several activities include the option of using specific web sites. These allow pupils to develop further topics introduced within the book itself, for example updating the Montserrat volcanic eruption, finding the latest world population data, or using recent weather maps provided by the BBC and the Meteorological Office.
- Any textbook must provide value for money. Many geography departments continue to have very limited funding and, once investment has been made in a text, it may have to be used for several years. Ideally, teachers should be given the opportunity to replace a series over a period of time, rather than having to make a bulk purchase at one particular point.

## What are the limitations in using geography textbooks?

There is a need to be aware of a number of potential limitations with geography textbooks.

### The reliance on a single series or author

If a teacher relies on one textbook for a year, or a textbook series for several years, then their pupils may get a restricted view of geography due to that author's perspective or approach. Earlier, the analogy of pupils having the same geography teacher throughout their school life was used. Yet, does it automatically mean that such pupils are disadvantaged compared with those who may have had several teachers during that time? Surely what matters is the quality of teaching involved. Similarly, what should be judged is the quality and effectiveness of the textbook, together with its ability to motivate pupils and to improve their geographical knowledge and understanding.

Some school textbooks can apparently have a considerable influence on classroom teaching. Roberts (1998) claimed that the Stanley Thorne Key Geography series, by Waugh and Bushell, had such an effect. Roberts states:

> For the majority of departments, the 'Key Geography' interpretation of the 1991 Geography NC became the Geography NC. They based their key stage 3 courses on it and they use the books in the majority of lessons, with students carrying out the activities in the books. To a certain extent, therefore, changes in classroom practice since 1991 can be attributed as much to the dominance of one textbook series as to the statutory requirements themselves. The impact of the 1991 GNC on classroom practice could have been very different had other key stage 3 geography series been used more widely.
>
> (Roberts, 1998: 24)

### Most books tend to be aimed at the mid-ability range

This, unfortunately, is often a result of the economics of publishing. The production of a complete mixed ability book with material capable of extending the full ability range of pupils would be both physically very large and, apart from possibly being unmanageable, certainly expensive. Unless a book happens to be widely adopted, something impossible to predict in advance, most educational publishers will not take such a risk. To produce a book for a limited ability range that covers a limited range of topics and used as an extension or an alternative to the core text, may be educationally beneficial but is unlikely to be economically viable. In the long term, a two-hundred-page book is likely to be considerably cheaper by bulk buying than three smaller books each of seventy pages.

## Over-reliance by some teachers on textbooks

There has been criticism of certain geography textbooks as some teachers seem to actually use them as their teaching syllabus, instead of developing their own resources and teaching scheme. I never envisaged, nor can I imagine, that a sizeable number of teachers begin at page four of one of my books and work through it page by page, lesson by lesson, until they reach the end. However, this is an impression given by some QCA officers, OFSTED officials and geography advisers. This is *not* how a textbook should be used. Indeed, such an approach would appear to be more a weakness of the teacher than of the book. Roberts pointed out that her research showed that:

> By 1995 two-thirds of geography departments were using textbooks in over half their geography lessons. The OFSTED inspections of 1993–94 suggest that these findings are valid nationally. However, OFSTED's comments that 'some teachers were over-reliant on textbooks' and that 'a few schools relied too much on textbook series as substitutes for coherent planning and the consideration of teaching methods' and that 'many schools relied on a limited, and sometimes limiting, single textbook series', were not quantified.
>
> (Roberts, 1998: 24)

## Bias and stereotyping

These may be viewed at three different scales.

Any place or example that an author chooses is bound to have bias. For example, the National Curriculum requests that 'two countries, other than those in the United Kingdom, should be studied. They should be in significantly different states of development.' The author chose Kenya, because of first-hand knowledge, and Japan, as that country seemed the most convenient of the three options available at Key Stage 3 – smaller area, more compact, less detail – compared with the sizeable and highly diverse USA and the complexities of changes within the USSR. Having made that decision, I revisited Kenya and later Japan, collecting current information, talking to local people and taking photographs on specific themes.

Of greater significance is when the curriculum requests a specific example, for example 'the geographical distribution of one economic activity' (National Curriculum) or 'choose one type of farming within the EU' (GCSE). Here, not only is there a likelihood of bias, but the much greater danger of both oversimplifying and stereotyping, such as the impression that *all* types of farming in the EU are similar to the example chosen and described. The dangers of over-simplification and stereotyping are problems of which, I am sure, most teachers are aware and which, in turn, they take into account when either using a textbook or producing their own teaching strategies.

Of considerable concern to the present author, if not always to certain pressure groups, is the danger of bias in the presentation of data and opinions. To provoke thought amongst pupils, I have always tried to present a balanced view. This enables them to make their own informed decisions and, most important, develop their own values and attitudes, e.g. the advantages and disadvantages of using certain types of energy or the role of transnationals or tourism in an economically developing country.

### Problem of topicality and dating published material

The problem of producing contemporary information and describing the most recent case studies is a major problem for both the geography author and the publisher. Authors take several months or longer to write a textbook and the publishers take at least a further six months for that material to be published. This means it is inevitable that a geography textbook is already out of date well before it reaches the market. With recent improvements in global communications and the increase in the quality and quantity of available information, this means that the effective life of a geography textbook is about three or fours years, which is probably half of what it was in the early 1980s. Consequently, books have to be revised, rewritten or replaced at increasingly shorter intervals. Whilst this means that teachers can keep their resources updated, it also means they have added expense as well as having to change lesson plans and schemes of work.

### Limitations in depth and range of case studies and of opportunities for investigations

Teachers, examination boards, publishers, authors, geography advisers and OFSTED officials all seem to agree that many geography textbooks contain insufficient case studies and that these are also often too short and over-simplified. Furthermore, they also feel they provide only limited opportunities for pupils to make personal investigations or to conduct their own enquiries. However, in reality, I feel that teachers rarely seem to have sufficient curricular time to look at many topics in depth or to allow pupils to conduct lengthy research. Also, the examination system does not encourage pupils to write at great length on any specific place or topic. There are also economic restrictions placed on publishers, especially as a book focusing on case studies or suggested enquiries rarely sells many copies. From an author's point of view the use of in-depth case studies or enquiry work can take up much space. This can only be achieved by a reduction in the number and, therefore, the range of case studies and investigations; these in turn, will make the book more prescriptive. Finally, though advisers and OFSTED officials can theorize, as indeed they should, about the ideal scenario, they do not face the practicalities of classroom teaching!

### Writing a geography textbook – a personal perspective

The textbook can either be a professionally produced set of lesson plans that form a scheme of work, or it can be a source of additional material. My first book *The*

*British Isles* (Waugh, 1983) consisted of my two years of lesson plans and resources that I was using in school to teach the Avery Hill project. At that time, before the availability of the photocopier (student teachers today do not know how lucky they are!), I had to resort to the self-production of semi-legible purple 'Banda' sheets with relatively poor diagrams and an absence of photographs. In *The British Isles*, my poorly presented worksheets were replaced by a well designed layout, a typed text and quality diagrams/artwork and photographs – half of which appeared in full colour.

There are three main stages in writing a textbook

## Stage 1. The book as a unit

Initial thoughts are on layout and design. I made a conscious decision from the outset with *The British Isles* to go for a double-page spread, an innovation which was welcomed and appreciated by teachers. This development arose from the considerable classroom management problems caused by the abundance of teaching resources provided for the trial period of the Avery Hill project. In one single lesson, the pupils, many of whom by the very nature of the project were the least able, were presented with a mass of resources. For any one lesson these might include maps, photographs, newspaper extracts, statistics and activities. A double-page spread was to help teachers with their classroom management, as pupils had all they needed for the lesson in front of them without the distraction of having to turn pages. The material itself gave guidance to the length and suggested structure of a lesson. I also fought long and hard with the publisher for the use of colour, since the limited range of textbooks available at that time tended to be either in black and white or with just a single 'colour' – often a sickly red or green! I believed then, as now, that most people would prefer colour to black and white. The publishers initially allowed me only one colour double spread in every eight, but later relented, agreeing first to every alternate spread in colour (*The British Isles*, 1983) and ultimately to full colour (*The British Isles*, Second Edition, 1990). Since then, I have discovered that if a book is designed before it is actually written, then it is more likely to be successful than one which is designed after the draft manuscript has been submitted. Additionally, an attractive design with a modern layout, high-quality artwork and clear photographs has become increasingly important. Success may be measured by the number of copies adopted by schools, the comments made by teachers and pupils, its contribution to raising standards, and if it enhances the number opting to study geography at each successive level.

Depending on the level of the book, I then look at either the relevant National Curriculum requirements or the full range of GCSE syllabuses. For Key Stage 3, I take the National Curriculum Programmes of Study (Statements of Attainment for the first book) and convert these to key questions. The key question represents the equivalent of the main aim of the lesson. By listing the key questions, it is possible to produce an overall plan for the book (Figure 7.2); this technique can be used by teachers when producing their teaching schemes of work. For the GCSE level book *The New Wider World* (Waugh, 1998), I reviewed all thirteen existing

| KEY GEOGRAPHY   Extensions   Matrix | | | | Foundations | Connections | Interactions | Places |
|---|---|---|---|---|---|---|---|
| Content | Page | Key Questions | Cross reference to . . . | | | | |
| **1 Tectonic processes** | 4-5 | Why is there a global pattern of earthquakes and volcanoes? | | | | 26-28 | |
| a Global distribution of earthquakes and volcanoes and their relationship to plate boundaries | 6-7 | What are the causes of earthquakes? | | | | 27-29 | 88 |
| b Nature, causes and effects of earthquakes | 8-9 | How do people respond to earthquakes? | | | | 24-25, 94-97 | 88-89 |
| c Human responses to earthquakes | 10-11 | What are the causes of volcanic eruptions? | | | | 20-21 | 88 |
| d Nature, causes and effects of volcanic eruptions | 12-13 | How do people respond to volcanic eruptions? | | | | 22-23 | 88 |
| e Human responses | | | | | | | |
| **2 Geomorphological processes** | 14-15 | How does rock type and weathering affect the development of landforms? | | | 4-5,10-11 14,97 | | |
| a Role of rock type and weathering in landform development | 16-17 | What are the main processes which produce river landforms? | | 30 | 6-13, 94-97 | | |
| b Landforms and processes associated with river valleys and drainage basins | 18-19 | What are the causes and effects of river floods? | | 32-34 | | | 80-81 |
| c Causes and effects of river floods | 20-21 | What can people do to try to control river floods? | | 35,42 | | | |
| d Human responses and attempts to control river floods | 22-23 | What are the main processes which produce coastal landforms? | | | 6,14-15 | | |
| e Landforms and processes associated with coastal landforms | | | | | | | |
| f Causes, effects and human responses to cliff collapse | 24-25 | What are the causes, effects and human responses to cliff collapse and coastal flooding? | | | 14 | | |

*Figure 7.2* Structure for 'Extensions' (Key Stage 3)

UK syllabuses to produce a matrix which listed every topic included in these examination syllabuses. This showed that several topics were common to most syllabuses, and many others to at least three of the syllabuses. By taking all these topics it was possible to determine the length and content of the book and its various 'chapters/units' (Figure 7.3). At GCSE A-level, I again begin by looking in depth at all existing examination syllabuses. Such initial planning is time-consuming, but, like planning a teaching syllabus or unit, the more time allocated to thinking it through carefully at the outset, the greater the time saved at a future stage. It also ensures that I do not run out of pages for the last topic – just as I invariably used to run out of time when teaching GCE O-level in my earlier years in the classroom!

Consideration is then given to the ability and age group for whom the book is intended. This helps determine the language level and the geographical content, i.e. knowledge, depth, skills and vocabulary. Most Key Stage 3 GNC books, like the 'Key Geography' series (Waugh, and Bushell, 1992a), were aimed at the middle of the ability range. Incidentally, of the teachers using this series, 25 per cent (including me) have claimed that this level was too easy for *their* pupils, 50 per cent that it was about right and 25 per cent (including Tony Bushell) felt it was too hard. These figures, which suggest an ideal normal distribution curve, are supported by QCA who claim that the Key Geography series was at the appropriate level for the entire cohort. To widen the ability range, I have since written *Extensions* (Waugh, 1999) for the most able and Tony Bushell has written *Basics* (Bushell, 1999) for the less able.

**THE WIDER WORLD** NEW GCSE SYLLABUSES GUIDE

| | | NEAB | | | ULEAC | | SEG | | MEG | | MEG WJEC | WJEC | SCOTTISH STANDARD | NISEAC |
|---|---|---|---|---|---|---|---|---|---|---|---|---|---|---|
| | | A | B | C | A | B | A | B | A | C | B | A | | |
| ✓ = Specific reference in Syllabus<br>? = Implied, or linked topic<br>✗ = Not specifically related to Syllabus | | | | | | | | | | | | | | |
| 1 POPULATION | | ✓ | ✗ | ✗ | ✓ | ✓ | ✓ | ✓ | ✓ | ✓ | ✗ | ✓ | ✓ | ✓ |
| Distribution and density | p4–7 | ✗ | ✗ | ✓ | ✓ | ✓ | ✓ | ✓ | ✓ | ✓ | ✗ | ✓ | ✓ | ✓ |
| Population growth | p8&9 | ✓ | ✓ | ✓ | ✓ | ✓ | ✓ | ✓ | ✓ | ✓ | ✗ | ✓ | ✓ | ✓ |
| Population structures | p10&11 | ✗ | ✓ | ✓ | ✓ | ? | ? | ✓ | ✓ | ✓ | ✗ | ✓ | ✓ | ✓ |
| Future trends | p12&13 | ✗ | ✓ | ✓ | ✓ | ? | ✓ | ✓ | ✓ | ✓ | ✗ | ✓ | ✓ | ✓ |
| Questions | p14–17 | ✗ | ✓ | ✓ | ✓ | ✓ | ✓ | ✓ | ✓ | ✓ | ✗ | ✓ | ✓ | ✓ |
| 2 SETTLEMENTS | | ✗ | ✗ | ✗ | ✓ | ✗ | ✓ | ✗ | ✓ | ✓ | ✗ | ✗ | ✓ | ✓ |
| Site,situation and functions | p18&19 | ✗ | ✗ | ✗ | ✓ | ✗ | ✓ | ✗ | ✓ | ✓ | ✗ | ✗ | ✓ | ✓ |
| Patterns | p20&21 | ✗ | ✗ | ✗ | ✓ | ✗ | ✗ | ✗ | ✗ | ✗ | ✗ | ✗ | ? | ✓ |
| Hierarchy | p22 | ✗ | ✗ | ✗ | ✓ | ✗ | ✓ | ✗ | ✓ | ✓ | ✗ | ✗ | ✓ | ✓ |
| Questions | p23 | ✗ | ✗ | ✗ | ✓ | ✗ | ✓ | ✗ | ✓ | ✓ | ✗ | ✗ | ✓ | ✓ |

*Figure 7.3* Matching GCSE syllabuses with *The New Wider World* (GCSE)

The layout or design is next considered. As previously stated, I have always worked in double page spreads for the 11–16 age group. Within this, a decision must be made on the proportion of space for artwork, i.e. maps, graphs, tables or photographs. This includes artwork and the size and number of photographs. For example, should there be two large (better for pupil interpretation) or three small (because teachers often want the extra resource)? Other considerations here include:

- What proportion will be text?
- Which geographical skills will be needed? Will they be newly introduced or revisited for reinforcement or revision?
- The degree to which knowledge is given to pupils or the amount that they have to discover for themselves. This, in turn, determines levels of explanation in the text.
- Will pupil activities be located at the end of each spread (probably more convenient for less able pupils and non-specialist or less experienced staff) or at the end of a chapter? This allows more space for extra text and resources on the actual spread (probably better suited to more able pupils and to specialist and more experienced staff).

Overall, I find it much easier writing to a predetermined template.

### Stage 2. The double page spread

Planning of this requires the following:

- Asking the key question or stating the aim of the spread.
- Determining the resources that are available or needed. These are placed onto an A3 sheet, virtually the size of my textbooks. I personally have always considered the quality and relevance of resources to be of even more importance than the text. This is based on the belief that whilst most

geography teachers are likely to have sufficient knowledge and understanding of a topic, they may not have the resources required to teach it.

- In my opinion, it is easier to begin with the resources and then use text to describe and explain what they show. Many other textbooks, however, appear to use their resources to explain the text.
- I also try to use my own photographs wherever possible. These are taken for a specific geographical purpose, and their availability is known rather than relying on a photographic agency. This strategy is also cheaper and therefore publishers are inclined to allow more photographs to be used within the book. It also provides greater credibility by showing I am writing with first-hand knowledge of a place.
- When writing, I always try to imagine that I am actually talking to a specific class – even to say to myself 'If I had said that, would those two sitting by the window have understood me?' In other words, I want individual pupils to feel that the book has been specially written for them. In this way I try to both motivate and engage pupils.
- Before sending the manuscript to the publisher, I have to type the text and, where appropriate, the questions and activities; draw or provide maps, diagrams and tables and give a clear description (for non-geographers) of any photograph still needed. Later, I have to check any alterations made by the editor, the final layout of each page, the quality, clarity and accuracy of the artwork and photographs, and the overall design of the book.

### Stage 3. Support material

These attempt to address the following:

- The need to extend the series by the addition of extra geographical material. For example, additional and in-depth case studies or the levels of academic ability (i.e. for the more and less able).
- Do teachers want or, perhaps even more important, have they the teaching time or money available to buy support or extension material?
- Will they use books aimed at different levels of ability with the same class at the same time?
- Can publishers afford to commission books that will be aimed at a limited range of ability or a limited section of the National Curriculum or GCSE syllabuses?

Teachers often request additional support material, especially for case studies to provide further choice, greater depth and more recent examples. However, in practice, schools rarely purchase such material in quantities that make it economically viable to the publisher. An exception to this is when a core book, or series, is adopted in sufficient numbers so as to give the publisher confidence to add to it. In other words, support material is often dependent on the success of the parent/core textbook. This can be illustrated with reference to the development of the Stanley Thorne Key Geography series.

It is encouraging that textbooks have increasing links to, and integration with, other forms of media such as CD-ROMs, the Internet and school educational programmes. Though these are intended to complement the textbook, in the short term, they are unlikely to replace it. Two examples from my own experience illustrate this.

In *Extensions* (Waugh, 1999) the final activity often has a reference to a known and proven web site. Such links, repeated on the publisher's own web site, save pupils and teachers having to search randomly for such material and then, perhaps, finding that it is either irrelevant, inaccurate or in an unusable format. Used appropriately, the Internet can help pupils to make personal investigations and conduct their own enquiries, to work alone or in groups to discover the latest data or description of an event. Such web sites can also help to prevent the textbook becoming dated, thus saving the department expenditure on purchasing revised or updated books. It should be emphasized here that I hope pupils are not encouraged to spend most of their school time looking at monitor screens, before returning home to spend their evenings watching television screens!

Reference was made earlier to the textbook–video link between the BBC's *Geography 2000* series and *The New Wider World*, (Waugh, 1998). This notion is being further developed in *Place and People – Comparative Case Studies*, which Thomas Nelson intend to publish, in connection with Channel 4, in the year 2000. Here the author, publisher and television company have worked together on the format of five television programmes based on China, together with a series of contemporary case studies. These use several recent Channel 4 schools geography programmes and the majority of the China series for broadcast in spring 2000. Material from the programmes will be used together with data I collected on a working visit to China. This book is intended to:

- describe the geographical background to China and each programme;
- use places and people seen in the programmes – this helps to motivate pupils who appreciate they are studying real places and real people;
- extend the number of case studies – production costs and timing result in these being limited in the programmes and additional case studies help reduce the danger of stereotyping when the programme can only use one example.
- add background knowledge, follow-up work and suggested activities to go with the television programmes.

Finally, the television programmes can go into greater depth in a particular topic and show, by moving images, geographical processes in action – a great advantage over the static photos of a textbook.

## Conclusion

It is my belief that a good textbook is a resource, albeit the most important resource. It should provide teachers with up-to-date, accurate, relevant and wide-ranging data and be presented in a way that should generate interest and motivate pupils.

It should suggest a route, or several if space allows, through the curriculum, whether this be the National Curriculum at Key Stage 3 or a GCSE/A-level syllabus. It should provide sufficient core material, together with case studies and questions, to allow teachers to extract what is relevant to their needs and to which they can add their own resources. By saving teachers time in syllabus and lesson preparation, it allows them time to put their energy into the exciting and valuable aspects of teaching, that is making the information come alive with personal enthusiasm and experiences and helping pupils understand and value the subject. To me, a well structured textbook imposes its own discipline. Pupils can see where they are going and know what is expected of them. This should, in turn, increase their awareness of the subject and confidence in themselves.

## Questions for further discussion

The following questions are aspects that are considered to be worth further thought and discussion for teachers' own professional practice.

1   Should the prime purpose of a textbook be to provide resources and up-to-date information, or should it allow and encourage pupils to conduct their own investigations and enquiries? Is it possible for a book to do both?
2   To what extent should a textbook be structured in its approach or is a more open-ended style more preferable?
3   Should teachers rely mainly on one textbook, or a textbook series, as the basis for their teaching syllabus? If not, what are the realistic, and economic, alternatives?
4   How can textbooks be supported by, and integrated with, other forms of the media?

## References

Bushell, T. (1999) *Basics*, Cheltenham: Stanley Thornes.
*The Little Oxford Dictionary* (1988) Oxford: OUP.
Roberts, M. (1996) 'Teaching styles and strategies', in Kent, K., Lambert, D., Naish, M. and Slater, F. *Geography in Education – Viewpoints on Teaching and Learning*, Cambridge: Cambridge University Press.
Roberts, M. (1998) 'Impact and legacy of the 1991 Geography National Curriculum at Key Stage 3', *Geography*, 83, 1: 15–27.
Waugh, D. (1983) *The British Isles*, Walton-on-Thames: Thomas Nelson.
Waugh, D. (1990) *The British Isles*, Walton-on-Thames: Thomas Nelson.
Waugh, D. (1998) *The New Wider World*, Walton-on-Thames: Thomas Nelson.
Waugh, D. (2000) *Place and People – Comparative Case Studies*, Walton-on-Thames: Thomas Nelson.
Waugh, D. and Bushell, T. (1992a) *Key Geography for Key Stage 3: Foundations, Connections, Interactions*, Cheltenham: Stanley Thornes.

Waugh, D. and Bushell, T. (1992b) *Foundations – Teachers Resource Guide*, Cheltenham: Stanley Thornes.
Waugh, D. and Bushell, T. (1999) *Extensions*, Cheltenham: Stanley Thornes.

## Television series

*Geography 2000*, Japan (1994), the USA (1996) and Brazil (1997), BBC.
*Place and People – China*, Channel 4 (2000).

# 8   Textbook pedagogy

## Issues on the use of textbooks in geography classrooms

*David Lambert*

This chapter is a slightly modified version of a paper which first appeared in
A. Kent (ed.), *Research Forum 1: Issues for Research in Geographical Education*
(London: University of London Institute of Education and the International
Geographical Union, 1998).

## Introduction

The main purpose of this chapter is to make the case for research which employs
a strategy to observe directly the use of textbooks[1] in geography classrooms. As
we shall see, the considerable research interest over many years into the contents
of geography textbooks has not been matched, at least in England (see Johnsen,
1993), by research and development of their classroom use, by which I mean the
pedagogy of geography textbooks including the notion of teachers *mediating* text.
Textbook use remains under-researched, a result according to Bill Marsden (1998),
of a British anti-textbook ideology and perhaps resulting in a 'strongly entrenched
antipathy' (Marsden, 1998: 13) towards textbooks among British geography
educators.

In 1985, John Lidstone identified a major discontinuity between the rhetoric
and reality regarding textbook use (Lidstone, 1985, 1992): he found that textbooks
were widely used and highly valued by geography teachers, despite an apparent
cultural orthodoxy among educationists that they were best avoided in the interests
of creative and imaginative teaching. I contend that such a mismatch has been
a persistent feature of secondary school geography in England and exists even
more prominently today since the advent of the Geography National Curriculum
in 1991. It is a matter which requires serious attention, for at best it leads to
vague feelings of professional guilt on the part of teachers who use textbooks –
much as drivers who use their cars to pick up the Sunday papers: 'I know I shouldn't,
but . . . '. At worst, it has reinforced a situation in which teachers and trainers
appear to exist in separate worlds, with the research community shut off from
the 'real world' of the practitioner. In the meantime, a woefully under-theorized
aspect of pedagogy (teaching with textbooks) continues to be propagated in
geography classrooms, unchallenged by any wider considerations or alternative
perspectives.

To emphasize my main point, there is virtually no research knowledge based upon direct classroom use of textbooks in UK secondary schools, despite their self-evident pre-eminent position in teaching. Even Lidstone's research did not observe directly the interaction of pupil, teacher and text. This chapter suggests that there is now a pressing need for such research.

Following quasi-autobiographical reflections on geography teaching, which provide a certain context giving rise to a number of questions and a possible research agenda, this chapter describes two small-scale research studies on textbooks undertaken in London. The second of these studies relied heavily on student teachers to make direct classroom observations, and it is in this way that the 'black box' of classroom interaction was opened up enough to provide the basis for the essentially descriptive account which follows.

The discussion finishes with some more speculative remarks about the potential of such research at all levels, for there are global trends at work which impel the whole education community to adopt a constructively critical stance towards habitual practices. For example, resources for education are being squeezed the world over, and as systems demand more and more measures of 'effectiveness', it would certainly help if educationists could develop internationally a language which could establish both quantitative and qualitative criteria to guide spending of scarce resources on books. In countries such as Britain there is growing concern and interest in raising levels of 'literacy' through the curriculum: What does this mean for classroom practice and the use of textbooks at school and at home? The findings of such research might also help authors and publishers produce better books.

## Textbooks: A changing personal perspective

As a geography teacher brought up on a rich diet of active learning (see Slater, 1982), changing geography (see Walford, 1973, 1981), and innovative curriculum thinking during the 1970s and 1980s (see Graves, 1996 for a summary), I became, in the early 1980s, the kind of secondary school subject leader who sought to generate resource diversity in his department. In practical terms such an attitude resulted in having to make a straight choice between purchasing the same textbook – or coursebook – for each pupil or buying class sets, half sets or even individual copies of books, and a range of other materials including video hardware and software, specialized 'packs', slide sets and so on. The geography teaching team worked hard producing its own materials. Often these were 'worksheets', but also maps, diagrams, information sheets, summaries and tests were produced. Such materials are precisely the kinds of printed material which a textbook publisher can deliver to a high standard – and certainly to standards exceeding those of the spirit duplicator and black and white photocopier (even when wordprocessed, which often, in those days, they were not). The irony of this position did not figure seriously in the department's management: any advantages in buying commercially produced materials were offset by a radically reduced departmental reprographics budget and subsequent perceived constraint on its creative potential. It is, I think, worth pondering further this state of affairs.

I did not really examine the purpose and role of the textbook in my teaching, nor of my departmental colleagues. Textbooks were a kind of 'given' school artefact. They were useful to 'fall back on'. They were useful for supply teachers. There was a vague assumption that textbooks could be used 'as and when' appropriate, but the one certainty was that they were not to be followed slavishly from cover to cover throughout the year. An unspoken professional anxiety lurked: at what point would regular textbook use be interpreted as 'slavery'?

In fact, any subjugation to the text had become impossible, for there were not enough copies to go around – certainly not to be taken home by the students – and, probably more times than I care to remember, diagrams, exercises and other extracts from textbooks were copied, either by or for the students, in order to facilitate homework. As well as being slightly absurd (and probably infringing the copyright law) such practice was, with the benefit of hindsight, damaging. If a book is conceived and written as a whole it surely does not serve the student well to dismember it and distribute it in tantalizing glimpses: sure, the student has the graph to examine and the questions to answer, but what is its context? What came before the graph and what follows it? What did the author have to say about it? Did we unwittingly encourage students to see textbooks as just a collection of information leaflets and worksheets, and ignore their greater pedagogic potential?

It could and perhaps should be argued (in self-defence) that the real villain here was the funding situation. In England virtually all learning materials, including stationery and textbooks, are supplied by the school. So long as the system, and parents, remain attached to such expectations, and education budgets remain tight, then heads of department in most state schools will have to continue to make choices of the kind I have described. Of course, it is desirable to have textbooks for all students *and* a healthy reprographics budget – and computer hardware and software, video and other audio-visual aids, fieldwork equipment and so on. It is worth noting in passing that recent figures from the Educational Publishers Council (1997) reveal that only 10 per cent of English secondary schools spend above £50 per student per year on books, against the EPC figure for a recommended or 'adequate' annual spend of £56. The proportion of the spend devoted to geography is often very small, some surveys showing departments in State schools functioning on £2.00–£3.00 per pupil per year (Thomas and Grimwade, 1996).

Another issue that remains clear in the memory was the issue of textbook selection. Unusually by international standards I had, as a head of department, virtually unfettered power to choose which books to purchase from an extraordinarily long list of possibles. Not that such a 'list' was ever supplied: one got to know what was available in a free market via publishers' catalogues, advertisements and the Geographical Association annual conference exhibition. One's selection, and therefore spending decisions, were influenced by notions such as value for money, design and appearance and the personal preferences (or prejudices) held at the time regarding the contents of geography. Teachers claimed to use 'topicality' and 'relevance' as criteria (though if you know about textbook production, you also know that from its publication date the material in a book is already at least eighteen months or two years out of date). Some also claimed to apply crude 'readability' analysis to the text as an aid to selection, though personally I was always dubious about the efficacy of such approaches – or at least how to interpret the scores. One criterion many geography teachers did attempt to apply, and one taken very seriously by many publishers and authors by the mid-1980s, concerned fairness in the way people and places were represented in the text and via diagrams and pictures: David Hicks's (1981) work was influential in this respect, though according to Winter (1997) and others, how such awareness is implemented still raises many questions even for the best selling Key Stage 3 geography textbooks of the late 1990s. For the purposes of this discussion, however, my point is that whatever criteria were used by teachers in the selection of textbooks for their students, pedagogic consideration was not one, at least not in a critical sense.

Such an assertion possibly requires further support or qualification. Still with my autobiographical reflections (but ones which I am confident are shared by many of the same generation of geography teachers), one of the principal interests of teachers in the mid-1970s was *learning*. Indeed, as a way of demonstrating one's commitment and sensitivity to the 'needs' of students, it was not uncommon to hear the revealing, self-conscious (somewhat pompous) claim: 'I do not teach geography – I teach children.' Active learning, doing, investigation, simulation, decision-making, role-play (etc.) were the watchwords representing the pedagogic practice to which to aspire. Not bad by any means, but is it possible, at least for the apochryphal teacher quoted above, that the content objectives were sometimes mislaid: The simulation is fun, but what is it for? This was a time when those advocating generic or transferable 'skills', as opposed to what they regarded as obscurantist, traditional subjects, were growing in influence on the curriculum. And it is just possible that some teachers inspired and enthused by 'geography as a *medium* of education' (Naish, 1986) and 'learning *through* geography' (Slater, 1982) (my emphases in both cases), were captivated by the medium and not the message (though personally I would deny this!). That is, the delicate balance that all teachers need to strike between process and product became skewed by the widely held perception that geography was not a sufficient 'end' in itself; as the difficult and controversial work of the National Curriculum Geography Working Group (GWG) in 1989–90 revealed, there was no commonly held understanding, even among the geography educationists on the GWG, of what the 'product' of geography was – though this is another story which is beyond the scope of this chapter (but see Butt, 1996; Lambert, 1994; Rawling, 1992; Walford, 1992, 1996).

There were two, apparently paradoxical, outcomes of adopting a form of pupil centredness such as that indicated in the previous paragraph insofar as textbooks were concerned. First, it reinforced the circumstances noted earlier in which the use of textbooks was deemed by some to be in some ways anti-educational. But second, it drove textbook authors and publishers to produce books which would be perceived by the market (heads of geography) and reviewers (teachers and educationists) to be educationally sound in terms of the variety of data and the arrangement of 'activities' on the page designed to 'involve' students. Thus, while new series in the early 1970s, such as the *Oxford Geography Project* (Rolfe *et al.*, 1975), were concerned at least in part to write innovative geography, by the 1980s it seems that process concerns dominated, as in, for example, the best-selling *Geography Today* series from Collins Education (Higginbottam, 1987). The general trend I am alluding to here has been discussed fully by Walford (1997) under the guise of tracing the 'case of the disappearing text'. It was as if a new formula were being hatched, and I remember a local in-service meeting for heads of geography at which books such as those in the latter series were authoritatively described as 'teacher proof': I still do not know whether this remark was made as a sign of respect and commendation for the books, but I do know that it was derogatory to teachers. But I also think the remark was accurate in the sense that teachers had little flexibility with such books: for instance, homeworks beginning with instructional terms such as 'read . . . ', or 'find out . . . ' were surprisingly difficult to set. Though clearly designed to be used, these books did not appear to be designed to be read! – at least not in the traditional sense of the word. Interestingly, Norman Graves concludes, in his editorial on an international collection of articles concerning textbooks and textbook research (Graves, 1997), that 'in attempting to make the books attractive to students and teachers – the double page spread for example – publishers are effectively limiting their explanatory and therefore intellectual potential' (p. 62).

In this section I have attempted through personal reflection to identify the somewhat uncertain, or troubled, status of textbooks in geography education – at least for lower secondary English school students. In so doing I hope to have been persuasive about the existence of a possible research agenda. This would include questions such as:

- How do students and teachers perceive the role and purpose of textbooks?
- In what ways does textbook provision – in both qualitative and quantitative terms – impact on teaching and learning?
- What are the characteristics of the teacher–text–student interface – that is, the nature of classroom dynamics in relation to the textbooks?

For the sake of convenience I shall refer to this agenda collectively under the heading *textbook pedagogy*. Perhaps significantly the term resonates with the call made by the chief executive of the Teacher Training Agency (TTA) of England (Millett, 1998), for teachers and teacher educators to think more about teaching and appropriate instructional techniques (and less about 'learning') and thus redress the balance which finds the English unable comfortably to 'talk pedagogy'.

The following section briefly reports the results of some small-scale research which may strengthen my claim that there is a need to 'open the classroom door' on a larger scale in order to learn more about how textbooks are used by teachers and pupils through direct observation.

# Geography textbooks in London schools

Full details of the two small-scale studies referred to here are reported elsewhere (Lambert, 1997, 1999). Suffice it to say that the schools providing the data were in effect an opportunity sample drawn from the initial teacher training partnership between the Institute of Education and around 70 London secondary schools. Whilst the earlier of the two studies was based almost entirely on a questionnaire, the second combined interview and lesson observation techniques undertaken by student geography teachers. The second study also had an 'experimental' aspect to its design in that a self-selected (i.e. volunteer) sub-sample of seven departments agreed to cooperate in a more longitudinal dimension (over the period of an academic year): these departments were able to augment, free of charge,[2] their textbook stocks in order to obviate any observed contraints on how textbooks were used which could be explained by perceived or real shortages. In other words, in exchange for this 'gift', the seven departments agreed to open their classroom doors to observation under what they perceived to be ideal conditions of textbook provision.

## *Study 1: Textbook choice*

This, the earlier study, identified (amongst other things) what was reported to be the 'Waugh Effect' in the London schools, a phenomenon by which around two-thirds of the sample departments used the series *Key Geography* (Waugh and Bushell, 1991) as a course book for years 7–9. The figure exceeded this for David Waugh's GCSE books (years 10–11). The 'effect' that this extraordinary market dominance describes (in which Waugh's total sales are counted in millions of units), is the quite familiar condition in which a market 'winner' can capture, and then continue to dominate for a protracted period, the individual spending decisions of free market consumers.[3] In the light of the personal reflections recounted in the previous section, however, it may be interesting to examine any links between that history and the establishment of the Waugh hegemony. To what extent does my story need bringing up to date – for the Waugh textbooks mentioned above post-date my period as a school teacher?

The research suggests that teachers were, following the introduction of a complex and hopelessly over-specified National Curriculum in 1991, somewhat intimidated. After all, the curriculum was introduced amidst a fanfare of what were perceived to be hostile noises towards teachers from the government and the press. The curriculum authors themselves, perhaps also under pressure from the centre, seemed to have been obsessed with the notion of geography as a 'content rich' subject and with the urge to specify what the content had to be, the implication being that teachers had until that moment been teaching the wrong material. The authors of *Key Geography* successfully met a widespread felt need. Not only was the series available in time for the implementation of the National Curriculum (September 1991), but it convincingly 'covered' its contents; further-more, it did so in highly legible and manageable bite-sized lesson chunks, using a rigid double-page spread formula. There is evidence that teachers spent a great deal of money buying such reassurance as these books seemed to provide. There is also evidence that *Key Geography* has emerged as the closest thing for decades to a national 'shared text' in geography. But, more than this, it has become the most influential *curriculum document*, for each double page was cleverly designed to be a self-contained geography lesson. Why design a scheme of work when you can buy one 'oven-ready', so to speak? The actual words of the National Curriculum Order remained, after the initial flurry of interest following its publication, largely unread in closed ring binders.

Thus, in the space of just a few years, school geography, which had been evolving in certain ways (see, for example, Rawling, 1993 for an analysis), was transformed into a subject deeply influenced by a single textbook series. I concluded, and continue to argue in this paper, that this, in itself, was not necessarily a bad thing. However, the particular form and design of the books in question *may be* a significant constraint on the development of creative, open and various classroom strategies for teaching and learning: The pages have a set formula for presenting material and heavily guide how this should be 'read'. But just as important is the role that teachers play in relation to the textbook. In the absence of critical reflection of the kind that arguably should take place during initial and subsequent training, teachers may not be fully aware of ways of using books other than those they have themselves experienced or observed – often adopting highly structured and closed approaches which assign to the book the role of manual and source of answers and ignoring (or at least undervaluing) other possibilities such as a stimulus, or a *text* to be interrogated, criticized or enjoyed.

### Study 2: Textbook use

The Waugh Effect represents a cultural shift in geography education, tantamount, almost, to the adoption of a shared National Curriculum textbook. This I argue has happened for pragmatic and organizational, not educational, reasons. Whether the invisible hand of the market has delivered a *high quality* national shared text is a moot point, however. Without actually naming the text, OFSTED went on record as judging Key Stage 3 to be over-dependent upon a 'limited and limiting' (OFSTED, 1995: 14) single textbook series. Anecdotal evidence suggests that some teachers bought into the series, expressing professional discomfort.[4] The series is criticized by practitioners: some find the textbooks have too high a reading level, and others that the books do not 'stretch' the faster and more accomplished learner. Whether this suggests anything more than the obvious – that a textbook cannot teach – or something more complex and hidden is unclear. For example, might criticisms such as these reveal cause for concern about how the design and format of the books might seriously limit how the books can be operated by students and teachers? Or were the textbooks not being used effectively as a result of other constraints such as resource limitations or indeed a shortfall in teaching skill?

The second investigation sheds some light on such matters. There is not the space here to provide anything other than a brief summary of the report (Lambert,

1999). The purpose was to gain some systematic observation of textbooks being used within the totality of the classroom context, and the findings, summarized most inadequately in the list below, are appealing enough, I believe, to indicate the potential benefit of a broader, deeper and indeed, longer study. Such a study would yield the following practitioner benefits:

- to provide authoritative information on desirable textbook resourcing levels and deployment;
- to create models of classroom practice relating to qualitative aspects of textbooks and their use;
- to identify pre-service and in-service training needs of teachers; and
- to suggest guidelines to textbook authors of the next generation of student texts and teachers' guides.

Among the findings of the small-scale London 'pilot' study were:

- that the inertial forces with regard to textbook choice are (understandably) strong. Even when departments in the seven experimental schools chose simply to add to stock, it took time (possibly more time than the study had at its disposal) to adjust practice to take advantage of a textbook-rich teaching environment;
- that a lack of 'home-working' with textbooks is commonplace. Some departments claimed 'school policy' prevented textbooks from going home (presumably for fear of damage or loss);
- that even when textbooks are issued one per student (which brought clear classroom management gains as students could focus better), very little independent reading was observed. Teachers heavily mediate the text, telling students which parts to read, reading out loud around the class and interpreting photographs and diagrams *for* the students. There was from this (admittedly very small) sample of lessons no evidence of wider reading or reading for enjoyment from geography textbooks;
- that teachers are not clear about the role of textbooks in their teaching. It seems that with their current design standards and formats, they cannot easily be used flexibly and it could be that this fuels a tendency recorded from this study of teachers expressing suspicion about the publishers' intentions or motives. There was strong resistance to the idea that any book might be followed as a course-book, as if in some kind of display of independence to be expected from a creative professional.

In general, the experimental study showed that teachers in the seven departments greatly valued their access to enhanced textbook provision. This was primarily for reasons of control (easier classroom management), for convenience and for ensuring curriculum coverage. In two of the schools, both with self-professed difficulties in establishing homework routines with students, class sets of books were ordered specifically for students to keep at home; students had a school and a home copy of the textbook. However, the statements of justification for this imaginative idea were opaque – 'to aid progression' was one such – revealing an absence of precision in articulating the pedagogic benefits of free and unhindered access to the textbook. What was even less forthcoming was a sense that books could inspire or motivate (and how they may contribute to these aspects of teaching). What was not considered at all was the potential of books to encourage independent learners and critical thinkers who can operate confidently with higher-order literacy skills such as scanning, skimming, synthesizing or evaluating.

## Conclusion

The final points in the previous section reveal perhaps most strongly the need to 'rediscover textbooks' in English secondary school geography. There is a need for research at the level of classroom interaction between student, teacher and text, because there still seems to exist a deep-seated presumed ineffectiveness of textbooks, especially among educationists, which is at variance with their widespread, but arguably not necessarily effective, use. We need to develop a confident and precise classroom language of textbook pedagogy. But first, what is the potential of textbooks in geography? As Soaniak, Lauren and Perlman have written:

> work with textbooks in the different subject matters suggest dramatically different potential for *empowering* students in their studies of the disciplines, for shaping classroom activity in such a way as to *engage* students intellectually and emotionally, and for *helping* students see connections between their school tasks and their life experiences.
>
> (Soaniak *et al.*, 1990: 436)

For geography their work strongly suggests that the textbook is undervalued as a means to introduce students to other worlds and to that which cannot be studied directly (p. 440).

We do not yet have sufficient research in England into the ways in which working with textbooks in geography may enable teachers to empower, engage or help students to learn. There is perhaps a need to share perspectives and experience on these matters internationally, for there are surely interesting comparative stories to tell. Other systems may also have a free market, but with different outcomes or response to a National Curriculum. Many systems have textbook approval procedures, or committees to oversee or advise on quality, a form of market intervention which has benefits and costs and which could usefully inform the Qualifications and Curriculum Authority (QCA) in England, which has recently shown interest in exploring some kind of involvement in curriculum resources and their production (see SCAA, 1997). And of course some countries have state-appointed textbook writers! For the practitioner, there are more immediate questions that may be considered, particularly during the times of the academic year when departmental resources are reviewed and spending decisions are required:

- What role does the department expect the textbook to fulfil? How flexibly can the textbooks on the market be used?
- How do teachers in the department use textbooks in their teaching? Are pupils encouraged to use books independently? Are the books designed to be used in this way? Are the books heavily mediated by the teacher?
- Who writes school geography textbooks? What kind of geography is written? What do the authors expect from readers?
- What are students' perceptions of textbooks? What do they expect from books? How are they valued? In what ways are they considered useful?
- How does the department ensure that students encounter the information age successfully and confidently through their geography? In what ways do books and computers interact with learners in different ways?

These questions begin to show the scope of an enormous possible research agenda – and encourage a particular focus for an increasingly widespread professional activity, namely, the peer review of teaching. But first things first. I hope the report and discussion in this chapter have made the case for 'opening the classroom door' and, through direct observation of the ways in which teachers, students and text interact, for geography educators and teachers to pursue a research programme in textbook pedagogy. This may help us move away from the 'teacher proof' – but very limiting – double page spread; but there is to date a surprising and perhaps damaging paucity of such research in England.

## Notes

1  I acknowledge that the term *textbook* can be problematic. To keep things simple I have adopted a pragmatic view, after consultation with the Publishers' Association. A textbook is any published book that is used in school in multiples, as a course-book, class set, study guide and so on. The *Times Educational Supplement* attempts to circumvent the issue in its annual national *schoolbooks* award, by specifying 'schoolbook' as a book which '*requires* the mediation of a teacher and which is published for the school market' (my emphasis).
2  This facility was made available by the generous agreement of member publishers of the Educational Publishers Council.
3  This is accomplished by judicious use of 'network externalities': big discounts, various add-on benefits, huge advertising and so on.
4  For example, the following quotation, taken from a formal written assignment of a student teacher in June 1998, serves to illustrate the continuing professional doubt about textbooks. This talented new entrant to the geography teaching community appeared to be expressing received wisdom, the professional equivalent of the 'well-known fact': 'The department's teaching is based on the Waugh series . . . teaching with the textbook leads to predictable lessons with formulaic, limiting tasks which do not stretch the pupils.'

## References

Butt, G. (1996) 'An investigation into the dynamics of the National Curriculum working group (1989–1990)', unpublished Ph.D. thesis, University of Birmingham.

Graves, N. (1996) 'Curriculum development in geography: an ongoing process', in Kent, A., Lambert, D., Naish, M., and Slater, F. (eds) *Geography in Education: Viewpoints on Teaching and Learning*, Cambridge: Cambridge University Press.

Graves, N. (1997) 'Forum: textbooks and textbook research in geography education: some international views', *International Research in Geographical and Environmental Education*, 6, 1: 60–105.

Hicks, D. (1981) *Bias in Geography Textbooks: Images of the Third World and Multi-ethnic Britain*, Centre for Multicultural Education, Working Paper No 1, London: ULIE.

Higginbottam, T. (ed.) (1987) *Geography Today* (Books 1–3), London: Collins Educational.

Johnsen, E. (1993) *Textbooks in the Kaleidoscope: A Critical Survey of Literature and Research on Educational Texts*, Oslo: Scandinavian University Press.

Lambert, D. (1994) 'The National Curriculum: what shall we do with it?', *Geography*, 79, 1: 65–76.

Lambert, D. (1997) 'The choice of textbooks for use in secondary school geography departments: some answers and some further questions', *Paradigm*, 21 (April): 21–31.

Lambert, D. (1999) 'Exploring the use of textbooks in the KS3 geography classroom: a small scale study', *Curriculum Journal*, 10, 1: 85–105.

Lidstone, J. (1985) 'A study of the use of geography textbooks by selected teachers in English secondary schools', unpublished Ph.D. thesis, University of London Institute of Education.

Lidstone, J. (1992) 'In defence of textbooks', in Naish, M. (ed.) *Geography and Education: National and International Perspectives*, London: University of London.

Marsden, B. (1998) 'Wrting a book about textbooks: some preliminary considerations', in Kent, A. (ed.) *Research Forum 1 Textbooks: Issues for Research in Geographical Education*, London: ULIE/International Geographical Union Commission on Geographical Education.

Millett, A. (1998) 'Let's get pedagogical', *Times Educational Supplement*, 12 June 1998, p. 28.

Naish, M. (1986) 'Geography in British schools: a medium of education', in *Festschrift zum 60. Geburtstag von Ernst Troger*, Vienna: Verlag Ferdinand Hirt.

OFSTED (1995) *Geography: A Review of Inspection Findings 1993/4*, London: HMSO.

Rawling, E. (1992) 'The making of a National Geography Curriculum', *Geography*, 77, 4: 292–309.

Rawling, E. (1993) 'School geography: towards 2000', *Geography*, 78, 2: 110–16.

Rolfe, J., Dearden, R., Kent, A., Rowe, C. and Grenyer, N. (1975) *Oxford Geography Project* (Books 1–3), Oxford: Oxford University Press.

SCAA (1997) *Analysis of Educational Resources: KS3 Geography Textbooks*, London: School Curriculum and Assessment Authority.

Slater, F. (1982) *Learning Through Geography*, London: Heinemann Education.

Soaniak, A., Lauren, A. and Perlman, C. (1990) 'Secondary education by the book', *Journal of Curriculum Studies*, 22, 5: 427–42.

Thomas, G. and Grimwade, K. (1996) 'Geography in the secondary school: a survey', *Teaching Geography*, 21, 1: 37–9.

Walford, R. (ed.) (1973) *New Directions in Geography Teaching*, Harlow: Longman.

Walford, R. (ed.) (1981) *Signposts for Geography Teaching*, Harlow: Longman.

Walford, R. (1992) 'Creating a National Curriculum: a view from the inside', in Hill, D. (ed.) *International Perspectives on Geographic Education*, Boulder: Center for Geographical Education, University of Colorado.

Walford, R. (1996) 'Geography 5–19: retrospect and prospect', in Rawling, E. and Daugherty, R., *Geography into the Twenty-first Century*, Christchurch: John Wiley.

Walford, R. (1997) 'The case of the disappearing text', *Paradigm*, 22: 1–11.

Waugh, D. and Bushell, T. (1991) *Key Geography* (Books 1–3), London: Stanley Thornes.

Winter, C. (1997) 'Reconstructing curricular and pedagogical knowledge about places and people in the geography classroom', in *Reporting Research in Geographical Education*, Monograph No. 5, pp. 28–48, London: University of London Institute of Education.

# 9  The resourceful geography teacher

*Chris Fisher*

## Introduction

In this chapter I seek to raise issues within the teaching of geography that relate to developments occurring both within the subject and beyond. It is a personal expression of concerns about geography teaching that, it is felt, should be considered by classroom practitioners of the subject at all levels of experience and expertise. The rationale is based on personal reflection and teaching experiences, work with experienced and newly qualified teachers and observed general trends. The ideas are expressed through a series of issues designed to provoke and to stimulate response.

## How resourceful are geography teachers in managing curriculum development?

Few involved in teaching would argue that a knowledge and understanding of the pupils being taught are crucial for effective teaching and learning. However, within the current climate of legislative prescription, to what extent is it possible for teachers of geography to produce a curriculum that is genuinely tailored to the needs of their own pupils? There is a growing need to motivate and interest pupils in our subject; we need to work harder to promote their interest and motivation. It is still the individual teacher in the classroom who best knows his or her own pupils, their interests, preferred styles of learning and what enthuses them. Yet the introduction of a National Curriculum has seen a stifling of opportunities to 'customize' courses to suit the particular needs of pupils. Even before the introduction of the National Curriculum, Huckle (1991) appealed to geography teachers to retain diversity: 'Radical teachers will do their best with it in the interests of their pupils, but they should continue to refine and work for alternatives' (Huckle, 1991: 117).

Despite this plea, there has been, sadly, a diffusion of sterile teaching of our subject, obsessed by the content, by both specialists and non-specialists alike. We have an extraordinary subject to teach, but how many of our lessons deserve this adjective? In too many schools the stimulating and innovative geography lesson has become a thing of the past, and our pupils and our subject have suffered as a result. Do our pupils really deserve this?

But was there ever a 'Golden Age' of geography teaching? Certainly, there was a time prior to the introduction of the 1991 National Curriculum, and even before the introduction of the General Certificate of Education (GCSE) in 1988, when the educational processes operating in schools allowed geography teachers considerable opportunities in curriculum development that are not available today. Fanciful reminiscences of 'experienced' geography teachers recall times when curricular autonomy was commonplace. To be a teacher of geography, at least in some schools, was to be a resourceful innovator of a subject that could in part be developed by the actions of those who actually worked with the pupils and who could devise courses appropriate to their specific needs.

Even prior to the introduction of GCSE, curricular developments had invited the involvement of classroom teachers and, by implication, contributed to their professional development. This was particularly true of those involved with 'mode two' and 'mode three' courses where schools could tailor public examination courses, at both Ordinary Level (O-level) and the Certificate of Secondary Education (CSE), for their own pupils' requirements. As a result, and under strict moderation systems, schools could develop whole courses and assessment structures either independently or through local consortia. However, the arrival of the new 'off the peg' GCSE examination system saw the swift demise of many such 'made to measure' courses. Those who had devised their own 'mode 3' GCSE courses were allowed to run them for only one year before being forced to adopt the national model. Disappointment with the changes was often tempered by optimism about the potential of the new single examination system with its emphasis on rewarding 'positive achievement', recognition of the value of coursework and the adoption of a summative assessment for all. There was a welcome shift away from the dominance of sterile facts and a growing recognition of the importance of understanding, skills, values and attitudes. Additionally, opportunities to develop coursework elements created exciting and new opportunities for those already well versed in designing their own curricula.

The era of curriculum innovation in geography was relatively short-lived. Norman Graves, in his examination of curriculum development in geography, begins his chapter: 'I am not sure that in the 1950s we really understood what curriculum development was about' (Graves, 1996: 72). He goes on to describe the emergence of the geographer's awareness of curriculum development in the 1960s and 1970s via 'a new thinking', presenting a model for curriculum planning in geography that was linked to the interactive version of Kerr (Graves, 1996: 74). At this time, curricular development in the natural sciences was based on research and this is seen in Graves's 'Paradigms of geography'. Experimentation resulted across many areas of the curriculum, and in 1964 the establishment of the Schools Council by the Department of Education and Science (DES) provided a platform for centralized development and collaboration involving Local Education Authorities (LEAs) and the teacher unions. In geography, teacher researchers developed, planned, experimented, modified and then initiated new projects. Most centred on a 'new' enquiry-based approach already seen in other disciplines, such as maths and science. These included 'Geography 14–18',

'Geography and the Young School Leaver (GYSL)' and 'Geography 16–19' (Boardman, 1985). These syllabuses were adopted by a good proportion of schools, although there was no compulsion for them to change from their more traditional courses. The overall effects of the Schools Geography Projects were even more widespread. At this time, despite many practical difficulties, curricular innovation could actually *involve* classroom teachers at all stages of the process and the effects were noted in a wide range of syllabuses offered to schools and in the teachers' own professional development, a point emphasized by Fisher when he states:

> These projects were significant in their impact on school geography, not only because they addressed the questions of geography's place and contribution to the curriculum, but also, importantly, because of their empowerment of teachers as curriculum developers.
>
> (Fisher, 1998: 12)

Looking back to this evolutionary period, Machon and Ranger also comment on these 'projects piloted by teachers in schools able to work with an autonomy that now seems unthinkable' (Machon and Ranger, 1996: 42).

Those committed to the rigorous demands of such activities amassed experiences and skills capable of enhancing their classroom teaching and professional development. The effects of teachers' involvement with coursework evaluation, examination writing, moderation and subject panels could broaden and enrich their capabilities to plan, teach and assess their own pupils. The value of such involvement extended from the ability to moderate accurately Advanced Level and GCSE work through to the concise wording of questions written on the classroom blackboard. For a few, such involvement enhanced their professional credibility to such an extent that enlightened governors and headteachers gave appropriate recognition of their refined professional abilities through promotion.

Such opportunities became more limited as the implications of the Education Reform Act of 1988 became apparent. Using an analogy from the motor vehicle industry, the September 2000 version of the Geography National Curriculum is the third 'model' manufactured by government in less than ten years. The first version was taught from 1991 and, although spawned from the 1988 Act, it had been planned in principle since the early 1980s. However, the long time spent 'on the drawing board', and the many planning changes it was subjected to, resulted in an extremely complex and fragmented piece of legislation, with each individual subject being written by subject groups in isolation from others. When it first arrived 'in the showroom' geography teachers immediately perceived the National Curriculum to be a 'poor runner' – unbalanced and cumbersome with in-built complexities and many potential flaws; these points are summarized by Walford (1997: 20–1). In operation, performance of the National Curriculum was erratic, often colliding with vehicles carrying other subjects and those 'exclusive features', the cross-curricular links, never operated satisfactorily. Its critics were numerous and this model would never have won an award for its design. Less than two years after departments had struggled to get this first model running, the manufacturers called in a master engineer to tinker with the workings and produce a successor. However, Ron Dearing's Mark II model bore few similarities to the original. This greatly streamlined version (Dearing 1994) was more economical on effort and far easier to service – although initial attempts to evaluate the performance of this 'political fix' (Lambert, 1997: 259) created problems for many. The reduction in prescription did offer teachers the opportunity to develop schemes of work more suited to their own pupils and resources. However, there was now often less time available in the week to teach the subject and, perhaps more significantly, teachers' attentions had been turned towards fitting the prescribed content to the lesson. Initially, at least, there was concern about external assessment of pupils' progression through each key stage, though for geography (as with other foundation subjects) this never materialized.

Almost inevitably, the instinct among teachers to adapt the curriculum and the way it was taught to best suit pupils' needs was quickly lost. Roberts (1997) examined the impact of the National Curriculum on three previously innovative departments of geography, and found that each had moved away from their previous 'enquiry-based' approaches towards teacher-led, didactic styles of teaching simply to cover the new requirements. Additionally, there was a growing trend for non-specialist teachers to be used to 'fill up' geography timetables. This often meant opportunities to adapt the new curriculum to the specific needs of schools and their pupils were largely ignored. There were fewer 'teams' of real geography specialists in schools than in the 1980s, and in smaller institutions often the only remaining experienced specialist was the head of department. The early 1990s was also a period with a growing burden of generic administrational duties and record keeping which took much of the teachers' focus away from their geography lessons. Therefore, unless actively pursued by tireless enthusiasts of curricular innovation, there was a growing tendency to follow the curriculum documents 'to the letter' simply because it was the easiest thing to do. With growing numbers of non-specialists used to teach geography, there was inevitably a lack of relevant experience, specialist training and awareness of what had been possible in previous years, and newly trained teachers had little awareness of what else was possible.

Strangely, an additional pressure came in the form of the new generation of 'whole Key Stage' textbooks; these tempted geographers away from devising their own, customized schemes of work and teachers instead tended to opt for schemes implicit within their adopted text. Growing administrational duties and generic tasks in schools also ate into teachers' finite reserves of the time and energy necessary to develop courses that really responded to pupils' needs. Returning to the 'vehicle analogy', September 2000 sees the introduction of the Mark III Geography National Curriculum. The adjustments have resulted in only a slightly modified model with greater opportunity for flexibility and less prescription. Some superficial bodywork changes have been made to reflect a more modern appearance, but the revision that many feel (if they were really honest) is most needed, that is a complete rebuild, if not a swift return to a new drawing board, has just not occurred. Therefore, geography teachers have to adapt their teaching to this latest 'model' and take the opportunities suggested by Graves's (1997) notion of consolidation:

> Consolidation does not mean stagnation, though, but being able to organise the smooth running of their teaching while at the same time having the professional freedom to undertake some experimentation – within the limits set by the National Curriculum – with content, teaching, strategies and assessment, in order to meet the particular needs of their pupils. More than ever, teachers need to bear in mind that the curriculum is a means to an end and not an end in itself.
>
> (Graves 1997:30)

There will inevitably be some speculation on the fortunes of the 'first National Curriculum generation'. The first National Curriculum cohort, i.e. pupils who began their state education in Year 1 when National Curriculum teaching began, commence the ninth year of their studies in September 2000. For the final three compulsory years of their state education, they will be studying a National Curriculum in geography that has been altered three times. Will their final achievements be adjudged an indication of National Curriculum success? Or will they be interpreted as accomplishments achieved in the face of constant curricular change and counter-change? The works of Pollard (1997), supported by David Leat (1999) suggest that pupils in the primary phase have already 'become increasingly instrumental in their learning' (Pollard, 1997).

Rawling, writing in both 1996 and in the introduction to this book, refers to a period of changing curriculum control, where geography's place has moved between control, prescription and autonomy (Rawling, 1996: 267). Rawling has a positive perception of an opportunity, with the 2000 revision, for geography teachers to once more become curriculum innovators. However, will teachers of geography be able to take up such a challenge? Or has the previous demise of opportunities for many geographers to be curricular innovators detracted from their ability to provide a teaching programme that best suits the needs of their pupils? Of course not – but whether colleagues now feel they have the autonomy, proficiency and confidence required for such adaptation is uncertain. It certainly could be inferred that the processes implicit in the implementation of the National Curriculum may have resulted in an overt 'de-skilling' of geography teachers in this respect. It is imperative that today's teachers of geography, at all levels of educational provision, need to be alive to the possibilities of developing the curriculum from the published programmes. This requires an awareness of the conceptual framework of geography as well as subject knowledge, and may not be helped by the high proportion of non-specialists now teaching the subject at Key Stage 3.

There is a need to look beyond the two-dimensional documentation into the three-dimensional subject that is geography. An outstanding headteacher, when advising his staff on how to implement the National Curriculum, encouraged them with the thought: 'There's no such thing as the National Curriculum police!' (James Quinn). This has always been useful advice, and it would be prudent for many to adopt this stance rather than feeling bound to adhere to every comma and full stop of the published criteria. Over the past two decades there have been major changes in who controls curricular development and this has certainly resulted in a loss of autonomy for teachers. I would further argue that this has reduced the opportunities for professional development within the subject, with the loss of opportunities to gain valuable experience through involvement in curricular innovation. However, in the face of regular change, what has always remained constant is the importance of the teachers in the classroom. They are in control of how the curriculum is presented to their own pupils through their own teaching and are capable of making adjustments accordingly. They are given the considerable responsibility of educating young people who only get one chance with their school education. During Initial Teacher Education, today's student teachers are encouraged to take the stance adopted by Capel, Leask and Turner who state that the route through the curriculum should provide: 'the best opportunities for pupils to learn' (Capel *et al.*, 1995: 56).

The National Curriculum, as with syllabuses for GCSE and A-level, still has to be *taught* and teachers should dwell on that key word, whose definition embraces the complex notion of the learning process. Teachers are not simple 'deliverers' of the curriculum, yet this term has slipped into parlance with politicians, the media and now, even, ashamedly, some in education. Writing in 1996, Rawling felt that 'the first version of the Geography National Curriculum seemed to require a reduction in professional input and the assumption of a "delivery mode" rather than a "creative mode" of operation' (Rawling, 1996: 255). Perhaps it should be remembered that 'delivery' is what happens when the newspaper arrives through your letterbox – education is surely a rather more complex process than that. If it were not, then the current crisis in teacher recruitment could be solved overnight by teenagers switching jobs from their paper rounds! Tony Fisher warns of this 'reductive view' of teaching, where the complexity required to achieve learning through teaching 'is thereby rendered unproblematic and misleadingly straight-forward' (Fisher, 1998: 27). He also cites the view of Stones (1992):

> Knowing one's subject assumes an unwanted pre-eminence in some discourses about education, and knowledge about that subject becomes the product which the teacher has to 'deliver' by telling.
>
> (Stones, 1992: 16 in Fisher, 1998: 27)

Teachers should not be afraid of using their professional expertise, skills and judgement to translate study programmes or coursework requirements to best suit the needs of their own pupils and provide genuine interest and motivation in the subject to maximize their pupils' chances of success. There is a need for many to re-focus on *how well* geography is taught. Other authors in this book have much to say on this and OFSTED inspection evidence supports this link between quality of teaching and attainment. Leat (1999) has promoted developments in classroom processes featuring the teaching of critical thinking skills to promote learning. This approach has built successfully on the improvements achieved in the Cognitive

Acceleration in Science project (see Adey and Shayer, 1994) and is proving a welcome and refreshing development for many teachers of geography. For the courses taught at Key Stage 4 and above, departments can still choose syllabuses that are best suited to their own cohorts, although the range of choice is decreasing due to amalgamations, economies of scale and greater centralization affecting examination boards. At National Curriculum Key Stages 1–3, the National Curriculum 2000 revision now gives greater flexibility in wording, a reduction in prescription and a wider choice of place to allow teachers to 'customize' their courses to best suit their pupils, skills and resources. Eleanor Rawling and others endorse the opportunities for greater school-based curriculum development following the 2000 revision. Those who visit many geography departments to observe lessons, be they advisers, inspectors or teacher trainers, look forward to seeing diversity and innovation in both the teachers' interpretation of the geography curriculum and its manifestation in geography lessons. They should consequently see interest, enthusiasm and motivation – in both the pupils and their teachers.

## Are geography teachers resourceful enough in their teaching?

Another feature of the pre-political 'Golden Age' of teaching and perhaps overlooked in affectionate staff room anecdotes, concerns the more tangible cognition of the term 'resource' when discussing the teaching of geography. The textbook has always been the major element of a wide range of resources used in geography lessons. Delving into the recesses of dusty stockroom shelves often reveals texts surviving from previous colleagues, regimes and even generations. Initial comparison with today's multicoloured and pupil-friendly volumes reveals startling contrasts; such an exercise conducted with younger teachers can produce responses verging on the incredulous! The 'Golden Age' teacher had to be a master of adaptation. Scarcity of funds, limited availability of appropriate texts, few televisual resources and the absence of satellite imagery and ICT meant the teacher *had* to utilize resourcefulness, initiative and ingenuity in the provision of appropriate learning materials for motivating and stimulating their pupils. Many teaching days started with long sessions on the ubiquitous 'Banda' machine or its monochrome accomplice, the ink stencil duplicator, as the teacher converted current events into digestible fragments for pupil consumption.

Today, however, newly qualified teachers enter schools where resources for the teaching of geography are far more diverse and task-specific than in the past. The wide range of commercially produced texts, models, equipment, audio-visual and ICT-related resources on show each year at the Geographical Association Conference would suggest to an outsider that geography lessons are characterized by the use of a wide range of diverse stimuli and data sources. Yet we all know that this is far from the reality of many geography lessons and classrooms. Why is this?

Financial resources are clearly an issue. As a subject, geography has been shouldered aside in the rush for the 'capitation doorway', as newer subjects and a plethora of national initiatives have absorbed much of the limited funding available to schools, whatever their status. Nevertheless, few departments today receive less, in real terms, than in the past, and the range and diversity of teaching resources available have, in many respects, never been better. However, in reality, the diversity of resources, especially textbooks, seen in departments remains very limited. There is plentiful evidence that the wholesale adoption of 'key texts', particularly for Key Stage 3, has resulted in them becoming virtually the sole teaching resource used in the majority of lessons. The texts themselves may, in many respects, be highly commendable, but there are clearly concerns about the ability of one volume to cover a whole Key Stage, GCSE or A-level syllabus; this was never attempted in the past when, arguably, our subject was less broad than it is today. OFSTED inspection evidence (OFSTED, 1995) is highly critical of the 'single text', linking weaknesses in observed teaching quality with departments that are over-reliant on single volumes. Also, the 'pupil tasks' or 'exercises' within the books tend to be aimed at those non-existent, imaginary, 'average' pupils – and certainly not *your* classes. Textbooks should be regarded simply as 'resources', but the commercial pressures of publishing dictate that pupil tasks are included to attract sales and make texts useful for non-specialist use. When choosing textbooks, and other resources, how many teachers consider the needs of their own pupils as well as the needs of the curriculum? There is, surely, a need to conduct some form of analysis based on pupils' needs prior to making the choice. However, it is not within the scope of this discussion to examine the role and changing nature of geography textbooks; for this, refer to chapters by David Waugh and David Lambert. It is the ability of the teacher to be resourceful that remains the focus of this discussion.

A peculiar inverse relationship appears to have developed between teacher resourcefulness and the availability of teaching resources – as the latter has increased over time, so the former appears to have declined. The teacher's ability to innovate and utilize resources efficiently has certainly changed, and possibly worsened. It is this ability to use such resources effectively that is the issue here. Earlier, Tony Fisher's notion of a 'reductive view' of teaching was cited (Fisher, 1998: 27). Is it possible that geography teachers themselves have suffered such a 'reduction' in their own perception of the teacher's role? The use of many highly diverse teaching resources has become rather 'mechanistic', lacking flair, creativity and imagination. Is this linked, perhaps, to the reduction in subject specialists now teaching geography, especially at Key Stage 3? Whilst recruitment of students to become teachers of geography has now become so difficult that it has officially become a shortage subject, there also seems to be a growing shortage of basic teaching posts for newly qualified teachers to find (RGS, 1999). There is a growing suspicion among some teachers that when geographers 'move on', growing numbers of schools fail to replace them and consequently more classes are taught by non-specialists. The burgeoning pre-eminence of the 'core' subjects, in terms not only of teaching time, but also in perceived importance by legislators and school management is surely partly responsible for this development. If there is a perception of the subject, by school managers and governors, as merely 'content to be delivered', then any able teacher (regardless of their subject specialism) can be regarded as being capable of achieving this. All geography teachers, therefore, have a responsibility to produce a balanced promotion of their subject for their senior managers. This should include an emphasis on both the principles of curriculum design (Rawling, 1992) and high-quality teaching processes as regularly demonstrated in the classroom. There should be an express avoidance of that anathema, the lesson that features 'occupancy geography' with little thinking and even less learning.

## Is resourcefulness recognized in a teacher's ability?

In the past decade, an abundance of 'descriptors' have been introduced to identify both the qualities and attributes required for teaching and also to provide a new professional structure for career development. These have included:

- Requirements for courses of Initial Teacher Education: *Teaching: High Status, High Standards* (TTA, 1998a);
- Standards for NQT year: *The Induction Period for Newly Qualified Teachers* (DfEE, 1999);
- OFSTED inspection criteria (HMSO, 1995);
- Standards for Subject Leaders: *National Standards for Subject Leaders* (TTA, 1998b); and
- Technical paper descriptors for teacher appraisal: *Teachers: Meeting the Challenge of Change* Green Paper (DfEE, December 1998).

Additionally, there have been a number of publications to promote the craft of teaching and boost flagging teacher recruitment figures. In its 1996 publicity brochure, the Teacher Training Agency asked the crucial question: 'What makes a successful secondary teacher?' (TTA, 1996: 4). The response was:

> It takes a special kind of person to be a successful secondary teacher. In addition to good academic qualifications many other qualities and skills are required. An accomplished communicator and administrator, you will also need to be creative, energetic, enthusiastic and flexible and have a good sense of humour.
> ... you must also be able to use and develop a range of suitable teaching techniques which grip the imagination of your pupils and enable them to learn from you.
>
> (TTA, 1996: 4)

There are certainly attributes described here which appear to concur with the sentiments expressed in this chapter – the need for resourcefulness, flair and imagination are among the teacher's repertoire of key skills. However, these qualities become lost in a sea of prescriptive description indicators when the analysis turns away from publicity brochures to the phrases used to describe teachers, from their initial training through to Subject Leaders and beyond. Such attempts to capture in words, and in turn quantify, the precise nature of the teachers' craft have generated considerable comment. For example:

> Discourses of competences attempt to repress certain conceptions of knowledge and understanding in order to sustain an agenda where competence-based qualifications appear to be the most appropriate response. A regime of truth is established which derides certain forms of knowledge as 'theory', irrelevant to 'getting the job done well'.
>
> (Usher and Edwards, 1994, in Fisher, 1998: 5)

Whilst the overall aims of the descriptors include notions of continuity and progression, it is acknowledged that there are limitations and they only indicate a minimum requirement. For example, the Teacher Training Agency in introducing its *Standards for the Award of Qualified Teacher Status* (TTA, 1992) does indicate that these only offer a starting platform for the development of new teachers:

> professionalism . . . implies more than meeting a series of discrete standards. It is necessary to consider the standards as a whole to appreciate the creativity, commitment, energy and enthusiasm which teaching demands, and the intellectual and managerial skills required of the effective professional.
>
> (TTA, 1992: 2)

This comment really may be regarded as only a token gesture towards such qualities, for the vast majority of the requirements are dominated by the identification of mechanistic 'performance indicators'. Throughout the document, along with its 1998 update (TTA, 1998), there is a preoccupation with 'outcome' and insufficient regard for the processes involved in achieving that outcome. This was a view shared by Burke (1990), who expressed the following view prior to the introduction of any of these measures:

> Whilst considerable attention is currently being paid to the issues of how competence is to be defined and standards expressed, the matter of how individuals can be helped to become more competent more quickly is comparatively neglected.
>
> (Burke, 1990: 100)

Since then, those involved in the implementation of standards and competences, for example those involved in Initial Teacher Education, have reflected on them in a similar vein:

> It is important to note that my view is that competence is a broad concept and is not narrowly focused on the routine aspects of the work activity. . . . Competence cannot be observed in its entirety. Real competence is concerned with inputs as well as outcomes and performance.
>
> (Field, 1995: 27)

Whilst all such sets of descriptors are generic, is it possible to identify those characteristics that are synonymous with the geography teacher who is innovative and creative in their teaching and whose classroom practice may be described as 'resourceful'? Initial Teacher Education competences now include specific Annexes for teachers of the 'core' subjects. Some other groups have also interpreted generic descriptors for their own specialism, for example careers teachers in Kent have 'translated' the Subject Leaders' standards to their own specific roles. The Geographical Association is involved in developing subject-specific statements to work alongside such documents, but most sets of descriptors remain 'generic'; to what extent do these sets of 'descriptors' identify 'resourcefulness' in teachers?

## Initial Teacher Education

The requirements for Initial Teacher Education leading to Qualified Teacher Status have been revised substantially in the past decade. There was initially *Circular 9/92* (DfEE, 1992) and then its subsequent revision *Teaching: High Status, High Standards* (TTA, 1998a). During their 'training', student teachers are required to demonstrate generic requirements for teaching under the headings of

A.    Knowledge and understanding
B.    Planning, teaching and class management
C.    Monitoring, assessment, recording, reporting and accountability
D.    Other professional requirements

There are additional, subject-specific requirements for teachers of the 'core' subjects of English, Mathematics, ICT and Science (DfEE, 1998: Annex A–H). Great emphasis is placed on attributes that are both easily discernible and dominated by 'knowledge acquisition'. 'To have a secure knowledge', 'be capable of' and 'can demonstrate' are persistent themes within the profusion of competence statements. However, recognition of the need to be innovative, enthusiastic, inspirational and creative can only be obliquely discerned. For example:

k.  use teaching methods which sustain the momentum of pupils' work and keep all pupils engaged through:
    i.   stimulating intellectual curiosity, communicating enthusiasm for the subject being taught, fostering pupils' enthusiasm and maintaining pupils' motivation;
    ix.  selecting and making good use of textbooks, ICT and other learning resources which enable teaching objectives to be met;
                    (from *Teaching: High Status, High Standards*, TTA, 1998a: 13)

These two statements are from over fifty found across the *eight* pages of 'Standards' that provide the current requirements for courses of Initial Teacher Education. Therefore, the emphasis on the most important skills and attributes required of teachers completing their training seems rather different from those cited in publicity and recruitment literature. Is it merely that the ethics involved here need questioning, or is it also that such crucial process skills are more difficult to easily appraise? Perhaps the current revision of the 'Standard' may address this issue.

## OFSTED inspection criteria

After a series of evolutionary stages, the current system awards a grade based on the stated criteria for the teacher's 'performance' during a lesson observed by an inspector. The criteria used in the judgement of teaching would appear to give little opportunity to identify and 'reward' innovation, creativity, energy or enthusiasm. However, some might argue that such features are implicit within some of the 'catch-all' descriptor phrases used. For example, a 'very good' teaching performance has teaching that: 'promotes very high educational standards' and has pupils who: 'show positive attitudes and behave very well' with 'most . . . achieving well above the national standard'.

It must be said that due to the reputation that has developed around such inspections, it is the tendency of many teachers to shy away from innovative features in their teaching during the 'inspection week'. Such characteristics are far more easily discerned in a teacher over a period of time and through their planning, than in the two or three lessons seen by inspectors every four years. There is a similarity here with the descriptors for Initial Teacher Education as considerable significance is laid on the 'outcome' rather than the process used to achieve it. This is, perhaps, a reflection of the 'snapshot' nature of the school inspection process today, where great emphasis is laid on an attempt to quantify the 'end product' with little attention paid, or credit given, to the complex processes by which this is attained. This also reflects, surely, the 'reductive' view of teaching as a mode for curricular 'delivery'.

## Standards for Subject Leaders

Produced in 1998, this is one of four new sets of National Standards introduced to the profession:

*   the award of Qualified Teacher Status (QTS)
*   the Induction Period for Newly Qualified Teachers
*   Special Educational Needs Co-ordinators (SENCOs)
*   Subject Leaders
*   Headteachers (National Professional Qualification for Headteachers – NPQH)

The intention of these standards was to identify, really for the first time in most areas, the expectations for teachers at key points in the profession. The emphasis was placed on planned professional development with appropriate training, improved pupil achievement and a professional recognition of teachers' expertise and achievements. They were also a way of emphasizing national policies in developing the profession with a keen eye on aspects such as literacy, numeracy and ICT.

It might be assumed that those given responsibility for leading a subject would be expected to exhibit teaching skills of the highest calibre, with the ability to inspire, enthuse and be innovative with the curriculum. This would particularly apply in a secondary school where there may be a large department and a number of subject specialists to motivate, manage and inspire. As seen earlier, such features may only be discerned through what is briefly implied:

> Effective subject leaders result in:
> b.  teachers who –
>     Make effective use of subject-specific resources [and] select appropriate teaching and learning approaches to meet subject-specific learning objectives and the needs of pupils.
> Subject leaders should have knowledge and understanding of:
> d.  the characteristics of high quality teaching in the subject and the main strategies for improving and sustaining high standards of teaching, learning and achievement for all pupils; . . .
> Subject leaders identify appropriate resources for the subject and ensure that they are used efficiently, effectively and safely.
>                 (*National Standards for Subject Leaders*, TTA, 1998b: 5, 6, 12)

Analysis of the entire 'standards framework' reveals a pattern similar to that seen earlier, as again much attention is paid to outcomes, but relatively little focus on the processes by which they are achieved. Another notable feature of these documents is the recurrent use of phrases such as 'good teachers' and 'high quality teaching'. Yet no real attempt is made to define what these terms actually indicate in terms of the actions and processes involved. Though any group of teachers might reach a general consensus on what being a 'good teacher' means, arriving at detailed descriptors would create much valuable debate. However, if we are to promote high quality and resourcefulness in our teachers, then surely some precise definition is needed to avoid reverting to the 'reductive view' of teaching discussed earlier. The Geographical Association has clearly stated its case on curricular issues at earlier times of national debate, for example Bailey and Binns (1987) and 'Geography in the curriculum; a position statement from the GA' (GA, 1999a). In mid-1999, the Geographical Association took a welcome lead in publishing *Leading Geography: National Standards for Geography Leaders in Secondary Schools* (GA, 1999b), along with an equivalent version for Geography Subject Leaders in the primary sector. This move suggests that geographers are prepared to consider their own subject-specific interpretation of such criteria and use them for informing those 'non-geographers' involved in educational management and administration. How many headteachers are aware of these documents?

### The 'new generation' of teachers

Another set of 'descriptors' for the craft of teaching was published in connection with a controversial Green Paper titled *Teachers: Meeting the Challenge of Change* (DfEE, 1998) which was characterized by persistent references to 'good' teachers. Within the body of the Green Paper, however, there was little attempt to define exactly what this term really meant. This document, though, announced a new category of 'Advance Skills Teachers', who were described as: 'demonstrating good classroom practice', 'designing and testing new teaching materials' and 'a particularly valuable resource for schools in need of excellent teachers' (DfEE, 1998).

Following the publication of this complex Green Paper, the ensuing months saw a growing concern among teachers that focused almost exclusively on the issue of staff appraisal and the proposal to link elements of future pay to pupil performance. This drew attention away from the way that the craft of teaching was described in the documentation that was meant to set the standards for teaching into the next century. To encourage higher-quality teaching in the classroom, the Green Paper sought to reward a high proportion of teachers, possibly as much as half, with higher salaries once they had proven themselves capable of working at 'threshold standards'. These require teachers to demonstrate a range of qualities. However, notions of 'resourcefulness' and 'innovation' can, once more, only be inferred from the standards to be used, for example:

> . . . use a range of appropriate strategies for teaching and classroom management . . . demonstrate they are effective professionals who challenge and support all pupils to do their best through . . . engaging and motivating pupils [and] . . . analytical thinking . . .
>
> (DfEE, 2000)

The Application Pack suggests that teachers who meet the threshold standards will be highly effective classroom practitioners who should command a wider authority across the school. They will possess an established record of good results and make significant contributions, through their teaching, towards the school's targets, policies, ethos and aims. They will keep up to date with developments in their subject and how to teach it. They will have a wide repertoire of teaching techniques and use relevant evidence and data to improve their teaching in order to raise standards of pupils' achievements. They will also demonstrate professional insight into the effects of their teaching and assessment approaches and will be proactive in working with others inside and outside the school to secure their pupils' progress. Though there are frequent references to 'targets', there appears little appreciation of the complexities of the craft of teaching, the processes involved and the need for high-quality teachers to be resourceful innovators.

The majority of the 'descriptors' referred to earlier rely on easily observed or measurable 'outcomes', discerned from either direct observation of practice or written evidence of policy, planning and evaluation. Though the notion of the 'resourceful innovator' may be extracted implicitly from some descriptors, its nature is not recognized as a key component of high-quality teaching, whether this be in geography or any other subject. It is important to re-emphasize that there is a need for geography teachers to arrive at a common understanding of what these 'descriptors' mean for their own specialist teaching. Such an interpretation should achieve national status and can be utilized by school senior managers and the educational system in due recognition of the unique contribution that high-quality geography teaching can make to pupils' lives.

## Questions for discussion

### *How resourceful are geography teachers in managing curriculum development?*

1   How can existing teaching programmes be adapted to best suit the needs of your pupils and provide them with diverse and innovative opportunities that promote learning, interest and enthusiasm in geography?

### *Are geography teachers resourceful in their teaching?*

1   What are the 'resource needs' of your pupils?
2   How can you adapt your teaching resources to create innovative and diverse pupil tasks for classroom and home use?
3   Does your teaching demonstrate high-quality processes conducive to learning?
4   Does your school's senior management team perceive geography lessons to be illuminating experiences where pupils acquire knowledge, understanding and skills that are valued both within the subject area and in wider applications?

### *Is resourcefulness recognized in a teacher's ability?*

1   How would you recognize 'resourcefulness' in a geography teacher?
2   List the features you would associate with:
    (a) a 'good' geography teacher,
    (b) 'high-quality' geography teaching,
    (c) an outstanding geography subject leader.
3   Does the Geographical Association's contribution to the Subject Leader debate help you, and your school, identify high-quality geography teaching from Initial Teacher Education through to Subject Leader?

## References

Adey, P. and Shayer, M. (1994) *Really Raising Standards*, London: Routledge.
Bailey, P. and Binns, T. (eds) (1987) *A Case for Geography*, Sheffield: Geographical Association.

Boardman, D. (ed.) (1985) *New Directions in Geographical Education*, London: Falmer Press.

Burke, J. (1990) *Competence Based Education and Training*, London: Falmer Press.

Capel, S., Leask, M. and Turner, T. (1995) *Learning to Teach in the Secondary School*, London: Routledge.

Dearing, R. (1994) *The National Curriculum and its Assessment: A Final Report*, London: SCAA.

DfEE (1992) *Circular 9/92*, London: Department for Education and Employment.

DfEE (1998) Green Paper *Teachers: Meeting the Challenge of Change*, London: Department for Education and Employment.

DfEE (1999) Circular 5/99 *The Induction Period for Newly Qualified Teachers*, London: Department for Education and Employment.

DfEE (2000) 3/00 *Threshold Assessment Application Pack*, London: Department for Education and Employment.

Field, C.D. (1995) 'A reflective, non-didactic development programme for tutors of modern languages to adults', unpublished M.A. dissertation, University of Kent at Canterbury.

Fisher, T. (1998) *Developing as a Teacher of Geography*, Cambridge: Chris Kington.

GA (1999a) 'Geography in the curriculum: a position statement from the GA', *Teaching Geography*, 24, 2 (April): 57–9.

GA (1999b) *Leading Geography: National Standards for Geography Leaders in Secondary Schools*, Pipes, R. (ed.) Sheffield: The Geographical Association.

Graves, N. (1996) 'Curriculum development in geography: an ongoing process', in Kent, A., Lambert, D., Naish, M. and Slater, F., *Geography in Education: Viewpoints on Teaching and Learning*, Cambridge: Cambridge University Press.

Graves, N. (1997) 'Geographical education in the 1990s', in Tilbury, D. and Williams, M. (eds) *Teaching and Learning Geography*, London: Routledge.

HMSO (1995) *The Ofsted Handbook – Guidance on the Inspection of Secondary Schools*, London: Her Majesty's Stationery Office.

Huckle, J. (1991) 'Reasons to be cheerful', in Walford, R. (ed.) *Viewpoints on Geography Teaching: The Charney Manor Conference Papers 1990*, London: Longman.

Lambert, D. (1997) 'Principles of pupil assessment', in Tilbury, D. and Williams, M. (eds) *Teaching and Learning Geography*, London: Routledge.

Leat, D. (1999) *Thinking Through Geography*, Cambridge: Chris Kingston.

Machon, P. and Ranger, G. (1996) 'Change in school geography', in Bailey, P. and Fox, P. (eds) *Geography Teachers Handbook*, Sheffield: Geographical Association.

OFSTED (1995) *Geography: A Review of Inspection Findings 1993/4*, London: HMSO.

Pollard, A. (1997) 'The basics and eagerness to learn: a new curriculum for primary schooling', SCAA Invitational Conference, 9–10 June.

Rawling, E. (1992) 'The making of the National Curriculum', *Geography*, 337, 77, 4: 292–309, Sheffield: Geographical Association.

Rawling, E. (1996) 'Geography 5–19: some issues for debate', in Rawling, E. and Daugherty, R. (eds) *Geography into the Twenty-First Century*, Chichester: John Wiley.

RGS (1999) 'Geography teaching: recruitment and supply', unpublished papers from the conference held at Royal Geographical Society, 21 April.

Roberts, M. (1997) 'Reconstructing the geography National Curriculum', in Helsby, G. and McCulloch, G. (eds) *Teachers and the National Curriculum*, London: Cassell.

Stones, E. (1992) *Quality Teaching: A sample of Cases*, London: Routledge.

TTA (1992) *Standards for the Award of Qualified Teacher Status*, London: Teacher Training Agency.

TTA (1996) *Secondary Teaching 96/97: Open Minds, Open Doors*, London: Teacher Training Agency.

TTA (1998a) *Teaching: High Status, High Standards*, London: Teacher Training Agency.

TTA (1998b) *National Standards for Subject Leaders*, London: Teacher Training Agency.

Usher, R. and Edwards, R. (1994) *Postmodernism and Education: Different Voices, Different Worlds*, London: Routledge.

Walford, R. (1997) 'The great debate and 1988', in Tilbury, D. and Williams, M. (eds) *Teaching and Learning Geography*, London: Routledge.

# 10 The importance of 'big' concepts and skills in learning geography

*David Leat*

## Introduction

Secondary school geography is bogged down in content. There were too many Statements of Attainment in the original Geography National Curriculum Orders, which encouraged a breakneck gallop through a forest of textbook double page spreads. Margaret Roberts in her research into the impact of the geography National Curriculum on three departments, reports the conclusion of one head of department, committed to enquiry-based learning, as follows: 'there is far more talk and chalk than there has ever been before. People are saying we haven't got time for group discussion . . . People are saying we must get through the syllabus' (Roberts, 1997: 109). The revised orders (DfEE, 1995) reduced the content and encouraged a more considered approach, but there remains a strong legacy that the Key Stage 3 geography curriculum is something that has to be delivered, 'got through' or even endured. Similar sentiments could be applied to Key Stage 4. We can have some optimism that the revisions for implementation in September 2000 will represent a substantial improvement.

It is important to make clear the assumption underpinning this chapter: that teaching geography should be about developing the capacities of the mind such that students who study the subject are assisted in becoming good learners. This is not to argue that content is unimportant or that any content will do. Research on expert problem solvers (Chi *et al.*, 1982) suggests that they have both excellent subject (declarative) knowledge and cognitive skills (procedural knowledge). Geography students need knowledge of major environmental systems, processes and patterns evident at a variety of scales. They also need map skills, graphical skills and data interpretation skills. However, such outcomes should not be the primary aim of geography teachers; the content is the vehicle: the development of good, motivated learners, who can transfer their learning is the destination. Without such an intention we have little claim to being a profession, because research evidence suggests that many pupils are unable to use in everyday contexts what they have been taught in school. Reflect on this: an analysis of answers by pupils on the Avery Hill GCSE (Battersby *et al.*, 1993) showed that approximately 40 per cent of candidates scored zero on the case study parts of questions. A substantial number also gained only one or two marks. This is not a good record for a subject which prides itself on developing a sense of place.

Lifelong learning is a current buzz phrase. It features prominently in political debate, which means that we should be wary of it! Nonetheless it provides a bearing on which we can fix to provide some judgement on whether we are going in the right direction. Candy, Crebet and O'Leary (1994), albeit in the context of the education of Australian undergraduates, propose five qualities for lifelong learners:

*An enquiring mind*
- a love of learning;
- a sense of curiosity and question asking;
- a critical spirit;
- comprehension, monitoring and self-evaluation;

*Helicopter vision*
- a sense of interconnectedness of fields;
- an awareness of how knowledge is created in at least one field of study and an understanding of the methodological and substantive limitations of the field;
- breadth of vision;

*Information literacy*
- knowledge of major current resources available in at least one field of study;
- ability to frame researchable questions in at least one field of study;
- ability to retrieve information using a variety of media;
- ability to decode information in a variety of forms;
- critical evaluation of information;

*A sense of personal agency*
- a positive concept of oneself as capable and autonomous;
- self-organizational skills (time management, goal setting, etc.);

*A repertoire of learning skills*
- knowledge of one's own strengths, weaknesses and preferred learning styles;
- a range of strategies for learning in whatever context one finds oneself; and an understanding of the differences between surface and deep-level learning.

Having recognized that this list was derived in relation to undergraduates, it does not follow that one should wait until students become undergraduates – partly because it may be too late and partly because this would marginalize the majority who do not proceed to higher education. The list is not a prescription for content, it is an agenda for how pupils are taught. Pascal and Bertram (1997) have argued in relation to the National Curriculum that there is an urgent need to define the characteristics of children which will enable them to become lifelong learners and to modify curriculum frameworks to ensure that they support and enhance the 'super skills' of learning.

The current onus of the curriculum appears to be on doing the opposite. The Primary Assessment and Curriculum Experience (PACE) project has studied a cohort of primary pupils as they progressed through the National Curriculum. Pollard (1997) reports that the evidence indicates that pupils are becoming increasingly instrumental in their learning. In relation to core subjects, the impact of statutory testing is to create a gulf between successful and 'failing' students, who quickly regard themselves as unable to learn. Pupils generally become aware of the importance of good marks and 'getting things right', with the result that many prefer to avoid challenge and have a low tolerance of ambiguity. Interestingly the most popular subject is art because pupils feel that they have a choice in what they do. Pollard argues that if the goal of education is a flexible, effective and fulfilled workforce, then there must be an emphasis from the early years on transferable skills, conceptual knowledge and self-confidence. The present National Curriculum structure is conservative in content and structure and may be undermining dispositions to learn. National Curriculum geography cannot escape criticism in this respect; it is part of the problem.

It is anachronistic, perhaps even ridiculous, to define a subject simply through the specification of content – for a number of reasons. First, the boundaries of the subject will always change as new paradigms emerge and new issues come into focus. Second, the information revolution is forcing a reassessment of the role of knowledge in school subjects, because pupils can readily access so much raw information through the Internet without the teacher as gatekeeper. Third, such an approach places limits on pupils' learning – it is part of the empty vessel approach to learning in which pupils are to be filled up with the requisite knowledge. If they do not learn it well, it is a failing of the pupil, rather than the subject. It is more optimistic to acknowledge that a subject has a duty to develop the learning abilities of pupils in a way that reflects the cognitive skills of good exponents of that discipline. Put more simply, geography should aim to help pupils think in the ways that the best geographers do. Geography should be defined as much by how geographers do their subject as by what they study (or used to!).

## Why is it important to provide a clear conceptual structure to the subject?

Learning is not simply a matter of somehow absorbing discrete facts and principles. Most of what we learn is learned through the framework of what we already know. If we have no prior experience or learning to assist us, new information is unlikely to make any sense. Contrast the likely outcome of listening to radio commentaries on sumo wrestling and football. As most of us have extremely limited knowledge of sumo wrestling we will make very little sense of the commentary because we do not have knowledge structures to interpret the commentary. Many readers, however, would understand references to 'a through ball', 'offside', 'a flat back four' and 'holding the ball up'. However, without contextual knowledge of football which provides a conceptual framework, they sound like nonsense. For many low-achieving pupils doing geography is analogous to listening to the sumo wrestling!

Bloom (1976) reports that 60–80 per cent of variance in achievement scores in a variety of contexts could be attributed to prior learning. What we learn is primarily determined by what we already know.

Learning contributes to developing knowledge structures, in which items of knowledge are connected to make wholes that are more significant than the sum of the parts. Wood (1988), drawing on the work of Miller (1956), underlines that adults in unfamiliar situations are overwhelmed if they are expected to react to more than a small number of unconnected items. They cannot make sense of them. Wood connects this fact with research on chess Grand Masters, which demonstrates that if they are shown a board in a state of play for only a few seconds they could register the positions of all the pieces and reproduce their positions on another board. By contrast, chess novices can only recall a few pieces and positions. The explanation offered is that what the expert sees is not individual pieces but configurations of pieces, meaningful patterns that are recalled to reconstruct the board. The Grand Masters do not have a greater memory capacity, but rather the chunks that they recall are not individual pieces but configurations or groups of pieces. As Wood puts it, the expert has developed an organized memory of typical states of play which enables her or him to recognize more of what they see and they are better able to plan and think ahead.

The Cognitive Acceleration through Science Education (Adey *et al.*, 1989) project, which has a considerable track record for raising attainment, is focused on improving pupils' thinking. This is deemed necessary because certain types of reasoning, which are crucial to success in science, are regarded as dependent on higher-order thinking. These reasoning patterns are: control of variables; ratio and proportionality; compensation and equilibrium; probability and correlation; and the use of abstract models to explain and predict. Put simply, if pupils do not understand, for example, the whole point and principle of the control of variables and fair tests, then much of GCSE science will remain a mystery and Grade C or above would be out of reach. It is through such reasoning patterns (or schemata) that more successful pupils will be able to recognize situations in which, for example, competing variables are in play and experiments have to control all but one of the variables, which will be the basis of the hypothesis to be tested. Pupils who can reason in this way are seeing pattern, just as the chess Grand Masters do. Pupils who cannot reason in this way are overwhelmed by the complexity of the situation and tend to make wild guesses about what is happening.

Two recent Teacher Training Agency-funded reports – *Effective Teachers of Numeracy* (Askew *et al.*, 1997) and *Effective Teachers of Literacy* (Medwell *et al.*, 1998) provide further validation of the thesis that pupil progress is considerably assisted by creating pattern. At Key Stage 2 (age 7 to 11) highly effective numeracy teachers believe that being numerate requires 'having a rich network of connections between different mathematical ideas' (Askew *et al.*, 1997: 1). These teachers believed that the discussion of concepts is important in exemplifying the teacher's network of knowledge and that classroom mathematics needs to be related to everyday contexts. Furthermore, these beliefs were represented in their practice: They ask pupils to explain their thinking and help them to link it to other topics and contexts. For the literacy teachers there was also a strong coherence in philosophies, so that grammar structures were not taught as discrete features but as connected parts of a whole. So that in both populations pupils were experiencing a curriculum that emphasized pattern and connection and which sought to link teaching to pupil experiences outside the classroom. They were being offered an insight into the threads or warp in a tapestry that run through it creating different pictures as they intermix with different weft.

## How do pupils benefit from such a framing of the subject?

It is important to be more explicit about the benefits that accrue to pupils from this approach to teaching. It is not just the ability to see pattern that brings advantage. Hatano and Inagaki (1992) use learning to cook, to illustrate the importance of mental models. When we start learning to cook we are highly dependent on recipe books and on having all the right ingredients and utensils. If something is missing, or if we cannot find the book, we are stumped. We progress through a stage of remembering parts of recipes and then whole recipes, thus using acquired knowledge, but the knowledge does not transfer, in that we cannot interchange parts of recipes. However, they describe a further stage that is qualitatively different, when we acquire conceptual knowledge 'which means more or less comprehensive knowledge about the nature of the objects of the procedures (i.e what they are like)' (p. 116). So, in the cooking example, once we know about the characteristics of eggs, flour and milk and what they do in cooking, what function they serve in recipes, how to combine them and how they can be treated differently in different contexts, we have conceptual knowledge and we have reached a new threshold as we now have a mental model. The conceptual knowledge can change in response to thinking and we can use it to predict and hypothesize (Halford, 1993) and make up new recipes. It might be possible with this mental model to make up a passable recipe for a quiche without a book to guide us. Mental models are representations of reality and as such they are the basis of understanding. Many users of cars and computers are totally stumped when they malfunction. One interpretation of this helplessness is that the user does not possess a mental model of the working of car engines or computer systems. We do not *understand* how they work.

Mental models are therefore implicated in some modes of transfer of learning, in that they suggest a way in which knowledge learned in one context can be desituated and applied to another. This reduces the amount of information that needs to be rote learned. In the following extract two able and articulate 14-year-old girls are being interviewed about how they have done the Kobe earthquake mystery (SCAA, 1996) in a simulated recall interview, in which a video recording of them doing the task is played back (some parts at fast forward). A mystery is a highly differentiated task in which pupils are given a very open question to answer by working with 12–30 data items each on a separate slip of paper. The data items vary – some form a narrative thread about people and events, whilst others are more abstract relating to socio-economic or physical geography factors.

| Interviewer: | You have one at the top there about Japan being a rich country? |
| First female pupil: | It was like a background (the interviewer and the teacher had not used this word). It was not in order, it was background, Japan is a rich country and the plates stuff, it's not in any order. |
| Interviewer: | You are forming groups? |
| Both pupils: | Yes. |
| Second female pupil: | I thought that they should end up in a line like a storyboard, but they didn't all go (storyboards had not been mentioned). |
| Interviewer: | Where have you used storyboards? |
| Both pupils: | In English. |
| Interviewer: | What didn't fit? |
| First female pupil: | The backgrounds. |
| Second female pupil: | There were the buildings and things that contributed to her death, but not directly. |
| Interviewer: | Have you done background before? |
| Second female pupil: | Once or twice in Y8. We did not realise that we were doing it. New things kept cropping up and things changed . . . so it changed. We were looking at evidence and sorting and resorting. |
| Interviewer: | Have you looked at evidence before? |
| Both pupils: | In history. In history we do sources, which sources are reliable and which are unreliable. |

There is considerable evidence that these two pupils are using mental models, important cognitive skills and metacognitive self-regulation. Although it does not appear first in the extract, it seems that their initial approach to organizing their explanation was based on storyboards. They have a clear understanding of the structure and role of storyboards from English, that is they have conceptual knowledge about storyboards. For instance they know that storyboards conventionally have a narrative thread in which events are time sequenced. They can see storyboards in their heads, so they have a visual representation of the model. They can use storyboards as a way of imposing order on the data, which allows them to start putting the data in a sequence. However, as the second pupil reports, 'I thought that they should end up in a line like a storyboard, but they didn't all go.' She made a prediction about the events, which they test and find that it does not fit. They are engaging in self-regulation.

So having failed with one mental model, they start using another, the idea of cause being understood in terms of trigger and background factors. This is an alternative mental model which does not use time sequencing in the same dominant way. She states that the 'backgrounds' did not fit. 'There were the buildings and things that contributed to her death, but not directly.' They see this as a contributory factor, but it does not fit the storyboard approach. Once again they appear to carry the mental model as a visual representation in the sense that they can recall data items arranged as trigger and background factors on a table top. They have conceptual knowledge about the characteristics of background and trigger factors. They know that background factors apply over lengthy periods of time and to many places and that they make certain events more likely. Trigger factors are more localized and episodic and spark particular events. This second mental model appears to be more successful in helping them impose order on the data. It would also allow them to make predictions, perhaps about how earthquake risk could be reduced in the future by examining how trigger or factors could be managed so as to reduce future damage by earthquakes.

However, they are not finished, for there is evidence that they use a third mental model – the reliability of evidence. It is possible to argue that checking reliability is a cognitive skill, but it is important to be alert to the fact that understanding and skills are not as separable as might first appear. Mental models are the basis of some cognitive skills. One's understanding of reliability is likely to be rooted in a particular example or examples, where it was first encountered. One will go back to such instances to check understanding and types. If you were introduced to reliability in the context of an environmental issue such as a quarry development in a National Park, you might well return to why you judged one person's evidence as reliable and somebody else's evidence as unreliable to check what these words meant. In other words, one has conceptual knowledge, which forms the basis of a cognitive skill. These two girls used experiences in history as the basis for sifting the importance of certain evidence in a geography context. Overall it can be inferred that these girls are monitoring and regulating their own performance (Flavell, 1976): 'New things kept cropping up and things changed . . . so it changed. We were looking at evidence and sorting and resorting.' Such self-regulation is extremely impressive and implies that they are matching many of the attributes for lifelong learners described earlier.

The picture that emerges is that these pupils have mental models which are based on learning experiences in the humanities and English. They allow them to deal with complex information and choose between approaches to generating a solution, and as Newton (1995) puts it, the models confer a certain 'cognitive autonomy'. It is this autonomy that has to be the hallmark of an educated pupil and adult. This autonomy is clearly exposed in a further short interview extract with another group of pupils, who are being asked how what they have learned recently in geography can help them in the future.

**Female pupil:**  In projects and stuff. It can help you. For writing essays and stuff, you have all the reasons, the background and the trigger reasons, it can help you sort of arrange an essay and write it.

**Second female pupil:**  And if you're going to college you can use it. I think this happened because of the background.

If you watch an individual or group really struggling with a task, ask yourself whether it is because they do not have a mental model or representation on which they can draw. The girls described above are at one end of the spectrum. Some pupils are fairly stumped when they start doing a mystery. They can read the data items and can infer some meaning, but they do not have the mental resources to proceed to impose any meaningful pattern. The TTG group has a video of another group of Year 10 pupils doing a mystery, in which they immediately sort the data into two groups – advantages and disadvantages – even though such an arrangement bore little resemblance to the question asked. Had this group become over-dependent on a dominant mental model, encouraged by the style of some GCSE texts? Teaching needs to encourage pupils to develop a wide range of mental models, from which they can actively and intelligently choose and always keep open the possibility of developing new ones.

This final extract in the section comes from an interview with a group of pupils from a Year 8 mixed ability class. They have just completed a lesson in which they were asked to identify suitable weather for a range of activites in Britain, such as painting a house, a cricket match, a farmer planting cabbages and a police search for a missing child. From here they were invited to imagine that in the future there are powerful computers which can control the weather. In this context they have been asked to generate as many ideas as possible about how the weather could be decided. Through discussing these ideas they begin to appreciate that the power to control the weather would in itself generate considerable conflict, because of the competing needs and interests of different groups.

| | |
|---|---|
| **Interviewer:** | Anything else that you've learned? |
| **Female pupil:** | We have learned like different ways that you can solve arguments. |
| **Interviewer:** | Keep going, tell me more about that. |
| **Female pupil:** | If you think about it, all the things we have put on the board leave some people unhappy . . . if, if there was like 6 weeks of sunshine and 6 weeks of rain then the farmers for one six weeks would be really unhappy because of all the crops . . . and if you've voted like say if they've voted for Prime Minister, even if one Prime Minister wins by a long way, there's still like the minority of people who aren't happy, cos the one that they wanted didn't win. |
| **Interviewer:** | OK, so keep going, what are you going to do? . . . Summarise that into what you think you learned . . . Just that it doesn't always suit everybody? |
| **Female pupil:** | Even if 99.9% of people think that there's got to be like sun on one day for like the 0.1% who don't think that there should be sun on that day . . . you don't get everyone agreeing. |
| **Male pupil:** | Cos if it's like sunny all the time all the people with hay fever and things like that, they wouldn't be able to go out of the house. |

(Slightly later)

| Interviewer: | Let me go back. She talked about the different ways you could manage the weather and she asked you a question . . . is there anywhere else you could use that in your daily life? How do you think that would help you? |
| Male pupil: | People have wars and it's not a very good idea to have wars . . . you get into trouble and you get wars with your mum and dad . . . |
| Second female pupil: | And sometimes when you fight with your brother and sister. You get upset and you say something you don't mean to them. |
| Female pupil: | You've just got to be common sensible about things, if somebody starts an argument with you, you've just got to try and see what their argument is about, and you can say we can put your idea down and we'll put mine underneath it. |

It can be argued that these pupils have been assisted to see a pattern which runs through a range of contexts – the lesson, politics and family life. For the first female pupil, in particular, one can see that she is developing a depth of conceptual knowledge about conflict and its resolution that is highly sophisticated and she is transferring this between contexts. This suggests the existence of a mental model, which is being used to run simulations of conflict in a variety of scenarios, to predict events and consequences. All these pupils are better equipped to impose meaning on other conflict scenarios and to understand how such conflict can be resolved in planning contexts. The ability to see pattern underscores the ability to transfer learning.

## What does a conceptual structure look like in geography and how does it relate to other subjects?

Earlier, the important reasoning patterns in CASE were outlined. What are the important concepts in geography? The very use of the word 'concept' invites confusion, but it has been used up to now because it is part of the language of teaching geography. It is my intention to outline a list that has the same function as the CASE reasoning patterns, that would encourage teachers to identify the connections between topics and between the subject and pupils' experiences. The concepts could be expected to have nested beneath them a number of mental models, which constitute the group or class of things the concept represents. One can always argue about such lists. However, many geographers would probably find a fair level of agreement. The most critical point in such a list is not its exactitude but having the list and working with it. The ultimate validity of the list is whether it includes the type of reasoning used by those pupils who are really successful in the subject. The list in Table 10.1 is tentative and those requiring further detail should consult Leat (1998).

*Table 10.1* Major concepts used in Thinking Through Geography

| Cause and effect | Decision-making |
| --- | --- |
| Planning | Systems |
| Development | Classification |
| Inequality | Location |

Planning will be taken as an example. Geography deals with many contexts in which planning is invoked. Planning can be defined here as human activity which deals with future goals or desired states where resources cannot meet all the wants of all interested parties. From the research by the TTG group with pupils thus far, it is evident that there are a number of important threads to be considered:

- planning in human contexts can be undertaken at a variety of scales, the range of which can be represented by the individual or household unit, the community or at government level;
- planning can be for the short, medium or long term – long-term planning tends to be undertaken more by government;
- a plan needs to take account of the context or environment in which it will operate;
- accurate prediction of future environmental conditions is important to good planning;
- plans are inevitably made up of parts, but these parts need to make a coherent whole;
- plans are limited by available resources;
- plans create conflicts which have to be resolved – power generally determines the manner in which the conflict is resolved and there are common strategies for sorting out the detail, such as zoning, replacement of losses, amelioration, monetary compensation (buying off) and sharing by time allocation;
- plans are only as good as their implementation.

Within these threads, different levels of understanding are possible. Lower-achieving pupils tend to consider only one scale and find creating plans for the longer term difficult. Lower-achieving pupils tend to take far less account of context when they draw up a plan and they are less successful at integrating parts into coherent wholes. Lower-achieving pupils are less perceptive of potential conflicts and tend to solve them in a cruder fashion. Higher-achieving pupils tend to be able to do the opposites. To put this another way, which links back to David Wood's work, higher-achieving pupils see configurations or patterns which allow them to attend to more information at once, because they have more available space in their working memory. However, once a pupil has added another piece of pattern to their long-term memory, they are adding power to their information-processing capacity. Thus if a pupil understands that planning features can be classified by their time scale, they can use this to impose order on information in new contexts in the future and make predictions from this basis. Alternatively one can conceptualize superior performance as having more powerful mental models.

It is important to make clear that the primary intention is not to teach pupils reasoning patterns. One is not saying 'Here is a way that you can successfully tackle all problems – learn it.' Nor is it the position that pupils are left to discover all thinking patterns for themselves. The indicated path lies somewhere in between. Pupils are encouraged to work things out for themselves. They are encouraged to share in whole-class discussion of their strategies and solutions, such that good thinking is made available to all, but they are not forced to adopt it as 'the method'. Furthermore, to extend and refine their thinking they need to be given new problems which challenge them, problems which cannot be solved effectively without reaching beyond their current levels of mental activity. Furthermore, if they struggle they may be given just enough help to get them moving again, which accords with Wood and Wood's (1996) notion of 'contingent teaching'. A further crucial role of the teacher is to give the pupils words to describe the reasoning that they used. With a language, thinking and talking about thinking is facilitated.

Teaching geography should encourage students to develop configurations derived from typical situations in geography. They would thus have templates through which to interpret more of the information that bombards them and be better able to plan and think ahead. The example of the Avery Hill GCSE syllabus for examination in 2000 graphically illustrates the point. The syllabus sets out to build on the foundation laid in earlier key stages through a number of features. Six are listed (seven for Wales). The first is 'reinforcing key concepts at increasing levels of generalization and abstraction'. The fourth is 'promoting a further development of skills and techniques appropriate to the developing cognitive abilities of the students' and the fifth is 'encouraging the use of a wide and appropriate range of learning/teaching strategies'. If one proceeds to the syllabus content, the central importance of key concepts is evident just below the surface (see Table 10.2). The key questions have been examined to determine how often an understanding of a 'big' concept underpins those questions. Classifying in such a way is an imprecise science, but Table 10.2 indicates the extent to which such concepts saturate a syllabus which is built around ideas, principles or questions.

*Table 10.2* Analysis of the presence of 'big' concepts in the Avery Hill GCSE syllabus

| Concept | Climate, the Environment and People | Water, Landforms and People | People and Place | People, Work and Environment |
|---|---|---|---|---|
| Classification | 6 | 2 | 7 | 0 |
| Planning | 2 | 8 | 3 | 1 |
| Decision-making | 0 | 1 | 2 | 1 |
| Cause and effect | 8 | 8 | 15 | 5 |
| Development | 2 | 0 | 4 | 1 |
| Inequality | 0 | 0 | 7 | 2 |
| Systems | 5 | 2 | 1 | 4 |
| Location | 0 | 1 | 3 | 0 |

One can begin to conceive of a whole curriculum which is mapped out in terms of the important concepts/reasoning patterns and information processing skills that are essential to being a good learner and then mapping subjects onto that framework. CASE represents important reasoning patterns in science, which are also highly relevant to mathematics. Nichol (1998) has listed seven structural concepts that are fundamental to history: *cause, continuity, change, consequence, chronology, situation* and *evidence*. Furthermore, he recognizes headings (taken from *Somerset Thinking Skills Course*, Blagg *et al.*, 1988) that encompass cognitive strategies that are important in thinking historically: *Gathering and Organizing, Recognizing and Defining, Generating, Planning, Monitoring and Checking, Evaluating, Transferring and Generalizing, Communicating*.

Feuerstein *et al.*'s (1980) intervention programme Instrumental Enrichment (IE) provides one of the best starting points for considering important cognitive skills which underpin achievement. IE starts from the premise that most underachieving pupils have suffered from a lack of quality interaction (mediation) with adults or older siblings. Ability is not regarded as an innate factor and thinking is seen as a set of cultural artefacts that are passed on from one generation to another through the process of mediation. IE aims therefore to remedy deficiencies in cognitive functions through a programme of instruments. Table 10.3 is an adaptation of IE's cognitive functions (Feuerstein *et al.*, 1980) to illustrate the skills that geography might seek to develop in pupils.

## Conclusion: What are the implications for teachers' thinking and practice of recognizing 'big' concepts and skills?

Black and Dockrell (1980) investigated the intended learning outcomes of Scottish teachers, including geographers. Their analysis, across subjects, identified three different levels of intended outcomes: *Modular, Longitudinal* and *Background*. Modular outcomes relate to the content of the unit or module being taught. In geography this might be knowing the characteristics of a waterfall and how it is formed, or knowing the difference between primary, secondary and tertiary occupations. These outcomes are assessed within the module and any remedial work needs to be done within the unit, because the content is not revisited. Longitudinal objectives can be taught, assessed and remediated across a number of units, because they are not tied to any particular content. Longitudinal objectives are more likely to relate to skills and values, such as the ability to draw and interpret line graphs, the ability to make an oral presentation or an understanding of how decisions are made. Background outcomes are more elusive. Black and Dockrell found that they were ultimately regarded by teachers as the most important to an understanding of the subject, but they were very rarely made explicit or taught. In theory they could be included in any module. An example would be a critical approach to the analysis of data. Big concepts and skills are longitudinal and background learning outcomes; they are the most important learning outcomes in the subject. Schemes of work are most commonly constructed with modular objectives as the framework, although some highlight key ideas which have a

Table 10.3 Cognitive skills to teach in geography (adapted from Feuerstein's IE cognitive functions)

*Taking information in*
1. Using all the senses, but especially looking and listening, to gather clear and complete information.
2. Using a plan or system so that we do not miss something or waste effort.
3. Giving a name to the things that we gather through our senses.
4. Recognizing where and when things are in space and time.
5. Recognizing as many characteristics of a thing or event as possible.
6. Using previous knowledge to make sense of the information.

*Using information once it has been gathered*
7. Making sure that you know what to do.
8. Sorting the relevant information from the irrelevant.
9. Use what you already know.
10. Making a plan of steps needed to do the task.
11. Looking for relationships that link together separate things, events and experiences.
12. Identifying the values or assumptions one is using.
13. Deciding on the class or set to which the new object or experience belongs (classifying).
14. Generating different possibilities, plans or solutions and evaluating them.
15. Checking the parts against the whole and the whole against the parts.
16. Using logic and evidence to prove things and defend your position.

*Communicating the results of your thinking*
17. Being clear and specific in your language.
18. Think of the audience, put yourself in their shoes.
19. Preparing and rehearsing answers.
20. Take account of what others have said or written.
21. Use all your thinking to support your expression, e.g. draw on mental images, examples, analogies.

broader relevance. Few popular textbooks at Key Stages 3 and 4 do much to emphasize connections between topics or ideas and skills that underpin the subject.

A further advantage of recognizing the importance of big concepts and skills is that it may encourage better assessment practice. Within the current context of target-setting there is a strong incentive to re-examine assessment practice so that it supports learning. The recent review by Black and Wiliam (1998) of classroom assessment demonstrates forcibly that improved practice can raise standards. Sadly the review also demonstrates that teachers' practice is weak:

(a) teachers' tests encourage rote learning; the questions and tasks set are not discussed between teachers and not critically assessed in relation to what they actually assess; and there is a tendency to emphasize quantity and presentation of work and to neglect its quality in relation to learning.
(b) the giving of marks is overemphasized, with useful advice to inform learning largely absent; pupils are compared with one another in a normative

fashion with the result that low achievers learn that they lack ability, rather than learning what they need to improve.

Above all, learning needs to be made more visible to pupils in classrooms. This does require a substantial shift in pedagogy, which in turn requires a reorientation in initial and in-service training.

## Questions

1   If you accept the assumption that the great majority of geography lessons are underpinned by a 'big' concept, or important cognitive skill, can you identify them in your lessons?
2   What does progression look like in 'big' concepts?
3   What mental models do pupils need to help them understand geography more effectively and how do we help them develop these models?
4   How can we assess in a way that will encourage pupils to make connections and become better learners?

## References

Adey, P., Shayer, M. and Yates, C. (1989) *Thinking Science*, London: Macmillan.
Askew, M., Rhodes, V., Brown, M., Johnson, D. and Wiliam, D. (1997) *Effective Teachers of Numeracy: Final Report to the Teacher Training Agency*, London: King's College.
Battersby, J., Webster, A. and Younger, M. (1993) *The Case Study in GCSE Geography: Experiences from the Avery Hill Project*, Cardiff: Welsh Joint Examination Committee.
Black, H. and Dockrell, W. (1980) *Diagnostic Assessment in Geography – A Teacher's Handbook*, Edinburgh: Scottish Council for Research in Education.
Black, P. and Wiliam, D. (1998) 'Assessment and classroom learning', *Assessment in Education*, 5,
Blagg, N., Ballinger, M. and Gardner, R. (1988) *Somerset Thinking Skills Course*, Oxford: Blackwell.
Bloom, B.S. (1976) *Human Characteristics and Student Learning*, New York: McGraw-Hill.
Candy, P., Crebert, G. and O'Leary, J. (1994) *Developing Lifelong Learners Through Undergraduate Employment*, Commissioned Report No. 28, National Board of Employment Education and Training, Canberra: Government Publishing Service.
Chi, M., Glaser, R. and Rees, E. (1982) 'Experience and problem solving', in Sternberg, R.J. (ed.) *Advances in the Psychology of Human Intelligence*, Volume 1, Hillsdale, NJ: Lawrence Erlbaum Associates.
Department for Education and Employment (1995) *Geography in the National Curriculum*, London: HMSO.
Feuerstein, R., Rand, Y., Hoffman, M. and Miller, R. (1980) *Instrumental Enrichment: An Intervention for Cognitive Modifiability*, Baltimore, MD: University Park Press.
Flavell, J. (1976) 'Metacognitive aspects of problem solving', in Resnick, L., *The Nature of Intelligence*, Hillsdale, NJ: Lawrence Erlbaum Associates.
Halford, G.S. (1993) *Children's Understanding: The Development of Mental Models*, Hillsdale, NJ: Lawrence Erlbaum Associates.
Hatano, G. and Inagaki, K. (1992) 'Desituating cognition through the construction of

conceptual knowledge', in Light, P. and Butterworth, G. (eds) *Context and Cognition*, Hemel Hempstead: Harvester Wheatsheaf.

Leat, D. (1997) 'Getting ambiguous', *Educating Able Children*, 1: 17–25.

Leat, D. (ed.) (1998) *Thinking Through Geography*, Cambridge: Chris Kington.

Medwell, J., Wray, D., Fox, R. and Poulson, L. (1998) *Effective Teachers of Literacy – Final Report to the Teacher Training Agency*, Exeter: University College of St Mark and St John and the University of Exeter.

Miller, G. (1956) 'The magical number seven plus or minus two. Some limits on our capacity for processing information', *Psychological Review*, 63: 81–97.

Newton, D. (1995) 'Causal situations in science: a model for supporting understanding', *Learning and Instruction*, 6, 3: 201–17.

Nichol, J. (1998) 'Thinking skills and children learning history', in Burden, R. and Williams, M. (eds) *Thinking Through the Curriculum*, London: Routledge.

Pascal, C. and Bertram, A. (1997) 'A curriculum for lifelong learning', SCAA Invitational Conference, London, 9–10 June, pp. 65–9.

Pollard, A. (1997) 'The basics and an eagerness to learn: a new curriculum for primary schooling', SCAA Invitational Conference, London, 9–10 June.

Roberts, M. (1997) 'Reconstructing the geography National Curriculum', in Helsby, G. and McCulloch, G. (eds) *Teachers and the National Curriculum*, London: Cassell.

SCAA (1996) *Key Stage 3 Optional Tests and Tasks: Geography Unit 2*, London: SCAA.

Wood, D. (1988) *How Children Think and Learn*, Oxford: Blackwell.

Wood, D. and Wood, H. (1996) 'Vygotsky, tutoring and learning', *Oxford Review of Education*, 22: 5–16.

# 11  Learn to debrief

*David Leat and David Kinninment*

This chapter started life with the title 'Learning to debrief'. It was meant to imply that here was something that you could do as a teacher of Key Stage 2, 3, 4 or post-16 geography, because it is not widely practised and might hold advantages for pupils' learning, especially where used with teaching thinking strategies (Leat, 1998). The title has become shorter and more imperative because it has become apparent in the work described here that debriefing is critical if teaching is to deliver outcomes related to autonomous learning and regain some of its lost shine. To be provocative – many lessons in geography and other subjects are parodies of what learning should look like: they are more concerned with teaching than learning. At worst they are exercises in control, where the teacher asks a rapid succession of closed and pseudo-open questions, in the name of checking for understanding, and pupils tackle low-level tasks which require the transferring of information from textbook to exercise book with very little thought. Homework is given and the bell goes. Ask yourself if this contributes much to the development of autonomous learners.

Compare this to the draft aims for the school curriculum prepared by the Qualifications and Curriculum Authority (QCA), which include:

- develop pupils' enjoyment of, and appetite for, and commitment to learning and achievement;
- equip pupils with . . . the skills to enquire and make connections across areas of learning;
- build on pupils' strengths and interests, and develop their confidence in their capacity to learn and work independently and collaboratively;
- enable pupils to think creatively and critically, to solve problems and to make a difference for the better.

In geography teaching, ten minutes of rambling introduction, interspersed with recall questions, followed by 30 minutes of tasks from a double-page spread and the setting of a homework does not come all that close to realizing those lofty learning ambitions. All of the preceding bullet points imply some role for the concepts of metacognition (Flavell, 1976; Nisbett and Shucksmith, 1986), which may broadly be understood as thinking about thinking, and transfer. Mayer and Wittrock (1996:

48) define transfer as 'when a person's prior experience and knowledge affect learning or problem solving in a new situation'. They recount four views of transfer: general transfer of general skill, specific transfer of specific behaviour, specific transfer of general skill and metacognitive control of general and specific skills. It is the last that they represent as the most promising, as it combines features of the other three. Thus Mayer and Wittrock argue that transfer is enhanced when students have learned general and specific processes or skills and the ability to select and monitor them. Furthermore they propose, on the basis of research evidence, that effective instruction ensures that students select relevant information, build internal connections between the information and develop external connections to other contexts and subject matter. They report a range of studies in which metacognitive ability has been linked with better performance.

There is evidence that teaching thinking/cognitive acceleration programmes can raise achievement. The strongest evidence for this effect in Britain comes from the CASE (Cognitive Acceleration through Science Education) project, although good evidence in relation to programmes such as Instrumental Enrichment and Philosophy for Children is available from other economically developed countries (Adey and Shayer, 1994). In the whole-class setting, pupils are asked to reflect on their thinking processes (as well as their answers) – to employ metacognition. A conscious effort is also made by the teacher to connect the new thinking to other contexts, so that the learning may be generalized and transferred by the pupil. This is the debriefing process.

The White Paper *Excellence in Schools* (DfEE, 1997) gave some prominence to teaching thinking;

> In particular, we want to see more examples of:
> - accelerated learning, based on the latest understanding of how people learn, which has enabled groups of pupils to progress at greater speed and with deeper understanding
> - the systematic teaching of thinking skills, which research has shown to be strongly associated with positive learning outcomes.

With strong current interest in thinking skills as a medium for addressing issues such as raising attainment, boys' underachievement and disaffection, there is a clear need to be able to describe the pedagogy and support its implementation. The research which forms the basis of this chapter was conducted by four teachers with the support of a PGCE tutor. All are members of the Thinking Through Geography (TTG – see Leat, 1998) group. The teachers made visits to observe one another conduct debriefing episodes, which were video recorded. Before leaving, the visiting teacher interviewed a small group of pupils, asking two core questions 'What did you learn in that lesson?' and 'What did the teacher do that helped you?' Analysis included transcribing and coding the debriefing episodes and the pupil interviews, and collective discussion between the teachers (in some cases stimulated by the video) of how lessons had been planned and delivered.

## What does debriefing look like in the geography classroom?

The analysis of the debriefing episodes shows two major distinguishing features – there are a large number of open questions and pupils give extended responses. This is in marked contrast to the pattern of talk in most lessons (Edwards and Westgate, 1987). Classroom talk is generally characterized by the I–R–E pattern (Sinclair and Coulthard, 1992): the teacher initiates, usually with a question (I), a pupil responds (R) and the teacher evaluates (E) before going on to ask another question. It is extremely common at the beginning of a lesson when the rationale is to rehearse the content of previous lessons and at the end of the lesson to check for understanding.

The debriefing episodes qualify rather than entirely overthrow this pattern. First, it is unusual for classroom talk to be dominated by open questions. Second, it is highly unusual for pupils to give extended responses, which in some circumstances go on for more than half a minute, often encouraged by the teacher saying 'go on'. It is far more common for pupils to speak for an average of two seconds only, at which point the teacher will cut in and either finish the answer or rephrase it.

However, delving below these surface characteristics there are other critical features:

- there are instances in all but one of the lessons of the teacher asking a pupil to justify their answer or reasoning (see the teacher's emphasis on 'why' in the dialogue that follows);
- in three of the lessons the teacher asks the pupils to reflect on or think about how they have done a task, prior to asking them for their inputs – thus they are given 'think' time;
- in two of the lessons the I–R–E pattern does break down as pupils respond spontaneously to other pupils' contributions – they initiate;
- in all but one of the lessons there are some references to cognitive or social skills, such as active listening, planning and comparing (see the last part of the dialogue, comparing Andrew and Craig);
- in all lessons the teacher makes at least one reference to other contexts and in one episode alone there are six.

Although they are either not numerous in frequency or present in only a minority of lessons, some features may be significant to the whole character of debriefing episodes. These include teachers' use of analogy and story, their reference to 'big' concepts, teachers asking pupils for transfer contexts, teachers referring to exemplary (overheard) comments or thinking. A final interesting feature, present in some of the lessons, is the teacher offering criteria to pupils by which thinking or work may be judged and expecting them to use these criteria (see the last part of the dialogue). In other words there is a critical quality to the discussion and although opinions and views are respected and valued, it is not a case of 'anything goes'. It is worth shouting loudly that these episodes are highly unusual in comparison to most classrooms. The videos of some of these lessons have been shown in many INSET sessions and one adviser/OFSTED inspector has commented that he has never seen those dimensions in whole-class discussion.

To help provide a more concrete picture of these generalizations in the classroom context, there follows some transcript of a debriefing episode from Lesson 7 in the sample of researched lessons. The class is a mixed ability Year 10 GCSE group in a school with a disadvantaged catchment in Northumberland. The topic is hurricanes and the lesson has two foci – the different effects of hurricanes on different places and the skills of comparing. The teacher has a specific concern that in GCSE examinations pupils often fail when asked to compare, and lose marks unnecessarily. The pupils have been doing a mystery (a card-sorting activity in which all the data to answer an open question is provided on slips of paper – see Leat, 1998) in which they have to investigate the nature and causes of the impacts of Hurricane Hugo on three areas – Puerto Rico, a coastal settlement in the USA, and a settlement further inland. (Some pupil answers are inaudible on the videotape.)

| | |
|---|---|
| **Teacher:** | OK, can I have your attention? Why does the same hurricane affect different people in different places in different ways? |
| **Female pupil:** | Because of proximity to the coast? |
| **Teacher:** | OK. Proximity to the coast. What does the word proximity mean again? |
| | Pupil responds. |
| **Teacher:** | How close it is to the sea. (Looking expectantly around the class) Why? . . . Why? |
| **Female pupil:** | Gives a whole sentence answer about the damage caused. |
| **Teacher:** | But the question was 'why?' |
| **Same female pupil:** | Because tropical storms get their energy from the ocean. |
| **Teacher:** | Because tropical storms get their energy from the sea. So how close it is to the sea is important. What about . . . give me another reason. |
| **Male pupil:** | How developed the country is. |
| **Teacher:** | How developed the country is. (Gesticulates with his hands to encourage the pupil, Andrew, to go on). |
| **Andrew:** | Because if it is an ELDC . . . |
| **Teacher:** | Sorry, you are baffling us with jargon . . . ELDC? What do you mean? |
| **Andrew:** | An economically less developed country. Because an ELDC has got less resources and money to repair the damage than an economically more developed country. |
| **Teacher:** | He just did a bit of good comparative work there. He compared an ELDC with an EMDC. Have a think about what he said . . . Craig of course didn't hear him (said unaggressively). |
| **Craig:** | I did. |
| **Teacher:** | Why was it good then, Craig? |
| **Craig:** | Because ELDC countries haven't got as good defences. |

| Teacher: | His (Andrew's) explanation was much better than Craig's. He did a good bit of comparative work. Don't go all huffy on me now, Craig (teacher smiles). |
| --- | --- |
| Teacher: | What do you think he (Andrew) did? Oh good another hand up. Emma? |
| Emma: | (inaudible, but gives a couple of sentences of explanation). |
| Teacher: | Ah! She wasn't doing too well there until she added something . . . that Andrew did. |
| Male pupil: | (mainly inaudible but finishes with) then said something about the developed country. |
| Teacher: | Yes, she looked at both types of country. |

This slice of debriefing comes after the first activity related to the mystery and concentrates on getting pupils to develop their skills in comparing in the context of the effects of hurricanes. There is a strong emphasis on pushing pupils to focus on what constitutes a good explanation, through getting them to critique each other's efforts. The second episode of debriefing near the end of the lesson gets them to expose the methods they have used to organize their information to make a comparison between the effects of the hurricane on contrasting areas. One group has just drawn three columns, two others have developed a matrix with column (places) and row (characteristics) headings, while a group of four girls have used a Venn diagram with three overlapping circles.

## What helped pupils learn from debriefing?

The previous section provided a general profile of observable features of debriefing episodes. This section concentrates on the effect that this has on pupils' learning. Analysis of the transcripts of pupil interviews has identified the following headings that begin to describe what the study teachers were doing that helped pupils learn. They may be considered as roles that the teachers perform. This analysis begins to provide a descriptive language for debriefing, through which professional practice can be developed. It is not to be expected that everything that pupils learn from debriefed lessons will be as a result of debriefing.

Brief details of the lessons are given below to provide some contextualization:

In Lesson 1 the Year 9 pupils have been doing a mystery concerning the death, apparently suicide, of a Lake District farmer whose personal life and financial circumstances have become severely strained.

In Lesson 2, a Year 10 class have done a Fact or Opinion exercise (see Leat, 1998) on Chinese population policies.

In Lesson 3, a Year 8 class have been doing a task in which they have been asked to devise possible methods of resolving conflicts if we had the power to control the weather, because different people would want different types of weather.

In Lesson 4, the focus has been on developing strategies for active listening with a Year 8 class, which pupils have identified after an activity in which they record the words of a song with a strong geographical relevance.

Lesson 5 has a focus on enquiry, encouraging Year 8 pupils to formulate questions about Japan.

In Lesson 6 a Year 7 class have been asked to select from a list what they would take on a trip to the Antarctic.

Lesson 7, described earlier, focuses on comparing the effects of Hurricane Hugo with a Year 10 class, also using a mystery.

In Lesson 8 with a Y7 class the focus is also on formulating questions, with an emphasis on what makes a good question.

### Collating ideas

In the debriefing process the teacher draws in a range of ideas which pupils have developed or strategies that they have used in tackling tasks so that they are available for all to consider.

*Lesson 4*

| | |
|---|---|
| **Teacher:** | When Miss J was talking about it, particularly at the end, did that help? |
| **Pupils:** | Yeah. |
| **Teacher:** | In what way? |
| **Female pupil:** | It showed you like more ways to be listening . . . and remember things. |
| **Teacher:** | Did you learn anything from other people? |
| **Male pupil:** | Like different stuff to do. |
| **Teacher:** | Different stuff to do. Like what, what? |
| **Male pupil:** | Like learning that we could symbolize? |
| **Teacher:** | . . . What was the word that was used? |
| **Male pupil:** | Abbreviated. |

*Lesson 5*

| | |
|---|---|
| **Female pupil:** | She was making us look at other people's work to understand, to see what they were writing about. |

### Promoting and managing discussion

Pupils made many references to the value of discussion, both in small groups and in the whole-class debriefing episodes. Pupils are at times explicit and adamant about the value of such talk. It is evident that both talking and listening are components of learning through talk. Wells (1989) has emphasized that 'all knowledge has to be actively constructed by the individual knower' and there is evidence in the following extracts to suggest that knowledge is being constructed through talk in these lessons.

*Lesson 1*

| | |
|---|---|
| **Male pupil:** | You can learn things from other people in the class. |
| **Female pupil:** | By listening. |
| **Teacher:** | You're sure about that? |
| **Female pupil:** | Yeah, you might not have heard it from that viewpoint. |
| **Second female pupil:** | Different points of view. |
| **First female pupil:** | Yeah. 'Cos someone may say something 'cos their father's a farmer or something like that and so you've got like an insight and you show it to the rest of the class. |
| **Third female pupil:** | What's good is like when other people put up like arguments you can see everyone's different point of view. |

*Lesson 3*

| | |
|---|---|
| **Female pupil:** | It's better to have someone else's opinion. |
| **Teacher:** | Why? I don't think that you are wrong. I want to know why? |
| **Female pupil:** | Because you can put your ideas and their ideas together and make it like better. |
| **Teacher:** | Why is it important to talk about your ideas? If you and I sat down now and talked about our opinions or some of our ideas, why is that better than you deciding on your own? |
| **Female pupil:** | You can find out better ideas than you had and make them better . . . and make them more exciting and more serious. |

*Lesson 6*

| | |
|---|---|
| **Teacher:** | So do you like saying your ideas? |
| **Chorus:** | Yeah. |
| **Teacher:** | So why do you think Miss E was getting you to talk about things? |
| **Male pupil:** | So you can mix ideas. |
| **Teacher:** | So do you think that is important? |
| **Male pupil:** | Yes. Because people might have better ideas than you've got. |

Thus while these pupils recognize the value of small group and whole-class discussion, they recognize that it is not just a matter of copying other people's ideas, it is the interaction between personal, original ideas and others' ideas that accelerates thinking. However, there was one occasion when a less positive view on discussion was made known.

*Lesson 5*

| | |
|---|---|
| **Teacher:** | Do you prefer that (discussion) to working by yourselves? |
| **Male pupil:** | I'd rather work by meself. |
| **Second male pupil:** | So would I. |

*Providing feedback*

A particular feature of discussion is the extent to which it provides feedback to individuals, on their thoughts and explanations. Though one might not immediately associate this feedback with a form of assessment, it can be argued that it is fulfilling the formative function of assessment that is so important in informing learning. Black and Wiliam's (1998) recent review article provides compelling evidence of the power of such feedback in raising attainment.

*Lesson 7*

| | |
|---|---|
| **Teacher:** | How did your teacher help you? What did he do that made you learn? |
| **Female pupil:** | He tried to make everyone make a comparison. |
| **Male pupil:** | . . . He was like getting one person to have a go and he was trying to get them to . . . |
| **Female pupil:** | To improve it. |
| **Teacher:** | How does he get them to improve it? |
| **Male pupil:** | Telling them that they were talking about one thing not both things. |
| **Teacher:** | He was trying to get you to put two things in one sentence. What else? |
| **Female pupil:** | How they were the same or different. |

Later in the same interview the pupils explain that the feedback can come from other pupils and why the feedback process is so useful.

| | |
|---|---|
| **Teacher:** | So what was Mr K doing then? |
| **Female pupil:** | Trying to get us to answer . . . add points to it. |
| **Male pupil:** | The next time we do it what things to do, what things not to do. |
| **Teacher:** | So it was helpful getting you in the class to improve Craig's point? |
| **Pupils** (strongly): | Yeah. |

*Attending to groups and individuals to promote self-esteem*

The debriefing process is not a separate entity and some of the success depends on the attention the teacher gives to groups and individuals in the introduction, as they work on the substantive task, or in the debriefing itself. This care seems to have the function of persuading pupils that the purpose of the lesson is to encourage them to think and to share that thinking. It provides them with confidence. This confidence is connected to an understanding on the part of pupils that to a large extent it is their reasoning that is being valued, although it is not the case that 'anything goes'. A probable consequence of this is improved self-esteem, which is so implicated in achievement (Muijs, 1997). Furthermore, the importance of interpersonal relations between teachers and pupils has been highlighted by Brekelmans, Wubbels and Levy (1993) who have shown that the cooperation scales of the Questionnaire on Teacher Interaction (Wubbels, Créton and Hooymayers, 1990) are positively related to student attitude.

*Lesson 3*

**Female pupil**:  She lets you have time to think about it.
**Teacher**:         Why do you like that?
**Female pupil**:  . . . if you don't understand what she meant, well she goes through it in stages.
**Teacher**:         And you said that she lets you think about it. Do you like that, do you like having a couple of minutes to think?
**Female pupil**:  Say if she went right . . . if you think about something and here's the answer straight away, if you have time to work it out, you can try and suss it how to do it.

Dillon (1988) strongly advocates the use of pauses and silences to give pupils space and time to explore and elaborate ideas.

*Lesson 1*

**Female pupil**:              Miss R treats you like an adult, not like a pupil, she treats you like an equal.

(Later in interview)

**Female pupil**:              She makes sure that you understand, like she makes sure that everyone understands before she moves on.
**Male pupil**:                When you're not quite sure what you're doing she doesn't like bite your head off like other teachers do.
**Second female pupil**:  She makes you feel more confident about answering questions. Anything you say is right as long as you can explain it.

### Making pupils explain themselves

A distinctive feature of many of the lessons was the extent to which pupils were asked to expand on their first few words, to explain fully, to 'go on' or 'say a bit more'. Pupils report positively on this process. This characteristic stands in contrast to research on classroom discourse, which shows a normal pattern of pupils uttering only a few words before the teacher evaluates or completes the response (Edwards and Westgate, 1987).

*Lesson 3*

**Female pupil:**    Instead of just letting us write down anything, she asked us why we
             wrote it down, why we thought it was a good idea . . . instead of just
             writing it down and saying that's right, like you've got to have a
             reason for thinking that's right.
**Teacher:**       Why is it important to have a reason for it?
**Female pupil:**    'Cos if you didn't have a reason why do you put it down?

(Later in the same interview)

**Male pupil:**      . . . when we had the vote for it, she asked us what we meant.
**Teacher:**       So again she asked you what you meant. So why did you find that
             useful? Why did you think that was a good way of doing it?
**Male pupil:**      Because you understand what you meant.
**Teacher:**       . . . so which bit, the writing down or the saying to someone?
**Male pupil:**      Saying it.
**Female pupil:**    . . . even if other people don't understand what we say and if she
             doesn't understand she'll just keep asking and asking what we mean
             and why we mean that.
**Teacher:**       So rather than give you the answer, she keeps saying 'Go on tell me
             more'.
**Female pupil:**    You get a better idea of what you are talking about in your mind.
**Male pupil:**      It's making you learn.

*Lesson 1*

**Female pupil:**    The good thing is, Miss R gets you to explain why you said it so you
             don't just think 'Oh, I'll put that in there'.

### Making connections

This is potentially one of the most powerful effects of debriefing, because it is the
foundation of helping pupils to transfer (Perkins and Salomon, 1988). The teachers
in some lessons are offering analogies or parallels in the context of pupils' everyday
lives which help them understand the geographical content and use that understanding elsewhere. For some pupils this is very successful and helps them make
sense of the content. This encourages the pupils to make their own connections.

*Lesson 7*

**Teacher:**       Is that the only way he got you to learn about comparisons?
**Female pupil:**    That question on the board . . . the jeans.

The lesson has been about comparing the effect of hurricanes and in the debriefing
process he generates a discussion about how pupils use comparing in the process of
buying a pair of jeans.

*Lesson 2*

| | |
|---|---|
| **Teacher:** | . . . anything else he tried to do? |
| **Female pupil:** | He gave examples. |
| **Teacher:** | Can you expand on that? What sort of examples? |
| **Female pupils:** | Like Newcastle United and the Spice Girls. |

In this case these two examples are used to show that opinions differ about these popular icons and that opinions may differ from factual statements. This connection is used to illuminate the difference between fact and shades of opinion in China on population policy.

*Lesson 1*

| | |
|---|---|
| **Female pupil:** | I know it sounds horrible but she's young, she does really try to connect with us, but she does. |
| **Second female pupil:** | That was another good thing. We were doing fair trade and she brought in fair trade chocolate and coffee. |

### Providing heuristics and alternative representations

A heuristic is a general problem-solving strategy. Strategies such as 5W (using Who, What, Where, Why and When as stems for questions in the process of enquiry), Fact or Opinion and Venn Diagrams are offered during lessons and to varying extents pupils recognize them as generic strategies that can be used in many other contexts. For some pupils, moreover, diagrams, which are constructed during the debrief, act as alternative representations for remembering and understanding. Drawings and diagrams are mentioned by Cooper and McIntyre (1996) as two of the strategies favoured by pupils for helping them to learn.

*Lesson 8*

| | |
|---|---|
| **Teacher:** | It was interesting what you said about the questions, do you want to add to that at all? |
| **Male pupil:** | . . . Use the 5Ws . . . It helped you know what sort of questions. |

*Lesson 5*

| | |
|---|---|
| **Teacher:** | In what way did she help you find more information? |
| **Female pupil:** | Like 5Ws. Some people didn't know about them. |

*Lesson 2*

| | |
|---|---|
| **Teacher:** | Anything else? |
| **Female pupil:** | The way he put diagrams on the board. |
| **Teacher:** | What sort of diagrams were you thinking of? |

**Female pupil:**   The lines for . . . like a fact line and an opinion line.
**Teacher:**   Do you think that helped you? Can you tell me a little bit more about how that helped you?
**Female pupil:**   So you know that a fact can be like probably true or can be in the middle.

Pupils had been given a range of statements on the population issue in China. They have been asked to classify them as fact or opinion. This led them to conclude that there are shades of opinion and degrees of proof in relation to facts. They had been offered two lines on which to place their statements. One had poles of definite fact and possible fact and the other of reasonable opinion and unreasonable opinion.

(Later in the interview)
**Female pupil:**   . . . on some of the exam questions, it was like the diagrams that he put on the board, it was like if you tried to picture them, then you could answer the questions.

In distinguishing between seven different roles performed by teachers which contribute to debriefing, one is inevitably atomizing a complex behaviour. Some of these roles overlap and it would be difficult to perform one without others. The feedback and collating of ideas could not easily take place without the discussion. Pupils explaining themselves would not be productive without the underwriting from the positive relationships with the teacher that makes them feel that their opinion is valued and their learning important.

## How to plan for debriefing?

This is a difficult question to answer because debriefing is so bound up in an approach to teaching that separating it out is problematic. It is necessary also to distinguish between planning that takes place on different time scales. All of the teachers in the project have beliefs about geography teaching that lead them to think about the outcomes of teaching thinking activities that pupils will benefit from talking about. Those in the TTG group usually plan to be explicit about concepts such as cause and effect, planning and decision-making and skills such as active listening, classifying, sequencing and checking whole and parts against each other. Thus some of their planning is long-term and underpins their whole approach to teaching. They are continually experimenting with the debriefing process. However, they also plan some elements of the debriefing of individual lessons.

Finally, some of the planning is interactive, as it is a response to what pupils say in the lesson. In the *Effective Teachers of Numeracy* report (Askew *et al.*, 1997) a model is presented of the interactions between teachers' beliefs, their subject and teaching knowledge, their classroom practices and pupil responses. It is suggested that effective teachers of numeracy work actively with pupils' explanations of the methods they have used, both refining them and drawing attention to differences in reasoning and methods. Thus listening to pupils' strategies and reasoning both help the effective numeracy teachers to understand good thinking and influence how they respond and proceed in whole-class discussions. This evidence lends credibility to the proposition that planning for debriefing is highly responsive to events in the classroom. Pupil explanations and strategies are not routinely judged by their closeness of fit to the teachers' template, but are judged on their merits as cognitive tools which can be shared. This requires considerable attention to listening to and watching pupils and skilled decisions about how to respond. Some new ideas are generated as the teacher is listening to or watching pupils. The consequence of this multi-layered approach is that planning for debriefing (Figure 11.1) becomes more complex over time. This chapter aims to encourage readers with practical pointers, but it needs to be recognized that one's thinking and practice will change over time.

Debriefing is only likely to be appropriate and successful if the pupils have done a stimulating and challenging task – one which has made them think hard and draw on mental strategies that they can see are personal. Group tasks are infinitely beter than individual tasks, because pupils will encourage and support each other in talking and thinking. Debriefing is unlikely to be successful following a simple comprehension activity based on a textbook. One needs a range of strategies to make lessons into rich learning experiences. Furthermore it is useful to distinguish between three intentions in debriefing:

(a) getting pupils to give their answers/solutions and the reasons and skills behind them, which helps;
(b) getting pupils to explain how they have done a task, both in terms of their individual cognitive processes and in terms of group processes and giving them a language for these processes;
(c) helping pupils see how these processes are or can be used elsewhere.

How to plan for debriefing will depend on what one's intentions are. Within the TTG group, there is a range of intentions. One teacher, for example, goes for very specific outcomes related to important skills in doing well at GCSE. This teacher is emphasizing intention (a) above. Another of the group feels that increasingly she does not have specific learning objectives for the debriefing episode and gives as evidence the extent to which the same teaching material can lead to very different discussions and points made by the pupils. Her global intention is to encourage pupils to become aware of what mental and cooperative strategies they were using in their work and then getting the pupils to analyse and evaluate them. In this way good thinking is shared. This teacher is highlighting intention (b). Despite this variance, planning will involve a decision about what concept or skill should be focused on in the debriefing. It is better not to have too many agendas in the debriefing. From here the issue becomes whether you are aiming to steer discussion in a particular direction to reach a predetermined outcome or genuinely wishing to explore and share the thinking of class members.

| Classroom activity (inc. content) | Concepts or skills focused on | Date: | Time: |
| --- | --- | --- | --- |
| | | Class information: | |

| | | Analogies/Examples to be used | Pupils' comments overheard | Used |
| --- | --- | --- | --- | --- |
| Focus<br>Whole group/Small group/Pairs/Individual | Briefing<br>Key features of task/launching | | | |
| Debriefing objectives:<br>For Pupils | | | | |
| For Self | | | | |
| Context:<br>Previous attempts | Debriefing<br>Debriefing questions:<br>Outcome = O<br>Interpersonal = I<br>Mental = M | Transfer contexts to be suggested | | |
| Class-related factors | | | | |
| Key words/terms/vocabulary: | | Follow up tasks/homework | | |

Figure 11.1 Planning for debriefing

It can be useful to have a number of questions, put on the board, an overhead projector or a large sheet of paper, which you give pupils three to five minutes to have a quick think about. This means that they have a chance to prepare their thoughts – they are not caught cold. These might include:

- What were your first ideas on this?
- What helped you do the task?
- Did you have any personal knowledge that helped with the task?
- Did you change your strategy or ideas as you worked?
- How would you do this differently if you did it again?
- Have you done anything like this in other subjects?

One would not pose all of these questions, two or three would be enough on any one occasion.

It is generally not productive to plan set sequences of questions. It is better to have stock questions which can be used as circumstances require. However, only practice can sensitize one to what question needs to be asked at what moment. For opening discussion, such questions/prompts might be:

- 'Let's hear someone's answer.'
- 'Debbie, what have you come up with?'
- 'What ideas have we got about this? Darren?'
- 'Remember the question/task was . . . What do you think?'

One develops a range of supplementary prompts and questions to encourage pupils to expand on their answers, such as:

- 'Go on.'
- 'Can you explain that in more detail?'
- 'Why do you think that?'
- 'Why?'

Alternatively, remembering not to interrupt, nodding, the use of hands to encourage continuation or other non-verbal communication can have the same effect.

One can also have a range of questions to help open up discussion:

- 'Everybody else agree?' or 'Anybody disagree?'
- 'Anybody do it differently?'
- 'Did he answer the question?'
- 'So we are all agreed that that is the best we can come up with?' This aims to provoke.
- 'What other ideas are there?'
- 'Kamal, I know you did something a bit different, can you tell everybody?'

Where more detailed planning is done, it tends to impede the debriefing because it makes it harder to respond to the flow of the discussion. The lessons need to be carefully planned, but it is important to retain the flexibility to respond to pupils' contributions. Hughes (1997) draws attention to this issue in a study of talk in early years classrooms, where she concludes that it is difficult for pupils to think aloud and explore ideas if pupils' questions are 'discouraged as an interruption to the pre-planned topic or squeezed out by teachers' over-dominant questions'. There is a balance to be achieved between teacher control of the overall discussion with allowing pupils enough space to make a significant contribution. Dillon (1988) gives a number of very valuable suggestions for helping teachers reform their approach to questioning.

One of the most important issues in the planning is developing analogies, stories, props, examples and likely contexts in pupils' lives that allow and encourage pupils to make connections between the outcomes of a lesson, in a bid both to encourage transfer and to present geography as a subject which can help pupils to make sense of the world as they experience it. So, for example, in one lesson which had a focus on planning as a cognitive skill, pupils were asked to consider how they planned what they would pack in their bags if they were going on holiday. In other lessons pupils have been asked to consider what 'things' influence decisions on where their family might go on a holiday or day-trip, which allows the introduction of the word 'factor', which gives an easy lead into other humanities subjects, for example What were the factors leading to the start of the English Civil War? Such contexts and representations make a substantial difference both to understanding and motivation. Mason (1994) summarizes some of the evidence relating to effectiveness of analogies in fostering understanding.

A bigger and longer-term issue is important here. If one is concerned about transfer and making connections to other subjects, then it opens a need to talk to other subject teachers about the use of reasoning and skills in their lessons. It can start an important dialogue about learning. Individual teachers within the TTG group have made important connections with teachers in science, English, history and art to explore wider issues in pupils' learning.

Finally on this point, try to make sure that the pupils see the point of the lesson. The analogies and transfer contexts are included to promote this, but do not feel shy about rounding up and summarizing the point of it all, although it is perhaps more powerful if the class can do it in their own words for each other. It is not vital that this be done at the beginning of the lesson as it can be very valuable to start with an element of intrigue.

It is vital that you protect time to conduct the debriefing, which may mean thinking very differently about the structure of lessons. You have to come to believe that the debriefing process is at least as important as the activity, that the learning processes are as important as the content. Without this belief there is no motivation to make it happen. Several teachers have commented on how difficult they find it to protect this time. One potential remedy to this is to start debriefing short activities which do not come at the end of the lesson.

Watching and listening to groups before the whole-class debriefing often provides important ingredients for this session. So, for example, if you overhear or have an interesting conversation with a group you can call on that group to contribute their thoughts. You may be able to 'seed' a particular contribution by prompting a group with subtle comments or questions which stimulate or nudge a particular line of reasoning. You can then draw on this investment in your debriefing. Pupils invariably respond very positively when you say 'I know that you three had an interesting approach.' It needs repeating that planning has to be interactive: teachers have global goals, but they should be sensitive to the thinking of pupils. To this end it is really very useful to write down some of what you hear or see. Do not routinely interrupt groups by approaching them with the words 'How are you getting on?' – it disrupts their thinking.

Over time you are better placed to observe groups, because you know how they might tackle a task. This allows you to plan for how you might offer them assistance if they get bogged down. This is another key component of diagnostic and formative assessment.

The most important thing to bear in mind as you start the session is that you want the best thinking to be shared. Therefore you have to keep asking pupils to respond to each other, to critique what has been said by others. However, this has to be done sensitively; it is not a competition to find the best, it is a collaboration.

One of the dilemmas you may face occurs when pupils' solutions or reasoning falls short of some predetermined notion that you have, despite all your best efforts to push them further. The question is whether you leave the pupils with the best solution or reasoning that they come up with or do you superimpose your own? There is a temptation and a tradition to do the latter because you are the 'font of wisdom and truth' as the teacher. Indeed this might be the right decision in the circumstances, because you are apprehensive about leaving them with a sub-optimal answer, especially if they are near exams. This is a decision based on modular intentions. If your intended outcomes really are longer-term and relate to developing their autonomy as thinkers and learners, then you might decide to settle for their solutions. The danger in suddenly introducing your answer, like pulling a rabbit from a hat, is that you undermine their willingness to participate. You have been offering them a different contract, their honest and hard thinking in return for your acceptance of and respect for their thinking. You are in danger of breaking the contract. There are three partial solutions to this dilemma:

- You can return to the same concept or reasoning pattern at a later date. Just get them to record their current solution for revisiting later.
- You can offer them criteria to judge whether their solutions and reasoning are robust. The easiest way of doing this is asking whether this solution would work in other similar contexts. For example, if pupils are coming up with ways of resolving conflicts between different interest groups in the Lake District National Park, you can ask whether the strategies would also work in a sports and leisure centre.

- You can press them hard by repeatedly asking such things as 'Have we answered the question?', 'Would that really work in reality?' or 'Has anybody else got a different answer?'

## Implications for professional development

The following are potentially powerful features of debriefing sessions:

- maintaining a high proportion of open questions which require the articulation of reasoning by pupils;
- encouraging pupils to extend and justify their answers, if necessary giving thinking time;
- encouraging pupils to evaluate each other's contributions to discussion;
- providing evaluative feedback to pupils, not necessarily in the form of 'that was good/not so good', but in terms of criteria that pupils can apply;
- using analogies, stories and everyday contexts to help pupils to understand the wider significance of their learning and encourage them to transfer it;
- drawing attention to the cognitive and social skills that the pupils have used and encouraging distillation of good practice in relation to these skills;
- relating thinking and learning described by pupils to the important concepts or reasoning pattern in subjects;
- drawing on what one has heard or seen during small-group work preceding the debriefing.

However, it must be reiterated that these features need to be built on in a climate that encourages trust and openness in discussion.

For PGCE students, NQTs and those still in the novice teacher stage, it is not easy to acquire these skills by learning from those around you because, with few exceptions, these skills are not routinely practised by serving teachers. This is a case where more recently qualified teachers may have to take a lead in practice development. In relation to professional development, the methodology outlined at the beginning of the chapter has much to recommend it that can be copied at departmental, school, authority or regional level. The important features include:

- be able to observe one another within a particular frame of concern and interest, in this case debriefing, which could well form part of an induction programme;
- the use of video for self-analysis, analysis of whole-class talk, stimulating discussion between colleagues and for dissemination;
- interviewing pupils about what they have learned, what has helped them to learn and whether particular lessons have been different in any respect;
- the time to plan, reflect and analyse which allows one to take thinking about professional practice on to another level and relate it to theoretical generalizations;

- working in a network, perhaps through the local education authority, or with a higher education institution, as equal partners, which provides support in terms of discussion and connections to broader issues;
- relating this professional development to your school development plan (perhaps even the LEA's Education Development Plan), because the issue relates strongly to raising attainment.

There is much more, of course, to be learned about debriefing, but a more pressing concern would seem to be finding ways of helping more teachers develop their practice in this important area, based on a body of research evidence. There are therefore a number of questions which might make useful points of departure for trainees, newly qualified teachers or those who want to extend and improve their professional practice at whatever stage of their career:

## Questions

1   Do your current teaching activities make your pupils think sufficiently so that you could ask them how they have tackled them?
2   If the answer is 'yes' (at least sometimes) do you have any insights into how they do them – what previous knowledge do they use, what cognitive and social strategies do they employ, are they impulsive or do they think things through? If the answer to Question 2 is 'no', you might try listening to and watching them as they work.
3   Assuming that you want to make a start on developing your debriefing skills, can you identify a good activity and a focus and can you identify in your planning the value and significance of the processes you think they will tell you about? Are you prepared to take the risk of creating risk and ambiguity in your classroom?
4   Is your department or school interested? There is something wrong if they are not.

## References

Adey, P. and Shayer, M. (1994) *Really Raising Standards*, London: Routledge.
Askew, M., Brown, M., Rhodes, V., Johnson, D. and Wiliam, D. (1997) *Effective Teachers of Numeracy*, London: Kings College.
Black, P. and Wiliam, D. (1998) 'Assessment and classroom learning', *Assessment in Education*, 5, 1 (special edition).
Brekelmans, M., Wubbels, T. and Levy, J. (1993) 'Student performance, attitudes, instructional strategies and teacher-communication style', in Wubbels, T. and Levy, J. (eds) *Do you Know What You Look Like? Interpersonal Relations in Education*, London: Falmer Press.
Cooper, P. and McIntyre, D. (1996) *Effective Teaching and Learning: Teachers' and Students' Perspectives*, Buckingham: Open University Press.
Department for Education and Employment (1997) *Excellence in Schools*, London: HMSO.

Dillon, J. (1988) *Questioning and Teaching: A Manual of Practice*, London: Croom Helm.

Edwards, A. and Westgate, D. (1987) *Investigating Classroom Talk*, London: Falmer Press.

Flavell, J.H. (1976) 'Metacognitive aspects of problem solving', in Resnick, L.B. (ed.) *The Nature of Intelligence*, Hillsdale, NJ: Lawrence Erlbaum Associates.

Hughes, M. (1997) *Teachers and Other Adults as Talk-Partners for Pupils in Nursery and Reception Classes*, Summary of Doctoral Thesis Findings, London: Teacher Training Agency.

Leat, D. (ed.) (1998) *Thinking Through Geography*, Cambridge: Chris Kington.

Mason, L. (1994) 'Analogy, metaconceptual awareness and conceptual change: a classroom study', *Educational Studies*, 20: 267–91.

Mayer, R. and Wittrock, M. (1996) 'Problem-solving transfer', in Berliner, D. and Calfee, R. (eds) *Handbook of Educational Psychology*, New York: Simon & Schuster.

Muijs, R.D. (1997) 'Predictors of academic achievement and academic self-concept: a longitudinal perspective', *British Journal of Educational Psychology*, 67: 263–77.

Nisbett, J. and Shucksmith, J. (1986) *The Seventh Sense: Reflections on Learning to Learn*, Edinburgh: Scottish Council for Educational Research.

Perkins, D. and Salomon, G. (1988) 'Teaching for transfer', *Educational Leadership*, 46: 22–32.

Sinclair, J. and Coulthard, M. (1992) 'Towards an analysis of discourse', in Coulthard, M. (ed.) *Advances in Spoken Discourse Analysis*, London: Routledge.

Wells, G. (1989) 'Language in the classroom: literacy and collaborative talk', *Language and Education*, 3, 4.

Wubbels, T., Créton, H. and Hooymayers, H. (1990) 'Discipline problems of beginning teachers, interactional teacher behaviour mapped out', paper presented at the American Education Research Association Conference, Chicago, April.

# Part III

# Wider issues in teaching geography

# 12 Aspects of global citizenship

*Roger Carter*

## Introduction

The central issue of this chapter is the extent to which geography teachers working to the prescribed National Curriculum can help develop in their pupils both a global perspective and the capability to become global citizens. In pursuit of this issue three questions are raised and considered:

- What is a global perspective and why is this important?
- What is education for global citizenship?
- What curriculum strategies might support global citizenship and how can geography develop these?

## What is a global perspective and why is this important?

All education is about the future. The National Curriculum for England and Wales, first established in 1988, asserted in the preamble 'There is an entitlement to a balanced and broadly based curriculum which promotes the spiritual, moral, cultural, mental and physical development of pupils at the school and of society, and prepares such pupils for the opportunities, responsibilities and experiences of adult life' (1988 Education Reform Act, section 1:1). This entitlement, frequently restated, has been reaffirmed with each subsequent revision to the original Order.

What is in question is the extent to which the statutory programmes will enable an appropriate preparation for youngsters who will live out their lives in the twenty-first century. Will the National Curriculum provide the knowledge, skills, understandings and capabilities to equip them for a world which we can only speculate on? When and where in the education of young people do we help them to look at the kind of future they want for themselves, for society and for the planet? Preparation for adult life is often perceived more narrowly, in terms of equipping society with a well qualified workforce able to compete in world markets, and equipping individuals with the means to progress and be self-fulfilled. Such aspirations fall far short of addressing the global questions, issues and challenges that this generation will leave to the next. Children in schools today will face huge problems which bear on the survival prospects of the planet: stabilizing a rapidly rising world population, protecting biological diversity, slowing the destruction of finite resources, bringing down the emission of harmful gases. Coming generations must learn how to use energy and materials more sustainably, reducing waste and pollution and reversing the damaging trends brought about by 200 years of industrialization – and they must do all this in a context of worsening social and racial inequities. Has any previous generation faced a more daunting agenda? Preparation for the opportunities, responsibilities and experiences of adult life requires focus, attack and urgency.

The National Curriculum looks increasingly unlikely to address such a challenge. Are the prescribed subjects the right ones? Is the content appropriate? The curriculum subject structure of the late 1990s looks not dissimilar to the Board of Education Curriculum Regulations of 1904. The National Curriculum has a feel of the past about it, largely defined by subject disciplines. It will need considerable mediation if it is to respond effectively to events outside the classroom which appear to develop at a far faster rate.

It is always difficult to predict the future, but current indicators suggest a context of growth, development and technological advance on scales never before experienced. Rapid change is ubiquitous – far outstripping the upheavals of previous industrial revolutions. The knowledge revolution expands to bear on work, recreation, the arts and family life. There are radical shifts in technology, capable of transforming our culture. The speed and intensity of change to all aspects of life carry with them the risk of uncertainty and loss of confidence. Events and issues such as BSE, AIDS, Chernobyl, and animal cloning are generating a loss of confidence in science and technology. The challenge of sustainability extends beyond the world of ozone layers and forest depletion, to the social sustainability of pensions, health provision and transport systems. Accelerated change may bring dangers of division and conflict – and the risk of a non-included world of crime, disorder, drugs and social breakdown.

All of these trends are global in scale and impact. No one is unaffected by them. Yet the National Curriculum makes only marginal reference to the forces of globalization. Part of the problem is its complexity. Although no one can be unaware of the importance of globalization, it remains a complex and largely unexamined phenomenon. Explaining globalization to young people is a daunting task for those on the edge of understanding it themselves. Consequently the images and understandings of globalization commonly propounded are incomplete, narrow and uncritical.

Globalization has been described as the creation of global systems where what happens in one part of the world affects people and places everywhere. Arguably the process has been continuous since human activity developed with the movement and trading of goods across land and sea between ancient communities. Improving transport and communication promoted migration and interaction. The global economy has burgeoned with the emergence of transnational élites, and the scale on which the global economy now operates has led to massive increase in power and influence of multinational corporations – not only over markets, but over political institutions as well. These businesses carry funds far greater than do many nations. They organize global manufacturing, trade and finance, promoting high profits, controlling and expanding markets, increasing production and consumption. Global financial élites have achieved political power through their economic dominance, negotiating directly with nation-states, over whom they have the whip hand. These corporations now control 70 per cent of world trade. Daily they demonstrate the ability to move jobs and assets from locality to locality and country to country, forcing ever greater subsidies along the way. Financial markets can move production to countries and localities where they can pay less than a living wage or use the threat of moving jobs to break up labour unions or break down wages. The large multinationals bear most responsibility for resource stripping – of forests, fisheries and mineral deposits.

Organizations such as the United Nations, the World Bank, the International Monetary Fund and the union of the world's richest nations under the G8 banner do have power to influence the world economy. However, far too often well-publicized summit conferences of these organizations have found difficulty in finding agreement on clear and decisive policies, preferring to set unambitious targets for the future. There is an apparent lack of will to make the bold commitment. Money talks.

If globalization is largely seen and explained in economic terms, the effects of the process are much wider. Impacts can be seen not only on trade, employment and finance. Equally significant is environmental degradation, international crime, and the impact on regional cultures. On the one hand globalization is producing greater diversity and a desire to stress distinctiveness (for example the revival of nationalism in Eastern Europe), whilst at the same time providing greater homogeneity in other respects. The relationship between globalization and world poverty is unclear, but certainly the growth of multinationals has coincided with a growing gap between the world's rich and poor. There are contradictions everywhere. Increasing world-wide communication goes hand in hand with rigidity in the labour market, and restricted movement across national boundaries. The geographer's mindset of regions, nations and states sits uneasily alongside this complex rearrangement of space.

Explanations in geography (of unemployment, famine, migration, social or economic patterns and processes) which ignore the global dimension are likely to be incomplete and misleading. The dimensions of globalization, economic, political, social and environmental, impact not only on a global scale. They reach right down to communities and individuals. Nobody is unaffected by them. Some of these dimensions are identified in Figure 12.1 'The globalization rose', developed as an aid to analysis and understanding by the Development Education Centre (DEC) in Birmingham, which is useful in making the global and local connection. There are interesting areas to study in the interface between the 'cardinal points', for example between the environment and the economy, between political and social perspectives (Robinson, 1988).

It would be wrong to perceive globalization as only a negative threat to world health and order. Global technology can make significant improvements to

**N – Natural and environmental**

How is the environment of the
nation or locality affected by
globalization?
What resources are coming in or
going out?
What effect is globalization
having on natural systems locally
(e.g. weather, geology, water
cycle, ecology)?

**W – Who decides?
Political**

Who are the players in
the global decision-making
that affects the nation or
locality? What part do
people from the nation or
locality play in global
decisions?
How are national or local
decisions affected by
globalization?

**E – Economic**

What is happening to
employment, wages,
wealth, investment and
finances as a
result of globalization?
What effect is this
having on consumers?

**S – Social and cultural**

How are people's values being
affected by globalization?
What is happening to religion,
language, culture, family life, and
leisure activities as a result of
globalization?
How are lifestyles and education
affected?

*Figure 12.1* The globalization rose – global to local

production, to yields, to health access, to communications, thereby substantially
improving the lot of individuals. Nor are the processes described here inevitable.
The systems are not immutable, in fact they are changing all the time. The world
cannot sustain the levels of consumption currently enjoyed by the affluent nations,
finite resources will see to that. Ceaseless capital accumulation cannot be sustained
forever. What would happen if an 'optimal' desirable growth of 2.5 per cent was
actually realized in the UK? If the economy grew at this rate over the next century
the GDP would have to grow tenfold. From an environmental perspective this
would be a disastrous prospect, but is unlikely to happen. Whether governments

and companies favour such growth levels is irrelevant since various factors will converge to stop it. On the environmental front there is the prospect of further shock oil price rises, a food shock when food production reaches the limit of food intensification, a water shock as ancient aquifers are exhausted. And multinationals can only survive if people buy their products. These corporations have great interest in consumer demand that cannot always be manipulated and they are therefore vulnerable to local opposition. Several multinationals in the genetic food industry, for example, are experiencing a society-wide collapse of support for radical technologies which would introduce genetically modified foods.

It should be possible to steer globalization processes towards more sustainable outcomes which will at the same time alleviate poverty. The aim should be to focus on and spread the benefits of global activity. Trade, finance and business can be controlled by politicians given the will and pressure from their constituents. Often change seems impossible until it happens, so although it may seem inevitable in its present form it would be counter-productive to take such a passive stance. It is important to move away from the negative and closed view of the process to identify beneficial alternatives and pursue them.

Education, both at school and in the community, can help to create a more open and active approach to the issues of globalization – indeed it has an obligation to do so. The next generation will need support to influence the way that globalization works and its effects. Teaching about globalization should be central to a subject like geography in the twenty-first century. It should also be fundamental to other subjects such as economics, science and technology, and never ignored elsewhere. Yet the National Curriculum makes only marginal references to it. Preparing pupils for the opportunities, responsibilities and experiences of adult life must mean raising their understanding of global forces in order that they may adapt to cope with them or shape them. Any notion of global citizenship should build on some understanding of what is happening in the world.

## What is education for global citizenship?

Looking ahead to the twenty-first century, the task of building a sustainable world order will require a substantial rethink of the present curriculum. The knowledge, skills and attitudes needed to compete industrially or commercially are not necessarily the same as those needed to build equitable, sustainable communities. A broader vision of the role and content of education is needed.

A better balance is needed between skills and knowledge on the one hand and values and commitment on the other. Schools should help produce leaders and citizens of the future whose mindsets operate automatically in a sustainability mode. The current preoccupation with standards in a narrow range of skills (important though they are) may allow politicians to set bench marks, measure value added, or publish league tables. It will not of itself encourage pupils to personalize their learning, to explore and reflect, or to develop the capabilities to function in the world outside school as citizens, users of the environment, potential employees or consumers. A stronger focus on the learners' needs as individuals and members of larger groups is called for. Pupils need time and space to think and talk through their own attitudes and value positions. Teachers need encouragement to take risks, to play with ideas with their pupils. Education for the twenty-first century should engender a real feeling by everybody that they matter in society and that they can influence decisions either directly or indirectly.

Any National Curriculum will be concerned to expose pupils to their own culture and heritage. The National Curriculum for England and Wales is by no means unusual or more insular than national programmes elsewhere – some would argue that it is less so. Few countries of the world have devised a syllabus that sets out to provide pupils with a comprehensive view of the world as an interconnected and interdependent system. A tension exists here. Any National Curriculum is likely to focus on what its pupils need to be active and informed citizens of their own society, and to know about those areas or aspects of the world in which their own country has strategic, economic or political interests. The message that their country and its interests are only a part of the global picture will be a softer one. The world-wide increase in regional studies, European studies, Australian studies, Asian studies, Pacific studies, both in schools and in higher education reflect this (Singh *et al.*, 1997). The danger is that to develop a sense of national identity and patriotism may become insular, perhaps nationalistic, and a distortion of the fact that any nation or region in the world today is inextricably connected to social, cultural and economic globalism. The subject structure of the curriculum is unhelpful in examining such a world. Discrete subjects may offer perspectives, but what is required is a greater degree of integration of global reference across the curriculum.

Within such a curriculum one may expect the geography Order, of all programmes, to take a broad perspective and help pupils make curricular connections elsewhere. The Order for geography pays insufficient attention to the global scale and global issues. How much of the programme focuses on global issues? Should there be so much attention on countries and their regions? Is school geography too preoccupied with the small-scale and local? In thematic geography is sufficient account taken of global patterns and processes? What places do we teach about and what do we teach about places? Currently schools are locked into syllabuses and text resources from which they can teach but a very narrow sample of the world. How valid are the theories, models and concepts we teach in helping children to understand a rapidly changing world? In time, theories of economic development, of industrial location, of core–periphery models, of settlement hierarchies may all come to be challenged. If space is largely annihilated through communications technology in a globalized world, then where will all the place-related theories go? Without constantly reappraising school geography the subject will become cluttered with dead information and outdated theory. It will ignore places, events and ideas that have become very important to pupils' lives. Greater flexibility is needed.

A geography programme that attacks head-on the issues of globalization is likely to raise such questions as the following:

- Why is globalization such a powerful force?
- Are there alternatives to globalization as it is?
- Who benefits from globalization?
- Why is the gap between the rich and poor widening?
- What is the ultimate result of global competition?
- Why is there so much money in the global system?
- What security have individual nations in the global economy?
- Can globalization be controlled?

If the National Curriculum fails to give a strong lead on education for global citizenship, there is nothing in the Order for geography to prevent such questions being pursued. The programme does provide some opportunities to pursue these matters, and these go well beyond just doing a Third World case study. Development occurs everywhere and the thematic requirement at Key Stage 3 reflects this. In investigating development pupils should be taught:

- about different ways of identifying differences in development;
- about differences in development and their effect on the quality of life of different groups of people; and
- how the interdependence of countries influences development.

There is certainly scope here to investigate aspects of globalization. Further opportunities occur in the skills specifications. Throughout the key stages the Order prescribes an investigative approach to developing enquiry skills. Questions such as 'Where is it?', 'How did it get like this?' permeate the content of each key stage. The question 'How is this place connected to other places?' should, when developed, enable pupils at all key stages to begin to develop the concept of interdependence, by exploring the many ways in which their own place relates to a wider world.

Beyond the National Curriculum a powerful influence on the curriculum is the examination boards, and there are encouraging signs that syllabuses are beginning to provide opportunities to strengthen global perspectives among older pupils. For example the new (AS) syllabus in World Development (WJEC) sets out its purposes as:

- reaffirming or developing a sense of identity or self-esteem;
- valuing all pupils and addressing inequality;
- relevant values and attitudes, and personal, social and health education;
- learning from others around the world;
- relevance to young people's interests and needs; and
- supporting and increasing the motivation to effect change.

This may be an appropriate set of objectives for young people in their late teens, but should complex issues be left until children are older and have achieved a greater level of individual development? Can a child of 7 grasp abstract notions about justice, rights, resource depletion, interdependence? Certainly there is a challenge here for those who teach younger children. Yet even in early years, children do try to make sense of global trends and problems that their parents and teachers struggle with at deeper levels. In their daily lives children have concrete experiences that contain elements to be found in larger world issues – calling names (prejudice), excluding others (discrimination), protesting that rules are unfair (human rights), arguing about toys (resource distribution), fighting (peace/conflict), using consumables sometimes unwisely (environment), benefiting from working or playing together (interdependence), negotiating a solution (perspective), being aware of who has power (Fountain, 1994).

Such behavioural patterns extend well beyond any geography programme, even if the subject has much to offer children in their early years. Geography teachers need to look across the curriculum for ways to connect to the whole curriculum. For example, in A *Curriculum for Global Citizenship*, Oxfam (1997) sets out ways in which key ideas and skills may be introduced to very young children and developed incrementally as they mature. Table 12.1 provides an example of its proposal to develop the concepts of globalization and interdependence. Although this work is essentially cross-curricular, there is much resonance with the geography Order and the capacity of geography to contribute.

There is also a role for geography in developing much that has been recommended by the Advisory Group on Citizenship as part of its contribution to curriculum discussions (Advisory Group on Citizenship, 1998). The group identifies four dimensions which should be developed in pupils of all ages within and beyond the National Curriculum. These dimensions are incorporated in the revised arrangements for the National Curriculum beyond September 2000:

- status, rights and obligations: e.g. residence, elections, benefits, mutual obligations, such as keeping the law;
- social inclusion: community, nation, state, supranational and transnational networks;

*Table 12.1* Globalization and interdependence: a curriculum for global citizenship

| | |
|---|---|
| Pre KS1 | sense of immediate and local environment |
| | awareness of different places |
| KS1 | sense of the wider world |
| | links and connections between different places |
| KS2 | trade between countries |
| | fair trade |
| KS3 | awareness of interdependence |
| | our political system and others |
| KS4 | power relationships |
| | north/south world economic and political systems |
| | ethical consumerism |
| 16–19 | complexity of global issues |

- sentiment and a sense of identity: a curriculum planned around the needs of the global citizen will need to develop children's sense of identity and self-esteem through a holistic approach to learning within the school environment, dedicated to valuing others and their experiences both locally and globally;
- political literacy: to be exercised not only in national politics, but in a wider context, keeping in balance the local and global, the personal and political.

Although much has been done by pressure groups, agencies and subject associations to raise the profile of global affairs within the education system, there remains much to do. Unsurprisingly, because of a lack of political direction in the past, there is a shortage of good examples of global education. Little has been written about sequence and progression in learning, or how such work may relate to theories of child development. There are few objective measures of learning outcomes to support teachers. If this is a whole-curriculum agenda there is little guidance as to how education for global citizenship may be developed across subjects. Geography has a key role to play, but it has still to clarify, far less to identify, ways in which the content of geography may complement other subjects and whole-school initiatives to reinforce learning. School geography is still at the stage of developing strategies, some of which will be explored in the next section.

## What curriculum strategies might support global citizenship and how can geography develop these?

The National Curriculum has had the effect of making teachers play safe with the prescribed content. Good geography should provide a view of the world that develops as knowledge and thinking changes. A more flexible Order should encourage a more experimental, innovative stance. If at the moment the approaches described later lack a strong theoretical basis, they may at least provide a pragmatic starting point from which to move forward. In time, action research should provide a stronger underpinning for such work.

### Developing large concepts

Various groups have made interesting contributions to the debate about National Curriculum revisions. It is interesting to set alongside each other the main concepts promoted by Oxfam's Development Education Programme, the Advisory Group on Citizenship, and the Panel for Education for Sustainable Development (QCA, 1998): see Table 12.2.

There is an apparent overlap and duplication within the table, although it would be necessary to examine further what these groups mean by the terms used. Any group of geographers would probably come up with a set of concepts that would differ one from another and from those in the table. However, it is also the case that there is a spatial dimension to all or most of the concepts listed here. Equally, it is helpful to develop a geography programme around a number of central underpinning concepts through which much of the subject matter is understood.

*Table 12.2* Identification of concepts by advisory panels

| Oxfam | Citizenship | Sustainable Development |
|---|---|---|
| Social justice and equity | Fairness, justice, the rule of law and human rights | Equity and justice |
| Diversity | Equality and diversity | Diversity |
| Peace and conflict | Cooperation and conflict | |
| Globalization/interdependence | | Interdependence |
| Sustainable development | | Needs and rights of future generations |
| | Democracy/autocracy | |
| | Freedom and order | |
| | Individual and community | |
| | Power and authority | |
| | Rights and responsibilities | Citizenship/stewardship |
| | | Uncertainty and precaution in action |

Pupils find this helpful. Otherwise the subject becomes a mass of rather disconnected content. It matters that such concepts are shared with pupils, so that they can understand and use them in a wide variety of contexts. Which of the concepts in Table 12.2 are central to geography? To which others could geography provide an important perspective? What important geographical concepts are not included in the table?

David Leat, in *Thinking Through Geography* (Leat, 1998), stresses the importance of bedding key concepts into curriculum planning by:

- being clear about the big concepts that each unit of work is trying to develop;
- developing teaching strategies as a checklist for ways in which pupils can develop these concepts; and
- planning and using debriefing sessions to encourage the development of transfer, particularly by offering other contexts to which the pupils' learning can be applied.

At both primary and secondary level the geography programme can be planned so as to develop in pupils a growing understanding of the concept of globalization and with it a heightened capacity for global citizenry. What is important here is the ability to connect new to previous learning, to transfer ideas to new situations, so as gradually to develop, deepen and refine the concept.

In this activity it is important to clarify the part that geography may play alongside perspectives drawn from other disciplines as they translate into classroom subjects. Stronger cross-curricular planning, particularly in secondary schools, where traditionally planning has been developed vertically through subject departments, would enable a sharper understanding of geography's contribution to global citizenship, and how it relates to other contributions. It would also aid transfer of learning for the pupil.

## The geography of futures

Children are interested in the future, but rarely do schools ask them what they think and feel about the future or consult them about their hopes and fears. When they do, the results are interesting. Hicks (1998) provides evidence of pupils' views about the future in his study of nearly 400 pupils from rural and urban schools in southwest England. The main issues that concerned these youngsters are shown in Table 12.3.

The pupils sampled were of both primary and secondary age. It is interesting that their hopes and fears, both for their own area and the wider world, closely mirror each other. Clearly, young people are aware of the major global issues of environment, conflict, poverty and hunger.

A relevant school geography should help children identify their hopes and fears for the future and encourage them to talk about these. Teachers should then ask themselves how these hopes and fears relate to the geographical places and themes that are taught, and how they help pupils to understand the world they live in. 'How is it changing?' becomes a particularly important question around which to organize thinking. What sorts of changes are pupils most aware of in their community? their country? their world? Can they identify them, examine them, and begin to understand how changes come about?

An exploration of future alternative scenarios should encourage ideas about preferred futures and challenge the notion that global forces are beyond the capability of human control. The global agenda is also about the local one – it is in the locality that younger pupils can draw direct experiences about change, how it comes about, who controls it, and what direct action they can take. Local Agenda 21 programmes may reinforce the important idea that individual and collective action can make a difference.

## Making spatial connections

Younger children sometimes find it difficult to understand the nesting of different scales in their lives. How can they simultaneously live in a street, a town, a region

*Table 12.3* Hopes and fears for the future

| Hopes for the local area | | Fears for the local area | |
|---|---|---|---|
| Less population | 56% | More crime | 41% |
| Better amenities | 36% | More pollution | 36% |
| Less crime | 30% | Terrorism | 29% |
| Greater prosperity | 25% | Unemployment | 22% |
| Less traffic | 25% | Homelessness | 9% |
| *Hopes for the global future* | | *Fears for the global future* | |
| Peace/no war | 49% | Disasters – natural/human | 46% |
| Less pollution | 45% | More wars | 35% |
| No poverty/hunger | 32% | More pollution | 20% |
| Good relationships between | | More poverty | 17% |
| countries | 19% | | |

*Source:* Hicks (1998)

and a country? How can they at one and the same time be English, British, European and a world citizen? The following quotation will have echoes in many readers:

> This is the way I would look at it: The world exists; I exist; how do I fit in to this world? This is the first thing that education does – it tries to link you with the world. I don't know whether you did it, but we did it when I was a child. Once you learned to write, the first thing you did was learn to write your name: Albert Chinua, Achobe, CNS Central School, Ogido, Onitsha Province, Eastern Nigeria, West Africa, World! You see? This is a widening awareness. You've got the tool of education – literacy; you can write now. And the first thing you try to do is locate yourself in the world.
>
> (Albert Chinua)

Our home address is a universal way of placing us all on earth. Each layer of the address represents the next larger tier of organization. At each level decisions are made which may affect the individual directly or indirectly. In turn, it may be that personal action may influence decisions made at these various levels. Even though a decision may be made at a great geographical distance, it may still influence personal life at the local level on a daily basis. For example, a change in international trade prices might swiftly affect the daily income of the farmer producer in another continent.

Studies in geography should therefore range across the scales. Local, regional or national case studies should connect to scales above and below. The study of any place needs to consider how this place is connected to other places at a variety of scales. If there is a regular practice of addressing these connections in geography lessons it will make the following ideas more accessible to pupils:

- Decisions made at one level can have an effect at other scales.
- Large-scale decisions may have a local impact.
- All individuals can exercise some influence.
- People in different places experience the same process.

## Posing the right questions

Many teachers have come to see the power of key questions when planning geography. A sequence of clear questions can provide direction to the study. In time, pupils can be encouraged to recognize geographical questions and initiate their own (QCA, 1998). When addressing issues of globalization as they impact on all scales from local to global, it is worth considering what questions are particularly helpful in structuring thinking about the world. All the programmes of study stress the importance of enquiry skills, and useful progress has been made in this area. Questions that take pupils into describing and explaining activities are particularly important in developing geographical skills and understanding. Some significant questions relating to globalization have already been identified. 'How is it changing?' is of particular importance in helping pupils begin to understand both the dynamics of the world and the forces that bring change about. 'How is it connected to other places?' is equally useful when exploring the complex network of interactions between any one place and the world outside it. There is scope, too, to strengthen pupils' personal response to their learning by raising question sequences such as the following:

- Why is this important to me?
- What would it be like if . . . ?
- What would I like to happen?
- What do others think and feel about this?
- What do I think and feel about this?
- Why do I think this way?
- What can I do about it?

Equally, in any issues-based work which explores the interface between people and places at different scales, a useful sequence of questions to develop lines of enquiry might be the following:

- Who has the power in this situation and how will they use it?
- Who will decide?
- How will the decision be made?
- Who will gain or lose from the situation?
- How can the decision-making process be influenced?
- What can I/we do about it?

### A critical response to information technology

The impact in schools of the information explosion is taking hold, giving access through CD-ROM and the Internet to knowledge for all pupils. Soon teachers will have no choice but to become net surfers, coaches and facilitators – not there to pass on knowledge, but to encourage the development of higher-order skills such as evaluation of sources, data interpretation and time management.

How will such change affect the teaching of development, when at a stroke pupils can access a vast database on the subject, with videos, animations and the constant updating of world-wide activity? The same goes for weather, Japan, rainforests, settlement patterns or any other geographical topic likely to be taught. Are pupils capable of handling this? Their problem will not be about finding the 'facts', but rejecting, sorting, verifying, balancing, summarizing information in a way that offers some sort of sensible balance between time spent and work accomplished.

Two skills will be at a premium. Already 'time management' is critical in schools. What lies ahead will be ever harder decisions about what to spend time doing. Coping with the information explosion will be no easy task for pupil or teacher. This is especially difficult because the material that pupils can call up from machines is totally undigested. Much more attention is needed for evaluating material. Already assumed truths and single viewpoints are found embedded and unchallenged in school geography. Texts (in the sense of resources that geography uses) are subjective. They are not a mirror on the world.

Geography lessons should give more time to interrogating texts. This calls for teaching which encourages scepticism and emphasizes discourse in order to create more critical, questioning learners. Ours is a complex subject. It takes us straight into issues which are complex and many-sided. Too often it is presented as black and white. Too many coursework projects claim to have proved something. There is a need to move away from notions of proof – from clear-cut simplistic generalizations to encouraging more critical thinking. Pupils need to talk to each other more in geography about what they think and feel. Increasingly a key question of importance in geographical enquiry is likely to be 'Is it true?'

As pupils become increasingly confident with ICT applications in geography, they will need to develop from using ICT to find things out, towards learning how to use ICT to try things out, to make things happen, and to understand how they happen.

## Education for global citizenship

Whatever the claims of geography for a curriculum place in its own right, the urgency of the task (preparing for a better world) requires a clear commitment to the wider aims of education. We need a stronger focus on the needs of the learner – they in turn need to be able to personalize learning and relate it to their own lives as individuals and members of the larger community. Pupils' capability to operate in the world outside school as citizens with individual rights and responsibilities and a respect for the democratic process is paramount. Emerging attitudes and values may then develop into a capacity to use and apply learning, to growing self-understanding and to active participation in adult life.

Initial Teacher Education providers have a responsibility to ensure that future teachers are equipped to understand the issues facing our globalized society and are enabled and motivated to promote a more equitable and sustainable world with their pupils. All teachers have a responsibility to bring global perspectives to their work. The Development Education Association (1998) asserts that their education and training should show them what this means and how it can be done. It identifies and advocates five principles. New teachers should:

- be encouraged to explore and understand the issues concerned with active global citizenship as part of their education and training;
- be shown how to translate their concerns for global issues into effective practice;
- experience a range of approaches and active learning strategies which contribute to active global citizenship;
- be taught the importance of an inclusive values base which respects diversity and intercultural understanding; and

- be encouraged to recognize that developing and refining their understanding of global citizenship are appropriate targets for continuing professional development.

This is a tall order given the current pressures of time on Initial Teacher Training, and the narrow political focus on core skills of literacy and numeracy, but 'if teachers are not among the first to become, in effect, citizens of the world, who will?' (Barber, 1997: 237).

## References

Advisory Group on Citizenship (1998) *Education for Citizenship and the Teaching of Democracy in Schools*, Sudbury: QCA.

Barber, M. (1997) *The Learning Game: Argument for an Educational Revolution*, London: Victor Gollanz.

Development Education Association (1998) *Training Teachers for Tomorrow: Vision Statement for Global Citizenship*, London: DEA.

Fountain, S. (1994) 'Learning together', in *Global Education*, Cheltenham: Stanley Thornes.

Hicks, D. (1998) 'Exploring futures', in Carter, R. (ed.) *Handbook of Primary Geography*, Sheffield: The Geographical Association.

Leat, D. (1998) *Thinking Through Geography*, Cambridge: Chris Kington.

Oxfam (1997) *A Curriculum for Global Citizenship*.

Panel for Education for Sustainable Development (1998) *Education for Sustainable Development in the Schools Sector*, Sudbury: QCA.

QCA (1998) *Geographical Enquiry at Key Stages 1–3: Discussion Paper No 3*, Sudbury: QCA Publications.

Robinson, R. (1998) 'Macro-fantasies, real sufferings', *Economic Awareness*, January, 17–20.

Singh, M., Fien, J. and Williamson Fien, J. (1997) 'Processes of globalisation and (re)new(ed) emphasis for global education', *Development Education Journal*, 4, 1: 26–30.

# 13 Learning about development

## An 'entitlement' for all

*Tony Binns*

## Introduction

'Development' is a key concept, which I would strongly argue is, or certainly should be, an integral element – indeed a 'student entitlement' – at *all* levels of the education system from primary through secondary to further and higher education, and well beyond in the context of 'continuing education' and 'lifelong' learning (Binns, 1995).

In this chapter I will examine the meaning of development and development education, and will raise issues and questions relating to how these are often taught today, and the potential for enhancing their position and role within the education system of the future. It so happens that either by design or default, teaching about development in primary and secondary schools has generally been the responsibility of geography and geography teachers, but at tertiary level the field of 'development studies' widens to involve practitioners from many social science disciplines, such as anthropology, economics, international relations, politics and sociology. But as such subjects are rarely taught in schools below A-level, it is geography which has a key role to play in laying the groundwork for more advanced study at a later stage.

## What is 'development'?

The concept of 'development' is both complex and constantly being contested. There is no single definition of development; as Sachs suggests, 'Throughout the century, the meanings associated with urban development and colonial development concurred with many others to transform the word "development", step by step, into one with contours that are about as precise as those of an amoeba' (Sachs, 1992: 10).

We might usefully examine just a few of the countless definitions of development which have been put forward:

- *Chambers English Dictionary*
  'The act or process of developing: state of being developed: a gradual unfolding or growth: evolution . . . Advancing through successive stages to a higher, more complex, or more fully grown state'
  (*Chambers English Dictionary*, 1988: 386)

- *Dictionary of Human Geography*
  'A process of becoming and a potential state of being. The achievement of a state of development would enable people in societies to make their own histories and geographies under conditions of their own choosing. The process of development is the means by which such conditions of human existence might be achieved.'

  (Johnston, Gregory and Smith, 1994: 128)

- *Collins Reference Dictionary of Environmental Science*
  'The process by which some system, place, object or person is changed from one state into another; the term carries the connotation that the change is in the direction of growth or improvement.'

  (Jones *et al.*, 1990: 123)

My own favoured definition of development comes from the well respected economist Dudley Seers (Seers, 1969, 1971, 1979), who suggested in his seminal 1969 paper that:

Development is inevitably a normative concept, almost a synonym for improvement. To pretend otherwise is just to hide one's value judgements ... The questions to ask about a country's development are therefore: What has been happening to poverty? What has been happening to unemployment? What has been happening to inequality? If all three of these have become less severe, then beyond doubt this has been a period of development for the country concerned.

(Seers, 1969: 4)

Seers felt strongly that a definition of development should also involve the 'true fulfilment of human potential', and in a later paper, written after the oil crisis and price hike of the 1970s, he suggested that 'self-reliance' should be another important goal of development plans (Seers, 1979). In considering the question of individuals and groups being able to fulfil their potential, this raises many issues relating to the nature and quality of governance, as reflected, for example, in aspects such as freedom of speech, democracy and transparency in the formulation and implementation of government policies. Furthermore, it could be argued that the fulfilment of human potential is also severely constrained in poor countries by high rates of infant and child mortality, lower levels of life expectancy, as well as such features as the frequently low level of female participation in education systems.

Most importantly, development is quite definitely a 'social' as well as an 'economic' process, and it is unfortunate that even after much debate over four decades, economic growth is all too commonly still regarded as being synonymous with development. Rostow's well known 'Stages of Economic Growth' model (Rostow, 1960), for example, is often wrongly interpreted as a development model. Rostow was more concerned with economic progress and increasing industrial investment, rather than with human welfare and variables regarded by those such as Seers as important indicators of development – poverty, unemployment and inequality. Furthermore, Rostow's model was based on the historical experiences of economic growth in Europe and North America, and it is, therefore, quite inappropriate to attempt to apply such a model to countries which have been subjected to colonial rule and whose economies (and societies) have been manipulated to serve the demand for agricultural and mineral resources from the growing manufacturing sectors in the metropolitan countries. Above all, it should be remembered that development both concerns and involves *people* and that development processes vary considerably in their impacts both socially and spatially.

Moving to the school curriculum context, it should be noted that the definition and understanding of the concept and process of development were not at all helped by reference to 'economically developing countries' in the first Geography National Curriculum Order for English schools. For example, at Key Stage 2, levels 2 to 5, students were required to 'study a contrasting locality in the United Kingdom and a locality in an economically developing country' (DES, 1991: 37). The term 'economically developing' is problematic, not least because there are many cases of countries with rapidly rising Gross National Products, but where true development, in terms of a reduction in poverty and inequality has just not occurred (Binns, 1993; Potter *et al.*, 1999). Rather than trickling down to the poorest and remotest communities, it is well known that increased economic wealth in reality often moves towards already wealthy urban-based élites, thus increasing inequality in a range of key development indicators such as life expectancy and infant mortality. So the term 'economically developing' wrongly implied both that economic progress is the essence of development, and also that such countries are actually 'developing', which is questionable, certainly in the case of a number of sub-Saharan African countries, which in relative terms are now far worse off than they were over thirty years ago at independence. Interestingly, the term 'economically developing' was not used in the 1995 revised curriculum, but instead reference is made to countries and parts of the world 'in various/significantly different states of development' (DFE, 1995).

## Contexts and perceptions

If we regard development as fundamentally a process which should lead to an improvement in living standards, then it is important to recognize that develop-ment can happen in so-called 'developed' countries as well as in poor Third World countries. Varying levels of poverty, unemployment and inequality are found even in the world's wealthiest countries, but too often we seem to find it convenient to ignore their existence at home. In schools, teachers far too often portray the poor Third World countries as riddled with economic and social problems, whilst showing reluctance to deal with such problems in the home context, regarding them, I would suggest, as too complex, politically sensitive and controversial. Yet poverty and homelessness are all too evident, for example, in large European and

US cities, and a report published in the mid-1990s indicated that income inequalities between 1977 and 1990 had increased in the UK further and faster than in almost any comparable country and were greater than at any time since the Second World War. In fact, only New Zealand registered a greater increase in inequality during this period (JRF, 1995). It is essential that in teaching about development, at whatever level in the education system, students be introduced to a wide range of locational contexts and case studies, including the home environment and society.

Another significant consideration in teaching about development concerns the different perceptions which both students and teachers have, particularly about unfamiliar peoples and environments. Even within the UK, those living in southern England, for example, through images conveyed in the media often have distorted perceptions of what life is like in northern England, Scotland, Wales and Ireland. In broader spatial and temporal contexts, a complex chronology of terms has evolved from the colonial period to the present day, and it is unfortunate that many outdated and stereotypical views still persist. Drummond, for example, writing in 1888, typified views held about Africa at that time when he commented,

> here in his virgin simplicity dwells primaeval man, without clothes, without civilisation, without learning, without religion – the genuine child of nature, thoughtless, careless and contented . . . The African is often blamed for being lazy, but it is a misuse of words. He does not need to work; with so bountiful a nature round him it would be gratuitous to work
>
> (Drummond, 1888: 55)

More recently, sub-Saharan Africa has become synonymous with famine, drought, poverty, civil war and many other seemingly insurmountable problems, a region characterized by little progress in economic, social or cultural development (Binns, 1994).

There has been a considerable, and indeed ongoing, debate on what is the best term to describe the world's poorest countries. In fact, the different terminologies present a semantic minefield, with many descriptive terms at best inaccurate and at worst pejorative. A recent text rejected all but three terms: 'South', 'Developing World' and 'Third World' (Robinson and Serf, 1997: 7). The idea of the North–South dichotomy was a creation of the Brandt Report in 1980, but it is inaccurate in the way that the all-important dividing line includes geographically southern countries such as Australia and New Zealand in the North (Brandt, 1980). Though the term 'Developing World' is positive and implies progress, it does imply that the rest of the world is not developing, and as we have seen there are many so-called developing countries which are also not developing!

Terms such as 'Third World' continue to be widely used long after they were invented, and their meaning has often changed with time. The concept of Third World was first used to describe the growing number of states that were neither aligned with the 'First, Western-capitalist world' nor the 'Second, Eastern-socialist world'. The French demographer, Alfred Sauvy, is sometimes credited with first using the term in 1952, but the Bandung Conference in 1955 has come to be regarded as the event which gave birth to the Third World (Berger, 1994). Since the term was first coined, the so-called Third World has become much more diverse, including some of the world's poorest countries, such as Ethiopia and Mozambique, as well as the oil-rich Middle Eastern states and the emerging 'Asian Tigers' (South Korea, Taiwan, Hong Kong and Singapore). Furthermore, the collapse of state socialism in Eastern Europe, which was Sauvy's 'Second World', makes the tripartite division of the world even more redundant. Although some writers have argued that the term 'Third World' is now obsolete (Harris, 1986), it is still widely used by non-governmental organizations (NGOs), and most people have some idea of the broad characteristics of Third World countries (Robinson and Serf, 1997). As John Toye comments,

> The Third World is not, despite all that the development counter-revolution says, yet able to be dismissed from our minds. It is not a figment of our imagination ready to vanish when we blink. It is a result of our collective lack of imagination, our inability in our present difficult circumstances yet to see ourselves as belonging to one world, and not three
>
> (Toye, 1987: 10)

So, in the absence of a more satisfactory label (if indeed a label is actually needed?), I would agree with others that Third World is the best we can do. As an albeit imperfect teaching tool, use of the term Third World could provoke useful educational debate on important issues related to development, such as perception and interdependence.

Perceptions are also changing as the process of globalization becomes ever quicker and more encompassing. Overseas travel, the growth and 'incorporation' of sizeable ethnic minorities in many 'rich' countries and, not least, the phenomenal success and potential of the Internet, are just three factors which have helped to gradually change perceptions of distant peoples and environments. Whereas just two decades ago, stories, films and television programmes provided the only images of distant places, the young people of today are much more travelled than previous generations. In most school classes there will be at least one child who has possibly been to Florida or has experienced a safari or beach holiday in Africa. The greater 'ethnic mix', which is now a feature of so many of our schools, also provides an invaluable resource for generating study units and discussions on other cultures and livelihoods in such diverse places as Bangladesh, Nigeria and the Caribbean. Even the youngest children are fascinated by distant places and have an entitlement to be able to discover more about them, not least through the diverse cultural heritages of their classmates. Older students might be able to gain first-hand experience through overseas field courses and 'gap years' before, during or after university. Lastly, the Internet now provides an invaluable resource for everyone to use (selectively!), as the facility becomes available to more students both in their school or college, and increasingly at home.

## Why should we teach about development?

A statement from the United Nations in 1975 in itself provides a strong justification for teaching about development:

> Development education is concerned with issues of human rights, dignity, self-reliance, and social justice in both developed and developing countries. It is concerned with the causes of underdevelopment and the promotion of an understanding of what is involved in development, of how different countries go about undertaking development, and of the reasons for and ways of achieving a new international economic and social order.
>
> (UN, 1975, quoted in Hicks and Townley, 1982: 9)

The Development Education Association (DEA) sees development education as:

> a process which explores the relationship between North and South and more generally the links between our lives and those of people throughout the world. It is also about recognising our global interdependence and that, for any change to take place, a change of attitudes and values is required by the North.
>
> (DEA, 1993: 1)

Both statements suggest that there is in fact a very fine dividing line between development education and what is sometimes referred to as 'global citizenship', which is currently the subject of much curriculum debate in the UK and is considered in some detail by Roger Carter in his contribution to this book.

There are a number of compelling reasons why development education should be regarded as a student entitlement in our education system. First, from a humanitarian viewpoint, global inequality has never been greater. Should it not concern us all that whilst average life expectancy in the UK and USA in 1995 was over 76 years, in the world's poorest country, Sierra Leone, life expectancy was under 35 years? (UNDP, 1998: 128–30). Is it just and fair that an individual in one country can enjoy a life which on average is 40 years longer than another individual elsewhere in the world, purely because of where they were born and live? Considering levels of economic wealth in the same countries, whilst the USA had in 1995 a per capita Gross Domestic Product of US$26,977 and the UK had US$19,302, Sierra Leone's per capita GDP figure was a derisory US$625 (UNDP, 1998: 128–30). Many of the world's poorest countries and people are heavily dependent on farming and livestock-keeping to provide family subsistence requirements and sustain their livelihoods. In Western Europe, where relatively few people now work in the highly mechanized agricultural sector, we have a situation of over-production of food, such that policies have been introduced to 'set aside' land for non-agricultural use. Yet in other parts of the world, including Eastern Europe, food shortages are a regular, if not everyday, concern. Commenting on Africa, Timberlake argues:

> Africa's plight is unique. The rest of the world is moving forward by most of the normally accepted indicators of progress. Africa is moving backwards . . .

The continent's living standards have been declining steadily since the 1970s. Its ability to feed itself has been deteriorating since the late 1960s.

(Timberlake, 1985: 7)

One might indeed pose the question, why is there such considerable social and spatial disparity in the availability and accessibility of basic foodstuffs in the world today?

In the area of basic education, as reflected in levels of adult literacy, the UK and USA both had adult literacy rates of 99 per cent in 1995, whereas the figure for Sierra Leone was only 31 per cent. However, a particular concern is the sometimes vast differential between levels of male and female adult literacy, which is the case in some of the world's poorest countries, as well as those which are predominantly Muslim. In Sierra Leone, for example, whereas the adult literacy rate for males is 45 per cent, it is only 18 per cent for females. Even some relatively better off countries show marked gender-based inequalities in educational attainment and literacy levels, such as Saudi Arabia, which with a per capita Gross Domestic Product of US$8,516, has a male adult literacy rate of 71 per cent, yet only 50 per cent for females (UNDP, 1998: 131–3). We need to encourage students to engage with such issues and ask what are the underlying causes of such inequalities and what strategies might be implemented (at different scales) to reduce them? Through introducing development issues, young people should hopefully develop empathy and concern for those less fortunate than themselves, and this should encourage consideration of the nature and significance of different 'personal geographies' in a development context.

A second reason why development education should be regarded as a student entitlement concerns the historical justification. The United Kingdom is today one of the world's leading economic powers and the home-base of many of the world's most powerful multinational companies, whose origins can often be traced back to the period of colonialism. Whilst the UK (like other European powers such as France, the Netherlands, Spain and Portugal) derived much of its wealth from the production of raw materials associated with colonial expansion, British culture and values were simultaneously disseminated throughout the colonies in the shape of structures and systems for the management of economies, health, education, law and order, transport and trade. Such influence also extended into areas such as the arts and sport – cricket is surely a good example of this! It is probably fair to say that long after gaining independence, in some countries and among some people who experienced British colonialism, there remains an enthusiasm for maintaining strong links with the 'mother country' through, for example, organizations such as the Commonwealth.

Development education can play a key role in promoting an understanding of Britain's (or indeed other rich and powerful countries') role in the world today and the historical processes which underlie this. Furthermore, present-day economic, environmental and social conditions can be located in a global context with a strong historical dimension. It has been a long-standing concern of mine that school history and history teachers have really failed to 'get to grips' with the origins of present-day inequalities in the world and temporal changes in development processes. Topics such as the growth of world trade, slavery, colonialism and neo-colonialism, receive remarkably little classroom time compared with aspects of British and European history, which in some cases are taught repeatedly as children progress through the four key stages and on to A-level. The position in schools is in sharp contrast to that in higher education, where issues such as the nature and legacies of colonialism are well up the agenda in both teaching and research undertaken by historians.

## Development education in the UK

Development education emerged in the UK during the 1960s with the establishment of a number of development agencies, and has become a remarkably strong field of interest and activity over the past three decades or so. The latest Oxfam education resources catalogue lists no fewer than 45 development education centres in the UK, together with a further 12 in Ireland, some of which, perhaps most notably the DEC in Birmingham, were established as long ago as the early 1970s and have an impressive list of resources to support teachers and youth workers (Oxfam, 1999). In addition to such centres, which are frequently operated by volunteers, various development agencies (NGOs: non-governmental organizations) also have sections working on development education and producing a wide range of resources, for example, Action Aid, Catholic Fund for Overseas Development (CAFOD), Christian Aid, Intermediate Technology, Oxfam, Save the Children, Voluntary Service Overseas and Worldaware. The strength of the development education 'movement' in the UK was reflected in the establishment in October 1993 of the Development Education Association (DEA), with some 250 affiliated member organizations and its headquarters in London. The DEA's twice-yearly *Development Education Journal*, together with its *Monthly Bulletin*, provide up-to-date news on events and publications as well as some stimulating articles. The DEA's stated mission is to:

- promote development education within all sectors of education
- support the network of practitioners through a range of events, publications and information service
- lobby key decision-makers to recognise the value of development education and to give it full support

(DEA, 1996: 7)

As far as government support for development education is concerned, in 1976 the Labour Government's Ministry of Overseas Development established a Development Education Fund to promote wider public knowledge of international interdependence and a better understanding of 'worldwide social, economic and political conditions, particularly those which relate to and are responsible for, underdevelopment' (MOD, 1978). An Advisory Committee for Development Education was also established to advise the Minister on the expenditure of funds for development education. However, with the coming to power of Margaret

Thatcher's Conservative Government in 1979, development education became an immediate casualty of financial retrenchment at the new Overseas Development Administration (ODA).

In its short lifespan, the DEA has worked hard to influence government policy, and before the General Election in May 1997 was particularly active in lobbying political parties for a greater commitment to development education both in a future International Development Department and also as an integral feature in the revised National Curriculum (DEA, 1996). In 1996, the UK Government's Overseas Development Administration allocated just £700,000 to development education, representing only 0.01 thousand US$ per capita, which was one of the lowest expenditures among developed countries, and well below the figures of 1.22 and 0.99 US$ thousand per capita allocated respectively in Sweden and the Netherlands. Following the 1997 General Election, the publication by the new Labour Government's Department for International Development (DFID) of its White Paper on International Development in November 1997, represented a significant step forward in recognizing the importance of development education. Section 4 of the White Paper (*Eliminating World Poverty: A Challenge for the 21st Century*) is concerned with 'Building Support for Development' and stresses the importance of popular education on development issues:

> The British people should have accurate, unbiased, accessible information about the causes of poverty and inequality in developing countries, and about what the international community can do . . . The Government therefore attaches great importance to increasing development awareness in Britain. Every child should be educated about development issues, so that they can understand the key global considerations which will shape their lives. And every adult should have the chance to influence the Government's policies.
>
> (DFID, 1997: 77)

The White Paper also proposed that the Government would establish:

> a working group of educationalists and others (including the business sector, trades unions, the churches, the voluntary organisations and the media) to consider and promote awareness and understanding. We will work to ensure that global issues are integrated into the national curriculum and that relevant teaching materials are available. We will examine ways of improving progress in other aspects of formal and informal education and youth work.
>
> (DFID, 1997: 78)

In addition, a Development Policy Forum would be established:

> to allow individuals and representatives from all parts of society – academics, research institutes, the voluntary sector, the private sector and others – to share thinking and ideas for development and to draw on their wealth of knowledge and experience.
>
> (DFID, 1997: 78)

In the latest proposals for the revised National Curriculum for English schools, published for consultation in May 1999, and to be eventually implemented in September 2000, much emphasis is placed on citizenship and sustainable development, which are arguably key elements of both development education and geographical study. In the introduction to the Qualifications and Curriculum Authority consultation document, it is suggested that curriculum changes being made will focus on a number of issues including 'helping young people understand the world in which they live, and ensuring that they have a stake in society and their community by providing citizenship education' (QCA, 1999a: 4). The Secretary of State's proposals on the revised curriculum, which accompany the QCA consultation document, suggest that:

> Citizenship encourages pupils to become helpfully involved in the life of their schools, neighbourhoods, communities and the wider world. It promotes their political and economic literacy through learning about our economy and our democratic institutions, with respect for its varying national, religious and ethnic identities.
>
> (QCA, 1999b: 28)

Such a statement is very much in line with the ethos of development education.

Similarly, in the new curriculum proposals for geography, it is stated that references to sustainable development 'have been strengthened to reflect the work of the (government-appointed) Panel for Sustainable Development Education' (QCA, 1999b: 8). Geography, the consultation document argues:

> provides a link between the sciences and the arts and humanities, and contributes to environmental education and education for sustainable development. Geography develops understanding of physical and human landscapes and introduces pupils to different societies and cultures, enhancing awareness of global interdependence. It also promotes exploration of issues about the environment, development and society, and provides opportunities for pupils to reflect critically on their place in the world and their rights and responsibilities in relation to other people and the environment.
>
> (QCA, 1999a: 144)

Even as early as Key Stage 1, pupils will be required to be taught the skills, knowledge and understanding through geography to appreciate 'environmental change and sustainable development' and develop 'a framework of locational knowledge, with an ability to recognise how a locality is linked with other places in the world' (QCA, 1999a: 146). With such objectives for the youngest school children, geography is making a valuable contribution to development education, which is further developed in subsequent key stages and beyond, through A-level and into higher education.

## Some practicalities of teaching about development

As we have already seen, geography is the most important vehicle for teaching about development issues in schools. I have examined in detail elsewhere a number of strategies which might be used with different age groups of children (Binns, 1993, 1996), but it might be useful to mention some possibilities here:

### Role-plays and simulations

With primary age children in particular, there is much to be gained from setting up a simulation in which they make a 'pretend visit' to a distant country. I was involved with one very successful initiative, where we took 90 6- and 7-year-old children from an infant school in Hove (East Sussex) to the West African state of the Gambia for a day! The event arose out of a visit by a Gambian teacher to the school some months earlier. For several weeks before their 'visit' the children had been learning about people, wildlife and environment in Africa and The Gambia, and were actively involved in reading, writing and artwork, as well as making passports and designing hats to keep off the tropical sun. With the essential support of a group of Secondary PGCE trainees from Sussex University, who assumed a variety of different roles during the day, the children were given medical and passport checks before boarding the plane, gained more knowledge about The Gambia during the flight and then visited three Gambian villages where they could ask questions about life and work, before dancing to Gambian music and listening to an African story at the end of the day (Binns, 1993). The event was followed up later when the children moved into the neighbouring junior school, through establishing a letter exchange link with a Gambian school and using a series of laminated photographs for a work unit on the village where the school is located.

With older students, it might be possible to set up a role-play or debate on an issue such as Third World debt, which is particularly topical in the light of the Jubilee 2000 campaign and its lobbying of Western governments to cancel this debt, which amounts to about US$209 billion, more than twice the figure for 1985 (*The Guardian*, 1999). The key 'actors' should be identified, such as the 'Heavily Indebted Poor Countries' (HIPCs), governments and local producers, global lenders such as the World Bank and International Monetary Fund (IMF), developed country governments and multinationals, and national and inter-national development agencies. Important and challenging questions to debate would include the history of world debt: How did such indebtedness arise? What are the causes of debt and who is to blame? Should the debt be cancelled? Can the debt be cancelled? How can the future growth of indebtedness be stemmed? What is the effect of debt, and its possible cancellation, on poor people in Third World countries? Is debt cancellation a necessary pre-requisite for the alleviation and elimination of poverty?

## Artefacts and food

Many museums, as well as organizations such as the Commonwealth Institute, have collections of ethnographic artefacts which in some cases may be loaned to schools. Artefacts may provide a stimulus for examining many aspects of livelihoods in Third World countries, such as farming, fishing, rituals, cultural heritage and gender relations. Work on farming and food production could be initiated by actually examining foodstuffs produced in tropical countries such as mango, yam or rice. A visit to the local supermarket should reveal just how many products are imported from Third World countries. An audit of such produce may be conducted and a debate developed around such questions as: Who benefits in Third World countries from producing food for export? Is it more appropriate for such countries and their farmers to grow foodstuffs for home consumption, rather than produce for export? What is the most appropriate strategy for alleviating poverty? Again, it is important to identify the 'actors' involved in such production and trade.

## Visual aids

There is no shortage of high-quality photo packs and videos produced by the development education centres, NGOs and television companies. Students may be divided into small groups to discuss a photograph and present their views to the whole class. A good video might be used to promote debate. For example, the International Broadcasting Trust (IBT) and Yorkshire Television produced for Channel 4 a five-programme series titled *Geographical Eye Over Africa*, the second programme of which, *Nigeria: Dammed Water* also has a linked photo pack (IBT, 1995). Both the film and the photo pack address the important question of who actually benefits from large dams and irrigation schemes in poor tropical countries. Is such a type of development appropriate? This is a topic of much current interest and concern, and for sixth-form and higher education students there is no shortage of additional material about such development schemes, which can be used to raise further questions and provide useful case study material (see, for example, Adams, 1992; McCully, 1996). The controversial Three Gorges dam project on the Yangtze River in central China has generated much interest (see, for example, *National Geographic*, 1997), and will be the subject of a programme in a forthcoming Yorkshire Television/Channel 4 series for schools to be broadcast in 2000. The points in favour and against this massive construction project, which will displace over a million people, yet at the same time help reduce flooding downstream and generate electricity sufficient to supply ten large cities, might be examined through debate or role-play.

## Poetry, books and music

These are particularly important types of resources which can help to truly 'engage' young people in a wide range of development issues. There is no shortage of poetry and novels written in English by African, Caribbean and Indian writers, for example Chinua Achebe's *Things Fall Apart*, *No Longer at Ease* and *Anthills of the Savannah*, which can help to shed light on many aspects of the colonial and post-colonial transformation in African countries, in this case Nigeria. With the phenomenal growth in interest and availability of 'world music' in the 1990s there is plenty of scope for building a unit of work on development around a particular song. For example, international migration from poor to rich countries might be studied, as epitomized in the song 'America' from *West Side Story*. Meanwhile, the Senegalese artist, Youssou N'Dour, in his album *Hey You!* sings about aspects of everyday life such as polygamy and the emancipation of women, as well as the problem of multinational companies dumping toxic waste in poor countries.

### School links

Establishing a link with a school or college in a poor country can do much to develop empathy and promote global citizenship. By exchanging letters, artwork and photographs, children can gain a rich and personal insight into local issues and family life. Exchange visits for teachers and pupils are also becoming increasingly popular. The Geographical Association's International Committee has done much to initiate such links and exchanges.

### Field courses

There is absolutely no substitute for direct experience. Having led many groups of sixth-formers and university students to Africa (The Gambia, Kenya, Morocco, Tunisia), I have never failed to be impressed by the indelible impact that such a visit can make on an individual. In the light of gloomy media reports about Africa, it is a great step forward in the learning process for students to become personally aware of the fact that though Africans may indeed live in extreme poverty, they are frequently positive and forward-looking and invariably greet visitors with a warm smile and handshake. With cheaper packages and greater accessibility, many schools and colleges are now taking students to Third World countries on fieldwork. Whilst there is so much to be gained from such visits, it is vital that they are sensitively placed in a broader learning context and that teachers should guard against them becoming predominantly voyeuristic. There is much to be gained from closely examining with students the ethics of such fieldwork.

## Conclusion

The concept and processes of development are fundamentally concerned with the quality of life at home and overseas. Geographical education, particularly in schools, has played an absolutely vital role in promoting interest, understanding and debate in this important area, whereas too often other disciplines have 'stood on the side-line', displaying much potential, yet considerable reluctance, about becoming more involved. Getting to grips with development issues can do much to engender a sense of global citizenship in young people, whilst also strengthening awareness and understanding of a wide range of issues and values. In the context of an even more crowded curriculum, with recent initiatives in literacy and numeracy creating increased pressures on schools and teachers, it is vital that sufficient attention and time be devoted to development issues. There is great potential for more cross-curricular work, but it is likely that geographers will have to take the lead and convince their colleagues of the value of such collaboration. Fortuitously, the current emphasis on citizenship and sustainable development might be viewed as a highly appropriate vehicle for strengthening the position of development work within the curriculum.

## Issues and questions for discussion

- Is there a Third World?
- What is the most appropriate definition of development?
- How can myths and stereotypes be most effectively challenged?
- How can we best develop empathy, concern and action in young people – a sense of global citizenship?
- Why is there such little interest from other school disciplines and practitioners in embracing development issues?
- How might the teaching about development issues be strengthened in geography, but also perhaps by exploring opportunities for more cross-curricular work?

## References

Adams, W.M. (1992) *Wasting the Rain: Rivers, People and Planning in Africa*, London: Earthscan.

Berger, M.T. (1994) 'The end of the "Third World"?', *Third World Quarterly*, 15, 2: 257–75.

Binns, T. (1993) 'The international dimension in the geography National Curriculum', in Speak, C. and Wiegand, P. (eds) *International Understanding Through Geography*, Sheffield: The Geographical Association.

Binns, T. (1994) *Tropical Africa*, London: Routledge.

Binns, T. (1995) 'Geography in development: development in geography', *Geography*, 80, 4: 303–22.

Binns, T. (1996) 'Teaching about distant places', in Bailey, P. and Fox, P. (eds) *Geography Teachers' Handbook*, Sheffield: The Geographical Association.

Brandt, W. (ed.) (1980) *North–South: A Programme for Survival*, Report of the Independent Commission on International Development Issues (Chairman: Willy Brandt), London: Pan Books.

*Chambers English Dictionary* (1988) Cambridge: Chambers.

DEA (Development Education Association) (1993) *Launch Broadsheet*, London: DEA (DEA, 29–31 Cowper Street, London EC2A 4AP).

DEA (Development Education Association) (1996) *The Case for Development Education: Why it Should be Funded and Supported*, London: DEA.

DES (Department of Education and Science) (1991) *Geography in the National Curriculum (England)*, London: HMSO.

DFE (Department for Education) (1995) *Geography in the National Curriculum (England)*, London: HMSO.

DFID (Department for International Development) (1997) *Eliminating World Poverty: A*

*Challenge for the 21st Century*, White Paper on International Development, London: The Stationery Office.

Drummond, H. (1888) *Tropical Africa*, London: Hodder and Stoughton.

*The Guardian* (1999) 'Deep in the red', *Guardian Education*, 25 May, pp. 10–11.

Harris, N. (1986) *The End of the Third World*, Harmondsworth: Penguin.

Hicks, D. and Townley, C. (1982) *Teaching World Studies*, London: Longman.

IBT (International Broadcasting Trust) and Yorkshire TV (1995) *Geographical Eye Over Africa* (five 20-minute programmes), and *Dammed Water: Nigeria* (a Photopack for Secondary Geography), London: IBT.

Johnston, R., Gregory, D. and Smith, D.M. (eds) (1994) *The Dictionary of Human Geography*, Oxford: Blackwell.

Jones, G., Robertson, A., Forbes, J. and Hollier, G. (1990) *The Collins Reference Dictionary of Environmental Science*, London: Collins.

JRF (Joseph Rowntree Foundation) (1995) *Income and Wealth*, York: JRF.

McCully, P. (1996) *Silenced Rivers: The Ecology and Politics of Large Dams*, London: Zed Books.

MOD (Ministry of Overseas Development) (1978) *Report on the Future of Development Education*, London: MOD.

*National Geographic* (1997) 'China's Three Gorges', *National Geographic*, 192, 3 (September): 4–33.

Oxfam (1999) *Oxfam Education Resources for Schools*, London: Oxfam.

Potter, R.B., Binns, T., Elliott, J.A. and Smith, D. (1999) *Geographies of Development*, London: Longman.

QCA (Qualifications and Curriculum Authority) (1999a) *The Review of the National Curriculum in England: The Consultation Materials*, London: QCA.

QCA (Qualifications and Curriculum Authority) (1999b) *The Review of the National Curriculum in England: The Secretary of State's Proposals*, London: QCA.

Robinson, R. and Serf, J. (eds) (1997) *Global Geography: Learning Through Development Education at Key Stage 3*, Sheffield: The Geographical Association/DEC (Birmingham).

Rostow, W.W. (1960) *The Stages of Economic Growth: A Non-Communist Manifesto*, Cambridge: Cambridge University Press.

Sachs, W. (ed.) (1992) *The Development Dictionary*, London: Zed Books.

Seers, D. (1969) 'The meaning of development', *International Development Review*, 11, 4: 2–6.

Seers, D. (1971) 'What are we trying to measure?', *Journal of Development Studies*, 8: 21–36.

Seers, D. (1979) 'The new meaning of development', in Lehmann, D. (ed.) *Development Theory: Four Critical Studies*, London: Frank Cass.

Timberlake, L. (1985) *Africa in Crisis: The Causes, the Cures of Environmental Bankruptcy*, London: Earthscan.

Toye, J. (1987) *Dilemmas of Development*, Oxford: Blackwell.

UN (United Nations) (1975) *Statement on Development Education*, New York: UN.

UNDP (United Nations Development Programme) (1998) *Human Development Report, 1998*, Oxford: Oxford University Press.

# 14 Environmental education

## A question of values

*Stephen Scoffham*

*This we know: All things are connected like the blood that unites us.*
*We did not weave the web of life,*
*We are merely a strand in it.*
*Whatever we do to the web, we do to ourselves.*

Chief Seattle's address to the government of
Washington DC (mid-1850s) (Seattle, 1992)

All over the world the environment is in crisis. The issues are complex and varied. They include pollution, urbanization, acid rain, loss of wildlife, nuclear waste, the ozone hole and global warming. Whether we are well informed or not, we are all aware that something is amiss. The message is beamed to us via television documentaries and news bulletins, it appears as headlines in daily newspapers and it is chronicled in detail in books and journals. The problem is how to respond. Small-scale actions such as recycling household waste or using more efficient light bulbs seem rather inadequate in the face of such vast issues. Despite the rhetoric of environmentalists who encourage us to 'think globally, act locally', most of us tend to feel helpless in the face of the problems we confront.

Schools have a similar difficulty. Any worthwhile curriculum needs to address environmental issues. Pupils who are at school today will be tomorrow's decision-making citizens. As the twenty-first century progresses, environmental issues are likely to have an increasing impact on both local communities and society at large. It is important that pupils be well informed about the causes and consequences of the problems they are likely to encounter. As David Orr puts it:

> The future generations must learn how to use energy and materials with great efficiency. They must learn how to utilize solar energy in all its forms. They must rebuild the economy in order to eliminate waste and pollution. They must learn how to manage renewable resources for the long term . . . And they must do all of this while addressing worsening social and racial inequalities. No generation has ever faced a more daunting agenda.
>
> (Orr, 1992: 16)

When confronted with this programme, it would be easy to become pessimistic. Yet this would be a mistake. If we dwell too long on negative scenarios students are likely to become overwhelmed with a sense of despair or turn off altogether. Instead, we need to build success stories into the curriculum and indicate solutions and positive ways forward. Hicks sums up the matter unequivocally when he declares:

> No problem, environmental or otherwise, should be taught about at any level of education without concomitant emphasis on positive strategies for its resolution.
>
> (Hicks, 1998: 173)

Without a sense of hope, education loses much of its purpose. However, inspiring students involves much more than simply promoting a sense of bland optimism. It also involves accessing deep levels of intellectual and emotional meaning. This is one of the underlying principles of education for sustainability.

Hicks reminds us that repression is a commonplace in psychology. We tend to suppress information which we do not want to consciously acknowledge, particularly if is unpleasant or traumatic. While denying what is happening can sometimes be understandable, it is also unhelpful. Therapy has an important role in enabling people to re-engage with experiences they have suppressed and can help integrate them healthily into everyday life. The same applies to society at large. We need to be aware of the numbing effect of unpleasant information. Conversely, by exploring current environmental issues, schools may be able to help rebuild our collective self-image and self-esteem.

## A question of values

We tend to think of environmental awareness as a modern preoccupation. While the scale and complexity of the current crisis are clearly unprecedented, people throughout history have sought to come to terms with their environment and establish a harmonious relationship with it. In the fifth century BC, for example, the first kings of Sri Lanka built their capital city along ecological lines with designated zones for different activities and reservoirs to supply water. They also established what is arguably the world's first wildlife park.

Kindness and compassion to living creatures are one of the tenets of Buddhist teaching. Environmentalism is also a major component of many traditional cultures from the Maoris in the Pacific to the Indians of North America. Most aboriginal people believed that they belonged to the soil of a particular place. Sacred wells, trees, hills and rocks gave spiritual meaning to the physical landscape. The Romans, too, were sensitive to the spirit or essence of different localities (their *genius loci*) and set up shrines to local deities.

Christianity took over many of these ancient rituals and customs. It also promoted its own version of environmentalism. Judeo-Christian teaching begins with the story of how God created the world. Later we learn from the Bible how humans were given 'dominion' over creation, and Adam was put in the Garden of Eden 'to till and keep it' (Genesis 2.15). This has come to be interpreted as the notion of 'stewardship', so eloquently propounded by St Francis of Assisi.

The rise of capitalism and the Industrial Revolution in Western Europe changed the relationship between people and nature. A new perspective evolved which regarded the Earth as a machine to be managed and improved by human beings. Nowhere is this shift of thinking more graphically illustrated than in cartography. Medieval maps of the world were typically centred on Jerusalem and portrayed Biblical events. From the seventeenth century onwards, maps have been drawn with a northerly orientation and in an objective and analytical style.

Technology has undoubtedly brought great advances in material prosperity, but today people are increasingly aware of the dangers of alienation and spiritual impoverishment. Human beings are part of the life of the planet, not separate from it. How we see ourselves and our values and beliefs are therefore fundamental to understanding environmental problems. As Jonathan Porritt, the environmental campaigner, puts it, the ecological crisis is in reality:

> a crisis of the human spirit, a crisis which coincides with a period when so many people are already seized by a sense of purposelessness and profound alienation . . . it is in learning to heal the wounds we have inflicted on the Earth that we may eventually learn to heal our own self-inflicted wounds.
>
> (Porritt, cited in Moses, 1992: 5)

## The global context

It is also important to place the environmental crisis in the wider context of global change. Finding a route through the plethora of current issues is a daunting task. However, two facts stand out above all the others. The first is the sheer pressure of human numbers. The second is the great inequality of wealth between nations.

At the time of Christ there were about 250 million people in the world. For centuries the population stayed at relatively low levels with disease and famine taking their toll. In the eighteenth century, however, the Industrial Revolution set off a chain of events which led to dramatic increases. The total reached 1,000 million in 1830, since when it has gone on growing. Today there are about 6,000 million people in the world and projections indicate that numbers could more than double before they stabilize. The pressure that this places on the environment is immense. As human numbers go on increasing, the earth, being a self-enclosed system, is coming under more and more strain (see Figure 14.1)

In addition to the growth in numbers, people are also consuming more and more natural resources. The United Nations Human Development Report (1998) shows that private and public expenditure on consumption has increased six-fold since 1950. Around the world more people are better fed, better housed and have more leisure than ever before. However, material wealth doesn't always translate into human satisfaction. The percentage of Americans calling themselves happy peaked in 1957, even though consumption has more than doubled since then. To take

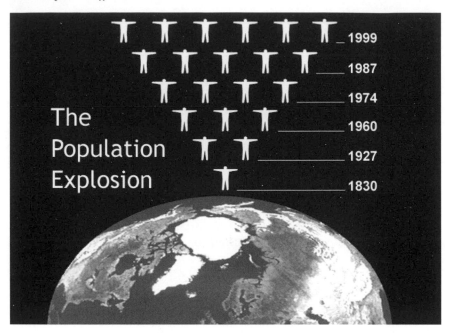

*Figure 14.1* Within a lifetime the population of the world has more than trebled to 6,000 million people (after Population Concern)

account of this the United Nations has now devised a range of indices which include life expectancy, educational attainment and gender empowerment as well as gross national product (GNP).

Wealth is also distributed very unevenly, with huge differences both within individual countries and between different parts of the world. A child born in Western Europe, for instance, will add more to consumption and pollution over his or her lifetime than 30–50 children in Africa or South America. Another way of expressing the same idea is to think in terms of ecological footprints. This measures the amount of land needed to support a particular life-style. The Dutch, for example, consume approximately fourteen times more than they could produce on the land in their own country. The deficit is made up by importing resources from other countries, leaving behind a deep 'ecological footprint'.

One of the most striking features of the world today is that whatever indicator is used, the same pattern emerges. A relatively small number of countries in North America, Europe, northern Asia and Australasia consume most of the world's resources and have high living standards. Meanwhile the majority of humankind can barely obtain the basic necessities of life and are trapped in a cycle of poverty, malnutrition and disease. This division has come to be known as the North–South divide.

The differences in wealth are so marked that they dominate any discussion of global environmental issues. While priorities in the North are to reduce pollution

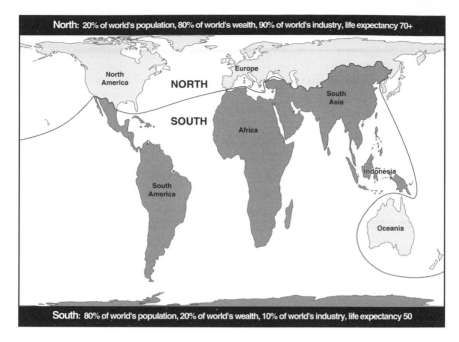

North: 20% of world's population, 80% of world's wealth, 90% of world's industry, life expectancy 70+

North
America

Europe

NORTH

South
Asia

SOUTH

Africa

Indonesia

South
America

Oceania

South: 80% of world's population, 20% of world's wealth, 10% of world's industry, life expectancy 50

*Figure 14.2* Global inequality (the North–South divide) is one of the main problems
facing the world today

and conserve wildlife, people of the South are struggling to repay international debts, provide basic education and health care and get enough to eat and drink. Many developing countries, especially those in sub-Saharan Africa, have been reduced to a state of virtual slavery by globalization, declining commodity prices and debt repayments. The weaker sections of society, particularly women and children, have been especially badly hit. In these circumstances the needs of the environment are likely to be given very little attention indeed (see Figure 14.2).

## Action for change

Politicians and governments around the world are well aware of the dangers posed by this dangerous cocktail of population growth, increased consumption and social inequalities. In recent years a number of major conferences have been held to discuss the problem and many new international laws have been passed to protect the environment. Sadly, these have tended to prove weak or ineffective.

Quite apart from anything else, environmental legislation is likely to be ignored if there is no suitable agency to enforce it. Also, governments which are democratically elected for relatively short terms have little incentive to take unpopular long-term decisions, especially if they are expensive or appear to run counter to national interests. More fundamentally, there are doubts about whether an economic system which is devoted to the accumulation of capital can ever be adapted to reflect ecological concerns. Underpinning all of these factors is an awareness that change is now happening so fast that it often exceeds our ability to adapt to it.

There are, however, some encouraging signs. The Brandt Report (1980) played a crucial role in drawing attention to inequalities between North and South and setting out an agenda that questioned the world economic order. This was reinforced by the Brundtland Report (Hinrichsen, 1987) which called for the conservation of resources and urged governments to adopt sustainable practices and a long-term perspective. Finally the Rio Convention (Quarrie, 1992) fashioned the first international agreements on pollution control. It also devised a global partnership for sustainable development. This has come to be known as Agenda 21 as it provides a blueprint for action in the twenty-first century.

## The school curriculum

Agenda 21 contains a chapter on children and youth in sustainable development. Among other things this calls on governments to 'promote primary environmental care activities', 'improve the environment for children', 'expand educational opportunities' and 'mobilise communities through schools and local health centres' (Agenda 21, Chapter 25). A subsequent chapter declares that 'education is critical for promoting sustainable development and improving the capacity of the people to address environment and development issues' (Chapter 36). Around the world educators have latched onto Agenda 21 and used it to help boost environmental education projects. Despite this, many teachers are still unaware of these opportunities.

Britain has a long and rather chequered tradition of environmental education which reaches back through nature walks and fieldwork to the painters and landscape gardeners of the eighteenth century. When the National Curriculum was introduced in 1991, environmental education featured as one of five cross-curricular themes. Although the themes have since withered, environmental education continues to attract strong support. There have been numerous ministerial statements extolling its value over the past decade. In 1996 the Schools Curriculum and Assessment Authority (SCAA) circulated a booklet to schools called *Teaching Environmental Matters Through the National Curriculum*. As well as a brief rationale, this contained descriptions of successful projects with children of all ages. More recently, in 1998, the Panel for Education for Sustainable Development submitted a report to the government which detailed the key concepts and learning outcomes for sustainable development education. This has informed the ongoing debate about citizenship and preparation for adult life.

One of the chief problems confronting environmental education is whether it should be treated as a subject in its own right or delivered through other curriculum areas such as geography, science and English. The question keeps on recurring. Environmental education is by its nature holistic and integrating. It fits rather uneasily into a structure based on traditional academic subjects and has therefore tended to be marginalized. Current advice fails to clarify the matter and simply suggests:

> It is for schools to decide how to teach environmental matters through the National Curriculum and how far to go beyond statutory obligations.
>
> (SCAA, 1996: 4)

Environmental education and geography certainly have many common interests. For example, environmental change and sustainable development are both components of the geography Programmes of Study at Key Stage 1 and Key Stage 2. At Key Stage 3 the thematic studies include both 'development' and 'environmental issues'. In addition, pupils are expected to develop an awareness of global citizenship and an understanding of people's attitudes and values.

Even more significantly, the geography National Curriculum is based on four major aims. These seek to:

(a) stimulate pupils' interest in their surroundings and in the variety of physical and human conditions on the Earth's surface;

(b) foster their sense of wonder at the beauty of the world around them;

(c) help them to develop an informed concern about the quality of the environment and the future of the human habitat; and

(d) thereby enhance their sense of responsibility for the care of the Earth and its peoples.

> (DES, 1990: 6)

Questions to do with the environment, citizenship and sustainablity therefore underpin the geography curriculum. No other school subject can make such a strong claim, although environmental education also has strong links with science (especially processes in the natural world), maths, ICT and English.

Indeed, there is a considerable body of literature which explores environmental issues. One of the simplest and most poignant stories for infants is John Burningham's *Oi! Get off our Train* (1989) in which different endangered animals climb aboard a young boy's train set to seek a ride to safety. Another is Michael Foreman's *One World* (1990). To find out more about the range of titles it is well worth referring to *The Green Guide to Children's Books* (Hill, 1991). This lists more than 400 books including poetry, stories and non-fiction for children of all ages from pre-school to the sixth form.

Besides working within the established timetable, there are a number of other ways in which schools can develop children's interest in the environment. These include taking part in award schemes and special events, visiting study centres and undertaking practical projects. All these activities have the advantage that they could form part of Local Agenda 21. Many councils have appointed Local Agenda 21 officers to facilitate environmental projects in the local community. Grass-roots action is central to this philosophy, so it is well worth enquiring to see if you can obtain support for your own initiatives (see Table 14.1).

*Table 14.1* Schools can promote environmental education in a number of ways apart from the established timetable (after Chambers 1995)

| | |
|---|---|
| Special events | Take part in seasonal events such as Riverwatch, Industry Week or Environment Week (organized annually at the end of May by the Civic Trust). |
| Environment clubs | Set up an environment club, either at lunchtime or after school. This is an ideal way of forging links with outside organizations such as WATCH, the RSPB or Groundwork. |
| Award schemes | Enter an award scheme or competition. One of the most successful is the Eco-School project, organized by the Tidy Britain Group. |
| Study centres | Arrange a visit to a Fieldwork or Environment centre. This could be either the focus for a study day or part of a residential school trip or journey. |
| Action projects | Undertake a practical project either within or beyond the school grounds. Small-scale, tangible activities, such as making a garden or trail are often particularly rewarding and have clear academic relevance. |

## Teaching complex issues

Environmental education involves the study of major global problems, many of which are extremely complex. Children can only learn about these issues from secondary sources and much of the information that they acquire tends to come from informal sources outside school. As a result, children often develop serious misconceptions.

Mason and Santi (1998) conducted an in-depth study of 22 pupils aged 10 and 11 years old to find out their ideas about the greenhouse effect. The children proposed six different causes:

- fumes from cars (2 children)
- hotter and hotter sun (4 children)
- straightening of the earth's axis (2 children)
- volcanic activity (7 children)
- ozone holes (5 children)
- a dome caused by sprays surrounding the earth (1 child)

The last explanation is perhaps closest to the truth, but all the suggestions are confused and need to be either developed or modified in some way. Mason and Santi argue that teaching will only be effective if it takes into account children's existing ideas. This should form the first step in implementing an ecology curriculum. They also stress the value of social interaction. Class discussions encourage questioning, criticizing and evaluating. Discussions also help to produce dissatisfaction with existing theories and ideas and are a fruitful breeding ground for conceptual change. Joint thinking processes, they declare, are much more effective than 'solo cognition'.

Similar findings underpin much current thinking in raising levels of attainment and understanding in other areas of science (Cavendish *et al.*, 1990; Harlen and

Black, 1990). In geography, Peter Knight (1993), David Leat (1996) and others have stressed the value of enquiry questions and cognitive conflict. The importance of problem-solving, games and simulations is also recognized. For example, HMI commented in their annual review of inspection findings that some of the best work with pupils in Years 5 and 6 'was based on debating local issues which required geographical knowledge and understanding. This was often successfully done by the pupils acting the characters in role' (HMI, 1993: 8).

As well as focusing attention on different aspects of the local area, enquiry questions can also be used for structuring studies about any locality around the world. In order to achieve a balance, a range of issues needs to be considered. The compass rose devised by Birmingham Development Centre is a valuable way of generating questions and drawing out parallels between people and places. In particular, it highlights change and social and environmental issues. Studies which fail to consider the needs of different sections of the community run the danger of being bland and simplistic. The way people interact with their surroundings also needs to be considered (see Figure 14.3).

One of the implications of taking a problem-orientated approach is that it often involves exploring controversial issues. On a local level this may lead to a conflict

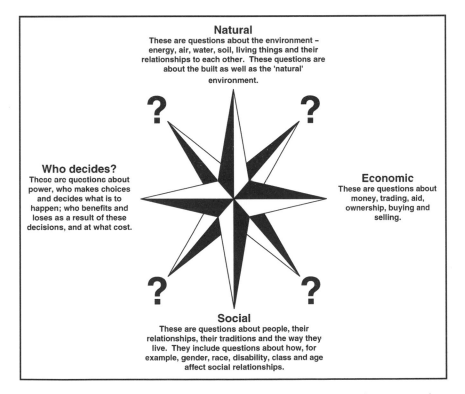

*Figure 14.3* Use the compass rose to help structure studies of places and issues around the world (after Birmingham Development Education Centre)

of interest between, say, the needs of the school and the needs of local businesses and organizations. On a global level any attempt to propose serious solutions to current issues is likely to involve a critique of wide-ranging social and political structures. In general, teachers need to consider each situation on its own merits and be prepared to use their common sense to strike a balance of interests or loyalties.

It is also important to consider different viewpoints and perspectives. Gough (1999) reminds us that the debate about the environment tends to be conducted by white, middle-aged males using English as their language of communication. Women and minority groups have a muted voice. The interests of developing countries are also often marginalized. We need to listen to the 'gaps' and 'silences' and be aware of the way that language can be appropriated by different interest groups according to their aims.

This may sound rather daunting, but even the youngest children can be introduced to different perspectives using stories and fictional accounts. For example, *Shaker Lane* by Alice and Martin Provensen (1993) considers the impact of a new reservoir on a small and powerless rural community. Conservation and direct action are also the themes in *The People Who Hugged the Trees* (Rose, 1990), an environmental folk tale from India by Deborah Lee Rose. Although the events in the tale happened nearly three centuries ago, it addresses some very modern concerns. Indeed, real lives and actual events provide the raw material for much inspired teaching in geography and environmental education. The activities of protest groups and 'eco-warriors' such as Swampy, who was famous in Britain in the early 1990s, are usually given considerable media coverage. Slightly further back in time, the murder of Chico Mendes, the rainforest campaigner, in Brazil in the 1980s still provides one of the most powerful and stirring environmental stories of the past few decades.

## Significant experiences

Another question which has been the focus of recent research is whether there are formative experiences or events which cause people to develop a sensitivity to the environment. A review of the findings by Chawla (1998) reveals generally consistent, if incomplete, findings. Some of the first studies were conducted in the early 1980s by Tanner who used a mixture of open-ended surveys and interviews to explore the background of those who either worked with environmental organizations or were engaged in environmental education. He found that the respondents cited interaction with the natural world (80 per cent), along with parents (49 per cent) and teachers (31 per cent) as key influences. Some years later, a much larger study by Palmer confirmed that childhood experiences out of doors were the single most important factor in developing personal concern for the environment. However, surveys in other countries (Slovenia and Greece) reveal the impact of negative experiences such as pollution. The question of what experiences *distinguish* those who are environmentally sensitive from those who are not still needs to be explored. Chawla concludes that there is probably no single, all-potent experience, but a mixture of factors. Interestingly, Palmer highlights the crucial influence of people, notably the family, teachers and other adults in awakening and fostering environmental concern.

These investigations suggest that committed and enthusiastic teaching can have a considerable influence on children, particularly when supported or reinforced by environmental activities at home and with grown-ups. Structured learning experiences are clearly vital in a classroom situation, but the importance of informal activities also needs to be recognized. Children relish the opportunity to linger, to explore places on their own and to indulge their imagination. Informal and unplanned spaces are particularly valuable. Titman (1994) in a summary of research on the school grounds and immediate surroundings, quotes an inter-war guide to infant activities which robustly declares:

> Waste ground, with trees and rubbish and perhaps a ditch, is the best plaything a child can be given. Geography is easily learned and wild fantasies worked out in the health-giving open air.
>
> (Boyce cited in Titman, 1994: 5)

Many other educationalists from Froebel, McMillan and Isaacs onwards have made similar observations. In an age when we are dominated by targets and achievements it is easy to forget that children sometimes simply need time to sit quietly on their own.

## Motivation

What is it that motivates children to explore and investigate their surroundings? Hart (1979) suggests that on one level we have a basic need to know about the world around us so we can find safe places in times of danger. But there are other reasons too. By exploring our surroundings we develop a sense of place identity and extend our control over the physical world, which in turn leads to a feeling of belonging. Through this process children learn as much about themselves as they do about the places they visit. Ultimately, we have a deep-seated desire to explore our oneness with nature and other creatures and hence better understand our place in the universe. We are all involved in this quest for meaning.

If this thesis is correct, it provides a powerful argument for giving a much higher profile to geography and environmental education in the school curriculum. Just as play is important in the development of the child, so environmental experiences meet a basic human need. Children have an innate affinity for the natural world. By developing and exploring this we may also be able to approach environmental issues at a root level. In the past many children developed basic physical, social and geographical skills through unsupervised interactions in their local neighbourhood. Fears of traffic and worries about molestation by strangers have led to youngsters being more and more restricted. Hillman (1998) has warned repeatedly of the danger of bringing children up in what he terms 'battery-reared' as opposed to 'free-range' conditions. Fieldwork and other outdoor educational experiences can help to provide some degree of compensation.

## The way forward

As we enter the twenty-first century there can be little doubt about the urgency of current problems. We need to educate children to be environmentally sensitive so they can participate responsibly in the affairs of both their own country and the wider international community. Oxfam (1997) has perceived the need for change and proposed its own version of the school curriculum. This aims to help children become global citizens who:

- are aware of the wider world;
- respect and value diversity;
- understand how the world works;
- are outraged by social injustice;
- contribute to the community;
- want to make the world more equitable and sustainable; and
- take responsibility for their actions.

Underpinning Oxfam's declaration is the belief that 'an education based on the principles of equity and social justice, with the development of the Global Citizen at its heart, is the key to a sustainable future' (Oxfam, 1997: 2). It is the kind of thinking which can help schools face the challenges which lie ahead.

Despite all the fine words and rhetoric of recent years, environmental education remains in an ambiguous and somewhat tenuous position in the school curriculum. Many commentators agree that schools need radical reorientation. Yet in Britain we have seen teaching increasingly co-opted by the language, practice and values of commerce in recent years. As Sterling puts it, not only are we educating children 'for a world that cannot be sustained in the future, we are also largely educating for a world that no longer exists' (Sterling, 1997: 24).

The notion of sustainability is one of the few positive environmental ideas which has emerged in recent years. Whether it will actually be possible to forge a link between technologies driven by commercial considerations on the one hand and ecological needs on the other is questionable. However, this approach does offer a way forward. Moreover, it reminds us about the importance of exploring values and attitudes at a time when discrete and measurable targets dominate the agenda. Restoring the human perspective will help to bring hope back to the classroom. Ultimately, it is through our vision and self-knowledge, not science and technology, that the environmental crisis stands the best chance of being addressed.

## Follow-up questions

1   What do you think are the most important environmental issues at the moment?
2   Is there a case for treating environmental education as a separate subject, rather than teaching it through other disciplines as at present?
3   What experiences have most influenced your own views towards the environment?

4 What do you think are the main features of good practice in environmental education teaching?

5 How would you justify fieldwork and outdoor work to an unsympathetic parent or teacher?

## References

Brandt, W. (1980) *North–South: A Programme for Survival*, London: Pan.

Brownlie, A. (1995) *Teaching About Localities*, Oxford: Oxfam.

Burningham, J. (1989) *Oi! Get off our Train*, London: Cape.

Cavendish, S. *et al.* (1990) *Assessing Science in the Primary Classroom: Observing Activities*, London: Paul Chapman.

Chambers, B. (1995) *Awareness into Action: Environmental Education in the Primary School*, Sheffield: Geographical Association.

Chawla, L. (1998) 'Significant life experiences revisited: a review of research on sources of environmental sensitivity', *Environmental Education Research*, 4, 4: 369–82.

DES (1990) *Geography for Ages 5 to 16*, London: HMSO.

Foreman, M. (1990) *One World*, London: Andersen.

Gough, A. (1999) 'Recognising women in environmental education and research: towards an eco-feminist post-constructuralist perspective', *Environmental Education Research*, 5, 2: 143–61.

Harlen, W. and Black, P. (1990) *Primary SPACE Project: Research Reports*, Liverpool: Liverpool University Press.

Hart, R. (1979) *Children's Experience of Place*, New York: Irvington.

Hicks, D. (1998) 'Stories of hope: a response to the "psychology of despair"', *Environmental Education Research*, 4, 2: 165–76.

Hill, R. (ed.) (1991) *Green Guide to Children's Books*, London: Books for Keeps.

Hillman, M. (1998) 'Neighbourhood safety', in Scoffham, S. (ed.) *Primary Sources*, Sheffield: The Geographical Association.

Hinrichsen, D. (1987) *Our Common Future: A Reader's Guide (The 'Brundtland Report Explained')*, London: Earthscan.

HMI (1993) *Geography Key Stages 1, 2 and 3*, London: HMSO.

Knight, P. (1993) *Primary Geography Primary History*, London: David Fulton.

Leat, D. (1996) 'Raising attainment in geography: prospects and problems', in Williams, M. (ed.) *Understanding Geographical and Environmental Education*, London: Cassell.

Mason, L. and Santi, M. (1998) 'Discussing the greenhouse effect: children's collaborative discussion, reasoning and conceptual change', *Environmental Education Research*, 4, 9: 67–84.

Moses, B. (1992) *Somewhere to Be*, Godalming: WWF.

Orr, D. (1992) 'Schools for the twenty first century', *Resurgence*, 160: 16–19.

Oxfam (1997) *A Curriculum for Global Citizenship*, Oxford: Oxfam.

Panel for Education for Sustainable Development (1998) *Education for Sustainable Development in the Schools Sector: A Report to DfEE/QCA*, London: DfEE/QCA.

Provensen, A. and M. (1993) *Shaker Lane*, London: Walker.

Quarrie, J. (ed.) (1992) *World Summit: The United Nations Conference on Environment and Development, Rio de Janeiro 1992*, London: Regency Press.

Rose, D. (1990) *The People Who Hugged the Trees*, Schull, West Ger: Rinehart.

SCAA (1996) *Teaching Environmental Matters Through the National Curriculum*, London: SCAA.

Chief Seattle (1992) *Brother Eagle, Sister Sky*, London: Hamilton.

Sterling, S. (1997) 'Education for change', in Huckle, J. and Sterling, S. (eds) *Education for Sustainability*, London: Earthscan.

Titman, W. (1994) *Special Places, Special People*, Godalming: World Wide Fund for Nature.

UNCED (1992) *Earth Summit 1992*, London: Regency Press.

United Nations (1998) *Human Development Report*, United Nations.

# 15 Europe matters

*Stephen Scoffham*

## Introduction

In Britain we are ambivalent in our attitude towards Europe. We joined the European Community only in 1973 after a long period of hesitation. The current debate over whether to participate in the European Monetary Union has revealed similar fault lines which have split the country and the main political parties. It seems that we are unwilling to contribute wholeheartedly to joint European ventures, but are sufficiently involved not to want to be left out.

This ambivalence is reflected in the school curriculum. As a nation we have subscribed to the various European directives, and there is undoubtedly considerable scope for teaching about Europe within the geography Programme of Study. However, these opportunities are often well concealed and it requires determination and careful reading to discover them.

In these circumstances there are many questions for teachers to consider. What are children's attitudes to Europe and when do they start developing their ideas? How do pupils find out about Europe? What are the boundaries of Europe and what does European identity actually mean? What are the most effective ways of promoting a European dimension? Above all, does Europe deserve a place in an already crowded curriculum? We need to have clear answers to these questions if we are to be effective and successful practitioners.

## Britain and Europe

Britain became separated from the mainland of Europe about 8,500 years ago at the end of the last Ice Age. As the ice melted, water broke through low-lying land between France and England. Although the Straits of Dover are as little as 30 km wide they have had a profound historical significance. Not only do they provide an important shipping route, but they have also served to protect Britain from invasion. There hasn't been a successful hostile landing on British soil since Norman times nearly a thousand years ago. It is hardly surprising, therefore, that the British have developed their own special sense of identity and a degree of insularity in their thinking. By contrast, the experience of our neighbours in Belgium and northern France has been markedly different.

The opening of the Channel Tunnel in 1994 symbolically ended Britain's isolation, creating a land route to the mainland for the first time in history. At the same time, the development of modern electronic communication systems has served to bring Britain closer to its European neighbours. Our links with Europe have proliferated through trade, holidays and cultural and political intercourse. Isolation is no longer possible in the modern world and national independence is a notion that has to be reinterpreted to take account of current realities. As Hamilton-Paterson puts it: 'Somewhere between 1945 and 1990 Britain lost consciousness of itself as an island' (Hamilton-Paterson, 1992: 76). This applies to education as much as to any other area of life.

## The concept of Europe

The concept of Europe dates back to the Greeks. The name itself comes from classical mythology. Europa, a beautiful princess was spotted by Zeus as she walked with her companions on the seashore. Zeus disguised himself as a bull and swam into the sea with Europa on his back, eventually reaching a new land (Crete) where he changed himself into the form of an eagle and ravished her.

While the rape of Europa belongs to mythology, the physical boundaries of the continent which bears her name are a geographical fact. Originally, the Greeks assumed that Europe ended at the Caspian Sea – a branch of the ocean that surrounded the world. Later they discovered that the Caspian was a great lake surrounded by land on all sides. As a result the boundary of Europe changed, becoming identified first with the River Don to the west and then with the Ural Mountains 1,000 kilometres to the east. Neither of these boundaries is particularly significant topographically.

In many ways Europe is best defined in political and cultural terms. The Greeks drew a division between their own 'civilized' world and the 'barbarians' who inhabited the lands beyond. The eastern and southern boundaries of the continent fluctuated according to events. From time to time waves of invaders have overrun vast areas. In medieval times Ghengis Khan laid waste to Kiev and large areas of surrounding land. A few centuries later the Ottomans conquered the Balkans and twice laid siege to Vienna. Only the Christian lands in the north and west seemed safe, forming a stronghold united by language and religion. The famous geographer Mackinder summed this up neatly when he declared 'European civilization is, in a very real sense, the outcome of the secular struggle against Asiatic invasion' (Mackinder, 1904: 12).

The fall of eastern and central Europe to Soviet domination in the present century has reinforced earlier myths of Western Europe as a haven of order and security. As Vujakovic argues, for much of the Cold War period 'Europe' came to mean Western Europe, and to 'become part of Europe' meant membership of the European Community (Vujakovic, 1999). Although there have been profound changes over the past decade with the break-up of the Soviet Union and the emergence of new countries in central and eastern Europe, the notion of Europe is still largely associated with the West. In addition, NATO (North Atlantic Treaty

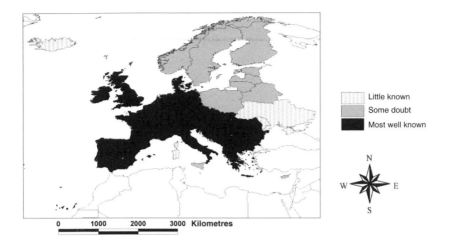

*Figure 15.1* Students' images of Europe

Organisation), from which eastern bloc countries used to be excluded, remains the cornerstone of European security arrangements.

An informal survey of students' images of Europe reveals the extent of this confusion. Forty-six first-year students who were following an Initial Teacher Training course (BA QTS) in primary education at Canterbury Christ Church University College were asked to shade Europe on a map of the world. The results showed a startling variety of images (Figure 15.1). One student shaded the whole of Europe and most of northern Asia, stopping only at the Pacific Ocean; another associated Europe with justy two countries – the UK and Ireland. Overall there was quite considerable doubt as to whether Scandinavia was a genuine part of the continent. The Mediterranean islands were also commonly omitted. Nearly all the students seriously underestimated the extent of eastern Europe. A further question about the location of Moscow showed that only three students (6 per cent) thought that it was a European city.

## Emotional involvement

One of the factors which may explain students' lack of knowledge about more remote parts of Europe is the geographical distance. Studies conducted at Stockholm University cited by Gould and White (1974) show how we tend to be most interested in local events and ignore things which do not affect us directly. Thus newspapers will report a cycle accident in a local side street, but dramatic events such as a motorway car crash or an aircraft accident only make the news if they happen further away. This can be expressed mathematically. On average, people's interest falls off with the square root of the perceived distance (Figure 15.2). It follows that Eastern Europe tends to be overlooked by both students and

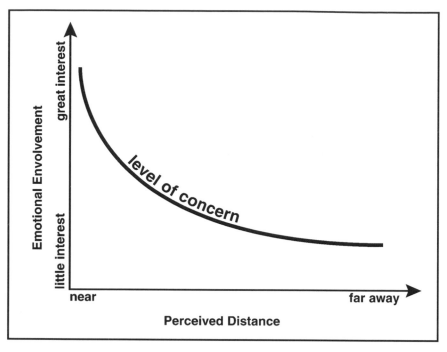

*Figure 15.2*  People tend to be most interested in local events (after Gould and
White, 1974)

the general public because it is so far away. It is interesting to note in this context
that many students failed to locate the Ukraine, the largest country in Europe, on
their maps.

Turning this argument around, one of the main arguments for teaching children
about Europe stems from this sense of emotional involvement. The countries of
mainland Europe are, together with the Irish Republic, our closest neighbours. We
belong to the European Community and share a common history and culture which
goes back to the Greeks and the Romans.

But there are other equally compelling reasons for promoting a European
dimension in the school curriculum. Common social, economic and political
structures are among the best hopes for promoting peace in a continent which has
suffered two devastating wars since the beginning of the century. These structures
are also essential when it comes to confronting environmental problems such as
acid rain and sea pollution which require international solutions. On a purely
pragmatic level, people travel much more nowadays than they did in the past and
are more likely to have friends abroad. Young people growing up in Britain today
will be taking their place in Europe and will need to fulfil their roles and duties as
European citizens as adults (see Figure 15.3).

Teaching children about Europe and preparing them for the future is part of
what Convery and others (1997) term an entitlement curriculum. This thinking

---

**The European Dream**

European nations have fought with each other almost continuously for the past thousand years. The EU has its roots in the determination of statesmen to build a new Europe after the Second World War. It is based on international trade, political cooperation and, above all, peace between nations.

Key events in the history of the EU

1951   Setting up of European Coal and Steel Community
1957   Signing of Treaty of Rome founding European Economic Community (EEC) and Euratom
1968   Completion of Customs Union
1973   Denmark, Ireland and UK join EC
1979   First direct elections to European Parliament
1981   Greece enters EC
1986   Portugal and Spain enter EC
1990   Unification of East and West Germany
1992   Treaty of Maastricht creates single market
1995   Austria, Finland and Sweden join the EC
1999   European monetary union

---

*Figure 15.3* The development of the European Union

has been given formal recognition by the European Union. A key resolution from the Council of Ministers for Education in 1988 identified the following policy objectives:

- to strengthen pupils' sense of European identity and civilization including democracy and human rights;
- to prepare young people to take part in the economic and social life of the Community;
- to improve children's knowledge of the Community and its member states;
- to highlight the importance of co-operation between member states and other countries of the world.

Following this resolution member states were required to publish their own policy statements on the European dimension. In England, the National Curriculum Council published a report in 1990 which emphasized the utilitarian value of teaching children about Europe. The European dimension also featured as part of 'education for citizenship', one of the five cross-curricular themes in the 1991 National Curriculum. These documents provide a valuable framework, but have nothing to say about teaching strategies and teaching techniques. To find out more we need to turn to research findings.

## What do children know about Europe?

Children start learning about Europe from an early age. Many 4-year-olds have heard of France and Spain and mention them when asked to list the countries they know. Seven-year-olds frequently add Greece and Italy to their repertoire. By the time they reach the age of 11 most children are aware of the countries of Western Europe. However, they still have great gaps in their mental maps. One of them covers Eastern Europe, which appears to remain largely unknown, even to 10- and 11-year-olds (Wiegand, 1993).

Research by Axia and others (1998) amplifies these findings. Three hundred 8- and 10-year-old children in British, Italian, Swiss and Spanish schools were asked to draw a map of Europe on a blank sheet of paper. Perhaps unsurprisingly, each national group proved best at drawing their own country and its immediate neighbours (see Figure 15.4). However, comparisons between nations showed that children from Italy performed significantly better than any other group. Axia speculates that proximity to other countries and the social, political and economic ties affect children's knowledge. The fact that children from south Italy failed to do as well as their north Italian counterparts, adds weight to this suggestion.

Axia's research also sheds light on the difference between age groups. While the 10-year-olds drew an average of eight countries on their maps, the 8-year-olds tended to show their own country and little else. They also tended to confuse countries, towns and other places, thinking of them all as separate and roughly equal areas.

The way children interpret the notion of a country has been fully investigated. Research by Piaget (1929) into the components of an address showed that below the age of 8 or 9 youngsters fail to appreciate how areas and regions fit together to make countries, which in turn combine into continents. The idea of a hierarchy or 'nesting relationship' appears to develop slowly over the primary years and may only actually be built up effectively during adolescence.

Weeden (1996) reports that even those children who have understood the idea of a settlement hierarchy appear to have difficulty placing a country within it. Part of the problem may be that the term 'country' has two meanings. It is used to refer both to the rural landscape (the countryside) and a nation state (a country). Words of this kind, which have a variety of meanings, tend to confuse pupils and impede their understanding.

This is significant not only in its own right, but also because there are some indications from studies undertaken with students that a knowledge of countries provides a basic framework for other locational knowledge such as rivers, mountains and cities (Catling, 1998). If this is true, then we need to take account of the developmental problems when teaching pupils about the map of Europe.

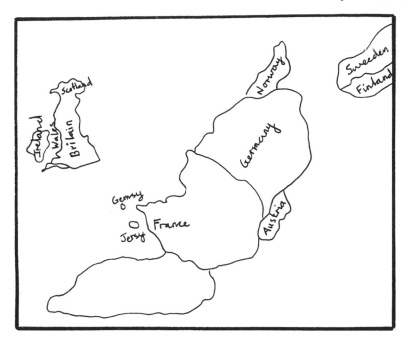

*Figure 15.4a* Map of Europe drawn by 10-year-old Scottish child (after Axia *et al.*, 1998)

*Figure 15.4b* Map of Europe drawn by 10-year-old north Italian child (after Axia *et al.*, 1998)

## Children's attitudes to Europe

Are young people interested in Europe and what attitudes do they have towards different nationalities? Barrett and Short (1992) conducted a study to find out what children in Britain think about the French, Italians, Germans and Spanish. They worked with two groups (ages 5–7 and 8–10), so they could see if the children's ideas changed with age.

With regard to the attributes and characteristics of different nationalities, they discovered that the young children generally failed to agree and were hampered by their lack of knowledge. By contrast, older children had much clearer opinions. In their view the Germans were 'white skinned' and 'aggressive', the Italians had 'smart clothes', 'lacked money' and 'ate spaghetti', the French were 'hardworking' and the Spanish were 'happy'.

When it came to attitudes and opinions the findings were even more illuminating:

> The two target nationalities about which the 5–7-year-old children had acquired the most information (French and Spanish) were also the two most well-liked nationalities. But despite the fact that these younger children had acquired comparatively little information about German and Italian people, this did not prevent them expressing affective responses to these two nationalities. German people, in particular were very positively disliked.
>
> (Barrett and Short, 1992: 356)

The fact that children express opinions about different nationalities and are often quite vehement in their views even before they have learnt anything about them has been widely noted (Scoffham, 1999). One possible explanation is that young children absorb attitudes just as they acquire other facts, and accept them without question or criticism.

## The link between knowledge and attitudes

What, then, is the link between knowledge and attitudes? In an international study of children aged 6 to 14, Lambert and Klineberg (1967) found that children were well informed about national groups which they liked and were ill informed about national groups that they disliked. Stillwell and Spencer (1974) too found a favourable shift in attitudes when they exposed children to a large classroom display on Germany.

In a more recent small-scale student study Baker (1995) explored pupils' attitudes to Germany. Careful questioning of a class of 8-year-olds uncovered an astonishing level of ignorance and confusion. Their stereotypical German was tall and skinny with brown or black skin and a funny hat. Some of the children also expressed some very strong negative opinions about Germans, with comments such as 'They're all Nazis' and 'They're disgusting people'. Associations with the Second World War were very much alive and were cited by 40 per cent of the class in brainstorms and association exercises. Encouragingly, the pupils tempered their views after a term's project and became much more neutral and balanced. Indeed, Baker noted that their actual attitudes were much harder to detect, 'seeming to disappear as they did behind the factual knowledge and snippets of information they had acquired' (Baker, 1995: 69).

It also seems that children are better able to understand the behaviour of people whom they like than those whom they dislike. In an ingenious study on reciprocity, Middleton, Tajfel and Johnson (1970) devised a simulation of a desert island rescue. The children were presented with a model of an island, together with dolls with labels round their necks to indicate different nationalities and four boats each 'captained' by a person from a different country. Which dolls would each captain choose to save? In their answers the children indicated they thought people from the countries they liked would behave more fairly than people from countries they disliked. In other words, the children's preferences influenced their ability to see other points of view.

One question which is worth considering further is the way children's attitudes change with age. It seems that infants select favourite countries on the basis of exotic or picturesque features. Their choices tend to be based on information that they have gathered at random. Past wars are often cited as the reason for disliking a country. However, their views are fleeting and liable to rapid change.

Later, at about the age of 8 or 9, children's preferences become more stable. People rather than places become increasingly important. Indeed, there is strong evidence from a major UNESCO study that children become more knowledgeable and favourably disposed towards people of other lands as they pass through the junior years. Friendliness to foreigners appears to peak around age 11, followed by a downward curve in international and interracial goodwill during adolescence (Carnie, 1972).

One of the reasons for introducing pupils to the European dimension is to challenge the negative stereotypes they may have acquired. There are powerful reasons for beginning this task at an early age whilst children's attitudes and opinions are still malleable. By the time they reach secondary school age prejudices are much harder to dislodge. A study of 3,000 American students reported by Hibberd (1983) lends weight to this view. Despite a course on the Third World, their views hardly changed between the ages of 12 and 17. 'Teachers need to work very hard indeed', Hibberd declares, 'to counteract false or unbalanced images already formed' (Hibberd, 1983: 68).

However, it is also important to remember that many pupils have no ideas at all about many places in Europe and other parts of the world before they are taught about them in school. As Wiegand points out:

in the primary school we are dealing as much with attitude formation as attitude change. Before learning about other countries many children are neither positively or negatively disposed towards those countries. They simply haven't thought much about them at all and don't have any clearly developed view.

(Wiegand, 1992: 55)

If this is the case, then the argument for presenting children with positive images becomes even more compelling.

## Sources of information

How do children find out about Europe and other parts of the world? Barrett and Short (1992) included a question about sources of information in the two hundred or so interviews they conducted. The children mentioned television as their main source of knowledge, followed by parents, books and holidays. While the accuracy of these results based on self-reporting may be open to question, they nevertheless seem significant. Baker (1995) comments on the enormous power of television to affect children's learning, and notes that the programmes she showed on Germany seemed to override everything else she tackled in class. A review of the research literature confirms that television is a key source of information about the wider world. What children glean from television programmes, the way they interpret different images and how they make sense of them are another issue.

The impact of travel on children's learning has also been hotly debated. About one-third of package holidays involve trips to southern Spain and the Balearic islands. Another third are focused on France and Greece. As a result, it is not uncommon to find children who have been abroad, even from relatively deprived areas. Quite how much children learn from these visits, which are often restricted to tourist resorts catering for the mass market, is open to question. Wiegand (1993) takes a positive view, concluding that at the very least children who have travelled will gain some idea of the distance they went, the route they took and the language, food and currency of the country they visited. Others, he claims, learn much more. They achieve a sense of balance in the way they describe places and recognize that the stereotypes which they previously held may not be true after all.

## Classroom considerations

How do schools affect children's knowledge of Europe? Barrett and Short note that the primary school children they interviewed rarely cited teachers as a source of knowledge. They conclude from this that 'there may be an important need for more attention to be paid to European issues in the primary school curriculum' (Barrett and Short, 1992: 360). Where teaching does take place, it appears to be effective. Axia found that those 10-year-olds who had been taught about Europe marked an average of eleven countries on their maps. Those who had had no educational input only marked about six. Axia observes: 'children seem to be highly receptive to the information' given by the school curricula on Europe' (Axia *et al.*, 1998: 436).

At secondary school level the situation appears rather more encouraging. An international survey of over 1,300 pupils (Convery *et al.*, 1997) indicated that 54 per cent of the pupils felt 'quite well informed about Europe' and they cited the media (55 per cent) and school (46 per cent) as their main information sources.

More detailed questioning about learning experiences revealed that teaching about Europe featured most strongly in the geography lessons (79 per cent), followed by history (69 per cent) and modern languages (60 per cent). Convery argues that students have a strong desire to learn about Europe:

> A powerful message to emerge from the research data is that young people living in the EU today would like to know more about the Europe they inhabit and would like to have the tools at their disposal to help them interpret the stream of data that comes their way via the media and their personal experiences.

> (Convery *et al.*, 1997: 74)

Looking to the future, Convery recognizes that greater openness and integration within the European Union will provide young people with an increasing range of opportunities. Females, whites, the better off and those who have travelled more will be able to seize these opportunities better than others. Education has an important role in promoting equality for disadvantaged groups that are already experiencing economic and social exclusion.

## Curriculum requirements

There are considerable opportunities for teaching pupils about Europe within the National Curriculum. In general terms, geography, history and modern languages are three subjects which have particularly appropriate content and skills. Cross-curricular dimensions such as environmental education are also highly relevant. The citizenship curriculum offers further, quite specific, possibilities.

Within geography, work on Europe can serve both as specific locality studies and to illustrate more general themes and issues. One of the principles under-pinning the geography curriculum is that pupils should work on a range of scales from local to global. Europe clearly features in this continuum. The curriculum also requires pupils to develop their knowledge of places and features around the world. A growing familiarity with the map of Europe should be one of the other learning outcomes.

It was never intended to set up separate courses to teach pupils about Europe. Following the 1988 Resolution of Ministers, all the members of the Union agreed instead that a European dimension should be incorporated into appropriate areas of the curriculum. The importance of using teaching materials with a European perspective was also stressed. In the United Kingdom journals such as *Teaching Geography* and *Primary Geographer* have carried regular articles on how to achieve these aims. There has also been a range of publications and official advice from government bodies (see Figure 15.5).

The enormous excitement and value of work on Europe are captured particularly well in some of these 'voices from the classroom'. Sara Stone, for example, is an infant teacher who decided to include a European dimension in her topic on food and farming. The work involved putting symbols on a map, learning a few words

- Make a survey of the local area for its connections with the rest of Europe.
- Find out about places in Europe which are featured in the news.
- Look at paintings of famous European landscapes.
- Prepare a meal using food and recipes from another part of Europe.
- Plan routes to holiday destinations in different parts of Europe.
- Read stories either traditional or modern with European settings.
- Organize a festival of Europe using costumes and music.
- Compare a typical school day in Britain and another part of Europe.
- Learn a few words in different European languages.
- Set up a display of postcards showing European cities and landscapes.
- Invite a parent or visitor who has lived in Europe to talk to the class.
- Use a locality pack to find out about a specific village or town.
- Record the weather across Europe over a period of a week using newspaper reports.
- Celebrate Europe Day (9 May) with workshops on different themes.
- Study satellite photographs and maps of Europe.
- Devise a quiz of European facts and figures.
- Watch a television programme about a place in Europe.
- Make up a game on a European theme or topic.
- Design a poster or leaflet to attract visitors to a European location.
- Find out about different European countries using information books and the Internet.
- Make a class-to-class link and exchange information by e-mail.

*Figure 15.5* Twenty-one ways of introducing a European dimension into the school curriculum

in different languages, setting up a class travel agency and finding out about the Single Market. Reflecting on the value of this approach, she concludes:

> It is important for social development that KS1 children experience working in activities that involve co-operation and empathy skills. It helps them to understand how, in a wider context, the member states of Europe (and beyond) have to work together too. They understand that countries do not always agree with each other but try to work things out because it is in the best interests of all the countries to do so. Quite sophisticated for five- to seven-year olds! By teaching them to accept and work with others at KS1 we set our children on the road to becoming 'good Europeans'. Europe is a state of mind!
>
> (Stone, 1997: 14)

Inevitably it takes time for a European dimension to become established within the work of a school. Halocha (1997) stresses the value of starting on a small scale and gradually building on success. He also argues that study visits to Europe for staff or pupils have a key role to play in helping to develop a sense of commitment. Wiegand makes the same point in a different way when he declares that authenticity is the essence and that 'there really does have to be some sense of contact with the place being studied' (Wiegand, 1992: 79). At primary level the idea of focusing on a locality is fundamental, as it helps pupils to make comparisons with their own area and avoids crude stereotypes and generalizations. Case studies and selected examples are equally valuable at Key Stage 3 (11–14 years).

Whatever approach you adopt, it is important not to overlook the children's own experience and to relate the work to their understanding and preconceptions. Donoghue (1998) notes how, when working with a number of different classes to conduct a student study, 'the teachers had all underestimated the level of the children's travel and as a result chose not to exploit the experiences in their teaching' (Donoghue, 1998: 28). This observation could be applied to many schools around the country.

One way of avoiding such oversights is to conduct your own action research before beginning any work with your class. This doesn't have to be complex and time-consuming. For example, you might ask the pupils to draw their own freehand map of Europe and to show ten places or features they know. Alternatively you could give them a blank map to complete. As well as being informative, the diversity of the response and range of errors is likely to be helpful in future lesson planning. Even simpler, you could get the class to brainstorm the things they know about the country or theme you are studying. Sort the information into categories using headings such as landscape, weather, people, transport and environment and repeat the exercise at the end of the project or lesson to see what they have learnt. Another approach is to provide a framework with three headings: *What I know*, *What I can guess*, *What I would like to find out about*. Apart from anything else, this approach is an excellent way of generating enquiry questions.

## Dismantling barriers

One of the questions Convery *et al.* (1997) included in their interview schedule was 'Do you think of yourself as European?' Forty per cent of English youngsters responded with the answer 'Not at all' , compared with 10 per cent in Germany and less than 5 per cent in Italy and the Netherlands. Other questions about current issues and decision-making revealed a similar pattern. Youngsters in mainland Europe seem to be significantly more pro-European than those in England.

Convery argues that teachers across Europe are struggling to introduce a European dimension to the curriculum. The lack of money, training and central government initiatives is limiting progress to a few enthusiastic schools and individuals. In Britain especially, teachers are overwhelmed by educational change. The pressure on the timetable has put Europe quite firmly at the bottom of a long list of priorities.

Yet teaching about Europe need not be time-consuming. If integrated with other subjects, it can be enriching and highly stimulating. There are powerful arguments for ensuring that pupils learn about Europe from the earliest age. These extend far beyond the utilitarian concerns of employment and economic success. What matters much more is to ensure that children develop a multinational perspective, that they appreciate the diversity of people and culture and that they acquire positive attitudes towards them.

The research evidence indicates that knowledge has an important part to play in changing attitudes. It also suggests that many children have acquired negative ideas and opinions about our European neighbours even before they come to school. These are most effectively challenged and moulded in the primary school years before they become too entrenched. This is also the best time developmentally to teach children about Europe as juniors (7–11-year-olds) seem to be particularly well disposed to foreigners.

At secondary level (age 11–16) there are exciting opportunities for extending pupils' knowledge and understanding. Not only are they able to learn more about different countries and gain increasing familiarity with the map of Europe, but they can also take on more abstract ideas to do with economics, politics, decision-making and citizenship.

The school curriculum needs to equip children for the needs and demands of the twenty-first century. It needs to be forward-thinking and pro-active. Learning about Europe and breaking through the xenophobic bounds which have restricted our thinking for so long are a vital part of this process. We live in the modern age where mass air travel and electronic communication have effectively eliminated geographical distance. Many of the world's most pressing issues can be dealt with only on an international and global scale. We need to see that we play our part in dismantling barriers.

## Follow-up questions

1   Is there any substance in the notion of Western Europe as the stronghold of European values?
2   How might research findings influence the way you teach pupils about Europe?
3   Why is it important to include a European dimension in the school curriculum and at what age should this begin?
4   Do you think of yourself as a European?

## References

Axia, G., Bremner, J., Deluca, P. and Andreasen, G. (1998) 'Children drawing Europe: the effects of nationality, age and teaching', *British Journal of Developmental Psychology*, 16: 423–37.

Baker, V. (1995) 'Children's knowledge and perceptions of Germany', unpublished student study, Canterbury Christ Church University College.

Barrett, M. and Short, J. (1992) 'Images of European people in a group of 5–10-year-old English schoolchildren', *British Journal of Developmental Psychology*, 10: 339–63.

Bell, G. (1991) *Developing a European Dimension in Primary Schools*, London: Fulton.

Carnie, J. (1972) 'Children's attitudes to other nationalities', in Graves, N. (ed.) *New Movements in the Study and Teaching of Geography*, London: Temple Smith.

Catling, S. (1998) 'Primary student teachers' world map knowledge', unpublished paper for UDE Geography Tutors' Conference, Bath.

Convery, A., Evans, M., Green, S., Macaro, E. and Mellor, J. (1997) *Pupils' Perceptions of Europe*, London: Cassell.

Donoghue, T. (1998) 'Travel as a factor in developing children's understanding of their address', unpublished student study, Canterbury Christ Church University College.

Gould, P. and White, R. (1974) *Mental Maps*, London: Penguin.

Halocha, J. (1997) 'The European dimension in primary education', in Tilbury, D. and Williams, M., *Teaching and Learning Geography*, London: Routledge.

Hamilton-Paterson, J. (1992) *Seven-Tenths*, London: Hutchinson.

Hibberd, D. (1983) 'Children's images of the Third World', *Teaching Geography*, 9, 2: 68–72.

Lambert, W. and Klineberg, O. (1967) *Children's Views of Foreign Peoples: A Cross-cultural Study*, London: Appleton-Century Crofts.

Mackinder, H. (1904) *The Geographical Pivot of History*, London: Royal Geographical Society.

Middleton, M., Tajfel, M. and Johnson, N. (1970) 'Cognitive and affective aspects of children's national attitudes', *British Journal of Social and Clinical Psychology*, 9: 122–34.

Piaget, J. (1929) *The Child's Conception of the World*, London: Kegan Paul.

Scoffham, S. (1999) 'Young children's perceptions of the world', in David, T. (ed.) *Teaching Young Children*, London: Paul Chapman.

Stillwell, R. and Spencer, C. (1974) 'Children's early preferences for other nations and their subsequent acquisition of knowledge about those nations', *European Journal of Social Psychology*, 3, 3: 345–9.

Stone, S. (1997) 'Taking key stage 1 into Europe', *Primary Geographer*, 29: 12–15.

Vujakovic, P. (1999) '"A new map is unrolling before us"!: Cartography in news media representations of post-cold war Europe', *Cartographic Journal*, 36, 1: 43–57.

Weeden, P. (1996) 'What is the capital of France and where is Burkina Faso?', *Primary Geographer*, 26: 12–13.

Wiegand, P. (1992) *Places in the Primary School*, London: Falmer Press.

Wiegand, P. (1993) *Children and Primary Geography*, London: Cassell.

## Further reading

*Primary Geographer* (1994) 19 (October) Focus on Europe.

*Primary Geographer* (1997) 29 (April) The European Context.

# 16 The place of assessment in geographical education

*Graham Butt*

## Introduction

In this chapter I will provide an overview of the role, function and practice of assessment in geographical education from ages 5 to 19 in English and Welsh schools since 1945. Given the inevitable restrictions on space within a publication of this size, it is only possible to provide a somewhat cursory exploration of what are, in many cases, large assessment issues. However, the aim is primarily to provide an introduction to a range of questions that face many teachers in their day-to-day teaching and assessment of geography. The myriad of assessment methods, qualifications and accreditations within geographical education is considered, as is the balance between individual teacher assessment and that undertaken by the 'assessment industry' which currently dominates the education world. It is the belief of the author that many important assessment issues still remain 'under-theorized' as Lambert (1996a: 262) and others (Black and Wiliam, 1998; Gipps, 1994) acknowledge.

There are a number of fundamental questions concerning assessment practices in geography which we need to explore. I will initially concentrate on two deceptively simple ones – first, 'What is assessment?', and second, 'Why do we assess?'

A definition of the term 'assessment' provides a useful starting point. Assessment is usually understood to be the process by which information is gathered on how students respond to the variety of educational tasks we set before them. It includes the interpretation of student performance, the recording of the evidence of that performance, and the use of such evidence either educationally or bureaucratically. Importantly, a range of different assessment tasks should ideally be employed if the evidence gathered is to be valid and reliable. There should also be some standards of performance stated at the outset against which the responses of the students can be measured.

Interestingly, the second question of *why* we assess is not posed very often, probably because assessment has increasingly become such an accepted cornerstone of education. Without question assessment has always been regarded as 'an inevitable and essential part of the education process' (Lambert, 1997: 255), but its role and function are rather infrequently held up to close scrutiny. Therefore assessment tends to be viewed simply as an accepted activity that teachers must undertake as part of their professional role. In fact, 'assessment' is not a single, straightforward, tangible activity, but exists in many different forms, each of which may serve different purposes. This diversity of forms is both a strength and a weakness. When an assessment activity is correctly targeted to a particular purpose which is understood by all those who are taking part in the process – and it has been trialled successfully – it may provide valid and reliable evidence of student attainment. However, all too often, the results obtained from different assessment methods are used to serve purposes for which they were neither designed, nor particularly suited.

In essence, the main purposes of assessment can be categorized into four key functions: formative, summative, certification and evaluation. These will be briefly described. Assessment can be either formative – helping teachers and students to decide on the most appropriate next steps in the education process; or summative – providing a statement of the level of student performance at a given point in the education process. In turn this assessment information may be used to decide whether certification (the award of a qualification recognizing attainment) can occur, or it can be used to evaluate how successful the education process has been for the student, the teacher and the school. However, the bureaucratic use of assessment evidence as a crude performance indicator, or in the creation of league tables, is regularly criticized for failing to take into account other significant factors within student and school performance.

Public examinations have traditionally been used as the major system of selecting young people for educational or employment purposes. As such, they predominantly perform a 'one-way' summative process – something which the 'assessor' does to the 'assessed'. The person assessed has little real involvement in the assessment process, apart from sitting an examination and then receiving a judgement at the end of it! This is quite different from the day-to-day formative assessments which serve broader educational, rather than bureaucratic, purposes. Here the teacher uses different methods of assessment to find out more about the student as a learner, and then uses the knowledge acquired to plan for future learning experiences. In both the summative and formative systems assessment and performance criteria should be explained to the students before the teaching starts. These criteria should also have been formulated as a part of the curriculum planning process.

The main danger, as stated above, is that we expect whatever assessment methods we have established to serve too many purposes. This usually results in none of the expected outcomes being performed well. Few, if any, assessment systems can simultaneously assess, measure, record, report and evaluate practice all at the same time – although in many ways this is what is currently expected of assessment within the National Curriculum.

## What is the history of assessment in geography?

A brief history of assessment practice in England and Wales since 1945 provides a useful background to any discussion of current and future developments in the context of geographical education. This section concludes with a more detailed examination of the National Curriculum assessment system, which provides a contemporary example of how assessment at a national scale can become conflated and burdensome. In this respect we can see how misconceived practices can serve to create false expectations of what a large assessment system is capable of.

It is perhaps wise to start by looking at public examinations, as these represent the most 'visible' and 'high stakes' forms of assessment used in England and Wales since 1945. In 1951 a two-tier system of Ordinary ('O') and Advanced ('A') levels was introduced to replace the existing School Certificate, following recommendations previously published in the Norwood Report (1943). These examinations were designed for the most able students, with O-levels created to assess the attainment of the top 20 per cent of young people. In view of the lack of certification for the 'less able', the Certificate of Secondary Education ('CSE') was introduced in 1963 to examine the next 40 per cent of the ability range, leaving the 'bottom' 40 per cent without any form of educational certification whatsoever. The CSE provided greater freedom for geography teachers to partly design their own curricula and assess their courses, subject to external moderation by examination boards. It was soon apparent that although more students could now gain some form of accreditation for their educational attainment, the existence of two qualifications at 16 was divisive and often led to hasty and pejorative judgements being made about students' abilities. As a result many schools, keen to delay decisions about which examination to enter students for and to maximize their chances of achieving a pass at the more prestigious O level, engaged in cumbersome and expensive 'double entry' of candidates. This nonsense was eradicated by the introduction of the GCSE in 1986, following a decade of 16-plus trials in schools where candidates were assessed against common, but differentiated, papers. However, the recent introduction of tiered papers in geography has meant a partial return to the situation which existed pre-GCSE, as geography teachers are again called on to decide whether to enter their students for the 'Higher' (grades A*–E) or 'Foundation' (grades C–G) GCSE papers. In 1998 another new examination, the Certificate of Achievement (CoA), was introduced to provide the lowest achievers with the opportunity of gaining a qualification at the end of Year 11. GCSE criteria do not apply to this certificate; therefore coursework components are not limited to 25 per cent of the final assessments and the grading of performance can be closely linked to National Curriculum levels. As such, the CoA offers a broadening of the educational opportunities for students who traditionally left school with few qualifications (Flinders, 1998).

The GCSE is generally perceived to be a successful examination. It is based on agreed National Criteria, both general and subject-specific, which have been developed for examining boards and groups to devise their syllabuses around. Grade criteria are made explicit within this examination (for grades A, C and F) and GCSEs are regularly updated enabling geography syllabuses to keep pace with changing concepts and key ideas. All the geography syllabuses include some aspects of social, economic, environmental, physical and political geography, often with an emphasis on enquiry methods, fieldwork/coursework and values and attitudes. Attainment in geography is assessed through the knowledge, understanding and skills which the candidates show. However, different geography syllabuses approach the subject in different ways and may emphasize particular geographical issues, themes and concepts to be taught and assessed. Similarly, they may stress that certain geographical skills and abilities should be tested – such as decision-making or competence in carrying out field investigations.

Despite its success, the future of the GCSE is difficult to predict, for it now sits rather uneasily within the 14–19 curriculum. Changes which have occurred 'around' the GCSE since its inception raise some interesting questions about the possible future role of this examination. The growth of Part 1 GNVQs for 14- to 16-year-olds also creates something of a tension – how easily do academic and vocational programmes of study and assessments now fit together within the existing curriculum framework? With the amalgamation of academic examination boards and vocational groups, what are the pressures from within the assessment system for large-scale change? Is the surge in the number of students 'staying on' in schools and colleges beyond the age of 16 forcing a reappraisal of the whole 14–19 curriculum, and the stage(s) at which assessment should occur within it? In essence, does a narrowly academic GCSE examination at 16 still continue to serve a useful purpose? Recent spectacular falls in the numbers of candidates entered for GCSE geography, from 303,858 candidates in 1996 to 267,533 in 1998, also need to be entered into the assessment equation for those involved in the teaching of geography at this level.

A-level examinations have remained as the 'gold standard' of academic assessment within the 16–19 age range since the 1950s, although throughout this period they have been subject to many attempts at reform. The reasons why these attempts have largely failed are reasonably straightforward:

> the fear that reduced specialisation at A level would mean more expensive four year degree courses; the additional costs of extra teaching and examining required to broaden the curriculum; and the reluctance of Governments to expose themselves to criticisms that they were tampering with the 'gold standard'.
>
> (*Times Educational Supplement*, 1999)

Nonetheless, geographers have been influential in the efforts to change this examination 'from within'. Perhaps the most notable example of such innovation has been the '16–19 Geography Project', which was based at the University of London from 1976 and funded by the Schools Council up until 1983, followed by funding from the School Curriculum Development Committee. The project achieved a radical reappraisal of the aims and practice of geography education and assessment at this level. The popularity of the geography A-level associated with the project bears witness to its achievements, as do the subsequent changes made to other A-level syllabuses in their attempts to mirror the success of this examination.

In the 1990s, the growing pressure to reform the A-level system, particularly because of the increasing recognition that vocational qualifications needed greater promotion within post-16 education, led to a series of national changes. These have involved the creation of an AS (Advanced Supplementary, then Advanced Subsiduary) examination which originally stood alone from that of the A-level, but which has now become a first stage on the route to a full A-level qualification. Recent attempts to broaden sixth-form education have resulted in suggestions that five subjects should initially be studied at post-16 level, instead of the current norm of three. With all students starting their course of study at AS level, decisions will be made after their first year about how many subjects they should study in their final year. These second-year courses, called A2 qualifications, will be slightly more demanding than those taken in the lower sixth and combine to create a full A-level. At the same time, GNVQ qualifications have been standardized with those of A-levels and repackaged into six and three unit awards, each graded A to E (Cassidy, 1999). These changes have been paralleled by efforts to introduce new literacy, numeracy and IT qualifications for all within the 16–19 curriculum.

Highlighting the development of the public examination system this century, Daugherty (1990) concludes that its role has mainly been one of selection, although examinations also serve to confirm each subject's status and establish a focus for educational priorities. In the past, external judgements of 'good practice' in geography education have been closely related to the skills of the geography teacher in knowing what and how to teach, rather than to the assessment of what the students had learned. Examinations were therefore taken at the end of a course of study to provide a summative measure of who were the high achievers, rather than to provide a formative guide as to what should be taught in the future, or an evaluation of the effectiveness of the teaching that had gone before.

## Assessment in the National Curriculum

Importantly, before the Education Reform Act (ERA) of 1988, governments had not seen assessment in education as a matter for their express concern or involvement. Assessment was previously viewed as a professional matter to be left to schools, teachers and examination boards, rather than to be directed by the government of the day. The basic principles which underpinned the national assessment system of public examinations and daily teacher assessment had, therefore, remained largely unaltered from the time of the last major Education Act in 1944. Inevitably, however, this system was seen by many as being somewhat harsh, given its obvious function of simply dividing students into groups of perceived successes and failures.

Following the growth in the number of comprehensive schools and the almost wholesale removal of the 11-plus examination nationally, the educational attainment of children remained largely unassessed by any external body until the age of 16 during the 1970s and 1980s. Ambitious and radical plans to assess all students at a national scale (around 600,000 in each year group throughout state schools in England and Wales) at regular intervals during their compulsory schooling began to emerge from the right of the Conservative Party in the late 1980s (Daugherty, 1995). The idea of a truly national assessment system – as much to assess the performance of teachers and schools, as that of children – began to develop alongside plans to create a National Curriculum, which would serve as the vehicle for its delivery. The Education Reform Act 1988, in tandem with the report of the Task Group on Assessment and Testing (TGAT) (DES, 1988), bound together a National Curriculum of subjects with a national assessment system for the first time. Teachers would in future be called on to make assessments of student performance against levels of attainment within Attainment Targets, or administer externally produced tests called Standard Assessment Tasks (SATs). Almost overnight a national assessment system was instigated, ostensibly tied to that which already existed at Key Stage 4 through the established GCSEs. Nonetheless, the government was unsure about both the means and practice of educational assessment – although by instinct it was not willing to give too much support to teacher assessment as opposed to external testing, either through the National Curriculum or GCSE. The major stumbling block appeared to be how far teachers could be trusted to assess reliably, compared to more 'rigorous' external means of assessment through publicly administered examinations or tests. The Conservative governments of the 1980s and early 1990s believed strongly that not only should the school curriculum be redefined, but also that educational change could be firmly led by national assessment. The (hopefully) reliable assessment evidence gained would then be used to justify various policies introduced to raise educational standards. Interestingly educational standards are notoriously difficult to define and equally hard to apply. Having often been created by professional consensus, such standards are not absolutes, and can only be used within agreed parameters of acceptable levels of performance. This makes their use and application rather more blurred around the edges than many politicians, and indeed some education-alists, would have us believe.

The original National Curriculum model of assessment was deeply flawed and became subject to rapid review (Dearing, 1994). The linking of aspects of knowledge and content to levels was problematic, as was the recording of student progress – even the then Department of Education and Science (DES) admitted that there was a danger that some of the more elaborate forms of assessment and recording schemes developed in schools would swamp teaching and learning. Walford's (1992) insider view on this period of development of assessment practice within the emergent Geography National Curriculum is significant:

> It's probably true that the full impact of assessment on the curriculum was never fully considered; but that was mostly because of a consistent steering away from the issue by the Secretariat who told us that it was not our business.
> (Walford, 1992: 99)

Statements of Attainment (SoAs) and SATs did not provide adequate assessment information to support children's learning; whilst the ability of the national assessment system to accurately describe attainment, measure progression and support educational development was poor. The Dearing Review (1994) introduced the concept of Level Descriptions (LDs) as a means of replacing the previously flawed and over-elaborate system of levels assessment against SoAs. Daugherty (1995) rightly commented that teachers would need a good deal of support in using these new LDs in their role as teacher assessors, and that moderation of some sort would be necessary to ensure standards at the national scale. Teacher assessment could not be expected to produce reliable attainment data 'without moderation arrangements which controlled both the tasks set by teachers and the way teachers interpret students' responses to those tasks' (p. 190). Problems of consistency of practice between schools and the need for some forms of comparison to be made across schools soon arose. However, the only real support given to teachers came from documents on teacher assessment produced by the School Curriculum and Assessment Authority (SCAA), the Qualifications and Curriculum Authority (QCA), and eventually through a series of Optional Tests and Tasks.

Arguably some of the biggest debates over the past decade concerning assessment in geography, and indeed many other subjects, have been about assessment in the National Curriculum. The government of the day introduced the National Curriculum before the means for its assessment were either fully thought through, or trialled in schools – a naïve act given that the whole curriculum was designed to be 'assessment led' from its conception. The original model of assessment for the National Curriculum, produced by Professor Paul Black's 'Task Group on Assessment and Testing' (TGAT) (DES, 1988), purported to provide a flexible, comprehensive framework for assessment – a claim which many commentators at the time felt to be at best optimistic (Daugherty, 1990; Lambert, 1996a). Despite the lack of evidence that the TGAT model could work, it was nonetheless predicated on some sound assessment principles, namely that assessment should be criteria-referenced, formative, moderated and linked to progression. The belief that assessment should be the servant, rather than the master, of the curriculum was also indisputable. The report heralded a system of assessment which acknowledged that:

> Promoting children's learning is the principal aim of schools. Assessment is at the heart of the process. It can provide a framework in which educational objectives may be set and students' progress charted and expressed. It can yield a basis for planning the next educational steps in response to children's needs.
> (DES, 1988: para. 3)

Unfortunately the reality of the unwieldy assessment system produced was rather different.

## The importance of the growth of teacher assessment

Teacher assessment has become an increasingly important facet of classroom practice, particularly since the implementation of the National Curriculum. The

National Curriculum forced a fundamental shift in both teachers' perceptions of their assessment roles and responsibilities, and in redefining the relationship between external examinations and teacher assessment. As a result, teacher assessment now has a greater status, importance and recognition than at any other time. The two distinct and separate cultures which had previously existed – that of the assessment 'industry', and that of daily 'teacher marking' (Lambert, 1996a, 1996b) – have now become rather blurred at the edges, with the once sharp distinction between the two finally being removed by the National Curriculum. Geography teachers are now responsible for assessing all of their students at Key Stage 3 against nationally identified levels and standards. Whereas in the recent past such judgements of attainment were largely for the consumption of the students themselves, their parents and other teachers, the audience for this assessment information is now much wider. Comparisons of such assessments on a national scale, both within geography and between subjects, make for interesting reading (see Butt and Smith, 1998).

Although early evidence showed that new teacher assessment systems started badly (Daugherty and Lambert, 1993; Fry and Schofield, 1993; Roberts, 1991, 1995), with Heads of Department feeling that bureaucratic rather than educational motives were driving the assessment process, things have gradually got better. OFSTED reports (1993a, 1993b) have provided official evidence that geography departments initially struggled with assessment, recording and reporting – a situation that has improved, but which is admittedly still less than satisfactory. In many ways this state of affairs is unremarkable, for in the early 1990s very little money was being directed into supporting teacher assessment compared with the considerable sums directed towards producing SATs for the core subjects. In addition, very little official guidance on teacher assessment was published in the early days of the National Curriculum, with teachers having either to devise strategies for themselves, or to rely on guidance from professional associations, working groups or educationalists. However, the die was already cast concerning the long-term relationship between teacher assessment and testing, for as Lambert stated:

> What is especially significant is the acceptance by the government that the only alternative to a prohibitively expensive and damagingly bureaucratic assessment system is to entrust teachers with the task of assessing level attainment of children in geography.
>
> (Lambert, 1996a: 273)

The government had realized that their one option was to trust teachers to make professional judgements on student attainment through teacher assessment as the only alternative to hugely expensive national testing. Teacher assessment within the National Curriculum is therefore much more central to the planning, organization and recording of learning than ever before and has given the day-to-day work of geography teachers a new emphasis and focus.

The growing significance of teacher assessment has been paralleled by a resurgence of interest in the whole area of assessment and classroom learning.

A major research paper by Black and Wiliam (1998) has successfully attempted to review the literature on formative teacher assessment published since 1987. The authors' findings are highly significant, concluding as they do that student learning responds positively to frequent, formative assessment feedback; that students' self-assessment is crucial to their educational progress; and that new theoretical models of formative assessment can assist in determining improvements in assessment practice. The considerable bank of evidence they draw on clearly states that formative assessment is potentially a powerful educational tool:

> attention to formative assessment can lead to significant learning gains . . . we have not come across any report of negative effects following from an enhancement of formative practice.
>
> (Black and Wiliam, 1998: 17)

The importance of students being able to critically reflect on their academic performance is also stressed, as they must:

> be active in their own assessment and [be able] to picture their own learning in the light of what it means to get better.
>
> (ibid.: 30)

## Conclusions

Despite the long, and largely successful, history of assessment within geography education, there are still many areas of controversy and weakness. Each year the announcement of GCSE and A-level results, and now National Curriculum levels, seems to attract negative comments from sections of both the popular and educational press about 'falling standards' and poor assessment practices. Though these often superficial debates may not warrant too much analysis, there are some fundamental questions about assessment that still remain largely unexplored. These often relate to assessment practice amongst teachers themselves. Black and Wiliam (1998) present a worrying picture of day-to-day assessment within the classroom, where:

- superficial rote learning often takes place, with classroom assessment based on the recall of details of knowledge which students soon forget;
- teachers fail to review the forms of assessment used, do not discuss assessment practices with other teachers and rarely reflect on what is being assessed;
- there is an over-emphasis on grading and an under-emphasis on learning;
- there is a tendency to use normative rather than criterion-referencing assessment systems;
- teachers emphasize competition through their assessment methods, rather than personal achievement and performance;
- assessment methods tend to reinforce perceptions of failure among the less able, leading to de-motivation and a loss of confidence in their ability to learn; and
- dominance of external, summative testing is still the norm.

Black and Wiliam (1998) also emphasize that students are at the centre of the assessment process and, like Gipps (1994) and Lambert (1996a), they believe that the social processes of assessment require further acknowledgement and research. These processes are significant because assessment takes place within social settings and between social actors where explanations and agreements about practice are gradually constructed. Further research is also needed into the assumptions we hold about assessment and learning; the composition and presentation of learning and assessment tasks; the assessment evidence drawn from students' work; interpretative frameworks used by teachers and students; the social setting for assessment in the classroom; and the general tensions between formative and summative assessment processes.

Lambert (1996a) defines the process of assessment as an art rather than a science, and notes the difficulties of making judgements about student *performance*, on which we base our ideas of their level of *attainment*, and which we then relate to their *ability*. Because this is not a simple relationship we cannot hope to fully understand it through using a single, simplistic assessment method. Often our expectations of what assessment can do are inflated and we tend to focus too quickly on what children are not capable of, rather than on what they are. In essence, Lambert believes that assessment is a process of 'getting to know' students, which involves dialogue with the learner in a variety of geography education settings. There is certainly no single optimum model of assessment that can be adopted, rather a set of guiding principles which must now centre on changing common classroom practices (Black and Wiliam, 1998).

## Follow-up questions

1   What role does assessment currently play in the teaching and learning of geography, and ideally what role should it play?
2   Is it possible to identify national standards in the assessment of geography either within the National Curriculum, at GCSE level or at A-level?
3   How will geography teachers best develop their professional practice with respect to assessment?

## References

Black, P. and Wiliam, D. (1998) 'Assessment and classroom learning', *Assessment and Classroom Learning: Principles, Policy and Practice*, 5, 1: 7–74.
Butt, G. and Smith, P. (1998) 'Education standards and assessment in geography – some cause for concern?', *Teaching Geography* 23, 3: 147–9.
Cassidy, S. (1999) 'Ministers under fire for A-level reforms', *Times Educational Supplement*, 19 March, p. P1.
Daugherty, R. (1990) 'Assessment in the geography curriculum', *Geography*, 75, 4: 289–301.
Daugherty, R. (1995) *National Curriculum Assessment: A Review of Policy 1987–1994*, London: Falmer Press.

Daugherty, R. and Lambert, D. (1993) 'Teacher assessment in geography Key Stage 3: a snapshot of practice', *Teaching Geography*, 18, 3: 113–15.

Dearing, R. (1994) *The National Curriculum and its Assessment: Final Report*, London: SCAA.

DES (1988) *National Curriculum Task Group on Assessment and Testing: A Report*, London: DES.

Flinders, K. (1998) 'The new Certificate of Achievement for geography', *Teaching Geography*, 22 1: 46–7.

Fry, P. and Schofield, A. (1993) *Teachers' Experiences of National Curriculum Geography in Year 7*, Sheffield: The Geographical Association.

Gipps, C. (1994) *Beyond Testing: Towards a Theory of Educational Assessment*, London: Falmer Press.

Lambert, D. (1996a) 'Assessing students' attainment and supporting learning, in Kent, A. *et al. Geography in Education: Viewpoints on Teaching and Learning*, Cambridge: Cambridge University Press.

Lambert, D. (1996b) 'Issues in assessment', in Bailey, P. and Fox, P. (eds) *Geography Teachers' Handbook*, Sheffield: The Geographical Association.

Lambert, D. (1997) 'Principles of student assessment', in Tilbury, D. and Williams, M. (eds) *Teaching and Learning Geography*, London: Routledge.

OFSTED (1993a) *Geography Key Stage 1, 2, and 3 (First Year 1991–2)*, London: HMSO.

OFSTED (1993b) *Geography Key Stage 1, 2, and 3 (Second Year 1992–3)*, London: HMSO.

Roberts, M. (1991) 'On the eve of the Geography National Curriculum: the implications for secondary school geography', *Geography* 76, 4: 331–42.

Roberts, M. (1995) 'Interpretations of the Geography National Curriculum; a common curriculum for all?', *Journal of Curriculum Studies* 27, 2: 187–209.

*Times Educational Supplement* (1999) Leader article, 19 March, London.

Walford, R. (1992) 'Creating the National Curriculum: a view from the inside', in Hill, A.D. (ed.) *International Perspectives on Geography Education*, Boulder: University of Colorado/IGU.

# 17 Geographical education and the vocational debate

*Graham Butt*

## Introduction

The vocational 'revolution' within the British education system, which started in the 1990s and continues into the new millennium, is recognized as a major force for change within the 14–19 curriculum. Its influence on secondary education has already been highly significant, affecting existing curriculum structures, widening student choice and introducing new forms of assessment and accreditation.

In recent years Conservative and Labour governments have both been keen to focus attention on the academic and vocational 'pathways' beyond the ages of 14 and 16. This has resulted in attempts to create a 'parity of esteem' between these two largely disparate educational traditions. Consequently, through efforts to promote vocational qualifications and to break away from an over-emphasis on academic achievement, contemporary British governments have tried to fundamentally alter the nature of our educational system. Most importantly, they have sought to change our perceptions of what constitutes 'achievement' in terms of academic education and vocational training within schools and colleges.

With respect to geography education, the impact of these changes is increasingly dramatic and we are currently experiencing the 'fall out' that accompanies such a large-scale realignment of educational priorities across the 14–19 age range. By the late 1990s many geography departments which had previously offered successful GCSE, A-level and AS-level courses found themselves under pressure for staff to deliver the new General National Vocational Qualification (GNVQ) courses. These courses often grew at the expense of geographical education, whilst subsequent changes to curricular options for students from the age of 14 often left geography out in the cold. The decisions that many children are currently making in state schools at 14 and 16, with respect to studying mainly vocational or academic courses, will potentially have a significant negative impact on the standing of geography within the 14–19 curriculum.

A series of broad questions arise, which this chapter will seek to address. First, how and why did the vocational 'revolution' occur, given that British schools and colleges had largely resisted such wholesale change throughout the twentieth century? Second, what are the implications of such changes for the educational experiences offered to young people, with particular reference to geography? Lastly, what is the longer-term future for geography education in such circumstances?

## How and why did the vocational 'revolution' occur?

The Conservative governments that held power during the 1980s, and much of the 1990s, became steadily more preoccupied with educational matters. The 1988 Education Reform Act, which in part introduced the National Curriculum, was a massive piece of government legislation which heralded radical change within the educational systems of England and Wales. Subsequent educational legislation, primarily designed to streamline this new curriculum and its assessment, also carried important messages about the way in which the government of the day visualized the academic and vocational routes that children should follow.

Two White Papers, *Education and Training for the Twenty-first Century* (DES, 1991) and *Competitiveness* (DFE, 1994), clearly indicated the government's intention that opportunities for educational attainment would in future be spread more widely throughout the 14–19 age group. Thus existing vocational courses were targeted for change and expansion, primarily through the introduction of GNVQs. This partly reflected a 're-emphasis on the relevance of school learning to employment' (Rawling, 1997a: 163) – a point symbolically underlined by the amalgamation in 1995 of the Department for Education with that for Employment. Post-16 education, with its traditional cornerstone of A-levels, had remained largely unaltered for forty years and had existed in the past mainly to serve the needs of relatively small numbers of students who wished to continue their education up to degree level. By contrast, the emergent vocational courses were expected to deliver new mainstream qualifications to as many as half of the 16–19 age group by the turn of the century. The 'staying on' rate in education amongst the post-16 population had continued to rise steadily throughout the 1990s, primarily as a result of the poor employment prospects experienced by this age group, making the introduction of new vocational courses a necessity. GNVQs were to be in the front-line of the government's efforts 'to expand education and training opportunities, to stress the relevance of school learning to employment and to link the improvement of economic performance directly to the raising of educational attainment' (Rawling, 1997b: 11). With talk of also introducing increased modularization and offering key skills across the whole post-16 education system, the prospect of creating meaningful comparability between vocational courses and A-levels looked possible for the first time. However, the Conservative government was itself unclear about such prospects, for whilst it ostensibly championed the cause of new vocational qualifications, it also highlighted the significant differences between the pathways and referred to A-levels as maintaining the 'gold standard' of educational achievement – hardly the actions of an administration keen to create parity of esteem between the two qualifications. This traditional lack of clarity about the purpose of vocational education extends, for some commentators, into a deeper ideological conflict as to whether vocationalism should seek to transform the current social order, or merely improve its effectiveness (Reeder, 1979).

By the mid-1990s, therefore, the 14–19 curriculum offered three educational pathways – the academic route (GCSE, AS and A-level), the general vocational route (GNVQ) and the vocational route (NVQs). It should not be forgotten that although legislation brought about a 'revolution' in general vocational education in schools, many existing vocational courses already had a long history stretching back to 'on the job' training and apprenticeships in specific work-related skills and competencies. At present some 17,000 vocational qualifications still exist that are neither GNVQs nor NVQs. By and large, schools had not seen these vocational pathways as being relevant to their students before the 1990s (in contrast to Further Education colleges) and had therefore only offered a limited range of Business and Technology Education Council (BTEC) and Royal Society of Arts (RSA) courses in the 1970s and 1980s. This situation might have continued into the new millennium had the divide between 'academic' and 'vocational' courses not been breached by the introduction of the more balanced 'general vocational' option of the GNVQ. This grew from the foundations of the Certificate of Pre Vocational Education (CPVE) and Technical and Vocational Educational Initiative (TVEI) launched in the late 1970s and early 1980s. Both of these innovations introduced a form of education based on general vocational skills and competencies, rather than vocational training linked specifically to a particular job or trade. Significantly, the success of these initiatives was somewhat hampered by confusion over their intended 'target group' and by varying curriculum interpretations of the term 'vocational' (see Chitty, 1989: 174). In the late 1980s the Conservatives had largely lost interest in TVEI, particularly as their attention had by this stage been drawn towards the larger goal of establishing a National Curriculum. As such, the GNVQ, established in 1993 following the implementa-tion of the National Curriculum, was launched as an innovative, broad-based, vocational alternative to A-levels which could potentially provide students with an access route to higher education. It is interesting to note that since their election in May 1997 the Labour government has broadly followed the inherited Conservative agenda with respect to the provision of vocational education.

## A troubled start

During the early 1990s deep-seated structural problems had begun to appear within the 14–19 curriculum, partly as a result of the very educational reforms that the Conservatives themselves had just initiated. The government sought to address these by commissioning a series of independent reports to target the major educational issues of the day. Essentially, these were the problems created by an over-crowded and inflexible National Curriculum that was difficult to assess. Reform of the National Curriculum provided opportunities to rethink and restructure the provision of both academic and vocational education, opening the door to new conceptions of the whole 14–19 curriculum. From the geographers' viewpoint the first Dearing Report (1993) took the significant step of making geography (and history) optional at the age of 14, reversing the original conception of the National Curriculum as being compulsory up to the age of 16. Despite the rhetoric that this reversal was because subjects such as geography and history had no particular claim for curricular space above other equally valuable subjects (including the creative arts, economics and religious studies), more pragmatic reasons for the changes were apparent. Additional space was badly needed within Key Stage 4 for new vocational initiatives, namely the introduction of a new 'Part 1' vocational course.

The Dearing Report (1994) made particularly strong recommendations for vocational options to be more prominent in schools from the age of 14 onwards. In essence, the compulsory curriculum for Key Stage 4 was now reduced to 60 per cent of timetabled time, leaving the remaining 40 per cent to be fought over by the new vocational courses, optional subjects such as geography, and other areas of curricular experience. This development was eminently sensible in educational terms, as it served to create a potentially wider choice for students across a broader curriculum. Unfortunately, it also had the effect of marginalizing geography (and history) in many schools – particularly where the option choices presented for students at 14 were insensitively arranged – and this may be a contributory factor in the 13 per cent decline in candidates sitting GCSE geography from 1996 to 1998.

Further advice was sought from Dearing when he was commissioned to sort out the 16–19 educational framework. This review (Dearing, 1996) recognized the value of A-levels, but pointed out that with almost one-third of 16–19-year-olds already studying for these qualifications they were at their limits of expansion. Dearing was again confident that the new growth area should be in the number of students taking vocational courses, and was clear that 'it is in the national interest that some of the nation's most able young people should follow a vocational pathway' (Dearing, 1996: 74). In a further attempt to create greater parity between academic and vocational pathways a new National Framework for Qualifications (in 4 levels) was suggested which encompassed all the new and existing qualifications. Importantly, equal status was to be given to both vocational and academic qualifications.

The Dearing Report and Revision (Dearing, 1994 and 1996) have therefore encouraged a reassessment of the 14–19 curriculum, sometimes in quite radical ways – for example, if most students are 'staying on' within education beyond the age of 16, then the current role and status of GCSEs could be questioned. Is this the most relevant qualification for students to take at 16 given that the majority have another two years of schooling in front of them? Is it perhaps more sensible to have a core curriculum up to the age of 14, followed by a reconceived 14–19 curriculum which offers a more balanced choice of academic and vocational options?

The introduction of any large-scale educational change is rarely smooth and the birth of the new vocational courses was no exception. Initially, GNVQs were widely criticized by educationalists, employers and OFSTED (see Butt, 1996; Capey, 1995; CBI, 1994; OFSTED, 1993, 1994, 1996a; Smithers, 1993) particularly with regard to their intellectual content, coherence and rigour, standards of assessment, course design and administration. Criticism was also partly due to the government's mixed messages within its own educational policy. It was easy to conclude in the mid-1990s that 'The creation of a credible, unified, academic and vocational education system with nationally agreed standards was not served by a government keen to "shore up" A levels and tinker with vocationalism' (Butt, 1996: 191). However, following the Dearing review of qualifications (1996) and the Capey Report (1995) all post-16 education, including GNVQs, began to undergo major reforms. Subsequent reports on the standards of vocational education have been more encouraging, as course specifications and assessment requirements have been redefined in the late 1990s. Increasingly, the styles of vocational and academic courses have therefore been drawn closer together which, ironically, may soon create problems of a lack of distinctiveness between the different qualifications.

## Do GNVQs offer anything new in vocational education?

GNVQs are designed to be 'something different' in the educational marketplace and have a particular emphasis on the 'world of work'. Students must achieve a national standard in the three mandatory key skills of Communication, Application of Number, and IT (which have recently also become a part of A and AS level courses) – as well as addressing the skills of Working With Others, Improving Own Learning and Performance and Problem Solving. The GNVQ units are classified into short-term learning goals where credit accumulation can occur at any stage. Optional units also allow opportunities for student choice and the creation of more 'personalized' study programmes. Students have to gain a range of knowledge and skills across a broad vocational area, develop key skills and a responsibility for planning their own work. They must clearly demonstrate that they can handle data, evaluate their own work and synthesize information. Flexible learning and supported self-study are also requirements of the GNVQ. GNVQs are currently available at three levels, Foundation, Intermediate and Advanced and these equate roughly to various levels of GCSE and A-level performance. Awards are graded as 'pass', 'merit' or 'distinction'.

- **Foundation** – usually taken as a one-year full-time course equivalent to 4 GCSEs at grades D–G.
- **Intermediate** – usually taken as a one-year full-time course equivalent to 4 GCSEs at grades A*–C.
- **Advanced** – usually taken as a two-year full-time course equivalent to 2 A-levels at grades A–E.

At the time of writing, the Foundation and Intermediate GNVQs were being redesigned to reduce their overall burden of assessment and strengthen what students needed to learn. A revision of the advanced GNVQ is due to follow.

The QCA consultation on post-16 qualifications, *Qualifying for Success* (1997), also suggested revisions to the full award GNVQ (12 units), as well as introducing the possibilities of a single award (6 units) and part award (3 units) GNVQ.

Assessment is based on the creation of portfolios of work and external tests and assignments. Each centre offering GNVQs must gain approval from an awarding body, nominate an internal GNVQ coordinator and be willing to coordinate internal and external verification and assessments. The distinctive philosophy of GNVQs means that once introduced, changes are necessary to the teaching, learning and assessment procedures previously adopted within schools and colleges. An important consideration is that GNVQ courses only gain credibility with students, employers and the wider community if they are perceived to be significantly different from the academic and vocational alternatives that have gone before. However, they must also be seen to be rigorous and useful. GNVQs are designed to introduce students to aspects of knowledge, understanding and skills related to vocational areas, such as health and social care, leisure and tourism and the business world.

## What are the implications of increasing vocationalism for geography courses within schools and colleges?

Any prospect that children of *all* abilities would automatically find the new vocational options attractive, or that vocational courses could rapidly achieve the same esteem as traditional academic ones, was ill-founded. Reorientating the perceptions of teachers, parents, employers and children towards accepting that vocational and academic courses are of equal status does not occur overnight. The traditional view that the academically 'able' should automatically pursue academic courses, whilst those who cannot aspire to such 'glittering prizes' should make do with something vocational and utilitarian, is too long-established to be quickly brushed aside. However, the creation of a new national perspective on vocationalism *is* occurring and may lead to the development of curriculum models similar to those currently operating within other European states, which have firmly established and well respected programmes of vocational education. In Germany, France and the Netherlands, schools rarely see a conflict of interest between the vocational and academic aims of their curricula. In such systems the options of pursuing a credible general, technical or vocational education, rather than one which is narrowly subject-based, are clearly apparent.

Reaction amongst most geography educators to the growth of vocational courses within this 14–19 curriculum in the mid-1990s was either cautious, or fearful. Bennetts saw Dearing's proposals for the National Curriculum, at a time of increasing pressure for schools to introduce vocational courses, as a 'setback for geographical education' (Bennetts, 1994: 60), whilst Rawling (1994) noted that geographers would have to fight to maintain their place in the curriculum in the face of greater curricular time, resourcing and status being afforded to the core subjects. The rapid growth of vocational courses was noted by Binns (1996) who stated that:

> with schools being encouraged to develop vocational courses for 14–16 year olds (Key Stage 4) as well as for post 16 students, vocational options could provide stiff competition for optional subjects, such as geography in the post

14 age group. Parents and students may perceive the new vocational courses as being more relevant in terms of future career prospects.

(Binns, 1996. 47)

In addition, Walford (1997) commented that the reforms re-shaped the whole pattern of post-16 education to such an extent that geography would have to 'reaffirm its enduring virtues and values if it is not to be squeezed out in favour of more narrowly focused or apparently "relevant" courses' (Walford, 1997: vii). Geographers quickly understood that they had a lot to lose, particularly with respect to the new vocational courses potentially whittling down their student numbers. As an optional subject at 14, geography had traditionally fared well in terms of student choice, ranking at around sixth place within annually produced tables of student entries for both A- level and GCSEs in the 1980s and 1990s. However, at a time when the list of compulsory curriculum subjects at 14–16 was expanding to include Design and Technology, Information Technology, modern foreign languages and physical education (as well as the core subjects), geography found itself squeezed by the introduction of new vocational options, as witnessed by declining candidate numbers for GCSE geography in the late 1990s.

The possible implications of the current growth of vocational courses on the standing of geographical education in schools can be gleaned from recent surveys. Grimwade (1997) has analysed the initial impact on the provision of geographical education of the Part 1 GNVQ pilot (for 14–16 year olds), which was first introduced in 1995. The growth in the number of schools and students opting for such courses is dramatic – from a pilot involving 253 schools in 1995, the uptake had grown by a further 243 schools by 1997. Indeed, in November 1996 the government was confident enough to announce that 'as a result of a favourable OFSTED evaluation report (OFSTED, 1996b) the Part One GNVQ would be opened up to all schools' (Rawling, 1997a: 167), underlining the successful start that this initiative had made. Most of Grimwade's analysis draws on the effects of the introduction of the Leisure and Tourism GNVQ which, although containing a limited geographical content, is the qualification most frequently taught by geographers. Many of the skills required of students studying for such GNVQs are similar to those expected of geographers – including undertaking enquiry work, involvement in out-of-school visits, and in some aspects of work-related experience. In addition, student-centred and flexible learning approaches, as well as the integration of key skills into schemes of work, have all been achieved by many geography teachers in the course of their day-to-day teaching of geography in the 14–19 curriculum.

Concluding his brief analysis, Grimwade (1997) states that 'the character and ethos' of different schools currently determine whether the GNVQs they offer become popular. If the impression gained by parents and students is that GNVQs are a qualification solely for the less able, then they are usually avoided, whereas in schools where they are afforded similar status to academic qualifications, they are generally more popular. Worryingly, Grimwade noted that in a number of schools 'GCSE Geography is already having to compete against a wider range of subjects in a smaller share of curriculum time. Competition from Part 1 GNVQs could be more than the subject could cope with' (Grimwade, 1997: 140). Some schools have already seen the removal of geography from GCSE option blocks because of the introduction of GNVQs, whilst in others certain students' choices may have been restricted as 'schools recognise the need for a more practically based curriculum for the less academically motivated' (Rawling, 1997a: 166). The reports from many Part 1 pilot schools concerning curriculum change have shown that accommodating the 20 per cent 'block' for GNVQ has meant the sidelining of the humanities options, despite calls for the maintenance of breadth and balance. As Rawling (1997b) comments, the timetabling arrangements made in many schools, such that vocational options can be offered from 14, have resulted in the creation of a GNVQ block in place of option columns which had traditionally contained geography and history. Indeed, there appears to be a false assumption within certain Senior Management Teams in schools that 'the geographical aspects of Leisure and Tourism . . . are sufficient to preserve geography's contribution [to the curriculum]' (Rawling, 1997b: 20).

Advice on what geography departments should do to ensure their subject's continued provision within the school curriculum has come from a Geographical Association working party, which was established in 1996 to consider the implications of the Part 1 GNVQ (Grimwade, 1997). This group suggests that geography teachers should fully engage in the discussions that schools are having about potential involvement in Part 1 GNVQs so that the case for geographical education is made. The first priority is to ensure that students can still study geography to GCSE level if they wish, although this does not preclude geographers from also becoming involved in teaching Part 1 GNVQs if these courses are introduced. Importantly, geography teachers should act to ensure that they, and their departments, do not lose their academic and professional identities. Similar points are made by Rawling (1996) (see Figure 17.1).

The advantages and disadvantages for geography teachers of being involved in the teaching of GNVQs are reasonably straightforward. As we are aware, geographers are already used to adopting investigative styles of working, can contribute to key skills provision and have experience of the 'work-related curriculum' – all abilities which transfer easily into vocational education. However, any argument which promotes the involvement of geographers in delivering GNVQs should also be balanced by a consideration of the ways in which GNVQs themselves either support, or undermine, the study of geography. The potential disadvantages of the expansion of GNVQ provision are perhaps more extensive, for in strictly 'geographical' terms they appear to have little to offer. The geographical content of GNVQs is minimal and they may lead to a de-skilling of the geographers engaged in their delivery – quite simply, vocational courses are no substitute for the study of geography. If the numbers of students opting for Part 1 courses increase, the numbers taking GCSE geography will continue to decline, which will inevitably have a 'knock on' effect on the uptake of A-level geography, higher education courses and teacher training.

**When consideration is being given to taking on GNVQs:**
- is the geography department fully represented in discussions about involvement in GNVQs?
- are senior managers aware of the range and potential of current geography GCSE courses?
- have the purposes and target group for GNVQ been clearly identified in the school and is the qualification recognized as adding a new dimension to the 14–16 curriculum?
- if the school runs vocational GCSEs which have strong geographical relevance (e.g. Travel & tourism), has the potential of these courses been fully explored?

**When the decision has been made to take on GNVQs:**
- will geography still be available to key stage 4 pupils as a full (and if appropriate short) GCSE course for those who want it?
- will those who opt for GNVQ Part One (or for units of a full course) still be able to take geography as well if they wish?
- is geography strong and expanding in the 16–19 curriculum (A/AS) and will its position be improved rather than threatened by the changes?
- will key stage 3 pupils be informed about the character and style of the different academic and general vocational courses available at 14–16, and about where geography fits in?
- will the GNVQ teaching team cover a range of appropriate subject specialisms and work related experience, so that geographers are not asked to teach inappropriate content or skills?

**When the GNVQ units are being implemented:**
- if geography teachers are asked to participate in teaching GNVQ, will their input be focused on knowledge, skills and understanding directly relevant to geography?
- will the geography department maintain its full complement of specialist teachers, its timetable allocations for geography and its status in the school?
- is the geography department able to maintain and extend the range of professional development opportunities open to staff?
- is it possible to develop links with geographers in other sectors of education (FE/HE) in order to address progression and continuity for students in both academic and vocational areas?

*Figure 17.1* Involvement in GNVQs: a checklist for geographers in schools
*Source*: Rawling, 1996

## What of the future?

It is a truism that the popularity of the new vocational courses has surprised many educationalists, particularly considering the comparatively short period of time in which they have existed. As Wright (1995) correctly stated in the mid-1990s, 'GNVQs have developed more rapidly than anyone expected, and more rapidly than government targets which were widely regarded as over-optimistic.' Importantly, we should be cautious about any educational initiative which grows too quickly, not least with respect to the effect that it may be having on other areas of our students' educational experience.

We have seen that with the reorganization of the school curriculum to embrace a fuller vocational component, a number of issues present themselves for 'traditional' subjects such as geography. On the one hand, there is the prospect that geography, by becoming too closely associated with vocational courses, will lose its intellectual identity and cease to function as a separate discipline. On the other, academic isolationism may mean the subject's demise as a result of dwindling student numbers and curriculum realignment away from the humanities. Will an increased involvement in the staffing and delivery of vocational courses by geography teachers inevitably erode the standing of their existing geography courses? Will geography still be able to contribute to wider cross-curricular areas in a curriculum where the status of vocational courses is growing? In essence, can geography survive on the periphery of a curriculum within which vocationalism is becoming more central?

Interestingly, the possible long-term effects of increasing vocationalism on the standing of subjects such as geography and history is not clear-cut. There will almost certainly be significant variations locally, regionally and nationally within schools and colleges in this respect. The general popularity of geography courses witnessed near the end of the twentieth century can only be maintained if geography teachers are given the opportunities to provide exciting, relevant and stimulating experiences within geography at all levels – but more particularly within Key Stage 3, at the end of which students face decisions about whether or not to opt for the subject at GCSE and beyond.

Geographers have always thought of themselves as being keen to embrace innovation. This commitment has been seen in their pioneering work in the development of academic and vocational courses over the past thirty years. Nonetheless an involvement in creating change should not be offered unconditionally, or blindly. Fundamental questions exist as to whether geographers will be expected to become the 'handmaidens' of vocational skills and utilitarian techniques for courses that are simply not 'geographical', effectively becoming the instruments of their own subject's decline. At the very least, the increased vocationalization of the 14–19 curriculum could be seen to create a refocusing of what constitutes 'a geographical education', or what is it to be 'a geographer'. As a result:

> a 'hierarchy' of different types of geography education and geography students [seems to exist]: the 'elite' students being those who have studied

geography GCSE, geography A level, and single honours geography; while the 'non elite' have taken GCSE/GNVQs in 'geography related' areas of study, GNVQs and/or A/AS levels, eventually leading to joint honours in geography.

(Butt, 1996: 191)

A dilemma is apparent. The British 14–19 educational system *does* need to have a viable commitment to vocational education. But should this be at the expense of geography, history and the humanities? Geographers already have a role in delivering GNVQs, but will this increasingly be to the detriment of their careers as geography teachers, their subject and their departments?

## Conclusions

It has become clear that the growing strength of GNVQs is having a direct impact in some schools on the numbers of students taking geography courses at both 14–16 and post-16 levels. This naturally has a resultant effect on the medium- and long-term staffing of their geography departments. Some geography teachers will take 'sideways' moves to become GNVQ teachers and coordinators, which will probably mean that they will not be replaced with geographers when they gain their next post. The loss of well trained geographers from the teaching staff has an immediate impact on how the subject is viewed by students. Any diminution in the strength of geography's appeal as an academic subject within compulsory education will obviously have dire consequences for recruitment to geography (or geography related) courses from the age of 14 up to degree level. The circle is completed as a declining cohort of graduate geographers provides fewer and fewer applicants to train to become the next generation of geography teachers. Difficulties in recruiting well qualified geography teachers into schools will also have an impact on the overall health of the subject and its popularity amongst students.

But maybe the prospects are not this bleak? Instead of seeing a rigid divide between academic and vocational courses, where vocational options are constantly viewed as being potentially more attractive than academic ones, there might be opportunities for healthy coexistence. For example, academic courses may be able to continue to introduce key skills and greater variation in learning styles, whilst still maintaining their academic integrity. Furthermore, Pring (1995) maintains that the academic–vocational divide is an unrealistic conception, as any education system should ideally encompass both practical and theoretical elements of learning for all children. This view is in part echoed by Hall (1996), when he states that A-levels are

an altar on which have been sacrificed the enthusiasms, the hopes and the capabilities of about half our young people in the past. A levels are long past their 'sell by date'. What we need is something now which links together the academic and the vocational.

(Hall, 1996: 170)

Certainly there has been recent evidence of the worlds of academic and vocational education being drawn closer together. The merging of SCAA and NCVQ into QCA, and the amalgamation of vocational and academic boards into new examination organizations, bear witness to a more than superficial realignment. Recent legislation has already narrowed the differences between certain academic and vocational courses, for if one looks at the syllabuses for GCSE Travel and Tourism and GNVQ Leisure and Tourism, for example, they contain many similarities. Both share almost identical skills and content, although their implied learning styles and means of assessment are still somewhat different. This has led certain observers to state that these qualifications may not now exist within separate and discrete 'pathways', but actually constitute a learning 'continuum' (Crombie-White *et al.*, 1995; Pring, 1995; Rawling, 1997b). The prospect of this continuum being extended is more credible following the publication of the Dearing and Capey reports, which have suggested the introduction of similar assessment models for both academic and vocational qualifications. If this is to be the case, then perhaps the separation of the academic and vocational pathways can no longer be defended?

Geography has, over the years, proved its academic and intellectual worth, but must still be clear about its contribution to children's education. In many respects vocational courses are, by comparison, still in the process of establishing their educational credentials. The separate pathways argument may now be unhelpful, and we should perhaps look towards the creation of a continuum of academic and vocational educational experiences for all students. However, what is currently true, and will remain true, is that the academic discipline of geography is not narrowly vocational. There may be areas of overlap and constructive dialogue with vocational courses, but the two will always seek to serve different educational purposes.

## Follow-up questions

1   How can geographers most successfully become involved in the dialogue about geographical knowledge, understanding and skills in the 14–19 curriculum?
2   How will the status, integrity and strength of geography at 14–16 level be maintained in an increasingly vocational curriculum?
3   What contribution should geographers be making to the development of the whole 14–19 curriculum?

## References

Bennetts, T. (1994) 'The Dearing Report and its implications for geography', *Teaching Geography* 19, 2: 60–3.
Binns, T. (1996) 'School geography: the key questions for discussion', in Rawling, E.M. and Daugherty, R.A (eds) *Geography into the Twenty-First Century*, Chichester: Wiley.
Butt, G. (1996) 'Developments in geography 14–19: a changing system', in Rawling, E.M. and Daugherty, R.A (eds) *Geography into the Twenty-First Century*, Chichester: Wiley.

Capey, J. (1995) *GNVQ Assessment Review*, London: NCVQ.

CBI (1994) *Quality Assured: The CBI Review of NVQs and SVQs*, London: CBI.

Chitty, C. (1989) *Towards a New Education System: The Victory of the New Right?* London: Falmer Press.

Crombie-White, R., Pring, R. and Brockington, D. (1995) *14–19 Education and Training: Implementing a Unified System of Learning*, London: RSA.

Dearing, R. (1994) *The National Curriculum and its Assessment: Final Report*, London: SCAA.

Dearing, R. (1996) *Review of Qualifications for 16–19 year olds: Final Report*, London: SCAA.

DES (1991) *Education and Training for the Twenty-first Century*, London: HMSO.

DFE (1994) *Competitiveness: Forging Ahead*, London: HMSO.

Grimwade, K. (1997) 'Part 1 GNVQs: what implications do they have for geography?', *Teaching Geography* 22, 3: 140–2.

Hall, D. (1996) 'Developments at A level', in Rawling, E.M. and Daugherty, R.A. (eds) *Geography into the Twenty-First Century*, Chichester: Wiley.

OFSTED (1993) *GNVQs in Schools: Quality and Standards in GNVQs*, London: HMSO.

OFSTED (1994) *GNVQs in Schools: Quality and Standards in GNVQs*, London: HMSO.

OFSTED (1996a) *Assessment of General National Vocational Qualifications in Schools 1995/6*, London: HMSO.

OFSTED (1996b) *Part One General National Vocational Qualification Pilot Interim Report. 1995/6*, London: HMSO.

Pring, R. (1995) *Closing the Gap: Liberal Education and Vocational Preparation*, London: Hodder and Stoughton.

QCA (1997) *Qualifying for Success*, London: HMSO.

Rawling, E. (1994) 'Dearing and the National Curriculum; what next for geography?', in Walford, R. and Machon, P. (eds) *Challenging Times: Implementing the National Curriculum in Geography*, Harlow: Longman.

Rawling, E. (1996) 'School geography: some key issues for higher education', *Journal of Geography in Higher Education* 20, 3: 305–31.

Rawling, E. (1997a) 'Geography and vocationalism: opportunity or threat?', *Geography*, 82, 2: 163–78.

Rawling, E. (1997b) 'Issues of continuity and progression in post-16 geography', in Powell, A. (ed.) *Handbook of Post-16 Geography*, Sheffield: The Geographical Association.

Reeder, D. (1979) 'A recurring debate: education and industry', in Bernbaum, G. (ed.) *Schooling in Decline*, London: Macmillan.

Smithers, A. (1993) *All Our Futures: Britain's Education Revolution: A Dispatches Report on Education*, London: Channel 4 Television.

Walford, R. (1997) 'Preface', in Powell, A. (ed.) *Handbook of Post-16 Geography*, Sheffield: The Geographical Association.

Wright, P. (1995) *Vocational Qualifications and Standards in Focus*, London: Higher Education Quality Council.

# 18 Geography in the early years

Kathy Alcock

## Introduction

'Look at that big puddle! Mummy, who put it there?'

This was the start of a conversation between a 3-year-old boy and his mother sitting opposite me on a recent train journey. It highlighted several issues for me. Children *are* interested in the world around them. They associate people with places. They ask questions and require answers. Many children understand far more than adults think they do. Children are entitled to the opportunity to build on the knowledge they already have and to be enabled to broaden their range of interest. The 'puddle' we were passing was what I would actually call a small lake, but my small friend's comments led me to question my own perception of it and ask myself – When does a puddle become a pond? When does a pond become a lake? When does a lake become a sea? Who decides these things? Are there any actual answers to questions such as these? Furthermore, is it necessary to know the answers?

Whether 4- or 5-year-olds should be in mainstream primary schools is an issue which is debated regularly, but is not the key issue here. In this chapter I am concerned with the geographical education of the 'early years', that is children up to the age of 6 years. It is, however, important to outline the standpoint from which I write at the outset.

I support many of the arguments for allowing children the freedom to learn, to experiment, to socialize, and to play without the restrictions or structures which the formal education systems brings. However, my experience of working with early years children and their parents in primary schools leads me to believe that the benefits can outweigh the problems. The proviso being that:

- the environment within that setting is one which allows for flexibility in terms of activities undertaken and time spent doing them;
- children are encouraged to succeed rather than compete;
- enough space and suitable resources are provided; and
- parents are urged to participate in their child's learning and are seen as co-workers with the teachers.

## Where does geography fit into the early years' curriculum?

Some people may think that geography cannot be taught to children of this age; indeed they may go so far as saying it is unnecessary to do so. However, if we accept that the curriculum for the early years needs to 'make sense' to the child, and that learning from real and relevant experiences is essential at this stage, then it is easier to see where geography fits into the picture. This has been recognized in that geography is part of 'Knowledge and Understanding of the World', one of the six 'Areas of Learning' in the 'Desirable Outcomes for Children's Learning' (SCAA, 1996) and the proposed 'Learning Goals' (QCA, 1999) although a note of caution must be added. We should not accept the change in emphasis from 'desirable outcomes' to 'goals' without questioning its validity. Bruce (1999), in arguing against the desirability of 'goals' as opposed to 'outcomes', draws on research evidence that affirms the view that an informally structured curriculum in the first six years, with the emphasis on well-thought-out play opportunities, communication and language, produces children who are better readers and writers later on.

## Why should early years children be introduced to geography?

The Geographical Association's *Primary Geography Handbook* (Carter, 1998) has highlighted the ways geography can contribute to the primary curriculum. Alcock (1998) has looked at this in relation to the early years. Nine reasons why young children should be introduced to geography are presented here, with an example of a lesson idea relating to each of them.

- Geography helps children find out about the people and places all around them.
  *Play games such as 'I spy out of the window' or 'Who is this?' giving clues of clothes worn or job done.*
- Children's personal experiences can be used and this can increase awareness of their surroundings.
  *Talk about holiday photographs and experiences away from the classroom.*
- Geography enhances children's understanding of the real world and helps them to make sense of the natural and built environments.
  *Take a walk around the locality, identifying natural and built features. Make a display using objects and materials 'found' with enquiry questions attached.*
- Geography focuses on the rich variety and diversity of human and natural resources.
  *Display food items both grown and processed. Chart achievements, ensuring there is something each child can succeed in doing.*
- Geography introduces the concept of sustainability.
  *Read a story such as* Rainforest *(Helen Cowcher).*
- Geography introduces mapwork skills.
  *Follow signs to get from one place to another or make a model of the room with labels.*

- Geography encourages greater global awareness, interdependence and citizenship and prepares children for the future.
  *Collect postcards and artefacts from other countries.*
- Good teaching will challenge stereotypes.
  *Arrange for a visit from someone from another culture to share their songs and traditions.*
- Geography works to enhance the holistic nature of young children's learning. Geographical knowledge is embedded in children's play activities; adults can identify and use this.
  *Build a town on a roadway map. Cars travel from one place to another following simple directions.*

## Our world is their world

From a very early age, children are aware of, and react to the environment in which they find themselves.

> Children are natural geographers. From the moment of birth they start to learn about their surroundings. First they become familiar with their own environment, then, through a variety of stimuli, they begin to form perceptions of other places beyond their direct experience.
>
> (Smeaton, 1998: 15)

How many of us, when our children have grown up, have discovered to our cost that when small children visit us, our homes are not safe places for them to be? Precious possessions are invariably the most attractive to investigative fingers. Children want to touch, to move, to bite, to feel whatever interests them. Rarely are these the items purchased or provided specifically for that purpose. At the same time, many young children seem to have an innate ability to sense whether people are friendly or hostile towards them. Their feelings need to be taken seriously and handled with care and sensitivity to prevent more deep-seated problems developing in the future.

Young children develop likes and dislikes regarding particular places. Many like light, open spaces; they like things which move and change. Many have fear of the dark, of noisy places or crowded environments. My 5-year-old son was terrified of walking down the dark passage leading to his first school classroom. I could feel the tension leaving his body as we entered the light, open playground. This is understandable and not unique to children in the early years of life. Hart (1979) conducted research over a two-year period and found that 2-year-olds may be frightened by almost any new situation. Many 6-year-olds expressed fear of high and unfamiliar places such as attics and cellars. By the age of 8 these fears are reduced to a certain extent.

Sometimes, prior explanation of what a place is going to be like or what is going to happen can help to allay these fears. Travelling in an open carriage on 'Le petit train jaune' through the mountains in Southern France illustrated this point.

The carriage was very full with no room for movement. One little boy began to tremble and cry every time the train entered a long, dark tunnel as he reacted to the whistles, shouts and screams of other travellers. He needed to be prepared for the fact that the tunnel would be dark and cold, that the people would make as much noise as possible, but that it wouldn't last long and the train would come out of the other end and then, on exit, the people would be quiet again. When older members of a family behave confidently, the younger children feel more secure. This child could not draw on that source for support. It is interesting to note that on the return journey, a family travelling with a large dog did sense the fear in their pet; they reassured it on entry to each tunnel and prepared the dog by covering its eyes and ears and talking in such a way as to give comfort – and it worked!

## How can we use young children's understanding of the world?

The world is an exciting, busy, varied and changing place. It is our duty as educators to introduce early years children to as yet unknown aspects of *their* world, but it must be acknowledged that children bring considerable knowledge and understanding of the world with them, when they enter the formal education system.

> The images of the world which children (and adults) carry about inside their heads are derived, on the one hand, from personal experiences of visiting places, and on the other, from vicarious experiences *via* media of various kinds.
>
> (Bale, 1987: 7)

Many children will have visited a range of shops, fast food outlets and restaurants. They will have experienced the car being filled with fuel, machines being repaired in their homes and letters and parcels being delivered. Visits will have been made to clinics, doctors, dentists. Television and videos will probably have been part of their life from birth and increasingly the Internet and CD-ROMs will feature. Places further afield will have been part of the world of some young children, whose families travel for holidays or work.

How often do teachers take an interest in, or use this vital knowledge and understanding or these valid experiences? Bale states that: 'It is from the worlds inside children's heads that school geography should build' (Bale, 1987: 30). Do we try to discover and *use* this information when planning our curriculum? Long-term planning in advance of teaching makes an audit of prior knowledge very difficult. Demands of inspection, continuity and progression may work against a teacher's ability to change, adapt and modify prepared plans in the light of circumstances, but this must not be used as an excuse. Children may become disaffected and disheartened if their contribution is undervalued. I have found that the hardest thing for young children to accept is the necessity to be quiet when they have something to say which they believe contributes to the discussion. One of the ways to mitigate this is to allow them as many opportunities as possible to share experiences with other children and adults, to encourage them to talk about places they have visited, people they have met, activities they have been engaged in. Titman (1994), during a three-year project into children and the school grounds, found that relatively few researchers had sought to understand the child's perspective. Are you one of those who realize the importance of seeing things 'through the eyes of a child'?

## Allowing children to share their knowledge and understanding

A teacher may provide a better opportunity for learning for a child, by asking the right question, rather than giving the right factual information. Time is an issue in this area, as there are children who need to be 'warmed up'. The approach 'Tell me about your visit to the dentist . . . ' may well be more effective than 'What happened when you went to the dentist?' It is also useful for a teacher, or another adult, to share a personal experience, for example, 'When I went across to France on the ferry last week, the sea was so rough that the tug boat had to be attached to the ferry as we left the harbour.' It is the 'prompts' you give a child which help them to recall knowledge. Even very young children can exhibit a surprising amount of knowledge. For example, Hugh, aged 4 years, when asked to talk about his holiday on a farm, was able to explain, in detail the process of obtaining milk 'from cow to cup' with few inaccuracies or misconceptions:

**Mum**:   What was on Anna's farm?
**Hugh**:   Some animals and Anna?
**Mum**:   What did Anna do?
**Hugh**:   She milked some cows.
**Mum**:   How did she milk them?
**Hugh**:   A machine went on their teats.
**Mum**:   What are teats?
**Hugh**:   The things that milk come out of. They've got a hole in them. They put a machine on them and the machine sucks it out. They put them really tight next to their teats.
**Mum**:   Oh right. Where does the milk go then?
**Hugh**:   It goes into a machine – a big machine, much bigger than the other machine. They pour that into a bucket then it goes into a plastic bin then you can buy the milk.
**Mum**:   Can you buy the milk at the farm?
**Hugh**:   Yes. In plastic bottles. It's in a real concrete place that's got wood which opens up and you pay. It's like a shop but not quite.
**Mum**:   Who else drank the milk?
**Hugh**:   I don't know?
**Mum**:   Did any other animals drink it?
**Hugh**:   Um! Oh Truffle did. He's a pig, a big, black, fat pig.

Encouraging a child to participate and to respond positively when incorrect answers are given is also important. So too is the issue of encouraging children to ask questions for themselves. This should be valued as it provides 'evidence that the child is playing an active, initiating role in learning' (Wray and Lewis, 1997). These are skills which need practising. The student or teacher in the early years of teaching should take advantage of opportunities to learn from others more skilled or experienced in these respects, noting what types of questions or approaches to a subject best allow children to contribute their knowledge and understanding.

## Where did you hear that before?

Listening in to young children engaged in role-play areas is a salutary experience. By doing this adults can discover what children hear and see, notice and consider to be significant in their world (as well as hearing themselves speaking, admonishing and, less frequently, praising through the voices of the young imitators). For example, a group of children 'playing' in the 'Travel Agents' had a conversation:

| | |
|---|---|
| **Child 1 (Travel Agent)**: | Good morning. Can I help you? |
| **Child 2**: | We want to go away? |
| **Child 1**: | Where? |
| **Child 2**: | *Anywhere* away from this dump. |
| **Child 3**: | Somewhere hot where it doesn't rain. |
| **Child 1**: | How much do you want to spend? |
| **Child 3**: | Five pounds. |
| **Child 2**: | That's not much. |
| **Child 3**: | It's all I've got. |
| **Child 1**: | Why don't you put it on your card? |
| **Child 3**: | What card? |
| **Child 2**: | Good idea. |
| **Child 1**: | Where do you want to go then? |
| **Child 3**: | Disneyland. |
| **Child 2**: | I've been there lots of times. |
| **Child 1**: | How do you want to travel? |
| **Child 2**: | Eurostar. |
| **Child 1**: | What's that? |
| **Child 2**: | Train – silly. |
| **Child 3**: | How long will it takes us? |
| **Child 2**: | 5 minutes. |

Young children may have misconceptions about time, space, money as is demonstrated in the preceding example. They will often 'pluck figures out of thin air', but if questioned more closely can be more specific. Some children associate distances with methods of travel. A group of 5-year-olds were trying to sort out places that were near and far. The criterion they initially used was whether they would travel by car or plane. This was suggested by John, who said: 'It *must* be a long way 'cos we went by plane.' One child said they went everywhere by car and he thought it was a long way if he went to sleep. Another said it was a 'far' place if her Mum drove for part of the journey.

## What is the right environment for learning?

It is important to create an appropriate environment for learning. Many of the richest experiences will come through play. Geography with its involvement in people and places can be the context for a range of activities one would engage in as part of the curriculum for the early years. This could be, for example, in the form of creating landscapes in sand, talking about scenes depicting aspects of the environment whilst completing jigsaw puzzles, using telephones in the role-play area, cooking and tasting food from other countries and cultures, playing board games or building a town with commercially produced construction materials or empty boxes and packages. Figure 18.1 shows an example of using a story book with a geographical context as a basis for a range of activities across several curriculum areas.

## What about fieldwork?

> Fieldwork gives pupils the opportunity, through a structured pathway, to become observant, to develop skills of recording, analysis and deduction and, hopefully, to develop enquiring minds.
>
> (Richardson, 1998: 181)

This is as true for young children as for older ones. Photographs are a useful resource for introducing children to places beyond their home area, but none of us who has taken children on fieldwork would underestimate the value of these direct experiences. Martin (1995), in supporting the case for fieldwork, states that it gives children the opportunity to gather information, to explore, observe and discover things that cannot be achieved in the classroom. Well organized and carefully prepared visits can maximize the opportunities for enjoyment, interest and learning.

It is not essential to go far from the school; in fact some of the most profitable work can be done actually within the school grounds. Young children may spend up to an hour each school day outside the building. They are able to say which areas they like and dislike and why. They have opinions about the features they see around them. They are able to say what they would like to add to or take away from the grounds. A map showing a few key features in the school grounds can be used to develop early mapwork skills. A local park can be used in the same way. Figure 18.2 is a map used by a reception class in a school in Dover when taking a walk around the school grounds. Children had to visit four places, each marked with a number, and say what they found there and whether they liked or disliked this place. Each group went with an adult and were also required to mark on the map the route they followed.

**Introduction**:  Story read to whole group followed by brief discussion.

**Group activities**:
*There should be at least two adults available, but preferably one with each group. Children will rotate so that they complete each activity during the session.*

**One**: Draw a map of the route taken by Webster and his friends. Children talk about the features they would pass during the journey. Maps to be annotated by an adult using children's descriptions whilst work is in progress. Some children will be able to record on tape or write a brief description of the journey.

**Two**: Using sand tray, toy ducks and other animals, trees and fences, create the environment of the story. Children feel the 'dry' earth. They re-enact the journey from the farm to the river. The water tray is used to depict the river environment. The ducks are helped by the children to 'jump' into the water, and experience the contrast between dry and wet places. A watering can is used to simulate rain and paper or thin card to simulate a bridge.

**Three**: A washing line is displayed with items hung on it using pegs replicating the scene in the orchard. Practical mathematics activities use these resources with questions such as 'How many socks are there?' or 'If I take away one skirt how many are left?' Some children will be able to record their answers.

**Four**: Role-play area is set up as a shop. Dressing-up clothes available for children to use to act out the story, particularly the part where Angus goes shopping with his family and then finds the ducks on their way back to the farm. This could also be done using puppets, either glove or stick types.

*Figure 18.1*  Example of a programme of work for one session for reception-aged children (based on the book *Webster's Walk* by Jill Dow)

Another example of an enterprising fieldwork activity involved linking two schools just five miles apart. One was in the town – Dover, the other in a rural setting – Shepherdswell. They were linked by a railway line. Children were able to walk to the station, passing *en route* many of the features and places they had talked and learned about as part of the study of their own locality. They travelled

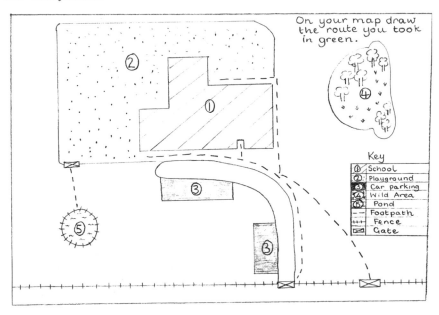

On your map draw the route you took in green.

Key
① School
②: Playground
③ Car parking
④ Wild Area
⑤ Pond
-- Footpath
+++ Fence
⊠ Gate

*Figure 18.2* Map showing some key features of part of the school grounds

by train (in the first class carriages!). The guard took groups in turn to the guard's van, explaining what the various instruments were used for. On arrival at Shepherdswell, the children took a prepared route, stopping at set places to complete tasks and making observations, before arriving at the partner school, which was the base for eating a packed lunch and using other necessary amenities. Children enjoyed playing with other children, and some rapidly made new friends. The afternoon comprised a visit to the church and recreation area, before making the return journey in time for the end of afternoon school. The cost for each child was £1 and this included money to buy an ice-cream at a local shop. The adult–child ratio was 1 : 5 and these children were 5 and 6 years old, but the visit would have been equally possible with 4- and 5-year-old children.

Maybe one of the most valuable experiences of fieldwork for a young child, is in making a journey, or going for a day out without their parents. Children talk to adults about different things when outside the familiar school environment. The social aspect is an important one; children interact with each other and, furthermore, activities such as these allow children to learn about themselves. Scoffham encourages the use of the local environment and states:

> Outings to the local surroundings can serve to develop a wide range of curriculum skills and help to promote the child's social and intellectual development.

> (Scoffham, 1981: 12)

Children may initially be afraid to engage in such an activity and this must be considered and taken account of within the preparation, but once completed, provided it has been successful, many of those who were fearful will be less so on another occasion.

## Gender differences

Reflecting now on my own practice as a reception-class teacher of children from just 4 to 5 years, I am aware that within my planning I rarely made provision for what I now consider to be important differences in the way young boys and girls react to activities provided to facilitate learning. These thoughts are not, as yet, supported by my own research evidence, but are based on experience. Matthews (1992) points to gender differences in the type and range of play, the boys' play being more exploratory and large-scale, the girls' being more home-orientated and small-scale.

Many of the 4-year-old boys I taught were more creative and imaginative with larger construction materials than the girls were. In sessions when choice was permitted, girls gravitated towards playdough, beads, drawing. Both boys and girls liked to dress up and play in the role-play area. The girls generally showed more interest in the fiction picture books rather than the non-fiction texts. Boys tended to show more interest when environmental issues were discussed. When issues involving people, particularly those less fortunate than we are, were discussed, the girls visibly showed a greater affinity to their plight. It was noticeable to me that the concentration span of the boys directly related to their level of interest in the activity. They were the ones who would resent having to stop what they were doing when the lesson needed to change. Maybe the girls felt the same, but they did not show their feelings as much as the boys.

A small-scale research project by Jodie Green (1994) found that Key Stage 1 children between the ages of 5 and 7 years, had gender stereotypical views of the workplace, but these were not rigidly fixed at this age, and could be challenged effectively. Surely it is at this stage in a child's education that this should happen.

Finally on this issue, my experiences of working with children over a period of twenty-five years have shown me that generally boys, particularly those in the early years age group, are more eager and willing to experiment, to question and to discover how things work for themselves. There is evidence from research (Hutt, 1972) that male brains and central nervous systems are generally less well developed at birth and are slower to mature than girls. For example, again, in general girls develop language faster. The implications of this are that girls will then use language to learn vicariously rather than through direct experience. Our gendered culture has exacerbated this gender difference, encouraging boys to be active, to explore, even if these explorations are sometimes destructive (they may smash toys or take things to pieces), and expecting girls to be more passive and learn through social interactions. If this is true, what are the implications for planning? Should different activities be planned for boys and girls at this age, or is it a case of providing opportunities for choice?

## A shared responsibility?

How much value do we place on the contribution parents make to the education of their children in the early years? Teachers often say all the 'right' things. During initial meetings with new parents, when they are introduced to the routines and philosophies of the school prior to their child's entry, many teachers and headteachers impress on parents that they are still the most important people in their child's life. In reality, is this actually the case? Is it the teacher who is always right or the parent? What happens if views, opinions or attitudes conflict? Who wins? Surely the answer is, the teacher when at school, the parent when at home. Where does this leave the small child?

Geography, with its focus on enquiry and investigation, with its relevance to all aspects of a child's life and with its focus on the people and places making up the child's world, presents real opportunities for shared learning and teaching. Parents and teachers are concerned to give children valuable learning experiences. There should never be competition, but cooperation. If there are differences in values and attitudes, in cultures and home environments, this surely reflects diversity which is present in our world and should be used creatively and celebrated.

Parents, as well as assisting in the classroom and with fieldwork, can contribute to the education process in a number of ways which relate to geography, for example:

- ask parents to talk to children about features in the local environment which they pass on the way to school;
- read story books which use issues as a theme, such as *Dear Greenpeace, Rainforest, Oi! Get off our train* or those which involve journeys, for example traditional tales such as *Little Red Riding Hood, The Gingerbread Man*, or more recent fiction such as *Webster's Walk* or *Postman Pat* stories;
- bring back artefacts from foreign holidays to use in school;
- encourage children to recycle;
- talk about where food comes from; and
- explain why maps and other reference material are being used when journeys are made and visits planned.

Taking children out of school during term-time for holidays is generally discouraged. For some people, if they want to take a holiday, it is necessary to take advantage of their legal entitlement to request leave of absence for their children. These situations may present difficulties for the school, but visiting a distant place, whether it be in this country or overseas, can be an experience which is beneficial to the child and can be used to provide a learning experience. A little time spent with the parents or guardians, giving some advice and suggestions for activities during the journey or at the holiday location may be welcomed. Here are some 'Home and Away' ideas:

- I can see – a tick list for the journey.
- Sign-spotting sheet.

- Make own jigsaws from pictures from magazines or holiday brochures.
- Telling a story with puppets; provide a vocabulary list.
- Find on a map the places you visit or the places which appear on television.
- Collect pebbles or rocks – describe the shape, colour, texture.
- Look for shapes and patterns in natural or built environment.
- 'Out of the window' – what can you see beginning with each letter, for example

  Houses

  Orange trees

  Tractor

  Entrance

  Lamp post

  or how many words can you think of beginning with one letter?
- Give a colour – find an object.

## Conclusion

This chapter has raised just a few of the issues in relation to geography and children in their early years. Readers are encouraged to relate what they have read to what they encounter in their own practice.

Young children are entitled to a rich, diverse and lively curriculum. As teachers, we need to offer experiences which will allow children to develop a sense of belonging and attachment. Geography can be the vehicle and the context for many opportunities for discovery and learning. It can enable children to build on what they already know and can enhance their understanding of the world. It also gives many opportunities for boosting children's self-confidence and self-esteem. New skills and concepts can be introduced in ways which are enjoyable and meaningful and, at the same time, prepare them for the future.

## Questions for discussion

1   What people and places are known and important to the children you teach?
2   Do you make use of the knowledge and understanding of the world which children bring with them when they join your class?
3   How do the children you teach view their world?
4   Where do the children you teach get their misconceptions from? Do you attempt to discover these before embarking on a programme of work? Do you evaluate your work to discover if you have made a difference and modify in the light of those findings?
5   Do you *really* value parents as partners in the educational process?
6   Do you provide opportunities for children to succeed and be challenged?
7   Are you in danger of underestimating the capabilities for learning of children in their early years?

## References

Alcock, K. (1998) 'Desirable outcomes?', *Primary Geographer*, 33: 14–16.

Bale, J. (1987) *Geography in the Primary School*, London: Routledge.

Bruce, T. (1999) 'Little choice', *Nursery World*, 12 (8 April): 6–7.

Carter, R. (ed.) (1998) *Primary Geography Handbook*, Sheffield: The Geographical Association.

Green, J. (1994) Unpublished small-scale research project for Canterbury Christ Church College.

Hart, R. (1979) *Children's Experience of Place*, New York: Irvington Press.

Hutt, C. (1972) *Males and Females*, Harmondsworth: Penguin.

Martin, F. (1995) *Teaching Early Years Geography*, Cambridge: Chris Kington.

Matthews, M. (1992) *Making Sense of Place*, Hemel Hempstead: Harvester Wheatsheaf.

QCA (1999) *The Review of the Desirable Outcomes: A Consultation Paper*, London: QCA.

Richardson, P. (1998) 'Fieldwork', in Carter, R. (ed.) *Primary Geography Handbook*, Sheffield: The Geographical Association.

SCAA (1996) *Desirable Outcomes for Children's Learning on Entering Compulsory Education*, London: DfEE.

Scoffham, S. (1981) *Using the School Grounds*, London: Ward Lock.

Smeaton, M. (1998) 'Questioning geography', in Carter, R. (ed.) *Primary Geography Handbook*, Sheffield: The Geographical Association.

Titman, W. (1994) *Special Places, Special People*, Godalming: WWF, UK.

Wood, D., McMahon, L. and Gaustoun, Y. (1980) *Working with Under Fives*, London: Grant McIntyre.

Wray, D. and Lewis, M. (1997) *Extending Literacy*, London: Routledge.

# 19 Towards the question-led curriculum 5–14

*Gill Davidson and Simon Catling*

## Introduction

The introduction of the first National Curriculum in England and Wales as part of the Education Reform Act in 1988 heralded important changes in conceptions of curriculum in English schools. Curriculum thinking since the mid-twentieth century had moved away from defining curriculum simply as syllabus content and recognized the need to consider the process of teaching and learning within the framework of a curriculum system. However, the 1988 Act changed the direction of curriculum development by dramatically reducing the role of teachers in curriculum decision-making. It also brought with it a new curriculum vocabulary. In particular, the term *delivery* has become ubiquitous. Although the DES (1989) claim that the National Curriculum is not intended to dictate how schools and individual teachers *deliver* the curriculum, we are reminded that the metaphors we use 'shape our conception of the problem we study' (Eisner, 1982: 6). A curriculum that is *delivered* conjures up images of teachers presenting packages of information as opposed to developing critical thinking in their pupils. A curriculum that is *delivered* embraces simplistic pedagogy based on a transmission–reception model with little regard given to the process of learning. A curriculum that is *delivered* is seen to be straightforward to assess, requiring only the measurement of the extent to which the information passed on has been retained by the recipients. Whitaker sums up the past fifteen years of educational reform:

> scarce attention has been given to the dynamics of learning, the methodologies of teaching and to the vital relationship between pupils and their teachers in classrooms and schools.
>
> (Whitaker, 1995: 7)

Our purpose in this chapter is to explore how this trend in curriculum development, arising directly from the way the National Curriculum has been developed, has adversely affected compulsory school geography. We highlight the issues facing teachers in seeking an appropriate curriculum planning model and suggest how some of these issues might be addressed. It should be pointed out that the existence of a central curriculum is not necessarily problematic. Naish (1992) refers to a study of the impact of centralization on the geography curriculum in 22 states and countries and concludes that there are several potential advantages to centralization. In particular, it can encourage a common body of knowledge, ideas and skills. However, an important prerequisite is sufficient flexibility to allow teachers in schools to contribute towards the process of curriculum development. In a later publication he warns,

> To simply be called on to deliver someone else's curriculum is to diminish the role of the teacher and can lead to a static, fossilised curriculum unresponsive to change.
>
> (Naish, 1997: 200)

## National Curriculum legacy

The form and structure of the initial National Curriculum Geography Order (DES, 1991), based as it was on a deficit model of the subject and children's understanding, encouraged a regressive model of curriculum, which failed to respond to the concerns and developments in geography of the previous two decades (Rawling, 1992). The emphasis on facts, place knowledge and traditional skills presented an outmoded view of geography as 'information about the world' that could be 'delivered' as uncontroversial and seemed to make further professional inter-pretation unnecessary (Rawling, 1996). The Schools Council projects of the 1970s and 1980s (see Blyth *et al.* 1976; Naish, Rawling and Hart 1987; Tolley and Reynolds, 1977) had encouraged professional autonomy and innovation in geographical education favouring an enquiry approach to teaching and learning. In contrast, the National Curriculum was prescriptive in content, with no attention given to the principles of curriculum design or teaching and learning. Teachers became confused about the aims of geographical education and their role in curriculum planning.

> More than twenty years of constructive curriculum development work was deliberately ignored and we were offered a curriculum which was content loaded and assessment led . . . there was a lack of emphasis on enquiry and a lack of an appropriate values orientation.
>
> (Naish, 1997: 205)

The emergence of a plethora of glossy, easy-to-use textbooks, which claimed 'comprehensive coverage' of the National Curriculum seemed, for many, to offer an easy way forward. Rawling (1996) points to OFSTED and HMI evidence which suggests that in these initial stages some teachers gave up the battle with the 'Order' and assumed a 'delivery' mode rather than a 'creative' mode of operation.

The reasons why we were presented with such a deficit curriculum model are many, and linked to the drive towards central control which pervades all sectors of education. The 'Great Education Debate' initiated by Callaghan's Ruskin College Speech (Callaghan, 1976) introduced a new democracy into curriculum planning. The working groups which produced the original National Curriculum draft sought the views of a range of people such as parents, employers, school governors, as well as people in the profession. What became clear in relation to geography was a dissonance between such groups about the nature of the subject. There was also a growing public unease that geography had lost its knowledge base; there was a feeling that the curriculum experiments of the 1970s and 1980s had placed too much emphasis on process by emphasizing skills, enquiry, values and attitudes. Hence the return to the focus on places, the emphasis on factual knowledge and the intervention of the Secretary of State, Kenneth Clarke, to remove reference to enquiry skills, issues and values from the Draft Order. Lawton (1992) claims that this whole exercise of curriculum change in the National Curriculum was seen by many politicians as an opportunity to re-emphasize traditional subject knowledge and basic skills. Such a trend is compatible with government criticism of so-called progressive methods of teaching linked to theories of 'child-centred learning'. Pressure to return to 'traditional' methods has pervaded government policy. The 'people-environment' approach to geography, with enquiry as the main style of teaching and learning, was associated with 'progressive methods' and was therefore seen as incompatible with this thrust of government policy.

Furthermore, the political agenda has focused on raising standards and improving quality in education through increased accountability. The National Curriculum model is fundamentally output-led, designed to provide data to judge education provision within and between schools. The success of a geography course is measured publicly by the achievement of predetermined objectives which have a strong impact on curriculum design. OFSTED criteria for inspection reinforce an objectives-led model. In the guidance for judging the quality of teachers' planning, inspectors are advised:

> Good planning means that teaching in a lesson or a sequence of lessons has clear objectives for what pupils are to learn and how these objectives will be achieved.
>
> (OFSTED, 1995: 72)

Roberts (1997) provides a valuable discussion of the merits and problems of the objectives model of curriculum and contrasts this to the process model that was the approach adopted by the innovative geography curriculum projects. One of the key criticisms of the objectives model is the tendency towards the use of a narrow range of objectives which can be easily assessed. Another is that little attention is given to the process of learning. Certainly, the National Curriculum model stressed learning outcomes linked to knowledge and understanding, as opposed to the capacities for developing critical thinking and values. It encouraged traditional approaches to both pedagogy and assessment which were outcome-orientated. Possibilities of using assessment evidence to plan for progression in individual learning were constrained by an over-emphasis on factual knowledge and the lack of conceptual clarity within and between the Statements of Attainment (SoA) and the Programmes of Study (PoS). The process model, on the other hand, focuses on learning and is closely associated with enquiry approaches:

> It recognises the role of pupils in shaping what they learn and in constructing geography for themselves. It recognises the complexity of classroom interaction.
>
> (Roberts, 1997: 46)

Increased central control has encouraged many teachers towards a linear model of curriculum which focuses on content and summative assessment, giving little consideration to the processes of learning. Where enquiry exists, it tends to be over-structured towards factual outcomes and narrowly sequential. In such a model there is a danger that the needs of the pupils become less important than the demands to deliver the curriculum and the learning process is not considered in curriculum planning. In effect, pupils are not fully engaged in the process of learning. Their needs are defined for them, while curiosity and enquiry are stifled.

The Dearing review of the curriculum (Dearing, 1994) was largely welcomed by geographers, as it afforded an opportunity to address the difficulties we have outlined. There was a demand for changes that would increase flexibility and open up opportunities for a greater professional input into curriculum planning by teachers. The changes to the geography curriculum were substantial. One was that the PoS described the content to be studied at each key stage. Aspects of the subject, skills, places and themes (incorporating physical, human and environmental geography) were headings in the PoS and not separate Attainment Targets. These were structured in paragraphs across each key stage, so it was possible to discern links and some progression across the curriculum. The introductory paragraph in each of the PoS gave a description of the overall entitlement for the key stage and offered some guidance on how to approach geographical study. Enquiry as a process for learning geography, although not mentioned by name, was inferred in each of the Programmes of Study. Pupils were required to undertake studies which focus on geographical questions and develop investigative skills. The level descriptions required that pupils become increasingly independent in defining questions and implementing effective sequences for investigation. There was one Attainment Target, 'Geography' and progression in attainment was described in the eight level descriptions (plus one for exceptional performance).

The second Geography Order came into effect in September 1995. It provided a much clearer basis for curriculum planning and afforded the opportunity for teachers to take an active role in curriculum development. However, it has been recognized that many teachers needed support to move into a new and creative role in curriculum development following a number of years of being de-skilled by the original Order. Such help has been slow in coming from government bodies (QCA, 1998a, 1998b). It has therefore been up to teachers and those involved in professional development, to develop this framework into a meaningful curriculum for pupils. Where teachers have had little experience of curriculum planning, this was not an easy task (Foley and Janikoun, 1996; Leat, 1998; Martin 1995). The authors have worked with a range of primary and secondary teachers and trainees in providing support for making sense of the National Curriculum Geography Order. We have also conducted periodic small-scale research involving surveys and interviews with teachers and trainees focusing, in particular, on their attitudes towards and practices in geographical enquiry and the use of questions with pupils. From this work we have been able to identify a number of concerns about the implementation of the Geography Order which are likely to continue unless they are addressed.

## Salient issues in National Curriculum planning

### Content driven

It is our view that a good deal of curriculum planning is still narrowly focused on *delivering* content. The starting point for planning has tended to be the places and themes and what children need to know about them, rather than processes of learning that might best engage children. The schemes of work have appeared as lists of content to be covered with references made to where resources can be found. Where there are objectives, these are often narrowly defined and predominantly relate to 'knowledge and understanding'. It is rare to see attitudes and values or the development of intellectual skills referred to explicitly in curriculum plans. Although sometimes these are emphasized in geography lessons, the fact that they are not planned for raises questions about progression and systematic coverage.

### Enquiry and key questions

One of the key problems seems to be that many teachers are unclear about the role and nature of enquiry in geographical learning and the way in which enquiry skills can be integrated with the study of places and themes. Evidence gathered from teachers showed a great variation in understanding of what is meant by enquiry. This is supported by surveys of primary and secondary teachers conducted on behalf of QCA, which concluded: 'teachers had different views of what geographical enquiry was and they interpreted it in different ways' (QCA, 1998a).

Though there are some variations in specificity, generally, geography educators agree that the enquiry process is fundamental to effective teaching and learning (Chambers and Donert, 1996; Foley and Janikoun, 1996; Naish *et al.*, 1987; Roberts, 1996a). Although many secondary teachers are familiar with and make use of the 'route to geographical enquiry', developed by Naish *et al.* (1987), in their Advanced level work, we have found limited evidence of this approach to planning for the National Curriculum. Enquiry requires the active involvement of pupils, not just in participation in planned teaching, but also in the development of the nature and patterns of enquiries. Enquiry builds naturally on children's interest and questioning of the world about them. Enquiry-based teaching and learning require the adoption of a question-led approach to geographical studies. However, many teachers seem to view it as an event and refer to 'an enquiry' as something separate from other ways of teaching the geography curriculum. Evidence that enquiry is not fully integrated into geography planning is highlighted in OFSTED reports (OFSTED 1999; Smith 1997a,1997b) and by SCAA:

> At all key stages, few teachers have given serious consideration to the integration of enquiry questions and skills into schemes of work.
>
> (SCAA, 1996a: 10)

We have found that even where key questions help structure planning, they are used to identify the content of the scheme of work and there is little recognition of why the question might be worth asking or that there may be a variety of possible answers. Just because questions are used to structure units of work does not therefore mean that it is not still a content-led, objectives model of curriculum that is employed. Much more thought needs to go into who is asking the questions as well as the type of questions being asked.

The questions indicated in the Geography Order are hierarchical and linked to the 'route to enquiry' defined by Naish *et al.* (1987) when developing the 16–19 Curriculum Project. It is, however, important to recognize that this is not a prescriptive model, merely a guide and that it can be adapted to suit different types of investigations. Flint (1994) identifies different types of geographical enquiry questions which can be linked to different stages in the enquiry process (see Table 19.1). In many schemes of work questions are not recognized as hierarchical, and there is often a concentration on descriptive and explanatory questions, so that there is little evidence of progression beyond the accumulation of information. Catling (1998, 1999) found a similar pattern in textbooks where the questions asked were generally descriptive and therefore limited in intellectual challenge.

Even when key questions are evident in planning, they are not always used in the classroom to structure learning. Pupils are seldom made aware of questions as a rationale for the information to be learned. Questions are nearly always initiated by the teacher and rarely by the pupils. It is rare to see teaching which concentrates on pupils' questions, which raises doubts about how they are to achieve the higher attainment levels which call for 'pupil independence in identifying geographical questions' (DFE, 1995).

## Skills

There has always been a tendency for some geography teachers to treat skills as separate from knowledge and understanding, and they are not always viewed as integral to the process of learning. For example, we have found mapwork separated as a unit of study from work on places and themes in primary and secondary schools. Teaching skills separately emphasizes technical rather than intellectual processes and does not give recognition to their role in developing understanding. There

*Table 19.1* Questions, learning and the enquiry process

| Enquiry Process (adapted from Naish et al., 1987) | Key Questions (adapted from National Curriculum 1995) | Type of Question (Flint, 1994) | Learning Process |
|---|---|---|---|
| Awareness | What do I think about it? | Speculative | Reception/Stimulus |
| Definition/ Description | What is it? Where is it? What is it like? | Descriptive | |
| Analysis/ Exploration | How did it get like this? How and why is it changing? What are the implications? | Explanatory Predictive | Information Processing |
| | What do different people think about it? What do I think about it? | Responsive | |
| Evaluation/ Decision-Making | What is likely to happen next? What do I think should happen? What are the consequences? | Predictive Evaluative | Storage |
| | What have I learned? | Evaluative | |

is a tendency to place emphasis on skills needed to present data, but there is insufficient emphasis on the intellectual skills needed to interpret, analyse, evaluate and explore meanings in data and information. Indeed, in primary schools there is a tendency to 'finish' work with a sound description of data rather than to engage children in analysing and evaluating it (OFSTED, 1998, 1999; Smith, 1997a, 1997b). Skills seem to happen with the activities rather than be planned for in a systematic and progressive way.

### Teaching and learning strategies

There is no doubt that good geography teachers do make use of a range of strategies and resources in their teaching. However, although there is variety, they focus on 'delivering content' rather than developing learning and understanding. There is a tendency for teachers to control the content and structure of lessons tightly. Questions asked by the teacher are predominantly factual. Though teachers use video resources, textbooks, CD-ROMs, newspapers and much else, tasks are intended only to extract factual information. There is much less emphasis on exploring ideas, constructing knowledge, giving opinions or comparing and critically evaluating different sources of evidence.

It also seems to be common practice to ask pupils to undertake tasks and activities without giving them a rationale or purpose. Pupils are rarely helped to see the significance of the work they undertake to their daily lives. The value of the understanding and skills they are developing is rarely made explicit. Friere (1972), when discussing the learning process, emphasized that pupils need to focus not only on the subject matter, but also on the means by which they bring their own developing learning capacities to bear on it. While teaching approaches may be active, it seems that there is little real engagement of pupils in the metacognitive aspects of exploring why, how and what is being learnt.

## Progression

Understanding progression seems to be the most challenging problem for the teachers we have worked with. It is hardly surprising if they plan simply from the content described in the programmes of study. Few teachers seem to make use of the level descriptors when planning geographical work and they have difficulty relating these to the programmes of study. This is particularly a problem in primary work because the level descriptors are not compulsory to use for assessment, recording and reporting. While recent materials on expectations for primary pupils (SCAA, 1997) and standards for assessment of secondary pupils (SCAA, 1996b) have been published, there is little clear indication that teachers have drawn specifically on them for planning purposes. There is little evidence of progression in curriculum planning and clearly this affects teachers' ability to plan for and assess individual pupil progress through the aspects of performance in the level descriptors.

## Assessment

OFSTED continue to highlight weaknesses in assessment practices in schools and within geography (OFSTED, 1998, 1999; Smith, 1997a,1997b). The most consistent criticisms are linked to assessment evidence not being used to inform curriculum planning or to identify learning targets for individual pupils. These problems are clearly linked to the issues in progression, and the difficulties in understanding the relationship between the level descriptors and the programmes of study. Many teachers have difficulties applying the levels to the content of their study units and lessons and the assessment evidence that emerges. The criteria for success in tasks are not linked to the aspects of performance and marking is often general rather than linked to specific attainments. It is also uncommon for pupils to be able to talk about their specific attainments or to fully understand what the feedback or marks mean. They are therefore, fully dependent on the teacher to guide their learning. Black and Wiliam (1998) have identified the important role of formative assessment in improving pupil attainment and the quality of learning. Such an approach to assessment must take into account the processes involved in learning and not just the outcomes.

## Summary

Though there is clearly some very good geography teaching, in which exciting and stimulating lessons make innovative use of strategies and resources, it has been noted that there are some concerns in teaching which must be addressed. Leat (1997) summarizes the problems as:

> Essentially, there is too much concern with teaching and not enough with learning, too much emphasis on substantive aspects of geography and not enough on the intellectual development of pupils.
>
> (Leat, 1997: 143)

It is our view that the way to address this problem is to re-emphasize the important role of questions and enquiry in geographical learning. We need to tap into the natural curiosity of children so that they are encouraged to observe the world around them and to ask questions about it. They need to know what information is available to answer their questions and where it can be found. Above all, they need to know that what they are learning is of value and to be able to recognize, apply and adapt their learning in new situations.

Enquiry is not an event, but the whole process of constructing geographical knowledge (Roberts, 1996b). It is especially important that children appreciate that a good deal of geographical information is contingent and contentious and they need to develop skills for critical evaluation. Enquiry promotes a view that knowledge should always be examined, questioned, re-examined and never be taken as absolute and it encourages children to develop their own ideas and to articulate them. What is needed is an approach to curriculum planning which is based on asking questions and which at the same time recognizes the statutory entitlement in the National Curriculum for children to have access to the common body of knowledge, ideas and skills contained within the Programmes of Study. Our view is that the move towards a question-led approach to curriculum planning can meet both these needs.

## The question-led curriculum

In such a short chapter it is impossible to address all of the issues or provide full and definitive answers to complex curriculum problems. However, we have begun to develop an approach to planning which is question-led and enquiry-orientated and focuses on learning.

A key starting point is to keep to the fore the nature of learning. There are of course a great number of theories about learning. Though it is still possible to identify a legacy of behaviourism in some approaches in the classroom and in government policy, it is true to say that constructivist theories of learning now predominate (Claxton, 1990: 20). In summary:

> a constructivist view of learning perceives children as intellectually active learners already holding ideas or schema which they use to make sense of their everyday experiences. Learning in classrooms involves the extension, elaboration or modification of their schemata. This process is one by which learners actively make sense of their world by constructing meanings.
>
> (Bennett and Dunne, 1994: 53)

There is a close link between constructivist theory and the enquiry approach in geography (Fisher, 1998). Working with teachers on curriculum planning, we have found it useful to think of the learning process in three stages and to approach planning using a series of questions:

- What is the topic?
- Why study it? What are the issues? How is it relevant to our lives?
- In what way can pupils' interests in the topic be stimulated?
- How can pupils be encouraged to raise issues and ask questions about the topic?
- How can the questions be structured into a hierarchical sequence?
- What resources will be needed to help answer the questions?
- What learning activities and tasks will pupils engage in to answer the questions and develop their understanding of the topic?
- Is there any need to differentiate resources and tasks to meet different learning needs?
- What are the likely learning outcomes in terms of key ideas, skills and attitudes and values?
- How do the learning tasks link to the aspects of performance in National Curriculum levels?
- Is there progression from previous learning and within the structure of the unit?
- What evidence will be available to judge pupils' progress in learning?
- How will the evidence be used and the outcomes recorded?
- How will the pupils become aware of their progress?

## The learning process

### Stage One: Reception/Stimulus

Motivation is vital for pupils to be receptive to new learning. At the start of units and lessons their interest in the topic needs to be awakened so that they have a desire to find out or know more about it. A teacher made this point:

> In this post-modern age, young people are very keen to question why they should study something. It is crucial that we have plausible and reasoned answers for them and show them our enthusiasm.

However, it is common for teachers to present topics to pupils without generating their interest or giving any rationale for why they should want to learn about it. Recent publications offering guidance for teachers on enquiry and planning schemes of work (QCA, 1998a, 1998b) seem to fail to recognize this vital stage in the learning process. There is an assumption that questions are decided by the teacher and structured into schemes of work, without any regard given to how to generate pupils' interest or involvement in the topic. In such circumstances pupils are less likely to engage with the material or link it to their previous learning.

We have worked with a number of teachers who have adopted the approach of 'stimulus' being the first stage in the development of a topic and they have found it successful in engaging pupils' interest. One teacher describes the way she approaches this:

> I first think about how I can make the topic interesting and relevant to the pupils. I ask myself, what is the point in knowing this? If I can't think of a good reason then why should my pupils? I then think of some way in which I can introduce the topic to them as something worth studying and relevant to their lives. I try to make them curious so they want to ask questions about it.

Many resources can be used as stimulus materials and these should be used in a flexible manner. Table 19.2 outlines some ideas used by a teacher to stimulate pupils' interest in topics. The key principle for using stimulus materials is to

*Table 19.2* Some examples of stimulus materials

| Topic | Stimulus ideas |
| --- | --- |
| Tectonic processes | video clips of earthquakes and volcanoes supported with dramatic classical music<br>the earthquake drill<br>diary of earthquake victim<br>newspaper articles |
| Migration | the song 'I want to be in America' from *West Side Story*<br>posters of paintings and stories by children in Sudan depicting forced migration (from Save the Children)<br>story adapted from *Tortilla Curtain* by T. Coraghessan Boyle |
| Development | photographs depicting different aspects of life around the globe<br>video scenes from aid appeals and Oxfam and Christian Aid<br>leaflets and material<br>The Trading Game |
| Ecosystems | audio recording of sounds from the rainforest<br>Sting's appeal to save the rainforest<br>desert survival game |
| Italy | TV adverts depicting different products from Italy and the images they portray<br>food tasting<br>video extracts from the *Holiday Programme* |
| South Africa | music from the Townships<br>sets of postcards<br>tourist brochures |
| Environmental issues | extract from the *Hound of the Baskervilles* (Dartmoor NP)<br>cartoons<br>newspaper cuttings and photographs<br>bag of waste to show opportunities for recycling |

encourage pupils to ask questions and identify issues that are worth studying. It is also important to relate these issues to something within their own experience or understanding and to make clear that their ideas and opinions are valued. Given the right stimulus, pupils will and do ask questions and the questions are often those we would like them to ask, although not all. Figure 19.1 shows the questions asked by a Year 8 group having watched five minutes of a video about flooding. Figure 19.2 outlines the questions asked by Year 4 children using photographs from a locality pack. Pupils need to be taught how to ask questions and what type of questions should be asked. One teacher described how she invests a good deal of time in her lessons focusing on questions:

> I start by demonstrating how to ask questions, setting a pattern for them. We do work on different types of questions and how to sequence them. I often use the example of when you first meet someone you begin with simple questions 'What is your name?', 'Where do you live?' Then later we might ask other questions like 'How do you feel?', 'Why did you do that?' I always ask them to come up with their own questions on a topic and we discuss the different types of questions and how best to sequence them. I often set homework to think up questions to ask. Training them in this way makes them enquiry orientated. They question everything in the end.

---

Why does it happen?
Where do floods happen most?
Are there any other types of flood other than flash or slow ones?
What will happen if the polar ice caps melt and global warming takes place?
Do people get killed in English floods?
Why can't people learn to swim?
How do they get rid of all the flood water?
How many floods does Britain get?
What is the largest number of people that have died in a flood?
Why do floods happen?
Do people get any warning?
What is the average length of time a flood lasts?
How can you prevent a flood?
Which town has had the worst flood?
How cold is the water?
Can floods always kill?
Where do people go if their homes have been destroyed?

---

*Figure 19.1* Questions about flooding asked by pupils

What are the buildings made of?
Do the children go to school?
How many are there in a class?
Do they have a play time?
Why are they doing lessons outside?
Do they watch television?
Is it hot there?
Could I play football?
Are their roads like ours?
How many houses are there?
Can children go to the shops?
What is it like carrying water?
Can you get a bus into town?
What do they grow?
Where do they shop?
Are there any shops?
Do they have a bathroom in the house?
Is it nice there?
Why are some houses made of bricks?
Does it rain?
How do people get there?
Can you get a doctor if you are ill?

*Figure 19.2* Questions about a locality by Year 4 pupils

It may not always be appropriate to involve pupils in formulating questions, but it is important to awaken their interest in a topic so that they understand the rationale for a sequence of lessons that follow. What is important is that children have the opportunity to consider the role, relevance and value of the questions that are investigated, whether 'set' by the teacher or formulated by themselves. Initially it is important for teachers to identify questions to guide geographical learning and for teachers to model this approach. Slater points out that 'No real understanding takes place unless the answers can be directly correlated to the questions' (Slater, 1993: 2).

It can be useful to identify an issue and to frame this as an enquiry question to structure the investigation of a topic. An enquiry question should provide scope for pupils to present their own ideas and answers, having investigated the issue. Examples of such questions include:

- Can anything be done to prevent earthquakes?          Tectonic processes
- How should the tropical rain forests be managed in the future?   Ecosystems

- Do you think there is a world population problem?            Population
- Should we be concerned about the future of our cities?       Settlement

In this initial stage the teachers' task is to engage pupils' enthusiasm for the topic and ensure they know what it is they are learning about, help them see how it relates to what they already know and enable them to appreciate why it is worth learning.

### Stage Two: Information processing

Much of what happens in geography units and lessons is covered by this second stage. There is a need to engage pupils in activities or tasks which involve them using skills and working with information to develop their understanding of concepts and ideas. This involves not only factual information but attitudes, opinions and ideas. However, it is important that questions be used as the basis and rationale for the tasks and activities and that pupils be actively engaged in pursuing answers to questions they recognize as worth asking. Slater makes a strong case for using questions in planning and teaching:

> No real understanding takes place unless the answers to questions can be directly correlated to the questions. The argument for the maintenance of a close link between questions and answers suggests that knowledge and understanding are incomplete when the generalised answers alone and in bulk are presented to learners. What is she getting at? is a familiar response to an activity in which the teacher has not made explicit the link between the question being explored and the answer or conclusion being presented.
>
> (Slater, 1993: 2)

If the pupils have been involved in generating the questions, they are more likely to see the relevance of the information and tasks. Teachers need to be aware of the nature of the questions being asked and to structure learning activities so that there is some variety and progression throughout the enquiry (see Table 19.1).

If pupils' questions are used as the basis for planning they can be grouped according to the type of question and the level of intellectual skill required to answer them. In this way there will be progression in the topic. The case study on Mt Etna (Figure 19.3) provides an opportunity to explore wider concepts involved in understanding tectonic processes. It moves from descriptive to explanatory, predictive, responsive and evaluative questions, building from examining information to engaging and challenging pupils' geographical ideas, the limits to their own understanding and the need to clarify their own values. Alternatively a variety of examples can be drawn on to answer more general questions, for instance those asked about flooding (Figure 19.1) can be answered by drawing on a variety of case studies.

The inclusion of questions in a scheme of work does not necessarily ensure that enquiry work occurs in the classroom. It is essential in planning to determine what kinds of experiences and pupil activities are needed to investigate those questions.

---

Theme:   Tectonic processes

Stimulus:   Video clips from the news

Enquiry question:
> Should people be evacuated from the Mt Etna region?

Definition and Description:
> What is the problem?
> What is a volcano?
> What kind of volcano is Mt Etna?
> Where is Mt Etna?
> Where are volcanoes found?
> What do volcanoes do?

Analysis and Exploration:
> Why do volcanoes erupt?
> What has caused Mt Etna to erupt?
> Why do people live near volcanoes?
> What are the dangers?
> How can the dangers be minimized – what are the available options?
> How will people be affected by different options?

Evaluation and decision-making:
> What do I think people should do?
> What are the consequences of the decision?

---

*Figure 19.3* Structuring pupils' questions in a Key Stage 3 enquiry

Enquiry learning involves pupils actively, identifying the information needed, where it might be found and working things out for themselves.

In a sequence of lessons looking at migration from Mexico to the USA, a Year 9 pupil established an Internet link with a border guard in the USA. The pupils in the class were then able to ask the guard questions using e-mail; he was very willing to respond. There are other examples where links have been established with schools in other countries and pupils have been able to gain information by questioning each other. As recognized by QCA (1998a), there are various levels and types of enquiry, and it is important to vary approaches and activities to incorporate a range of skills and information sources. A further variable is the degree of structure and guidance provided by the teacher, which can range from a high degree of control through structured problem-solving, to open-ended pupil-led investigations. At all levels, initially pupils will need to be guided in generating and sorting questions. Very young children will tend to ask any question, so selecting helpful questions will be important. Older primary pupils will need guidance in broadening the range of questions and focusing them on what can be investigated with limited resources. Pupils in Key Stage 3 will need support in selecting and structuring questions to use, for example, in drawing on a range of case studies to support a balanced explanation. The point is that consistent experience from early in Key Stage 1 throughout Key Stages 2 and 3 will enable pupils to become both autonomous and more sophisticated in formulating and pursuing their own questions.

A key principle for developing learning activities is for them to engage the pupils in developing thinking skills. Leat (1997,1998) describes a variety of valuable activities and principles which focus on developing classroom strategies designed to 'help teachers move away from statements like "Pupils should be taught that" . . . away from the view that geography is a load of content to be delivered' (Leat, 1998: 1). The strategies are targeted towards motivating pupils by encouraging them to ask questions, and become independent learners who are excited by learning (Leat, 1998). Leat also stresses the need for teachers to develop debriefing skills so that they can help pupils to recognize the way in which they think and learn and to identify appropriate strategies and reasoning patterns. By focusing on the 'how' of learning, pupils can learn to apply learning skills to new situations. They can also become more able to engage in self-assessment and target-setting and take more responsibility for their own learning as Black and Wiliam (1998) advocate.

Table 19.3 gives an example of a framework for planning based around the questions listed at the beginning of this section. These are a sequence of lessons about earthquakes. The stimulus for this sequence was a TV news clip, without sound, of the effects of the Kobe earthquake. Pupils were asked to write down what they could see, and what questions they would like to ask about it. The enquiry question 'Can anything be done to protect people from earthquakes?' forms the basis for the investigation and the pupils were then involved in agreeing the sequence of key questions which would guide their learning. The teacher then devised appropriate tasks and activities to investigate the questions. These involve the pupils in finding out information, using a variety of resources and identifying relevant information and ideas themselves.

This framework facilitates planning for progression and assessment. The key questions are hierarchical, so that there is progression in the development of cognitive skills within the topic. If all schemes of work are planned using this structure then it is straightforward to identify where pupils can make progress as the key questions can be correlated to the aspects of performance within the level descriptors. For instance, answering the question 'How did it get like this?' involves developing understanding of human and physical processes. The questions, therefore, provide the signposts for teachers to identify where opportunities exist in the curriculum for pupils to make progress in various aspects of geographical understanding. The last column in the model scheme itemizes the assessment evidence which can be used to judge pupils' understanding and skills.

Table 19.3 Geography planning for enquiry

Theme: Tectonic Processes    Stimulus: Kobe Video Clip    Year: Seven

Enquiry question: Can anything be done to protect people from earthquakes?

| Key Questions | Learning Activities | Key Ideas | Skills/Attitudes | Resources | Assessment/Evidence |
|---|---|---|---|---|---|
| What do you think is happening? What is an earthquake? What is it like? | Show clip from Kobe Earthquake without sound. Write down words to describe what you see and questions you might ask Discuss with the class Write commentary for the video in pairs H/wk Find out where other earthquakes happen | Earthquakes involve violent shaking of the earth's crust They cause a great deal of damage | Observing from video Identifying questions Constructing commentary Working collaboratively Respect for natural forces | Kobe Video Clip | Written commentary |
| Where do earthquakes occur? | Locate Kobe in the atlas/ draw onto map Ask for other examples of earthquakes H/wk Locate these onto the map Raise questions about the distribution Show video clip of plate boundaries Draw plate boundaries onto map Write a description of where earthquakes occur | Earthquakes occur in particular locations The earth's crust is divided into plates Plate boundaries are cracks in the earth's crust Earthquakes occur close to plate boundaries | Using an atlas Locating places on a map Describing a distribution | Atlases Blank world map OHT of plate boundaries Textbook | Completed maps Descriptions Explanations |

Table 19.3 continued

| Key Questions | Learning Activities | Key Ideas | Skills/Attitudes | Resources | Assessment/Evidence |
|---|---|---|---|---|---|
| Why do earthquakes occur? | Task to prepare a drama for primary children to explain what happens at a plate boundary and why earthquakes happen. Work in groups Use resources to prepare drama Act out dramas H/wk Prepare explanation of why earthquakes happen | There are three types of plate boundary Earthquakes occur as a result of tectonic activity at plate boundaries | Extracting information Selecting information Devising a drama Transforming information Writing an explanation | Textbooks CD-ROM and video Handout | Drama presentations Written report |
| How are people affected by earthquakes? | Refer back to video and discuss impact Examine seismograph and stages in an earthquake in pairs. Complete exercise Groups: Mystery exercise – Mr and Mrs Endo Who died and why? Feedback and debrief | A seismograph shows the pattern and severity of an earthquake There are different effects at different stages in an earthquake It is possible to identify factors which make the impact more severe | Interpreting graphs Selecting information Analysing information Presenting information Working collaboratively Debriefing/reflection Empathy | Seismograph handout Endo Mystery (SCAA) | Seismographs Group work Presentations |
| What factors affect the impact of earthquakes? | Examine video clips, newspaper articles, photographs of the Armenian earthquake. In groups, discuss the earthquake. identify the factors affecting | The impact of earthquakes varies according to severity and geographical location There are a number of factors which affect the impact of an earthquake | Extracting information Group work Grouping information Analysing information Evaluating information Presenting information | Video clips Newspaper articles Photographs | Posters |

Table 19.3 continued

| | | | | |
|---|---|---|---|---|
| | the impact and severity of the earthquake. Sort out the information into headings. Prepare a poster using the headings. Identify the similarities and differences to the Kobe earthquake | There are contrasts between ELDCs and MEDCs | | |
| What are the ways in which people can be protected and prepared for earthquakes? | Preparation for role-play. Different groups prepare presentations making a case for money to be spent on different protection and preparation measures (architects, geologists, emergency services, information services, city planners). Packs of information provided. Hold public meeting | There are a number of ways in which people might be protected and prepared for earthquakes. People have different viewpoints about priorities. Financial constraints mean that choices must be made | Adopting a role; Developing an argument; Using relevant information; Presenting an argument; Evaluating evidence; Developing empathy; Recognizing the validity of different viewpoints; Asking questions | Information packs; Role cards; OHTs and pens; Role presentations; Discussion |
| What do you think should be done to protect people from earthquakes? | Divide class in two – Kobe and Armenia. In small groups devise a list of priorities you would advise the government of the country to adopt in protecting people from future earthquakes. Justify your choices to the class. Discuss any differences | The priorities for earthquake protection will vary according to location and development | Evaluating information; Decision-making; Prioritizing | Priorities; Discussion |

Key questions are also important for planning individual lessons. The lesson plan shown in Figure 19.4 was planned by a trainee teacher, to prepare pupils for a fieldwork activity investigating microclimates around the school. As pupils entered the room the music from *Mission Impossible* was played and sealed envelopes had been placed on desks. The investigation or 'mission' was to discover if there were different microclimates around the school and it was presented to pupils in an exciting way. The key questions which had been generated by the pupils in the previous lesson were written on the envelopes and then the lesson proceeded through a series of tasks contained in the envelopes which were designed to answer the questions. The tasks were structured by the teacher, but involved the pupils in investigating, making their own decisions, for instance, selecting sites and devising recording sheets and drawing conclusions for themselves. At no point in the lesson did the teacher provide information other than instructions. The key questions give a purpose for the tasks, and they help to provide structure and pace in the lesson.

The examples illustrated show how by focusing on questions and the enquiry process it is perfectly possible to cover the content prescribed in the programmes of study. A number of teachers claim not to do enquiry because it is too time-consuming and they are also afraid of losing control of the lesson. We have found this not to be the case; pupils are generally more motivated and interested in the topics and are therefore keen to learn.

### Stage Three: Storage

If learning involves 'a modification of what you already believe or know' (Claxton, 1990: 6), then it is important to give pupils an opportunity to express how their thinking has changed and developed. If a topic is begun by identifying an issue or enquiry question, it is appropriate to conclude it by giving a personal response to it. Pupils should be encouraged to recognize what has influenced their thinking and how this relates to the values they hold. For instance, having studied the one-child policy in China, the final task in a sequence of lessons was for Year 9 pupils to express their own viewpoint on the policy and to identify three reasons to support their opinion. They were then required to identify two reasons that would make them change their mind. The purpose of this was to reinforce the fact that many issues are complicated and there are no simple solutions. In another topic, Year 8 pupils had been looking at the effects of migration from Mexico to the USA and at the end of the unit were asked to decide what they think the future policy should be and why, then to express their views in a letter to the US President.

At the end of a unit of work pupils should be encouraged to reflect on their learning and this should be encouraged through self-assessment techniques and debriefing led by the teacher,

> Teachers encourage pupils to explain their work, help them to understand the significance of what they have done, and put names to the reasoning patterns that they develop. This can be likened to providing pupils with a filing system to help them retrieve knowledge concepts and ideas.
>
> (Leat, 1997: 146)

Topic: Microclimates around the school

**What are the key questions which will guide the lesson?**
• What is a microclimate?
• Why is it important for us to study them?
• What factors affect microclimates?
• How shall we measure microclimates around the school?
• Where shall we take our recordings?
• How shall we record our measurements?

**What will the pupils learn in the lesson?**
*Knowledge/concepts*
• To know and understand how buildings, physical features, shelter, surface and aspect can affect the microclimate of an area
• To know and understand how to investigate the area around the school and its microclimate

*Skills*
• To recognize how equipment can be used to measure aspects of microclimates
• To identify appropriate sites using a large-scale map
• To create an appropriate recording instrument
• To collaborate with others in small groups

*Attitudes*
• To realize that a number of factors can influence the local microclimate and to appreciate the value of fieldwork in measuring the microclimate

**What resources will be used?**

| | |
|---|---|
| Envelopes | Card-sorting exercise |
| Compass | Handkerchief |
| Tape recorder | Anemometer |
| Jigsaw game | Thermometer |
| Map of the school grounds | |

**What assessment evidence will arise from the lesson?**
Answers to questions
Accuracy of card-sorting
Site identification
Recording sheets

*continued . . .*

| Time | Teacher activity | Pupil activity |
|------|------------------|----------------|
| 2.00 | Give out pieces of jigsaw | Find group to make up jigsaw |
|      |                  | Sit at tables in groups |
|      | Play *Mission Impossible* music | Listening |
|      | Refer to sealed envelopes on desk | Open envelopes – read 'mission' |
| 2.05 | Introduce 'mission' – 'To discover if microclimates vary around the school' Refer to preparation questions on sheet which will guide the rest of the lesson | Listening |
| 2.10 | Recap *What is a microclimate?* Share some definitions with the class | Discuss in groups and reach a definition. |
| 2.15 | *Why is it important for us to study?* Take feedback from the class | Examine cartoons and identify reasons for studying microclimates |
| 2.25 | *What affects microclimates?* Take feedback. Summarize factors Check understanding | Card-sorting exercise matching factor with definition |
| 2.35 | *How shall we measure microclimates around the school?* Give each group a handkerchief, thermometer, compass, anemometer. Explain task. Take feedback. Explain equipment | Identify what can be measured with each piece of equipment. Record answers. |
| 2.45 | *Where shall we take these measurements to get a good variation?* Give out maps. Discuss site selection | Look at maps and select four sites Give reasons for site selection |

*continued . . .*

| | | |
|---|---|---|
| 2.55 | *How will we record our measurements?* Take feedback. Identify best practice Homework – to prepare a recording sheet using IT | Devise a recording sheet in rough |
| 3. 05 | *How shall we conduct our investigation?* Explain procedures for fieldwork next lesson | Listening |
| 3.10 | *What have you learned in the lesson?* Recap key points. Ask questions | Answering questions |
| 3.15 | End lesson | |

*Figure 19.4* Lesson plan (Lesson devised by Katie Turner, King Alfred's School, Wantage)

## Conclusion

The geography curriculum for the twenty-first century must be focused on pupil learning, provide opportunities for critical enquiry, and stress the importance of attitudes and values through an appropriate range of teaching and learning approaches. There have been government initiatives and some worrying trends which threaten the position of geography in the curriculum, such as the literacy and numeracy hours in primary schools, and the introduction of vocational courses at secondary level. There is room for improvement in the quality of the teaching of geography in the National Curriculum (OFSTED, 1998, 1999; Smith 1997a, 1997b). These improvements need to focus on engaging pupils in high-order thinking skills, building from explanations into predictive, responsive and evaluative analysis. There needs to be a variety of teaching approaches used and a range of materials to stimulate and motivate pupils. At all levels they need to be actively involved. A question-led curriculum is founded on the rationale that enquiry and investigation are fundamental, both to harnessing effectively pupils' learning and curiosity and to develop a better informed understanding of geography as a way of exploring the world about us. Unless schools develop courses which stimulate and motivate young people, the supply of geographers in the future may decline. Geographers need to adopt a questioning approach and promote the subject as relevant and topical. OFSTED has recognized that with such an approach 'geography appeals to pupils' (OFSTED, 1998). If geography in the twenty-first century becomes a marginal field of study in schools, it will largely be because we have driven pupils away by employing an unhelpful model of curriculum. It is important now to recognize the full potential of the subject across the whole curriculum.

> Young minds of the present day do not take easily to long spells of passive learning and geography is better placed than most subjects to provide stimulation and enrichment of experience on the one hand, while maintaining purposefulness and relevance to contemporary life on the other.
>
> (Walford, 1998: 140)

## Acknowledgements

We would like to thank all those teachers who have contributed ideas to this chapter. Special thanks to Katie Turner, King Alfred's School, Wantage.

## References

Bennett, N. and Dunne, E., (1994) 'How children learn – implications for practice', in Moon, B. and Shelton Mayes, A., *Teaching and Learning in the Secondary School*, London: Routledge.

Black, P. and Wiliam, D. (1998) *Inside the Black Box*, London: King's College.

Blyth, A., Derricot, R., Elliot, G., Sumner, H., and Washington, A. (eds) (1976) *Curriculum Planning in History, Geography and Social Science*, Bristol: Collins/ESL.

Callaghan, J. (1976) 'Towards a national debate', *Education*, 22 October.

Catling, S. (1998) 'Views of distant localities in UK primary geogrpahy textbooks', in Ferreira, M., Neto, A. and Sarmento, C. (eds) *Culture, Geography and Geographical Education*, Vol. 1, Lisbon: Universidade Aberta.

Catling, S. (1999) 'Developing intercultural understanding through primary geography textbooks: some comments', *Geography Education*, 12: 15–23.

Chambers, B. and Donert, K. (1996) *Teaching Geography at Key Stage 2*, Cambridge: Chris Kington.

Claxton, G. (1990) *Teaching to Learn*, London: Cassell.

Dearing, R. (1994) *The National Curriculum and its Assessment: Final Report*, London: SCAA.

DES (1989) *National Curriculum: From Policy to Practice*, London: HMSO.

DES (1991) *Geography in the National Curriculum (England)*, London: HMSO.

DFE (1995) *Geography in the National Curriculum*, London: HMSO.

Eisner, E. (1982) *Cognition and Curriculum*, London: Longman.

Fisher, T. (1998) *Developing as a Teacher of Geography*, Cambridge: Chris Kington.

Flint, D. (1994) *Oliver and Boyd Geography Teacher's Book 5*, Harlow: Longman.

Foley, M. and Janikoun, J. (1996) *The Really Practical Guide to Primary Geography*, London: Stanley Thornes.

Friere, P. (1972) *Pedagogy of the Oppressed*, London: Penguin.

Lawton, D. (1982) *Education and Politics in the 1990s: Conflict or Consensus?* London: Falmer Press.

Leat, D. (1997) 'Cognitive acceleration in geographical education', in Tilbury, D. and Williams, M. (eds) *Teaching and Learning in Geography*, London: Routledge.

Leat, D. (1998) *Thinking Through Geography*, Cambridge: Chris Kington.

Martin, F. (1995) *Teaching Early Years Geography*, Cambridge: Chris Kington.

Naish, M. (1992) 'Geography in the secondary curriculum', in Naish, M. (ed.) *Geography and Education*, London: Kogan Page.

Naish, M. (1997) 'Geography and education – knowledge and control', in Convey, H. and Nolzen, H., *Geography and Education*, Munich: University of Munich.

Naish, M., Rawling, E. and Hart, C. (1987) *Geography 16–19: The Contribution of a Curriculum Project to 16–19 Education*, London: Longman.

OFSTED (1995) *Guidance on the Inspection of Secondary Schools*, London: HMSO.

OFSTED (1998) *Secondary Education: A Review of Secondary Schools 1993 1997*, London: HMSO.

OFSTED (1999) *The Annual Report of Her Majesty's Chief Inspector of Schools*, London: HMSO.

QCA (1998a) *Geographical Enquiry at Key Stages 1–3*, London: QCA.

QCA (1998b) *Geography: A Scheme of Work for Key Stages 1 & 2*, London: QCA.

Rawling, E. (1992) 'The making of the National Geography Curriculum', *Geography*, 77 4: 292–309.

Rawling, E. (1996) 'Impact of the National Curriculum on school-based curriculum development', in Kent, A., Lambert, D., Naish, M., and Slater, F. (eds) *Geography in Education: Viewpoints on Teaching and Learning*, London: Cambridge University Press.

Roberts, M. (1996a) 'Teaching styles and strategies', in Kent, A., Lambert, D., Naish, M. and Slater, F. (eds) *Geography in Education: Viewpoints on Teaching and Learning*, London: Cambridge University Press.

Roberts, M. (1996b) 'An exploration of the role of the teacher within enquiry based classroom activities', in van der Schee, J., Schoenmakeer, G., Trimp, H. and van Westbhenen, H. (eds) *Innovation in Geographical Education*, Amsterdam: University of Amsterdam.

Roberts, M. (1997) 'Curriculum planning and course development', in Tilbury, D. and Williams, M. (eds) *Teaching and Learning in Geography*, London: Routledge.

SCAA (1996a) *Monitoring the School Curriculum: Reporting to Schools*, London: SCAA.

SCAA (1996b) *Exemplification of Standards: Key Stage 3: Geography*, London: SCAA.

SCAA (1997) *Expectations in Geography at Key Stages 1 and 2*, London: SCAA.

Slater, F. (1993) *Learning Through Geography*, Pennsylvania: NCGE.

Smith, P. (1997a) 'Standards achieved: a review of geography in secondary schools in England 1995–1996', *Teaching Geography*, 22, 3: 125–6, Geographical Association.

Smith, P. (1997b) 'Standards achieved: a review of geography in primary schools in England 1995–96', *Primary Geographer*, 31: 4–5, Geographical Association.

Tolley, H. and Reynolds, J.B. (1977) *Geography 14–18*, London: Macmillan.

Walford, R. (1998) 'Geography 5–19 retrospect and prospect', in Rawling, E. and Daugherty, R. (eds) *Geography into the 21st Century*, Chichester: Wiley.

Whitaker, P. (1995) *Managing to Learn*, London: Cassell.

# 20 Wider issues for the future

*Rex Walford*

## Introduction

> I therefore want you to make the bold claim that geography is an essential part
> of education, whatever forms education may take, and there can be no question
> of dropping it in any considered course of study; it is, in my opinion, more
> important than a foreign language or a science, highly important as these are,
> for the simple reason ... that the intelligent person must understand
> something about the world and the country and the district in which he is set
> to live his life.
>
> (Norwood, 1946)

These unequivocal words of Sir Cyril Norwood, a leading educationalist, but not
himself a geographer, are a testament to the perceived value of geography in schools
– but they were uttered fifty years ago. Where, geographers may wonder, is the
equivalent Norwood of influence in the present climate of uncertainty?

As geography and geography teachers move into the new millennium, there
may be a certain wistful nostalgia for years past, – for the post-World War One years
of rising international consciousness which gave geography examination status in
secondary schools, for the mid-century years of steady development in both primary
and secondary sectors, for the excitement and vigour of the 'spatial analysis'
revolution, leading to the high-water mark of statutory geography for all between
the ages of 5 and 16 specified in the National Curriculum of 1988.

The advent of the National Curriculum has provided first hope and then regret
for geographers as the Kenneth Baker vision of a 5–16 'broad and balanced
curriculum' which included geography, history and arts subjects was initiated, but
then carelessly dismantled by a combination of pragmatism and power politics.

And yet, looking back over the longer term, it is clear that much has happened
to enhance geography in schools in the past 130 years. From being a collection
of travellers' tales, cosmography and some informational bric-a-brac, it has matured
into a major school subject at all levels, passing through several stimulating
intellectual debates on the way, and gaining something of lasting value from each
of them. Its place in the curriculum of schools, once unimportant, is now established, though not secure.

Primary school geography, after a period submerged in topic work, when it was often more honoured in the breach than in the observance by non-specialist teachers, was given a fillip by the 1988 National Curriculum requirements to teach specific material, though in practice its quality was variable because of teachers' lack of specialist knowledge. Primary teachers of the 1990s discovered that geography is more than just the immediate locality and began to rehabilitate the study of other countries through detailed case-studies.[1] There are indications, however, that an increase in other curriculum prescriptions (notably the 'literacy hour' and 'numeracy hour') and a lack of time for specific geography modules in Initial Teacher Education courses are currently working to geography's disadvantage. A recent OFSTED Annual Report was specific in stating that in the primary school 'Pupils' progress in geography does not compare well with other subjects' (OFSTED, 1998).

In the secondary sector, geography remains, for the most part, a popular and well liked subject with most pupils, though increasingly at GCSE and A-level they may not always be able to exercise their inclinations to choose it for study. At Key Stage 3 (11–14 years) the National Curriculum seems to have encouraged a return to 'safer' textbook learning compared with what has been going on in the past twenty years. OFSTED reports suggest that, in most schools, the proportion of 'unsatisfactory' lessons is low compared with other subjects, but that, conversely, geography does not have so many 'good' lessons.[2] Only at the post-16 stage does the quality of geography teaching appear to be superior to that of most other major subjects. At other levels, a 'middle-of-the-road' mentality appears to have overtaken current classroom practice.

Examination statistics suggest that geography remained buoyant in recruiting candidates to take the subject at GCSE until recently, but that current timetable restrictions are now beginning to bite. Candidature has declined from a high point of 302,298 in 1996 to 265,573 in 1998 and 257,214 in 1999 with geography now the seventh most popular GCSE subject. Given a 'free choice' of subjects, there is little doubt that GCSE geography numbers would remain at least at the 1999 figure, but, because of other statutory requirements, many schools now require students to choose between studying geography and history at GCSE level. Even where this system does not operate, there is usually considerable restriction on what students may choose beyond the 'core subjects' of English, maths and science.

At A-level, where a genuine choice of subjects is more freely made, the figures for geography remain encouragingly high. The high point was in 1994 when 46,339 candidates took the subject, but in 1998 the figure had only dropped marginally to 44,881 and geography was (excluding General Studies) the fourth most popular A-level subject choice in that year. In 1999 the entry was 42,181. For many years geography was the junior partner to history, but geography numbers overtook those of history in 1993. Since then the gap has continued to widen, so that geography now has 10 per cent more candidates than history. However, depending on circumstances, the picture can change very quickly, as the decline of economics at A-level shows. In 1992 economics had 40,194 candidates, but the figure had dropped to less than half that number (18,670) six years later.

Thus, at the turn of the century, things can go either way for geography. The current National Curriculum (given only minor revision by the 1999/2000 exercise) will, it is said, be considered for more radical revision in 2005. Will geography's presence be confirmed or challenged then?

The hope that geography might be restored as a compulsory subject at Key Stage 4 (as it was between 1988 and 1993) is probably over-optimistic, though it may eventually regain a stronger place in the primary curriculum if the 'literacy and numeracy hour' strategies turn out to be transitory phenomena.

In the upper forms of secondary schools, the subject's future looks problematic. Will GCSE numbers stabilize, or continue to drift downwards, as geography continues to be marginalized in the Key Stage 4 curriculum? Can A-level geography maintain its numbers in the light of a decline in students taking it as an examination subject at lower levels?

Fewer students taking A-level would mean, in all probability, a diminished flow of students for university courses. Fewer university students would have implications for adequate teacher provision; fewer well trained specialists would emerge. In consequence, the quality of school geography teaching could be affected adversely – and this would reduce further the number of students who might freely choose the subject for the purposes of examination. In other words, if weakness shows in one part of the system, a cycle of decline may follow.

If geographers wish to see the essence of their subject survive in schools into the twenty-first century (in whatever form), they need to be fully aware of all the current nuances of curriculum politics which are at work in schools and in government. They may also need to rethink some long-cherished beliefs. In the rest of this chapter, some key issues and possible strategies for action are considered in both the short and longer term.

## Immediate issues

### Should geographical educators change tack and back the 'deficit model'?

In the primary school, recent government concern about perceived deficiencies in the basic education of young children in Britain has led to the imposition of prescribed strategies relating to 'literacy and numeracy hours'. The Department for Education and Employment (DfEE) appears to have been moved to introduce these specialist hours on the basis of what has been shown to be *not* known – in other words they have been persuaded to act from a 'deficit model' of literacy and numeracy in relation to school pupils.

In the USA, the alarming deficiencies in geographical knowledge of American students revealed by national surveys provided the springboard for a high-profile Resolution promoted in Congress in 1987 (see Figure 20.1). The Resolution, approved by acclaim and signed by President Ronald Reagan, the Speaker of the House, and the President of the Senate, highlighted some of the deficiencies, affirmed that 'national attention must be focused on the integral role that

One Hundredth Congress of the United States of America

AT THE FIRST SESSION

*Begun and held at the City of Washington on Tuesday, the sixth day of January, one thousand nine hundred and eighty-seven*

### Joint Resolution

To designate the period commencing November 15, 1987, and ending November 21, 1987, as "Geography Awareness Week".

Whereas the United States of America is a truly unique nation with diverse landscapes, bountiful resources, a distinctive multiethnic population, and a rich cultural heritage, all of which contributes to the status of the United States as a world power;

Whereas geography is the study of people, their environments, and their resources;

Whereas, historically, geography has aided Americans in understanding the wholeness of their vast nation and the great abundance of its natural resources;

Whereas geography today offers perspectives and information in understanding ourselves, our relationship to the Earth, and our interdependence with other peoples of the world;

Whereas 20 percent of American elementary school students asked to locate the United States on a world map placed it in Brazil;

Whereas 95 percent of American college freshmen tested could not locate Vietnam on a world map;

Whereas 75 percent of Americans responding to a nationwide survey could not locate El Salvador on a map, while 63 percent could not name the two nations involved in the SALT talks;

Whereas over 20 percent of American teachers currently teaching geography have taken no classes in the subject and, therefore, do not have the training necessary to effectively teach geographic concepts;

Whereas departments of geography are being eliminated from American institutes of higher learning, thus endangering the discipline of geography in the United States;

Whereas traditional geography has virtually disappeared from the curricula of American schools while still being taught as a basic subject in other countries, including Great Britain, Canada, Japan, and the Soviet Union;

Whereas an ignorance of geography, foreign languages, and cultures places the United States at a disadvantage with other countries in matters of business, politics, and the environment;

Whereas the United States is a nation of worldwide involvements and global influence, the responsibilities of which demand an understanding of the lands, languages, and cultures of the world; and

Whereas national attention must be focused on the integral role that knowledge of world geography plays in preparing citizens of the United States for the future of an increasingly interdependent and interconnected world: Now, therefore, be it

*Resolved by the Senate and House of Representatives of the United States of America in Congress assembled,* That the period commencing November 15, 1987, and ending November 21, 1987, is designated as "Geography Awareness Week", and the President is authorized and requested to issue a proclamation calling upon the people of the United States to observe such week with appropriate ceremonies and activities.

APPROVED

JUL 24 1987

*Ronald Reagan*

*Speaker of the House of Representatives.*

*Vice President of the United States and President of the Senate.* Pro Tempore.

*Figure 20.1* Resolution of the US Congress regarding geography

knowledge of world geography plays in preparing citizens of the United States for the future of an increasingly interdependent world' and proclaimed a 'Geography Awareness Week'. Backed by National Geographic Society money, and a portfolio of supporting strategies including the creation of State Geographical Alliances and the foundation of numerous summer in-service Institutes for teachers, there has been a considerable improvement in the fortunes of geography in US schools since then.

Until now geographers in Britain have eschewed this approach, believing the subject to be stronger in health and presence on this side of the Atlantic and therefore better able to justify itself through student achievement, rather than student deficiency. But even if this is true, a 'deficit ' of basic national and world knowledge amongst students can also be revealed.

A recent survey (one of many with similar findings in the past decade[3]) showed that fewer than half of the sample of British schoolchildren surveyed could place London correctly on a map of Britain, only 42 per cent could identify Germany on a map of Europe, and only 18 per cent knew that the Acropolis was in Greece. It is significant that, commenting on this, government advisers admitted that the findings were 'surprising and disturbing'. Are these the first signs of official concern about geographical deficiencies to put alongside the worries about children being able to read properly and do mental arithmetic? If so, could not such concern be harnessed to a campaign to argue for the need of a 'global hour' to supplement the literacy and numeracy time periods, especially if subsequent OFSTED investigations confirm the situation? The key factor to the success of this strategy is that those in high places must care sufficiently to acknowledge that the lack of such 'basic' geographical knowledge is a matter of importance.

In May 1999, in the days immediately before the consultation for the National Curriculum 2000 was published, the *Sunday Times* ran a story which suggested that the basic 'location' maps instituted in the 1988 National Curriculum might be dropped (*Sunday Times*, 1999). The Secretary of State for Education, David Blunkett, was moved to respond very quickly to the story. He pre-empted the views of the Qualifications and Curriculum Authority and the whole consultation process, by issuing a statement saying that the maps would definitely remain.[4] Quite apart from the rights and wrongs of the matter, the fact that the Minister cared enough to intervene should be seen as an encouragement for geographers. Though some argue that locational knowledge is not 'the heart' of geography as they know it, it is surely both unwise and unrealistic to dismiss the teaching of basic facts with contempt or to minimize their importance – and the Blunkett intervention underlined the point. The aim of schools is not to turn pupils into specialist geographers, but to teach everyone some basic geographical knowledge and understanding.

### Is the supposed advantage of 'curriculum flexibility' an 'Achilles' Heel'?

When the first draft of the National Curriculum was published, a frequent early complaint was that a tight specification of knowledge would disadvantage teachers in their freedom to choose the topics they wished to teach. The plan, for instance, that all pupils should study the geography of three major world powers, USA, Russia and Japan, in Key Stage 3 was criticized as restrictive; it was removed in the first set of revisions. The Dearing-inspired revisions of 1993 were dominated by the need to squeeze a quart into a pint pot (or to reduce the quantity specified altogether) and the revising group proposed 'options' as an obvious way of solving the problem. The solution proposed means that in the 1995–2000 geography National Curriculum teachers have had the absurdity of having to choose rivers *or* coasts, volcanoes *or* earthquakes for study. This current flexibility of topic choice is being further extended into the geography formulation by the proposed 1999 revisions. In the document summarizing the proposals four of the nine paragraphs describing the proposed geography revisions speak of 'increasing flexibility' (QCA, 1999). Such good intentions may eventually turn out to be geography's Achilles' heel and lead to its demise.

Though such flexibility may be attractive for teachers, it sends a message to others outside the subject that at heart little or nothing in the subject is deemed essential. If more and more is made optional then the implication is clear – there are few fundamentals that all need to learn. If and when the subject comes under further pressure, geography will have few trump cards to play as questions about curriculum priorities are raised. Might it not be better, whilst there is time, to stake out and justify an absolutely essential core territory for the subject which all should learn, rather than bask in the dubious (and possibly transitory) freedom of curricular flexibility?

### Are the 'citizenship' and 'sustainable development' initiatives misleading directions for geography?

The Labour government post-1997 has sought to remedy perceived weaknesses in the original formulations and to cater for particular topical matters by setting up working parties on non-subject-specific aspects of education about which there is current concern and debate – citizenship, personal moral and spiritual education, sustainable development. The Working Party on Citizenship, chaired by Professor Bernard Crick, David Blunkett's former tutor, has achieved the aim of getting 'citizenship' a special place on the curriculum, i.e. added to the list of subjects, rather than being permeated through existing ones (Crick *et al.*, 1999). A Working Party on 'sustainable development' may achieve similar results. Some geographers see it as important to hitch their wagon to these reports, reshape their syllabuses accordingly and make strong claims on those particular pieces of curriculum territory.

The citizenship issue is an interesting case-study of relevance to geography. Most geography teachers would see their role as already including the encouragement of an element of citizenship. They seek to imbue a sense of identity amongst their pupils as they teach about the United Kingdom, a sensitivity to diverse national and ethnic groupings and beyond this a 'global citizenship' as they teach about other countries and the nature of the world environment. Though their teaching might stretch to covering such matters as the way in which the organization of the European Union works (or is supposed to work) and what the environmental responsibilities of a local council are, they would not see themselves as covering such elements of citizenship as understanding the legal system or the constitution.

The assumption would be that this was done in other subjects (notably history or general studies) and that geography makes a contribution to a theme which is, in essence, cross-curricular. Geography teachers would not want geography to be responsible for teaching all aspects of citizenship, any more than they would wish geography to be reduced to teaching *no* citizenship.

To re-cast the subject in order to take more account of these particular initiatives may, however, be an unwise move. The citizenship document has a whiff of *Brave New World* moralism about it which may, in time, make it thoroughly unpopular with students as well as teachers and difficult to teach; if pushed too hard, its ideology may turn out to be counter-productive. The citizenship plans and the proposals to encourage students to be positive about 'sustainable development' are, at present, also vague, relatively unresourced and untried.

Far better, perhaps, for geographers not to be deflected from concentrating on what they do better; providing a sound base of world knowledge, stimulating interest in places near and far, and getting pupils to appreciate the wonder and diversity of the world in both its physical and human manifestations. Pupil support for this educational enterprise is likely to be deeper and more constant. It is tempting to tailor teaching to passing governmental initiatives, but they may not prove a dependable long-term base.

## Should geographers now support less statutory provision, not seek more?

Geographers were originally surprised by the broadness of the statutory provision of the National Curriculum. They had assumed that a core of English, maths and science would be prescribed and were delighted to find themselves inside the 'broad and balanced' proposals of the 1988 Act, as one of the ten foundation subjects, rather than on the outside looking in. The proposals for wide statutory provision seemed for geography, at that time, a good idea. The loss of statutory geography in Key Stage 4 by the Dearing revisions of 1993 was a subsequent disappointment.

Ten years on, government thinking about secondary education seems to point towards a relaxation of National Curriculum prescriptions in Key Stage 4, rather than a stiffening of them, and so hopes that geography may be restored for all at that stage are unlikely to be fulfilled. Rather than press for the restoration of geography as a compulsory subject at Key Stage 4, it may be more advantageous for geographers to now support proposals for the decrease in statutory provision in this sphere. Geography might expect to benefit from a larger 'open' playing-field on which choices of subjects would be made.

The arguments for such a relaxation are strong. At the practical level, there are long-standing teacher shortages in design and technology and the science subjects, which the Teacher Training Agency has been unable to remedy fully despite sustained advertising campaigns. Though some of the future population undoubtedly need to be designers, technologists, scientists and speakers of Western European languages, it is not clear why all of them do. Britain's industrial base is now rooted firmly, *not* in science and manufacturing, but in the tertiary and quaternary service sector; the tourist and leisure industries employ the largest percentage of Britain's workforce and the tourist and information industries are the fastest growing. The need for language learning extends beyond French and German in today's global village; research suggests that most effective learning of language is through intensive and specialist tuition near the time of need, rather than through the 'long-haul' of a five-year course. The need for schools to give some priority to building a knowledge of and a sensitivity to a multicultural Britain in their pupils is graphically outlined by the 1999 Macpherson Report on the Stephen Lawrence killing.

The goal should be to have a citizenry not only literate, numerate and scientifically informed, but also culturally aware (in both time and space) and with respect for and an understanding of the environment. It is not suggested that the study of geography and history is *more* important than the study of science and technology up to the age of 16; but it surely is *as* important? If so, it deserves equality of treatment. Echoes of Norwood reverberate . . .

### Will geography be disadvantaged in the proposed changes for post-Key Stage 4 education?

At the post-16 level, there are plans not only for a new set of A-level examinations, but also for provision of a wider curriculum base for many pupils in England and Wales from September 2000 onwards. (In Scotland such a broader base already exists through the Certificate of Sixth Form Studies.) The proposals provide for pupils in academic pathways to study up to five subjects (working to a revised and re-targeted Advanced Supplementary (AS) level examination) in the first year of their 'sixth form' studies. Standing midway between the sciences, humanities and arts subjects, optimists suggest that geography may well benefit from being seen (both by students themselves and by parents and school tutors) as an 'extra' broadening subject to be taken, as one of five. But there may be a downside; more AS-level candidates may mean less A-level candidates if geography is seen as a pleasant leavening of the lump in a predominant arts or science cluster of sixth-form subjects, but no more than this. The intellectual fibre of the subject will be closely inspected. Geography teaching in sixth-forms will have to be intellectually stimulating and the narrow horizons of some careers advice importantly widened, if A-level numbers are not to fall in the long term.

Geography's position in the vocational and technical pathways is not so clear. The 'Leisure and Tourism' option of the GNVQ examination has proved popular, but those who take this examination have found that they have only a small segment of geographical knowledge at the end of it. There may be more geographical meat in other proposed GNVQ options, but these have yet to be put on to general offer.

### Is geography well placed to benefit from the ICT initiatives?

One area where school pupils of all ages seem to be well ahead of their teachers is in the use and understanding of information and communications technology.

Babes surf the Internet with equanimity, whilst their elders look nervously on from the book-favoured shore. Many geography teachers appear to have embraced innovation with a relatively greater enthusiasm than their colleagues in other subjects (as they have done on many occasions through recent educational history), and the considerable potential of Internet sources, remotely sensed images from satellites, and interactive video technologies is already being explored. ICT in schools is destined to be a growth area in the first quarter of the twenty-first century and it will be relatively well financed.[5] Any subject which grasps the opportunities offered and shows its willingness to explore and experiment will be looked on with favour. Geography is well placed to do this.

## Keeping the fences mended

Another set of key issues for the future relates to geography itself and its internal and external relations. However well geography does in classroom practice, its value and appeal will need to be demonstrated to those who see the subject from the outside. Parents, school governors, school curriculum committees, employers and especially key national decision-makers need to have an accurate image of what is being taught. They should not be working from some past antique image of the subject.

Regular national initiatives such as Geography Action Week (which has been observed with increasing enthusiasm each autumn since 1996) and the major surveys organized by the Geographical Association (Land Use–UK 1996: Coastline 2000) are useful vehicles for such broad publicizing. There is also considerable opportunity for geographers to advance understanding of their subject by taking up local and topical opportunities beyond the immediate context of the school curriculum – for example providing informative and imaginative maps for the school prospectus and noticeboards; carrying out surveys and analyses of key local conservation or traffic issues; publicizing the work of past pupils who have studied geography at university, or of geographers prominent in public life.

The Royal Geographical Society and the Geographical Association (helped by sponsorship from the Ordnance Survey) collaborated in April 1998 to run a seminar and dinner-meeting for government Ministers, key civil servants and executives from a range of quangos and large charitable organizations.[6] Such pro-active lobbying and networking have to be part and parcel of the work of professional organizations in today's world.

The Geographical Association has been a model for many other subject associations in this respect since its baptism into curriculum politics following the 'Great Debate' of the late 1970s. Its skill in presenting a good case for geography at the time of the National Curriculum formulation was at least a partial influence in shaping the mind of the Minister and it has kept up a steady stream of activity in this sphere since. Most recently, the appointment of its first salaried Chief Executive, Martin Curry, in December 1998 (after a century of devoted service from academics as voluntary Honorary Secretaries), has indicated a further step along the road from service association to professional institute.

The renewed interest and vigour of the Royal Geographical Society in the world of education (following a largely passive role for much of the century) owe something to its recent merger with the Institute of British Geographers (the body to which most university geographers belonged from its founding in 1933). But it owes as much to the purpose of its first woman director, Dr Rita Gardner, who has rapidly transformed the Society's administration and forward planning and enlarged its sphere of active operations since taking office in 1996. The RGS–IBG further strengthened its educational role by appointing its first full-time Education Officer in May 1999.

Both the RGS–IBG and the GA now work with comprehensive strategic plans to guide them, professional management approaches, and a clear perception of the need to be something more than providers of meetings, magazines and services for those who choose to join. The present harmonious relationship between the two bodies (with the GA seen as the 'leader' in policy matters concerning schools and the RGS–IBG as the 'leader' in higher education issues) has made geography more agile and energetic than many other subjects in dealing with issues and challenges. There is regular contact between the two professional associations, as they negotiate the quickly changing educational landscape. One day, might both see the advantage in unity?

Both GA and RGS–IBG in England, along with their Scottish and Welsh counterparts,[7] and working within the Council of British Geography (COBRIG), are now aware of the need to go beyond the narrow aspiration of servicing the immediate needs of their own members. They are coming to realize that their task is no less than to nurture a geographical consciousness (and a sense of the importance of that consciousness) in the community as a whole. There is some way to go in the present context before that aim can be said to be anywhere near achievement.

The need for professional bodies to generate policy discussion, to see ahead to issues on the horizon and to represent the interests of their members effectively on major matters is a key factor in preventing teachers from becoming beleaguered. Hurried individual reactive responses to central initiatives are rarely effective. And over the past twenty years, the amount of central intervention in educational matters has grown by leaps and bounds.

One other vital strategy for survival (or for the justification of survival) is for geography teachers to teach well. On present evidence, the number of 'satisfactory' lessons in future OFSTED inspections of geography needs to diminish and the number of 'good/exceptional' lessons needs to increase. Given the wealth and range of lively material available to geography teachers and the richness of life in the real world, it ought to be rare for a geography teacher not to be able to interest or stimulate students in some part of the subject on its own merits. The strongest justification for any educational enterprise is that it engages the freely given attention and goodwill of the learner; in the last resort, the survival of geography will depend on the day-by-day professional competence and enthusiasm of those who represent it at the chalk-face.

## Taking a longer-term view

These suggested courses of action are predicated on the belief that, at least for the next decade, whichever political party is in power in England and Wales, there will be, in essence, a continuation of the post-1988 policies hammered out in the wake of the Education Act. These stemmed from the speech of a Labour Prime Minister, James Callaghan, about the future of education at Ruskin College, Oxford in 1976: the period has encompassed long Conservative rule (1979–97), buttressed at either end by Labour governments, who have continued similar policies.

### What will be the prevailing philosophy for education in the future?

The dominant philosophy of the education policies from all three major parties in the past three decades has been commonly utilitarian – education is conceived primarily in terms of 'helping young people to be prepared for the job market'.

The wider concerns of transmitting knowledge of a cultural heritage, of enabling children to grow into mature self-knowledge through their own active participation in 'discovery learning' and of giving young people the tools to make a critique of their own society (the 'reconstructionist' view) have, for the most part, been underplayed, though there was an element of the 'cultural heritage' position emphasized as plans for a subject-centred National Curriculum emerged in the mid-1980s.

It is significant that the most distinctive clashes of opinion in curricular terms have been the ones about the 'broad and balanced curriculum' espoused by Kenneth Baker, and about the advisability of returning to the idea of separate pathways post-14. These opened up clashes not between the Conservative and Labour parties, but within them. The policies of David Blunkett, Secretary of State in the Labour government elected in 1997 have been, in most ways, educationally as 'conservative' as those of his Conservative predecessors, if not more so.

The utilitarian cast of mind has coincided with much greater central intervention than before and so its impact has been greater. Geography's role, as a generalist subject, in such a curriculum is an ambivalent one. The subject may be valued mostly for whatever 'practical usefulness' it provides to job preparation and creation. There are certainly elements of world knowledge and skill development (for instance with maps) which can be paraded as distinctive geographical contributions to education for the world of work; but these (probably rightly) are not seen as of major importance compared with the knowledge and skills provided in maths and English, neither are they the 'heart' of geography for most people who have studied it.

The need to have a general understanding of patterns and processes, of the way the world works spatially and economically, of how landscapes and townscapes come to be the way they are, even more the need to feel wonder, awe and respect for the physical world, are occasionally paid lip service at present but not raised to high priority. One must hope that the wheel will turn.

*Should school geography mirror academic geography?*

John Huckle wrote recently that:

> at a time when academic geography engaged with diverse philosophies and social and cultural theories in order to explain the contribution of space, place and geography, to the profound social changes which were taking place, the school subject's professional establishment turned its attention to a reinterpretation of the school subject which seemed to be little informed by these developments.
>
> (Huckle, 1997)

This raises the issue of whether one should expect the objective of school geography to be the same as that of academic geography, or to borrow uncritically themes and passing preoccupations from it. Schools have to offer an appropriate basic geography for all pupils; university academic communities don't.

School teachers do, of course, profit from expeditions to the frontiers of the subject; good teaching depends on informed subject knowledge and there has certainly been too little time to pursue that in the blizzard of bureaucratic papers which have blown into staffrooms in the past two decades. But academic geography appears to be at present in a fragmented state, and admitted to be so by its practitioners. A recent contribution to AREA offered this pessimistic view:

> If penetrating, insightful and prospectively useful geographical work is produced within academia, why does it often have little in common with what passes for people's perceptions of the subject outside of university geography departments? . . . over the years some commentators have attributed the blame for . . . poor communications to the fragmentation of the discipline . . . however . . . any likelihood that geography will – or should – consolidate its fragments is at best minimal.
>
> (Shaw and Matthews, 1998)

The traffic between schools and higher education might be better represented as desirably two-way; for schools, there is much to glean from new academic directions and discoveries; for Higher Education there may be lessons to be learnt from the re-examination of the essence of the subject induced by the spur of the National Curriculum. Such a National Curriculum (however unwelcome) might be devised for major subjects in Higher Education one day, especially if fragmentation continues unabated; it has already been discreetly installed in a large part of teacher education.

*Will the subject-centred curriculum survive?*

A key question generated by the work of Professor Crick's Working Party on Citizenship was: 'Are the rights and responsibilities of citizenship conveyed satisfactorily through the teaching in existing subjects?' The answer was 'No' and they sought (and were given) extra curricular time for the topic as a result. The way may now be open for other bolt-on additions. It is just possible that, in the longer term the whole notion of a subject-framework for the curriculum may gradually be called into question. The shape of the curriculum in Britain could in time become more like that of the states of Australia or the USA where particular hybrid formulations (e.g. Society and Environment, Government and Community, Social Studies) form modular-based courses. These, in turn, affect what is offered in universities.[8]

This question (and others which look to the mid-term future) have lately been considered by a new informal gathering of geography teachers and teacher-educators in England, who call themselves the GeoVisions group (GeoVisions Group, 1999). In a workshop led by members of the group at the 1999 Geographical Association conference at Manchester the question was posed: 'Is geography best seen as a *resource*?; instead of denying its eclecticism and trying to promote from the centre some kind of unified curriculum subject, (should we not) delight in it and exploit its propensity for permeable and mobile disciplinary boundaries?' In the next period of curriculum change, this may exactly become the key issue. What has to be weighed in the balance is the advantage of a continuing subject identity to the value of the community which sustains it, and the issue of what is lost if it withers.

So, what is it about geographical study which might make it deserve to survive in any form in the longer term? Some argue that it will be better in the future to describe the curriculum not by subjects, but by a series of 'entitlements', targets for particular ages. Others say that modularization or unitization of the curriculum is inevitable because there will be pressures for more flexible course arrangements. Still others argue for not only the linkage but the submergence of subjects into wider thematic groupings.

But also, by the nature of past educational events, there is a strong subject-identification and subject-loyalty which British teachers have developed. On balance, this has been a strength rather than a weakness, since it has ensured the development of a sound base of academic knowledge, an evolutionary approach to change and (for the most part) a corporate intellectual integrity. It has also led to a sense of 'belonging' and a focus for study. The existence of an army who assemble under a recognized flag provides coherence and mutual support even if the members of it do not always quite march to the same beat. An understanding of a discipline is more likely to be effective when it is mediated by and through a community of scholars rather than an *ad hoc* pragmatic collection of principles. 'Subjects' are not divine creations – but they have shown themselves to be practical and durable ways of marking out the intellectual landscape.

But do pupils see it that way? The case is sometimes made that subject-boundaries are 'artificial' and that, in reality, learning is a seamless robe which has no divisions. (Such a philosophy prevailed in primary education in the post-war period, though plenty of parents and children were happiest when assured that what they were doing was 'maths' or 'geography'.) The point is rhetorical rather than securely founded in epistemology either way.

Subjects (whether conceived philosophically or organically) provide convenient and identifiable segments of learning that help learners to find their way; and they have, on the whole, proved their usefulness as components of an organizational framework from the time that the earliest formal educational institutions were devised. They are neither benign nor malevolent in themselves, despite what some 'social constructionist' critics seem to imply (McLaren, 1993). There is no over-whelming reason (or evidence) to believe that what goes on in 'subjects' is any more obscurantist or a deterrent to learning than that which goes on in curriculum innovations conceived in other ways.

The Geography for the Young School Leaver project, begun in 1970, took a fresh line about what was appropriate geographic content for 15-year-olds. It was centred on spatial/geographical ideas, but it borrowed freely, using material and insights from other subjects. Its eclectic approaches remain influential with many teachers (and not only geography teachers) and pupils thirty years on. It is a good example of how a low-walled, subject-centred curriculum development can be as innovative and relevant as any recasting of material beyond subject-boundaries.

## What can geography contribute to school education in the twenty-first century?

So we return eventually to what may be the most important issue of all: What is the essence of geography? More exactly, what – within the generally accepted canon of the school subject that we call geography – will be of interest, and relevance to the education of pupils in the twenty-first century? What could justify or will justify the continuation of school geography in the future? Here is one sketch of what it could be, to encourage discussion and further formulations:

The most fundamental point may be the easiest to overlook. The study of geography deals with a key dimension of life – space and place in the real world: without an understanding of that dimension no young person is properly educated. 'Without geography, you're lost' may be better known as a T-shirt slogan than an educational aphorism, but its truth is self-evident. If there is no education about spaces and places, an appreciation of society and environment is unlikely to be developed properly. Concepts such as 'near' and 'far' look as if they are simple and innocent terms, scarcely worthy of any educational consideration, but that is a misapprehension; not understanding them has sometimes been the undoing of nations, let alone the inconvenience of individuals.

Geographical education is not alone in educating about the dimensions which enwrap human consciousness, but it is a vital component in doing so. Historical education (dealing primarily with the dimension of time) and religious education (dealing primarily with the dimension of the numinous and the spiritual) have equal claim to be partners in this function. Education about these dimensions broadens, fulfils and matures; schemes which do not appreciate the importance of these dimensions are seriously deficient in their education of the whole person.

Geography is also ordinarily regarded as the guardian of a particular language – the language of maps, which in more recent times has come to be known as 'graphicacy'. Research has shown that the facility to understand maps is independent of linguistic skills and that young children at the age of 3 can be competent map or map-model users (Blaut and Stea, 1974). Competence in the use of maps (and diagrams) in the modern world is of increasing significance, as any industrialist or manager will confirm, and all school pupils need to have a grounding in it. It is within geography lessons that this is usually done, though in the future, in Britain, it will need to go beyond the consideration of particular scales of Ordnance Survey maps and delve extensively into the many other map forms which are used in everyday life. Map-making as well as map-reading needs to be on everyone's basic curriculum.

Just as literacy, numeracy and graphicacy will need to continue to be taught as a base, so too will a knowledge of the planet we inhabit. Starting in primary school, as land and sea are distinguished on the globe, and continents and oceans named and remembered, an expanding mental portfolio of world knowledge is needed for everyday use now more than ever. Not every chance conversation can be conducted with repeated reference to an atlas or an encyclopaedia and so it is vital that future citizens carry around in their heads some general information about the world – a point which was made with some trepidation by the original Geography Working Group in 1989 (fearing an anti-'capes and bays' backlash), but one which has been quickly accepted as an uncontroversial aspect of National Curriculum formulations at all key stages.

The framework of world knowledge is a kind of coat-hook on which other things may be hung. The mastery of key spatial concepts (such as diffusion, migration, the theory of central places, the connectivity of networks) can then be tied in to the acquisition of understanding about the human and physical environment (such as the agricultural capacity of particular landscapes, patterns of world resources and trade, the growing hole in the ozone layer). It is the two major aspects of geography taken together (knowledge and conceptual understanding) which lead to a realistic appreciation, credible analysis and explanation of real-world situations (such as the limitations to economic development in a region, the impact of pollution, the predicaments of particular nations and peoples).

Thus, future citizens may move towards tackling such fundamentally important but apparently intractable twenty-first-century questions as 'Why are there food mountains in some parts of the world, whilst people are starving in others?', 'Are we going to run out of energy?', 'Why don't we colonize the oceans?'

The pedagogy attached to all this is likely to be as important as the content, since no education lastingly takes place without the motivation, cooperation and goodwill of the learner. There is a place for teacher exposition, and for the guided class viewing of visual material as well as for role-play, discussion, individual and group enquiry learning in the progress of these topics; an undue emphasis on one style is likely to be less productive than a skilful mix of varied approaches.

## Conclusion: What is the ultimate goal for geographic educators?

Beyond all this lies the necessity to make future generations of school pupils aware of what it is they inherit in the physical and human world, in order that they may be aware of the need to save it from ultimate destruction through human thoughtlessness or malevolence.

Increased technological power, increased mobility and increased population combine to put greater pressure on the physical environment and to demonstrate its ultimate fragility. Global warming is just one example of what may, as yet, be a dimly glimpsed potential apocalypse.

But it is not all gloom and doom. Geography teachers should not be ashamed to take the lead in schools in seeking to inspire their pupils with the continuing beauty and wonder of the natural world, as well as making them marvel at the complexity and liveliness of the human one. Not all things on earth are 'problems', as some current geography syllabuses seem to imply.

Geography teachers in Britain have, over the past hundred years, played a significant part in opening the eyes and widening the horizons of those who have sat in their classes. In the new century, the need to draw attention to those horizons is surely not diminished?

## Notes

1   The sales success of the Geographical Association's *St Lucia* pack (an initial leader in this field) is now being paralleled by other 'overseas locality' packs produced by other organizations and publishers.

2   The Annual Report of the Her Majesty's Chief Inspector for Schools 1996–97 HMSO reports:

> 30% of the geography teaching at Key Stage 1 was considered good/very good; 64% was considered satisfactory; 6% was considered unsatisfactory/poor. Comparable figures for English were 43, 52, 6; for History, 34, 61, 5; for Maths, 40, 54, 6; for Science, 41, 52, 6.

> 32% of the geography teaching at Key Stage 2 was considered good/very good; 61% was considered satisfactory: 8% was considered unsatisfactory/poor. Comparable figures for English were 44, 50, 6; for History, 42, 53, 5; for Maths, 43, 50, 7; for Science, 44, 49, 7.

> 50% of the geography teaching at Key Stage 3 was considered good/very good; 44% was considered satisfactory; 6% was considered unsatisfactory/poor. Comparable figures for English were 57, 39, 4; for History, 54, 39, 6; for Maths, 49, 44, 8; for Science, 51, 42, 7; for modern foreign languages, 50, 43, 8.

> 59% of the geography teaching at Key Stage 4 was considered good/very good; 38% was considered satisfactory; 3% was considered poor. Comparable figures for English were 66, 32, 2; for History 63, 34, 3; for Maths, 50, 45, 5; for Science, 55, 40, 5; for modern foreign languages, 48, 44, 8.

> 75% of the geography teaching post-16 was considered good/very good; 24% was

considered satisfactory; 1% was considered unsatisfactory/poor. Comparable figures for English were 73, 25, 2; for History, 76, 24, 0; for Maths, 66, 34, 0; for Science, 68, 30, 1; for modern foreign languages, 67, 31, 2.

3   The survey was carried out by NOP for Microsoft electronic publishers on 900 children between the ages of 8 and 16. It was reported on page 8 of *The Times* of 23rd January 1997. There have been many surveys which show similar lack of locational knowledge in the past two decades, e.g. 'Where are we? One in six thick Britons don't know', a survey of 1,000 adults by Mori, reported as the leading front-page story with an eight-column width headline in *Sunday Times*, 7th January 1988; a major survey of locational knowledge carried out in twelve countries by the Gallup Organisation in 1988, reported as 'British know little about the world and care even less' in The *Independent*, 29 December 1988.

4   'Blunkett reinstates landmark maps for geography pupils', *Daily Telegraph*, Tuesday, 4 May 1999, p. 9. The quotation from a 'spokesman' for Mr Blunkett was as follows: 'David Blunkett has already personally intervened in the authority's proposals. Greater flexibility in the naional curriculum is certainly under consideration but the removal of practical and necessary identification of physical landmarks and capital cities does not form part of Government thinking.' A full-page feature 'Revenge of the progressives' featured the story further in the *Sunday Times*, 16 May 1999, News section, p. 19.

5   The government has announced plans to link all schools to the Internet before 2001 and also to give every teacher a laptop computer, though the financial implications of this and the proportion of the cost which will need to be shouldered by the schools themselves remains unclear.

6   A summary of speeches and points made at the seminar was published jointly by RGS–IBG, GA and OS as *Education for Life*, a well illustrated glossy pamphlet, distributed free to all secondary schools in England and Wales.

7   The Scottish Association of Geography Teachers (SAGT) and the Royal Scottish Geographical Society (RSGS) play a similar role to the GA and RGS in Scotland as do the Association of Geography Teachers in Wales (AGTW) and the Universities Council for Welsh Geography (UCWG) in Wales. All belong to the Council of British Geography (COBRIG) and meet regularly to discuss matters of mutual concern.

8   There is a clear antecedent of this in Scotland, where 'Modern Studies' has been a secondary school course alongside geography and history since the 1950s and is often seen as an alternative to them. It comprises elements of history, geography, sociology, politics, and current affairs.

# References

Blaut, J.M. and Stea, D. (1974) 'Mapping at the age of three', *Journal of Geography*, 73, 7: 5–9.

Crick, B. *et al.* (1999) *Report of the Working Party on Citizenship*, London: HMSO.

GeoVisions Group (1999) 'Co-operative research', *Teaching Geography*, April: 70–1. See also articles about the group's work in October 1998 and January 1999 issues.

Huckle, J. (1997) 'Towards a critical school geography', in Tilbury, D. and Williams, M. (eds) *Teaching and Learning Geography*, London: Routledge.

McLaren, P. (1993) 'Foreword to the third edition', in Goodson, I. *School Subjects and Curriculum Change*, 3rd edn, London: Falmer Press.

Norwood, C. (1946) 'Address to the Geographical Association', *Geography*, 31, 1: 1–9.

OFSTED (1998) *The Annual Report of the Her Majesty's Chief Inspector for Schools 1996–97*, London: HMSO.

QCA (1999) *The Secretary of State's Proposals for the National Curriculum*, London: QCA.

Shaw, J. and Matthews, J. (1998) 'Communicating academic geography the continuing challenge', *Area*, 30, 4: 368.

*Sunday Times* (1999) 'Geography loses the place in new PC lessons', 2 May, News section, p. 7.

# Index